Foundation 3ds Max 8 Architectural Visualization

Brian L. Smith

friendsof ™

DESIGNER TO DESIGNER™

an Apress® company

Foundation 3ds Max 8 Architectural Visualization

ISBN-13: 978-1-59059-557-2

ISBN-10: 1-59059-557-2

Printed and bound in the United States of America 9 8 7 6 5 4 3 2 1

Trademarked names may appear in this book. Rather than use a trademark symbol with every occurrence of a trademarked name, we use the names only in an editorial fashion and to the benefit of the trademark owner, with no intention of infringement of the trademark.

Distributed to the book trade worldwide by Springer-Verlag New York, Inc., 233 Spring Street, 6th Floor, New York, NY 10013. Phone 1-800-SPRINGER, fax 201-348-4505, e-mail orders-ny@springer-sbm.com, or visit www.springeronline.com.

For information on translations, please contact Apress directly at 2560 Ninth Street, Suite 219, Berkeley, CA 94710. Phone 510-549-5930, fax 510-549-5939, e-mail info@apress.com, or visit www.apress.com.

The information in this book is distributed on an "as is" basis, without warranty. Although every precaution has been taken in the preparation of this work, neither the author(s) nor Apress shall have any liability to any person or entity with respect to any loss or damage caused or alleged to be caused directly or indirectly by the information contained in this work.

The source code for this book is freely available to readers at www.friendsofed.com in the Downloads section.

Credits

Lead Editor	**Production Editor**
Chris Mills	Laura Cheu
Technical Reviewer	**Compositor**
Mark Gerhard	Dina Quan
Contributing Author	**Artist**
Thomas Livings	Kinetic Publishing Services, LLC
Editorial Board	**Proofreader**
Steve Anglin, Ewan Buckingham, Gary Cornell, Jason Gilmore, Jonathan Gennick, Jonathan Hassell, James Huddleston, Chris Mills, Matthew Moodie, Dominic Shakeshaft, Jim Sumser, Keir Thomas, Matt Wade	Lori Bring
	Indexer
	John Collin
Project Manager | Production Director	**Cover Image Designer**
Grace Wong	Corné van Dooren
Copy Edit Manager	**Original 3D Cover Artist**
Nicole LeClerc	Oleg Melnyk
Copy Editors	**Interior and Cover Designer**
Damon Larson, Heather Lang	Kurt Krames
Assistant Production Director	**Manufacturing Director**
Kari Brooks-Copony	Tom Debolski

This book is dedicated to my lovely wife, Shari, and our two great kids, Laken and Kegan. Without their support, this book would simply not have been possible.

CONTENTS AT A GLANCE

About the Author xvii
About the Technical Reviewer xviii
About the Cover Image Designer xix
Acknowledgments xx
Introduction xxi

PART 1 **GETTING AROUND INSIDE 3DS MAX** 1
Quick Start 1 **Getting Started** 3
Chapter 1 **Navigating the 3ds Max Interface** 15
Chapter 2 **Working with Objects** 37

PART 2 **MODELING** **57**
Quick Start 2 **Getting Started with Modeling** **59**
Chapter 3 **Modeling Basics** **73**
Chapter 4 **The Critical Compound Objects Types
(Loft, Boolean, Terrain, and Scatter)** **107**
Chapter 5 **The Critical Modeling Modifiers** **129**

PART 3 **MATERIALS** **143**
Quick Start 3 **Getting Started with Materials** **145**
Chapter 6 **Material Basics** **163**
Chapter 7 **The Critical Map Channels** **189**
Chapter 8 **The Critical Map Types** **207**
Chapter 9 **UVW Mapping** **229**

PART 4 **LIGHTING** **241**

Quick Start 4 **Getting Started with Lights** 243

Chapter 10 **Basic Lighting** 263

Chapter 11 **Photometric Lighting** 291

Chapter 12 **Global Illumination** 307

PART 5 **CAMERAS AND ANIMATION** **321**

Quick Start 5 **Getting Started with Cameras and Animation** 323

Chapter 13 **Camera Basics** 329

Chapter 14 **Animation Basics** 341

Chapter 15 **Animation Controllers** 351

PART 6 **RENDERING** **371**

Quick Start 6 **Getting Started with Rendering** 373

Chapter 16 **Rendering Basics** 387

Chapter 17 **Scene Assembly** 415

Chapter 18 **Effect Basics** 433

APPENDIXES **461**

Appendix A **Marketing Your Services** 463

Appendix B **Top 20 Production Tips** 473

Appendix C **Customizing 3ds Max** 497

Appendix D **Keyboard Shortcuts** 503

Index 511

Gallery Credits 554

Gallery

CONTENTS

About the Author . . . . **xvii**

About the Technical Reviewer . . . . **xviii**

About the Cover Image Designer . . . . **xix**

Acknowledgments . . . . **xx**

Introduction . . . . **xxi**

PART 1 GETTING AROUND INSIDE 3DS MAX **1**

Quick Start 1 **Getting Started** **3**

Chapter 1 **Navigating the 3ds Max Interface** **15**

   The interface elements 16
      Menus 17
      Toolbars 17
      The Command panel 18
      Viewports 18
      The Lower Interface bar 18
      Quad menus 18
      Floaters 19
      Dialog boxes 19
   Using the Command panel 19
      The Create panel 20
      The Modify panel 20
      The Hierarchy panel 21
      The Motion panel 23
      The Display panel 23
      The Utilities panel 24
   Using the viewports 25
      Perspective and axonometric views 26
      Learning the viewports 26
      Zooming, panning, and rotating in a viewport 28
      Grids 30

Viewport refreshing and disabling 30
Rendering levels 31
Enabling Fast View 32
The viewport layouts 34
Undoing and saving view changes 35
Summary 35

Chapter 2 **Working with Objects** **37**

Selecting objects 37
The Select icons 37
The Select Objects dialog box 38
Select by region 40
Selection filters 43
Named selection sets 43
Selection lock 46
Other ways to select objects 46
Isolate selection 46
Displaying objects 47
The Display floater 48
Layers 50
Using the Layer Manager 50
Transforming objects 51
Move 51
Scale 52
Rotate 53
The Transform Type-In dialog box 54
Status bar type-in fields 55
Summary 55

PART 2 **MODELING** **57**

Quick Start 2 **Getting Started with Modeling** **59**

Chapter 3 **Modeling Basics** **73**

Setting up the work environment 74
Units 74
Display drivers 76
Configure paths 77
Preference settings 79
Customization 81
Working with shapes and splines 81
Shapes and splines defined 82
Shape basics 83
The Rendering rollout 85
The Interpolation rollout 86
Spline basics 88

Working with meshes and polys 88
   Creating mesh objects 89
   Editing mesh objects 90
      The Selection rollout 92
      The Soft Selection rollout 95
      The Edit Geometry rollout 98
   Important features available anywhere 99
      Attach 99
      Explode 101
      Remove Isolated Vertices 102
      View Align and Grid Align 102
   Important features available only in sub-object modes 103
   Detach 103
      Delete 104
      Weld 104
Summary 105

Chapter 4 The Critical Compound Objects Types (Loft, Boolean, Terrain, and Scatter) **107**

Creating Lofts 108
   The Creation Method rollout 108
   The Surface Parameters rollout 110
   The Path Parameters rollout 112
   The Skin Parameters rollout 114
   The Deformations rollout 116
Creating Booleans 116
   Union 117
   Subtraction 117
   Intersection 118
   Cut 118
   Suggestions for creating Booleans 119
Creating terrain 120
Creating scatter objects 123
   Distribution object parameters 124
   The Transform rollout 125
   Summary 127

Chapter 5 The Critical Modeling Modifiers **129**

The Extrude modifier 129
The Smooth modifier 131
The Noise modifier 132
The Optimize modifier 133
The TurboSmooth modifier 135
The Displace modifier 136
The Lathe modifier 138
The STL Check modifier 140
The Cap Holes modifier 141
Summary 142

PART 3 **MATERIALS** **143**

Quick Start 3 **Getting Started with Materials** **145**

Chapter 6 **Material Basics** **163**

The Material Editor 163
    Sample slots 164
    Changing the sample slot background 164
    Changing the sample slot object type 165
    Magnifying a sample slot 165
    Naming materials 167
    Creating new materials 167
    Assigning materials to objects 167
    Loading materials in the sample slots 169
    Removing materials and maps 169
    Selecting objects by material 171
    Showing maps in a viewport 172
Material Editor icons 172
    The Material/Map Browser 174
    Material libraries 175
    The Material/Map Navigator 177
Material Editor rollouts 177
    The Shader Basic Parameters rollout 178
        The Wire option 178
        The 2-Sided option 179
    The Blinn Basic Parameters rollout 180
        The Ambient, Diffuse, and Specular Color swatches 181
        The Specular Highlights section 181
        The Self-Illumination section 182
    The Extended Parameters rollout 183
        The Advanced Transparency section 184
        The Wire section 184
    The SuperSampling rollout 184
    The Maps rollout 187
    The Dynamic Properties rollout 187
    The Mental Ray Connection rollout 187
Summary 187

Chapter 7 **The Critical Map Channels** **189**

The Maps rollout 190
The Diffuse Color channel 190
The Opacity channel 192
The Bump channel 195
The Reflection channel 197
The Displacement channel 200
The Refraction channel 202
Summary 204

Chapter 8 **The Critical Map Types** **207**

The Bitmap map 207
The Coordinates rollout 208
Offset and tiling 209
Angle 210
Blur and blur offset 211
The Noise rollout 213
The Time rollout 214
The Output rollout 214
The Gradient map 215
The Gradient Ramp map 216
The Mix map 218
The Noise map 220
The Smoke map 221
The Waves map 222
The Falloff map 223
Summary 227

Chapter 9 **UVW Mapping** **229**

Generating mapping coordinates 229
The UVW Map modifier 230
Working with the UVW gizmo 231
Sizing and tiling 232
Alignment 232
Map channels and multi/sub-objects 235
Summary 240

PART 4 **LIGHTING** **241**

Quick Start 4 **Getting Started with Lights** **243**

Chapter 10 **Basic Lighting** **263**

Standard lights vs. photometric lights 264
The standard light source types 264
Omni lights 265
Spotlights 265
Direct lights 266
Creating lights 266
Viewport navigation controls 268
Light placement 269
Align Camera 269
Place Highlight 270

Light parameters 270
   The General Parameters rollout 271
      Shadow map 272
      Area shadows 274
      Raytraced shadows 274
      Advanced raytraced shadows 275
   The Intensity/Color/Attenuation rollout 276
      Intensity 276
      Color 277
      Decay 277
      Attenuation 277
   The Advanced Effects rollout 279
   The Shadow Parameters rollout 280
Rollouts for specific shadow types 282
   The Shadow Map Params rollout 282
   The Area Shadows rollout 285
   The Ray Traced Shadow Params rollout 286
   The Adv. Ray Traced Params rollout 286
   The Optimizations rollout 286
   The Spotlight and Directional Parameters rollouts 287
Summary 289

Chapter 11 **Photometric Lighting** **291**

Exposure control 291
   Types of exposure control 292
   Exposure control parameters 292
Photometric light types 293
   Point, linear, and area lights 293
      Intensity/Color/Attenuation rollout 294
   Preset Lights 297
IES Sun 298
IES Sky 299
Daylight 301
   Standard lights vs. IES Sun and IES Sky 303
Sunlight 304
Summary 304

Chapter 12 **Global Illumination** **307**

Principles of global illumination 308
   Shaders 308
Radiosity 309
   Radiosity Processing Parameters rollout 310
      Initial Quality 310
      Refine Iterations 312
      Light filtering 314
   Radiosity Meshing Parameters rollout 315
   Considerations when using radiosity 318
Summary 319

PART 5 CAMERAS AND ANIMATION **321**

Quick Start 5 **Getting Started with Cameras and Animation** **323**

Chapter 13 **Camera Basics** **329**

Camera types 330
Creating cameras 331
Viewport navigation controls 332
Camera placement 333
   Align Camera 333
   Place Highlight 334
Basic camera parameters 334
   Lens length and field of view 335
   Environment ranges 337
   Clipping planes 337
Summary 339

Chapter 14 **Animation Basics** **341**

Basic animation interfaces 342
   Time Configuration dialog box 342
   Time slider 344
   Animation playback controls 344
Keyframing 345
Creating keyframes 346
Creating basic motion 347
Summary 349

Chapter 15 **Animation Controllers** **351**

Controllers 352
   Constraints 353
Motion panel 354
Parameters 355
   Assign Controller rollout 355
   Assigning and changing controllers 356
   PRS Parameters rollout 358
   Position XYZ Parameters rollout 358
   Euler Parameters rollout 358
   Key Info (Basic) rollout 359
   Trajectories 363
Curve Editor 364
Summary 370

PART 6 **RENDERING** **371**

Quick Start 6 **Getting Started with Rendering** **373**

Chapter 16 **Rendering Basics** **387**

The Render Scene dialog box 388
   The Common tab 390
      Time Output 390
      Output Size 391
      Options 391
      Render Output 392
   Email Notifications 394
   The Renderer tab 394
      Options 395
      Antialiasing 395
      Global SuperSampling 396
      Object and Motion Blur 396
      Auto Reflect/Refract Maps 396
      Color Range Limiting 396
      Memory management 396
Choosing file dimensions 396
   Prints 397
   High-definition and standard DVDs 398
   Internet images 398
   Internet video 398
Additional rendering tools 399
   The Print Size Wizard 399
   The RAM Player 400
   The Panorama Exporter 402
Video Post 404
Network rendering 409
Summary 413

Chapter 17 **Scene Assembly** **415**

Computer power vs. scene complexity 416
   Transferring files 416
      Instance vs. copy 418
   Refreshing and rendering viewports 420
Assembly tools 422
   Save Selected 423
   Merge 424
   Import 425
   Export 426
   Export Selected 426
   XRef Objects 426

XRef Scenes 428
File Link Manager 428
File Properties 428
Summary Info 429
Archive and Resource Collector 430
Summary 431

Chapter 18 **Effect Basics** **433**

Atmospheric effects 434
The Fire effect 435
The Fog effect 437
Standard fog 439
Environment ranges 440
Layered fog 442
The Volume Fog effect 443
The Volume Light effect 445
Render effects 448
The Lens effect 449
The Depth of Field effect 452
The Motion Blur effect 453
Multi-pass effects 455
The Multi-Pass Motion Blur effect 455
The Multi-Pass Depth of Field effect 457
Summary 460

APPENDIXES **461**

Appendix A **Marketing Your Services** **463**

Your clients 463
Developers 464
Architects 464
Continuing education 465
Individuals 465
Contractors 466
Real estate agents 466
Your tools 466
Websites 467
Brochures 468
Phone books 468
DVDs 469
Phone calls 469
E-mails 470
Summary 470

Appendix B **Top 20 Production Tips** **473**

1. Build a network of subcontractors 474
2. Inspect the architectural drawings 475
3. Write a good script as soon as possible 477
4. Question poor designs 478
5. Master the keyboard shortcuts 478
6. Use additional input devices 479
7. Write a good contract 480
8. Break up projects into smaller jobs 480
9. Use the Loft feature 481
10. Save incrementally and save often 481
11. Use advanced raytraced shadows and know when to use advanced lighting 482
12. Purchase the best available model and material libraries 483
13. Create assembly lines for doors and windows 484
14. Use material libraries 486
15. Use standard scene elements 487
16. Use the top third-party plug-ins 487
17. Use the Scatter command and Spacing tool to create vegetation 489
18. Use artificial shadows 490
19. Participate in website forums 492
20. Attend trade shows, seminars, and classes 493
Summary 494

Appendix C **Customizing 3ds Max** **497**

The Customize menu 497
UI schemes 498
Custom UI and Defaults Switcher 498
Customize User Interface 500
Summary 501

Appendix D **Keyboard Shortcuts** **503**

Default keyboard shortcuts 503
Additional keyboard shortcuts 507

Index **511**

Gallery Credits **554**

Gallery

ABOUT THE AUTHOR

Since 1997, **Brian Smith** has worked as a CAD manager and animation specialist in architectural, engineering, and landscaping firms in southwest Florida. He started his own company in 2001, specializing in the production of architectural animations and renderings in 3ds Max. He is the cofounder of 3D Architectural Solutions in Sarasota, Florida, and is currently an instructor at the Autodesk Authorized Training Center, Planet Digital Education, in Orlando (www.planetdigital.com), where he teaches 3ds Max for the visualization industry. A portfolio of his work can be seen at www.3das.com.

Brian graduated from the U.S. Military Academy at West Point with a major in aerospace engineering. He served on active duty, and later in the Florida Army National Guard, including two years as a battery commander, responsible for a short range air defense battery of over 100 soldiers. Following 9/11, he served in Washington, D.C. as an air defense artillery fire control officer, working closely with the US Secret Service, the US Air Force, and the FAA to provide air defense coverage of our nation's capital. In 2005, he deployed numerous times with his unit to provide humanitarian relief to hurricane victims along the Gulf Coast.

ABOUT THE TECHNICAL REVIEWER

Mark Gerhard is a creative professional with over 15 years experience in the field of 3D modeling and animation. He was the first artist hired by Autodesk to test the initial release of 3D Studio in 1990, and spent six years as the lead writer for the tutorials that ship with the product. He has taught at Santa Rosa Junior College, Napa Valley College, Academy of Art University, Sonoma State University, Sonoma Country Day School, and Petaluma High School; and has lead countless classes and demonstrations of this software throughout the world. He has also been an author, illustrator, and technical editor for books on 3ds Max for Pearson Education, Wiley, Macmillan, and other publishers. He holds a BA in Practice of Art from UC Berkeley.

ABOUT THE COVER IMAGE DESIGNER

Corné van Dooren designed the front cover image for this book. Having been given a brief by friends of ED to create a new design for the Foundation series, he was inspired to create this new setup combining technology and organic forms.

With a colorful background as an avid cartoonist, Corné discovered the infinite world of multimedia at the age of 17—a journey of discovery that hasn't stopped since. His mantra has always been "The only limit to multimedia is the imagination," and this mantra keeps him moving forward constantly.

After enjoying success after success over the past years—working for many international clients, as well as being featured in multimedia magazines, testing software, and working on many other friends of ED books—Corné decided it was time to take another step in his career by launching his own company, Project 79, in March 2005.

You can see more of his work and contact him through www.cornevandooren.com or www.project79.com.

If you like his work, be sure to check out his chapter in *New Masters of Photoshop: Volume 2* (friends of ED, 2004).

ACKNOWLEDGMENTS

I would like to thank the entire team at friends of ED for making my writing sound far more intelligent than it originally started: Grace Wong, Nicole LeClerc, Damon Larson, Heather Lang, Kari Brooks-Copony, and Laura Cheu.

A special thanks to Chris Mills for believing in my idea of a book dedicated to the architectural visualization industry, and for helping make that dream a reality.

Thanks to my mom for beating proper English into me from the time I could write. Before any of these chapters ever made it to the team at friends of ED, she got first crack at correcting my writing—and she made plenty of markups.

Thanks to my long-time friend and business partner Brian Zajac, who keeps me steered in the right direction with all things graphical.

Thanks to my friends at Visarty and Catapult, whose 3D services helped my business stay in production during the crunch phase of this book. If you need some good subcontracting work done, these are two of the best companies out there. Their work can be seen in the gallery of this book.

Last but not least, I would like to thank Randall Stevens (ArchVision/VisMasters) and Jeff Mottle (CGarchitect.com) for their support of this book and the donation of valuable content.

Brian L. Smith

INTRODUCTION

I feel fortunate to be part of the 3D world at a time when it appears that the real world is completely embracing our work. My long-time friend Brian Zajac started in the 3D business a long time ago, when a typical workstation cost $100,000, and a simple animation that today would take only minutes to render took weeks. He gave up 3D and turned his sights to a career in web design where he wouldn't have to wait so long to see the fruits of his labor. Many architectural visualization companies struggled to survive these early days of 3D, when the software lacked the quality that many clients demanded, and the cost of equipment was a great a burden to manage. But just like the conversion from hand-drawn architectural blueprints to computer-aided drafting in the 90s, 3D visualizations have gained the necessary backing to make our work the standard—before long it will be the norm. Now anyone with enough drive and desire can start a 3D visualization business from their own home with just a single computer. With new developments in chip technology on the horizon, such as the much anticipated Cell chip, the near future promises even greater power for all of us to build better scenes and render them in a fraction of the time it takes today. Before you know it, we will be able to render our scenes in real time!

The idea for writing this book started sometime in the first few days of teaching myself 3D Studio Release 4 for DOS. I was amazed at all the books available for users in the entertainment industry, yet not one could be found for those of us in the visualization industry. I wasted countless hours learning things I found out only later that I didn't need to know, and I made up my mind that if someone else didn't have a visualization book on the market when I had learned the program, I would write one myself. And here it is. I hope you can benefit from what I believe to be the foundation for those of us using 3ds Max for architectural visualizations.

Tutorials

There are two types of tutorials in this book: the Quick Start tutorials that begin each major part of the book, and the tutorials within the chapters.

The intent of the Quick Start tutorials is to take you through the process of creating an animation from start to finish. Though the final product contains less detail and complexity than most visualizations, the process is still the same, and many of the steps are identical. Whenever possible, the Quick Start tutorials were designed to provide visibility of as many features as possible in the shortest number of steps, rather than having you redo the same steps over and over for the sake of building up the scene's content.

The tutorials within the chapters are designed to maximize the clarity of selected features and the speed at which you can learn the material. Whenever possible, you'll be asked to reset 3ds Max and create scene elements from scratch, rather than simply opening preconstructed scenes. By taking you through a tutorial that starts from scratch rather than a preconstructed scene, you'll be apt to feel a greater sense of confidence that the steps in the tutorial work independently of any pre-arranged settings or elements. Also, I've kept the complexity of the tutorials to a minimum and incorporated mostly simple objects (such as primitives) so that you can gain a greater sense of clarity of what exactly is going on. The end result is a tutorial that maximizes the transfer of knowledge in a minimal amount of time.

Layout conventions

To keep this book as clear and easy to follow as possible, the following text conventions are used throughout:

Important words or concepts are normally highlighted on the first appearance in **bold type**.

Menu commands are written in the form **Menu ➤ Submenu ➤ Submenu**.

Screen text is used to draw your attention to on-screen elements in the 3ds Max interface.

Part 1

GETTING AROUND INSIDE 3DS MAX

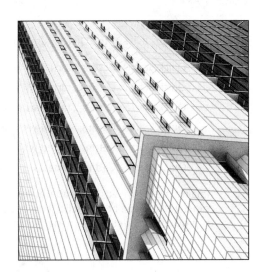

Quick Start 1

GETTING STARTED

If you've ever been frustrated with computer books that require extensive reading before giving you the knowledge to get your feet wet, fear not—the Quick Start tutorials in this book will allow you to jump right in and get soaked with knowledge relevant to architectural visualizations. There are six major parts to this book, each of which begins with a Quick Start tutorial designed to familiarize you with the material presented in subsequent chapters. Each tutorial is a continuation of the previous tutorial, and walks you through the creation of a virtual 3ds Max welcome center. The final product of the combined tutorials will be a ten-second animation of the welcome center.

This first tutorial, "Getting Started," is intended to be simple enough to be completed by someone with absolutely no experience with 3ds Max 8. It is also sophisticated enough to allow you to quickly set up 3ds Max and your new scene, similar to the way veteran users in the architectural visualization industry would. The remaining tutorials build upon the material in the preceding chapters and allow you to jump right into the next major part of the book, although it is possible to complete all six Quick Starts before reading any chapters.

Following is a list of the Quick Start tutorials that begin the six major parts of this book:

Quick Start 1: Getting Started

Quick Start 2: Getting Started with Modeling

Quick Start 3: Getting Started with Materials

Quick Start 4: Getting Started with Lighting

Quick Start 5: Getting Started with Cameras and Animation

Quick Start 6: Getting Started with Rendering

Images are provided for nearly every step of the tutorials, and annotations are included showing exactly where you need to click on the screen. Whenever a left-click is called for, the circle annotation is provided; right-clicks are designated with a diamond-shaped annotation.

Before starting the tutorials, you will have to download the Quick Start support files from the friends of ED website, www.friendsofed.com. These files include a 3ds Max scene with a few preconstructed elements and images used in the materials that are applied to the objects in your scene. There are also files for each subsequent Quick Start tutorial that you can use in lieu of the files that you save along the way. The ultimate goal of these tutorials is to walk you through some of the most important features, and eliminate, as much as possible, the need to use the same commands over and over. So let's get started!

The very first thing you need to do is download some support files needed for this tutorial and save them to a unique folder within the 3dsMax8 directory.

1. Create a folder named Friends_of_Ed in each of the two directories, 3dsMax8\scenes and 3dsMax8\images, as shown in the images below.

2. Go to www.friendsofed.com.

3. At the top of the website, click **books**.

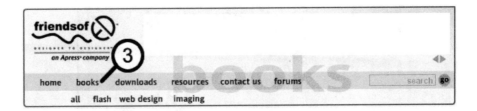

4. In the list that appears, click the link **Downloads** to the right of **Foundation 3ds Max 8 Architectural Visualization**.

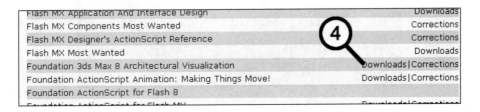

5. Click the file link named **Scene files** and save to your computer. Click the file named **Image files** and save to your computer.

6. Unzip **Scene files** into the **3dsMax8\scenes** folder you created and then unzip **Image files** into the **3dsMax8\images** folder you created.

7. Start 3ds Max 8.

The first thing you need to do within 3ds Max is tell the program where to find all the support images that are going to be used in this tutorial, i.e., the image files you just downloaded.

8. Click the **Customize** menu and select **Configure User Paths**.

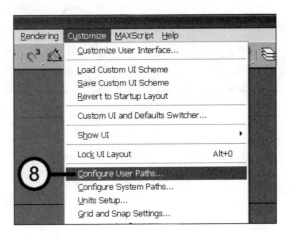

9. Click the **Add** button.

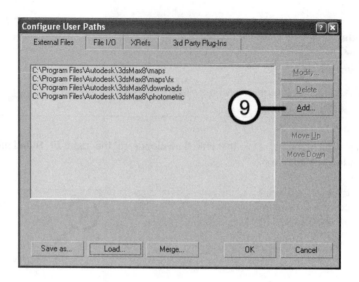

10. Go to the 3dsMax8 directory and highlight the Images folder.

11. Enable the **Add Subpaths** option.

12. Click the **Use Path** button twice. This tells 3ds Max to always look in the Images folder when it's looking for support files referenced in a scene. Click OK to exit.

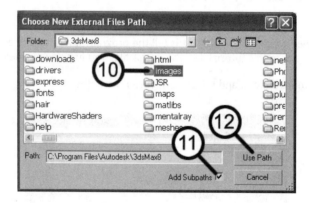

Next, you need to set up 3ds Max to use architectural units.

13. Click the **Customize** menu and select **Units Setup**.

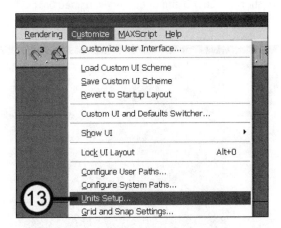

14. Select **US Standard**, **Feet w/Decimal Inches**.

15. Select **Inches** for **Default Units**, and click **OK** to exit.

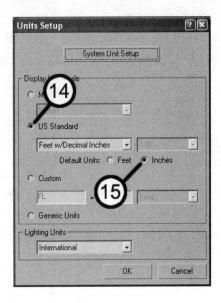

Rather than starting a 3D scene completely from scratch, you'll open a scene with some existing linework to speed up and facilitate the creation process for this tutorial.

16. Press the keyboard shortcut Ctrl+O and open the file named QuickStart01.max, located in the 3dsMax8\scenes\Friends_of_Ed folder. 3ds Max opens a scene with four viewports.

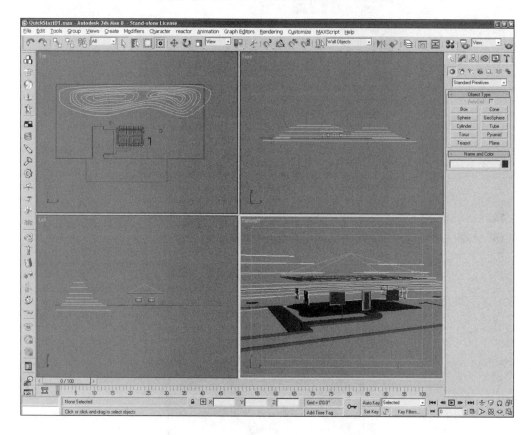

You're going to change the layout of the viewports so that there are two large viewports rather than four small ones. This will make seeing and working with the objects a little easier.

17. Right-click the word **Camera**, shown in the upper-left corner of the Camera viewport. This opens the **Viewport Properties** menu.

18. Select **Configure** from the menu. This opens the **Viewport Configuration** dialog box.

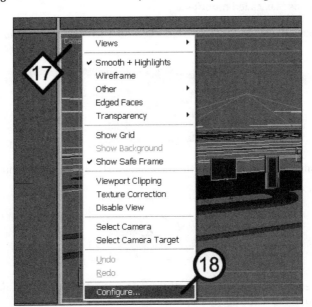

19. Click the **Layout** tab.

20. Select the viewport layout that shows two rectangular-shaped viewports, one above the other, and click **OK** to complete the command. The viewport layout changes to two viewports.

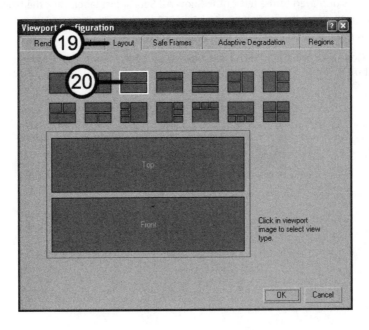

The last configuration you need to make is to change some shortcut buttons that give you access to powerful features in 3ds Max called **modifiers**.

21. In the Command panel, on the right-hand side of the screen, click the **Modify** tab.

22. Click the **Configure Modifier Sets** icon. The **Configure Modifier Sets** menu opens.

At the top of the menu, a check must be displayed next to **Show Buttons**, but not next to **Show All Sets in List** (as shown in the following image).

23. If a check is not displayed to the left of the **Show Buttons** label, click the label—if a check is displayed, press the Esc key on the keyboard to close the menu.

24. Click the **Configure Modifier Sets** icon again.

25. If a check is displayed to the left of the **Show All Sets in List** label, click the label—if a check is not displayed, press the Esc key on the keyboard to close the menu.

26. Click the **Configure Modifier Sets** icon one final time.

27. Select **Configure Modifier Sets** from the menu. This opens the **Configure Modifier Sets** dialog box.

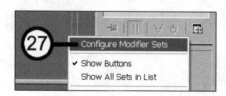

28. In the left-hand **Modifiers** window, scroll down in the list to the area labeled **MAX STANDARD**, and highlight the word **Extrude**. Click and drag the **Extrude** modifier from the left-hand window into any of the eight available modifier shortcut slots on the right-hand side of the dialog box.

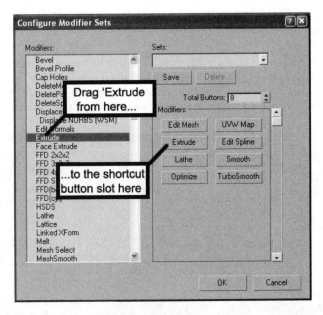

29. Repeat step 28 for the following modifiers, which you'll use throughout the Quick Start tutorials in this book. As shown in the preceding image, these are the **Edit Mesh**, **Edit Spline**, **UVW Map**, **Lathe**, **Smooth**, **Optimize**, and **Turbo Smooth** modifiers.

30. In the top-right corner of the dialog box, type **My Buttons** in the **Sets** drop-down field, and click **Save**. Click **OK** to close dialog box. This saves your shortcut button layout. You can save multiple layouts and select a layout from the drop-down list later.

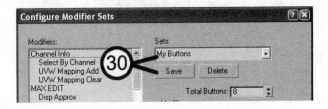

Before ending this tutorial, let's make one more change to the viewports.

31. Activate the Front view by right-clicking anywhere in the viewport. If a menu appears at your cursor's location, then the viewport is already activated. If so, press the Esc key to close the menu.

32. Press C to change the Front view to a Camera view. You'll use a preexisting locked camera in the scene to prevent inadvertent view changes to the viewport you'll be working in most often. Clicking and dragging in a viewport that's not locked can easily cause the viewport's perspective to change.

33. When your view changed to a Camera view, it should have also changed to a shaded view, a viewport setting known as **Smooth + Highlights**. If it did not, press the keyboard shortcut F3 to change the Camera view from wireframe to shaded (**Smooth + Highlights**). Now you can see surfaces in your scene. Your viewports should look like the image that follows.

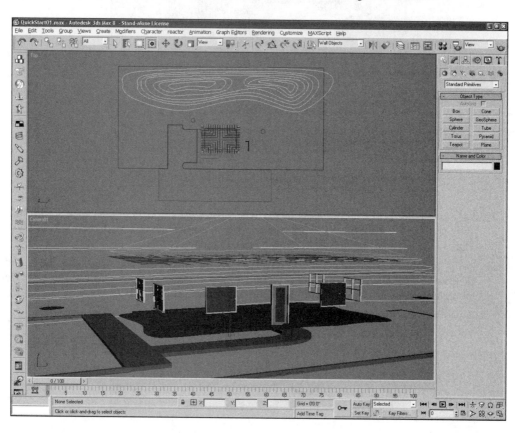

34. Click the **Zoom Extents All** button in the bottom-right corner of 3ds Max. This maximizes all your views, except Camera views. In this case, it only changed the Top view.

35. Click the **File** menu and select **Save As**. The **Save File As** dialog box opens to the Autodesk\3dsMax8\scenes folder.

36. Name your file MyQuickStart01.max for use in the next Quick Start tutorial.

This concludes Quick Start 1. In Quick Start 2, you'll jump right into the creation of your virtual welcome center!

Chapter 1

NAVIGATING THE 3DS MAX INTERFACE

The interface of any computer program is the means with which you command the program to perform a task. It stands to reason, therefore, that an interface should be designed in a way that allows the user to command the program as quickly and efficiently as possible. Did Autodesk succeed in creating that perfect interface? They did a great job; however, the default interface was created to benefit all 3ds Max users, not just those specializing in architectural visualizations. This chapter shows you how to best make use of the interface provided, and Appendix C demonstrates how to pick up where Autodesk leaves off, by showing you how to customize the 3ds Max interface to your specific needs.

Why put customization in an appendix at the end of a book? Simple. Until you have a firm grasp of at least the fundamentals, you won't know how to best customize the interface, and you'll probably end up changing it anyway. That being said, this chapter will focus on how to interact with the program as it is.

Autodesk did an outstanding job of making the 3ds Max interface user-friendly and efficient. As with many programs, there are numerous ways to tell the program to do the same thing. The trick is knowing which way is best—and this 3ds Max user defines *best* as the way that's fastest. It's a cliché, but time is money.

The interface elements

There are eight main screen interfaces through which to communicate with 3ds Max and get your work done, as shown in Figure 1-1. They include the Menu bar, toolbar, Command panel, viewport, Lower Interface bar, quad menu, floater, and dialog box. But before you can even use them, you have to work through at least one of two other interfaces: the keyboard and the mouse. Most users rely almost completely on the mouse—at least at first—and although using the mouse is a must in many ways, you should never overlook the power and usefulness of the keyboard.

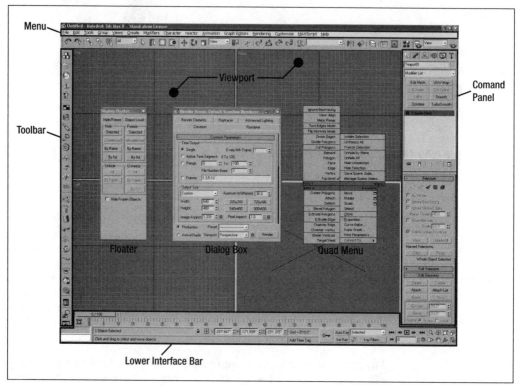

Figure 1-1. The eight main screen interfaces of 3ds Max

Most commands in 3ds Max can be executed with shortcut keystrokes. For example, to change the active viewport from Top view to Left view, simply press L. Keyboard shortcuts make using the keyboard a fast and efficient way of executing commands. If you find yourself using the screen interfaces to execute the same commands over and over again, it would be wise to invest a small amount of time learning the keyboard shortcuts for those commands and try using them for a while to see how beneficial they can be. Refer to Appendix D to see a list of all of the keyboard shortcuts relevant to architectural visualizations. If a shortcut doesn't exist for a particular command, Appendix C will show you how to create your own.

The mouse is also a critical interface through which you work. One feature on a mouse that's an absolute must, as any serious user would agree, is the scroll button (often in the form of a wheel between the left and right buttons). This additional feature allows you to pan and zoom, which are probably the two most frequently used commands in 3ds Max. Without the scroll button, you have to interrupt other commands to execute a zoom or pan.

A scroll button gives you two additional benefits. First, you can easily rotate your view by dragging the mouse while holding the Alt key and the scroll button on your mouse. Second, if you press and hold both Ctrl and Alt, you can zoom in and out of your scene by dragging the mouse up or down.

Menus

Although most commands in 3ds Max can be executed through the use of menus, the time needed to execute this way is much greater than with other interfaces. With the exception of a few tools not found in any other interface, I don't use the menus at all.

Notice the underlined letters in the default menus shown in Figure 1-2. You can use the keyboard to quickly open a menu by holding the Alt key and pressing the key of the letter that's underlined. You can then execute a command by pressing the key for an underlined letter of a submenu command. Holding the cursor over a submenu command that has an arrow to the right of it opens another submenu for that command. I dislike menus so much because it takes several keystrokes or precise and slow movements of the mouse to get to the command you want. There are better ways. For this reason, I avoid using menus whenever possible and won't spend time covering them here. Certain features that can only be accessed through the menus, however, will be discussed in the chapters that cover those features.

Figure 1-2. The default 3ds Max menus

Toolbars

Toolbars contain groups of icons that require only a single click of the mouse for command execution. However, with the exception of the **Main** toolbar (shown in Figure 1-3), I avoid using toolbars almost entirely because they simply require more time to use than keyboard shortcuts. Icons require moving the mouse cursor and your eyes away from the object or Command panel feature that you're working with, and making a precise selection over a small area of screen space. I prefer using keyboard shortcuts because I can keep my eyes on the object, and with one hand already resting on the keyboard, I can execute the command in a fraction of the time—without the risk of selecting the wrong command and having to spend time backing out of it when I do. Although the difference in time between the two interfaces may seem insignificant, when you consider that you may execute several thousand commands in one day, it becomes very significant.

Figure 1-3. The Main toolbar

17

The Command panel

The Command panel, shown in Figure 1-4, is an immense and complex interface with which to execute commands. It features six tabs at its top that you can click to access other panels. Each of these panels contains a vast array of features that sometimes are found only here. The Command panel, like toolbars, can be undocked and redocked—however, undocking results in a partial blockage of the viewports, and for that reason, I don't recommend undocking the Command panel.

Figure 1-4. The Command panel

Viewports

Viewports are the windows through which you can view your creations. By default, 3ds Max loads with a Front, Left, Top, and Perspective viewport. The arrangement of viewports and what you see within them can be easily changed or customized, as you'll learn later in this chapter.

The Lower Interface bar

Along the bottom of 3ds Max is a collection of some of the most important and frequently used controls in 3ds Max (Figure 1-5). These controls include the Time slider and the Track bar, as well as animation playback and viewport navigation controls.

Figure 1-5. The Lower Interface bar

Quad menus

Quad menus are quick-access menus that appear when you right-click within the active viewport. The menus change depending on what type of object (if any) is selected, as well as the cursor location. An example of a quad menu is shown in the right-hand side screenshot of Figure 1-6.

Floaters

Floaters are a type of interface that can remain open anywhere on the screen while you work. They're only available for certain commands, but for those they apply to, the benefit is that they don't take up too much screen space and you can continuously execute the same commands without having to leave other interfaces or open and close dialog boxes. An example of a floater is shown in the left-hand screenshot of Figure 1-6.

Dialog boxes

Many commands in 3ds Max open another type of interface, called a dialog box. Dialog boxes can contain their own menus, toolbars, spinners, or other means of user input. An example of a dialog box is shown in the center screenshot of Figure 1-6.

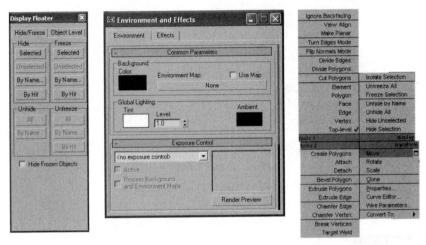

Figure 1-6. From left to right, an example of a floater, dialog box, and quad menu

Using the Command panel

With the exception of the viewports, you'll find that there's no area on the screen where you spend more time than the Command panel. Within the Command panel are six other panels that you access through tabs immediately under the Command panel header. The six tabs are **Create**, **Modify**, **Hierarchy**, **Motion**, **Display**, and **Utilities**. Each panel contains areas in which common controls are grouped together in what's called a rollout. To access a rollout's controls, the rollout must first be opened. Some rollouts are by default open, and some are closed. To the left of each rollout is a plus or minus sign—the plus sign indicates that the rollout is closed, and the minus sign indicates that the rollout is open. You can open or close a rollout by clicking on the rollout title. If the entire rollout exceeds the screen space available to the rollout, a small vertical scrollbar will appear to the right of the rollout—you can use this scrollbar to access the part of the rollout that can't be seen. Alternatively, if you move the cursor over an area of the rollout where no controls appear, a hand symbol will appear, which you can click and drag to scroll up or down. You can also click and drag the left edge of the Command panel to expand its width. Doing so can eliminate the need to pan. Like many options, this is a matter of personal preference.

The Create panel

When you click the **Create** panel tab, seven other icons will appear below it, as shown in Figure 1-7. Clicking these icons allows you to add all of the following categories of objects to your scene: **Geometry, Shapes, Lights, Cameras, Helpers, Space Warps**, and **Systems**. Immediately under the category icons is a subcategory drop-down list. Each subcategory displays an **Object Type** rollout, as well as a **Name and Color** rollout. Different subcategories display different objects available for creation. Immediately under the **Object Type** rollout is the **Name and Color** rollout, which allows you to change the default object name and color.

Figure 1-7. The Create panel

Creating an object

This exercise demonstrates use of the **Create** panel by creating a simple teapot. The teapot is a special object type often used for demonstration purposes.

1. Reset 3ds Max by selecting **Reset** from the **File** menu.
2. In the **Command** panel, click **Create ➤ Geometry ➤ Standard Primitives ➤ Teapot**.
3. Click and hold the left mouse button and drag anywhere in the Perspective view to place the teapot and increase its radius. Release the mouse button to complete the creation.

The Modify panel

There are several ways to modify an object, the most obvious of which is with the **Modify** panel (see Figure 1-8). When you select an object and click the **Modify** panel tab, the object name appears immediately below. Below the name is the **Modifier** drop-down list. Clicking this list opens all the available modifiers for the selected object. Modifiers are functions that contain parameters and change the appearance or structure of an object. Each type of object has a specific set of modifiers that can be applied. Below the **Modifier** drop-down list is the **Modifier Stack**, which contains the history of all modifiers applied to an object. Once applied, you can change the parameters of the modifier using the controls found in the **Parameters** rollout, located directly below the **Modifier Stack**.

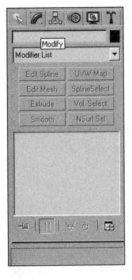

Figure 1-8. The Modify panel

Modifying an object

This exercise demonstrates use of the **Modify** panel by adjusting the teapot's radius parameter and then adding a simple modifier.

1. Continue from the previous exercise (or reset 3ds Max and create a teapot of any size in Perspective view).

2. Click the **Modify** tab.

3. With the teapot object still selected, click and hold the up arrow to the right of the **Radius** field to increase the radius of the teapot.

4. Click the **Modifier** drop-down list, scroll down, and select **Spherify** to add the **Spherify** modifier to the teapot. The teapot becomes more spherically shaped.

5. Click the **Undo** icon to undo the command and remove the modifier. (The **Undo** icon is the leftmost icon in the **Main** toolbar; it looks like a counterclockwise arrow).

The Hierarchy panel

The **Hierarchy** panel, shown in Figure 1-9, contains three buttons that give you access to several new rollouts and controls for an object. These buttons are **Pivot**, **IK** (Inverse Kinematics), and **Link Info**. The **Pivot** button gives you access to an extremely vital set of tools for creating architectural visualizations. The rollouts contain controls that allow you to change the location and orientation of an object's pivot point—the point about which transformations are applied. The **IK** button gives you access to controls that create inverse kinematics, which is a term describing the way motion is inherited up the hierarchy of a linked system of a body of objects, from the extremity objects to the objects closer to the body. The use of IK in architectural visualizations is very limited and the only use I've ever found for it is to simulate the motion of trees swaying in a wind (as such, I won't be covering IK in this book). Finally, the **Link Info** button gives you access to rollouts that contain locks, which simply prevent objects from being transformed (moved, scaled, or rotated) along a specific axis.

Figure 1-9. The Hierarchy panel

Changing an object's pivot point

This exercise demonstrates use of the **Hierarchy** panel by changing an object's pivot point.

1. Continue from the previous exercise (or reset 3ds Max and create a teapot of any size in Perspective view).

2. Select the teapot if it's not already selected.

3. Click the **Hierarchy** tab.

4. From the **Adjust Pivot** rollout, click the **Affect Pivot Only** button.

5. Click the **Center to Object** button. This moves the teapot's pivot point from the bottom of the teapot to the center of the teapot.

The Motion panel

The **Motion** panel, shown in Figure 1-10, simply provides access to tools that control the motion of objects or sub-objects. Within the panel are two buttons, **Parameters** and **Trajectories**. The **Parameters** button opens rollouts that allow you to assign controllers that affect the translation of objects in pre-set ways, or assign constraints that limit the translation in certain ways. The **Trajectories** button opens a single rollout that gives you access to parameters that govern animation paths. If this sounds confusing, don't worry, it can be—and we won't cover that until Chapter 12.

Figure 1-10. The Motion panel

The Display panel

The **Display** panel (shown in Figure 1-11) is perhaps the simplest and most straightforward of the six panels that make up the Command panel. This panel controls how objects are displayed within the viewports. You can change the display of individual objects or change the display of all objects at once. Clicking the **Display** panel takes you to six rollouts. The two that you'll most often use are the **Hide** and **Freeze** rollouts.

I'd also like to make brief mention of the **Display** floater, which is a handy feature (found in the **Tools** menu) that contains most of the same features found in the **Display** panel. It should be no surprise that the only things you see when you first open the **Display** floater are the **Hide** and **Freeze** features, which, as mentioned, you'll be using often. Good use of the **Hide** and **Freeze** features are essential for efficient work in 3ds Max.

Figure 1-11. The Display panel

Changing the display of an object

This exercise demonstrates use of the **Display** panel by hiding all scene geometry, including the simple teapot.

1. Continue from the previous exercise or reset 3ds Max and create a teapot of any size in Perspective view.

2. Click the **Display** tab.

3. In the **Hide by Category** rollout, click the **Geometry** option. All of the geometry in the scene will be hidden from view, including the teapot.

4. In the **Hide by Category** rollout, click the **Geometry** option again. The teapot will reappear.

5. In the **Hide** rollout, click the **Hide Unselected** button. All unselected objects will be hidden from view.

6. In the **Hide** rollout, click the **Unhide All** button. All scene objects will be unhidden and once again visible.

The Utilities panel

The **Utilities** panel (shown in Figure 1-12) is the last of the six that make up the Command panel. It contains a large assortment of utilities that do many different things. If you ever add a plug-in to 3ds Max, access to that plug-in might only be found by clicking the **More** button, which opens a dialog box with many other utilities. With the exception of specific plug-ins that I have installed, the only utility I've found useful on a regular basis is the **Asset Browser**, an extremely useful tool that allows you to scan your computer or the Internet for files. A couple of others tools will be discussed later, but for now, the **Asset Browser** is the only one you should concern yourself with. Almost all others require extensive knowledge of the program and only do very specific tasks that simply aren't needed in architectural visualizations.

Figure 1-12. The Utilities panel

The **Asset Browser** opens to a display much like Windows Explorer; however, the **Asset Browser** has many more features. It can display thumbnails of many file types related to graphics, such as files with the .tga extension. The **Asset Browser** also allows you to filter and display specific file types and choose from three different thumbnail sizes to display file content. You can double-click an image file to display it at full size, drag-and-drop files into your 3ds Max scene, and explore online content with many of the same types of buttons that you would find within Windows Explorer.

As you'll soon start to realize, there's an enormous portion of 3ds Max that you don't need to spend time learning if you're working strictly on architectural visualizations.

Using the Asset Browser

This exercise demonstrates use of the **Utilities** panel by utilizing the **Asset Browser** feature.

1. Reset 3ds Max.
2. Click the **Utilities** tab.
3. Click the **Asset Browser** button.
4. After a few seconds, a message will appear; when you see it, click **OK**.
5. Explore the directories within your computer to view thumbnails of your files.
6. Select **File ➤ Exit** from the **Asset Browser** menu to close the **Asset Browser**.

Using the viewports

There's no other place in 3ds Max where you'll spend more time than in the viewports. Viewports are the windows to your 3D world, through which all your work is performed. The importance of learning efficient use of viewports can't be overemphasized. Like all interface elements in 3ds Max, viewports have numerous settings that allow for customization; however, this section will focus on the fundamentals of viewport usage. You can refer to Appendix C at any time to learn how to customize the 3ds Max interface.

If you find learning a 2D CAD program difficult, then you'll probably find learning a 3D CAD program impossible. Adding that third dimension changes everything, and weeds out many 2D users who aren't up to the challenge of conceptualizing their creations in a third dimension. Most 2D CAD users operate through only one viewport, but in 3ds Max that's not even an option. Luckily, 3ds Max has developed a highly effective viewport interface that enables you to view your creations from four different perspectives at the same time. This section will show you how to work in viewports in ways that will maximize your efficiency in manipulating your creations.

Perspective and axonometric views

All viewports in 3ds Max show one of two types of views, perspective or axonometric. **Perspective views** mimic how your eyes perceive the real world, in which objects in the distance converge to a single point (as shown in the left pane of Figure 1-13). **Axonometric views** show objects from an infinitely distant perspective so that an object's parallel lines remain parallel regardless of the distance from the observer (see the right pane of Figure 1-13). In a perspective view, for example, a street that an observer stands on would vanish in the distance with both sides of the street converging to a single point, whereas in an axonometric view, both sides would remain parallel all the way to the horizon. In 3ds Max, the only perspective views are the Perspective, Camera, and Target Light views. All others, including the default views of Top, Left, and Front, are axonometric views.

 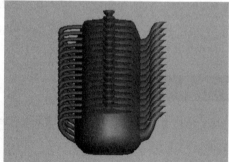

Figure 1-13. Perspective view (left) and axonometric view (right)

Learning the viewports

The default viewport layout shows four viewports, with the currently active viewport marked with a yellow border. In the top-left corner of each viewport is the viewport type, which you can right-click to bring up a menu, as shown in Figure 1-14. You can change the viewport type by selecting **Views** from this menu and selecting the view type from the flyout menu that appears.

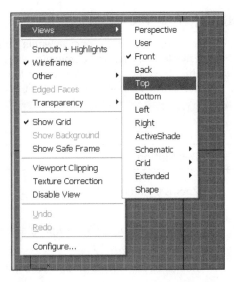

Figure 1-14. Viewport types

Several viewport types have shortcut keys that can be used to change the current viewport to a desired viewport type. These include T (Top view), B (Bottom view), F (Front view), L (Left view), P (Perspective view), and U (User view). Notice that when a Target Light or Camera is present in a scene, you can change a viewport to show the view from the perspective of either. The shortcut for Target Light view is $ (Shift+4), and the shortcut for Camera view is C.

Another way to change the viewport type is by selecting one of the viewport navigation controls, such as **Arc Rotate** or **Pan**. Using these tools will automatically change, for example, a Front view into a User view. User views are axonometric views that aren't constrained to a single axis and can show the scene from any location—but unlike perspective views, all parallel lines remain parallel.

Changing views within a viewport

This exercise demonstrates how to change the view of a viewport to some of the most commonly used view types.

1. Reset 3ds Max and create a teapot of any size in Perspective view.
2. Within any viewport, type "T" to change to Top view.
3. Type "L" to change to Left view.
4. Type "U" to change to User view.
5. Type "P" to change to Perspective view.
6. Right-click any viewport name and select **Views ➤ Front** from the drop-down menu to change the viewport to Front view.

Zooming, panning, and rotating in a viewport

You'll probably spend a significant amount of time changing your perspective within a viewport to get a better look at an object. The three methods available to do so are zooming, panning, and rotating your view. Table 1-1 lists and describes each of the different icons on the Lower Interface bar that allow you to zoom, pan, and rotate. If you use these three tools as often as I do, it would be wise to perfect their use.

Table 1-1. Viewport navigation controls

Icon	Name	Description
	Zoom (Alt+Z)	Zooms in and out of a viewport
	Zoom All	Zooms in and out of all viewports at the same time
	Zoom Extents (Ctrl+Alt+Z)	Zooms to the extents of all objects in the scene
	Zoom Extents Selected	Zooms to the extents of a selected object
	Zoom Extents All (Ctrl+Shift+Z)	Zooms all viewports to the extents of all objects
	Zoom Extents All Selected	Zooms all viewports to the extents of the selected object
	Region Zoom (Ctrl+W)	Zooms to a specific area that's selected by dragging the mouse
	Pan (Ctrl+P)	Pans within a viewport when the mouse is dragged
	Walk Through	Lets you move through a viewport by pressing a set of shortcut keys, including the arrow keys (similar to navigating in many 3D video games)
	Field of View	Changes the width of a Perspective or Camera view
	Arc Rotate (Ctrl+R)	Rotates the view around the world origin
	Arc Rotate Selected	Rotates the view around a selected object
	Arc Rotate SubObject	Rotates the view around a selected sub-object
	Maximize Viewport Toggle (Alt+W)	Toggles between one maximized viewport and four smaller viewports

Although there are keyboard shortcuts that allow you to zoom, pan, and rotate within a viewport, and I am an outspoken advocate of keyboard shortcuts, I would be doing you an injustice to endorse keyboard shortcuts in this particular instance. By far, the most effective way to move around inside a viewport is with the use of a mouse scroll button that has zoom, pan, and rotate capabilities. With such a mouse, zooming in and out of a view can be accomplished by simply scrolling the mouse wheel up or down. Alternatively, you can zoom in and out by dragging the mouse while pressing and holding its scroll button and the Alt and Ctrl keys on the keyboard. Panning is accomplished by simply dragging with the mouse while holding down its scroll button. Rotating is accomplished by dragging the mouse while holding its scroll button and the Alt key. If the scroll wheel on your mouse isn't working, check the settings in the **Viewports** panel in the **Preference Settings** menu.

Let's examine the viewport navigation icons a little more closely, because you may find that while there are some you may never use, there are some you can't live without. You can refer to Table 1-1 as you read. First, as I mentioned, I recommend avoiding the **Zoom** and **Pan** icons altogether, but they're there if you desire to use them. The very bottom-right icon, the **Min/Max** toggle, makes the active viewport larger (it takes up the space of all viewports combined), thus giving you an enlarged view of the active viewport.

To the left of the **Min/Max** toggle is the **Arc Rotate** icon. If you click and hold this icon, you're presented with two other flyout icons: **Arc Rotate Selected** and **Arc Rotate SubObject**. **Arc Rotate Selected** rotates about the pivot point of any object or objects selected. **Arc Rotate SubObject** allows you to rotate about an individually selected sub-object, such as a vertex or a multiple selection of sub-objects. When either of these icons is selected, a rotation guide appears in the active viewport. This guide looks like a circle with a square located at each quadrant. Clicking either the left or right squares rotates the view from side to side, while clicking either the top or bottom squares rotates the view up or down. Clicking inside this circle allows you to rotate about a point without tilting or banking the view from side to side. Clicking outside the circle allows you to rotate about a point while simultaneously causing the view to tilt or bank; however, tilting your view is usually unwanted in the visualization industry, and you should be careful not to tilt your view accidentally.

To the left of the **Pan** icon is the **Region Zoom** icon, which allows you to zoom in to a specific area by dragging the cursor over the region of the viewport that you want to zoom in to. When a viewport is in Perspective mode, this icon has a flyout icon called the **Field of View** icon. The **Field of View** icon lets you change the width of a view much like changing the lens of a camera. Unlike the **Zoom** feature, increasing or decreasing the field of view distorts the perspective, just as a wide angle or telescopic lens does.

The very top-right icon is the **Zoom Extents All** icon, which zooms all viewports to the extents of all visible objects in the scene until the objects fill each viewport to its entirety. This icon has a flyout, the **Zoom Extents All Selected** icon, which zooms all viewports to the extents of all selected objects.

To the left of the **Zoom Extents All** icon is the **Zoom Extents** icon, which zooms to the extents of all visible objects in the active viewport. This icon also has a flyout icon, the **Zoom Extents Selected** icon, which zooms to the extents of all selected objects in the active viewport.

To the left of this icon is the **Zoom All** icon, which simply zooms in to or out of all the viewports simultaneously, which is achieved by dragging the cursor in any of the viewports.

Changing views within a viewport

This exercise demonstrates how to use some of the important viewport navigation tools.

1. Reset 3ds Max and create a teapot of any size in Perspective view.

2. In the Lower Interface bar, click and hold the **Arc Rotate** icon, and select **Arc Rotate Selected** from the flyout menu.

3. Click and drag inside the rotation guide that appears in the active viewport. The view should rotate around the selected teapot.

4. Right-click inside any viewport to end the command. To reinitiate the command, you can use the keyboard shortcut Ctrl+R.

5. Click the **Min/Max Toggle** icon (Alt+W) to change views from four small viewports to one large one.

6. Click the **Zoom Extents** icon (Ctrl+Alt+Z) to zoom to the extents of all objects in your scene.

Grids

When 3ds Max opens to its default views, a grid appears in each viewport. The grid is simply a guide to help you establish your bearing in the viewports. Grids consist of lines that represent increments of space. You can change the lines within a grid to appear closer together or farther apart, and you can change the value that each increment represents. This book, however, won't cover this form of customization, as it's not crucial to the content of the book. I usually find myself disabling this feature before I even start a project, as it appears to clutter the viewport more than it benefits me to keep it active. You can disable the grid in the active viewport by pressing G.

Viewport refreshing and disabling

When you work in a program like 3ds Max, it's easy to build scenes that quickly get out of control in terms of file size and scene complexity. Although it's optimal to work in a way in which you don't have to wait on the computer to crunch the numbers, this is not always possible. Fortunately, 3ds Max gives you several ways of displaying objects in viewports that lessen the graphical burden on the computer. Each of these ways changes how quickly objects can be regenerated or refreshed in a viewport, which translates into how long you must wait to see the changes.

By default, all viewports in 3ds Max are **active**. (Don't confuse this word with the same term that describes which viewport is current, though.) When you make a change to your scene, every viewport that displays the part of the scene that gets changed has to be updated. Some changes are small and don't burden the computer. Other changes can take several seconds to refresh in each viewport. You can disable a viewport to prevent such updates by pressing D. You can also right-click the viewport name and select **Disable** from the pop-up menu.

Another setting that you can change to increase the viewport update speed is the **Update During Spinner Drag** option from the **View** menu. Spinners are the up and down arrows that appear next to an object's parameters. Every time you drag on a spinner to change an object's parameter values, each viewport that displays the object is updated. For complex objects, changing a spinner rapidly can cause even a powerful computer to crash. By disabling this option, you force the viewports to wait for the spinner to stop changing before updating the display.

Rendering levels

Another way to speed up viewport refresh rates is to reduce the rendering levels. Rendering levels describe the level of detail and display provided by a view. Several rendering level choices are available for each viewport, as shown in Figure 1-15, but I've found that there are only three I typically need to use: **Smooth + Highlights**, **Wireframe**, and **Bounding Box**. **Smooth + Highlights** is the highest-quality viewport display—it shows smooth surfaces with all lighting highlights. This rendering level takes the longest to regenerate. The second level that I use is **Wireframe**, which shows polygon edges only, and is somewhat quicker to regenerate. Lastly, the **Bounding Box** level, which is the quickest to regenerate, just shows a box in place of the object whose extents would completely enclose the object.

By default, 3ds Max opens with four viewports, three of which have a **Wireframe** rendering level. The fourth viewport, which displays the Perspective view, is displayed in **Smooth + Highlights** mode. Good management of rendering levels is critical for working efficiently in large scenes, and can prevent you from having to wait long periods of time for viewport regenerations.

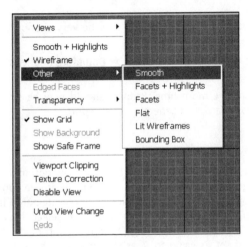

Figure 1-15. Rendering levels

I'll rarely have more than one viewport showing a **Smooth + Highlights** level, and that's usually the one displaying the Perspective or User view. As I develop very large scenes, I try to view as many objects as I can with the **Bounding Box** level. You'll probably find it rare to get any benefit out of turning the rendering level for an entire viewport to **Bounding Box** because you won't be able to recognize which objects are which (and you might even have trouble remembering which way is up). A much better use of the **Bounding Box** option is to view select *objects* in **Bounding Box** mode. These objects should be the most complex objects in your scene, and should remove a substantial burden from your graphics card. They should also be objects that you won't have to manipulate regularly. As I said, other levels are available for your use, but their benefit in architectural visualizations is questionable. Knowing when and how to use the three levels mentioned here will suffice.

Changing a viewport's rendering level

This exercise demonstrates how to change a viewport's rendering level to enhance object visibility within a scene. It also demonstrates the importance of rendering level management in maintaining acceptable viewport regeneration time.

1. Reset 3ds Max.

2. In the Perspective viewport, create a teapot.

3. Place the cursor over the Perspective viewport, click and drag using the mouse's scroll button, and pan around the viewport. With only one object in the scene, containing only a small number of faces, panning should be very smooth.

4. Click the **Modify** tab and change the segments to a maximum possible value of **64**.

5. In the Perspective viewport, create 5 more similar teapots, each with 64 segments. After the first teapot is changed to 64 segments, each successive teapot will be made with 64 segments automatically.

6. Pan around the Perspective viewport again. Panning should now be very choppy in a shaded viewport with this many faces visible.

7. Right-click the Perspective viewport name and select **Other ➤ Bounding Box** from the drop-down list.

8. Pan around the Perspective viewport one more time. Panning should now be smooth again because 3ds Max doesn't have to work hard to regenerate the viewport.

Enabling Fast View

Another way of achieving quicker viewport refreshing is to enable the Fast View option. I've made a point to avoid highlighting too many configuration options in this book, but this is one configuration feature that's too valuable to pass up. This option speeds up refreshing by displaying only a fraction of the faces in a scene. To enable this option, right-click the viewport name (or select the **Customize** menu) and select **Viewport Configuration**. Within the **Rendering Options** section of the **Rendering Method** tab, select **Fast View Nth Faces** and set its value to **5**, as shown in Figure 1-16. To change all the viewports in the same way, select the **All Viewports** option from the **Apply To** section of the same tab.

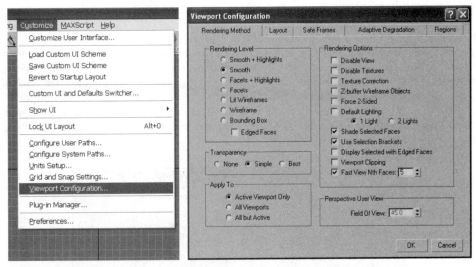

Figure 1-16. Enabling Fast View

Enabling Fast View within a viewport

This exercise demonstrates how to enable Fast View within a viewport to speed up viewport regenerations.

1. Continue from the previous exercise.

2. Right-click the Perspective viewport name and select **Wireframe** from the drop-down list.

3. Pan around the Perspective viewport. Even though the viewport is in **Wireframe** mode, panning should be choppy with such a large number of faces displayed.

4. Right-click the Perspective viewport again and select **Configure** from the drop-down list. The **Viewport Configuration** dialog box will open to the **Rendering Method** tab.

5. In the **Rendering Options** section, enable the **Fast View Nth Faces** option.

6. Click **OK** to close the **Viewport Configuration** dialog box. Now, only every fifth face will be visible inside the Perspective viewport.

7. Pan around the Perspective viewport one more time. Panning should now be smooth again because 3ds Max doesn't have to work as hard to regenerate just one-fifth of the previous number of faces.

The viewport layouts

At times you may decide you want to change the number or arrangement of your viewports, or you may want to quickly change their size or aspect ratio. The default layout displays four equally sized viewports, which can easily be changed by right-clicking the viewport name, clicking **Viewport Configuration** from the menu, and selecting **Layout**. Choose from any of the available layouts (as shown in Figure 1-17). An even easier way to change the size or arrangement of your viewports is to click at the intersection of two viewports and drag the edge to a new location. You can return to the original layout by right-clicking any of the viewport borders and selecting **Reset Layout** from the pop-up menu.

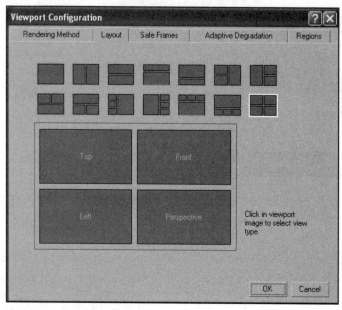

Figure 1-17. The viewport layouts

Changing the viewport layout

This exercise demonstrates how to change the viewport layout to suit your particular needs.

1. Reset 3ds Max.

2. Right-click the Perspective viewport name and select **Configure** from the drop-down list.

3. Select the **Layout** tab.

4. Select any of the 14 different viewport layout options and click **OK**. The viewport will change to match the option you selected.

5. Place your cursor over the border of any two viewports. Arrows will appear.

6. Click and drag any viewport border to resize any two viewports. You can also click and drag the border of any three or four viewports at one time.

7. Place your cursor over the border of any two viewports and right-click.

8. Select **Reset Layout** to reset the layout to the default 3ds Max layout.

Undoing and saving view changes

In the course of a project, you're bound to make several inadvertent changes to a viewport's display. When this happens, you can simply undo the view change by pressing Shift+Z or right-clicking the viewport name and selecting **Undo View Change** from the bottom of the pop-up menu, as shown in Figure 1-18. The menu will display the actual view type that can be changed. In the example in Figure 1-18, the user can undo the view rotate feature just implemented.

You can also save a specific view in any viewport by selecting **Save Active Viewport** from the **Views** menu. To restore this view later, select **Restore Active Viewport**. I don't find much use in this feature, however, because only one view can be saved per viewport.

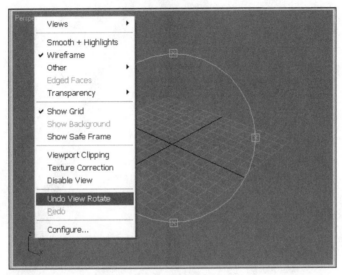

Figure 1-18. The Undo View Change command

Summary

By now you should know that 3ds Max is simply too large a program to learn comprehensively and that it's wise to focus on those features that are relevant to your industry. An underlying theme of this book is to teach you what you need to learn to be productive in an architectural visualization firm and avoid learning too many features that serve no purpose or function. Although I have always strived to learn as many new features as I can, my first priority has always been to perfect the tools that truly pay off in a production environment.

This chapter has covered the basics of navigating the 3ds Max interface, with a strong emphasis on efficient viewport navigation and keyboard shortcuts. Hopefully, you're ready to take the next step—working with objects!

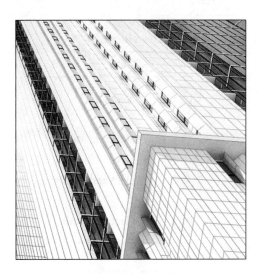

Chapter 2

WORKING WITH OBJECTS

Now that you understand the basics of the 3ds Max interface, it's time to learn how to work with objects in a scene. The concepts discussed in this chapter are critical because they represent the most common tasks that most 3ds Max users will perform: selecting objects, displaying objects, and transforming objects. There are numerous tools available and a seemingly infinite number of ways to accomplish the same task in 3ds Max. However, no task can be performed without utilizing the concepts covered in this chapter. Efficient use of the select, display, and transform features can save you countless hours over the course of any architectural visualization.

Selecting objects

Selecting objects in your scene is one of the most common and repeated tasks you will perform in 3ds Max. It would make sense, therefore, to ensure that the method you use to select an object is efficient and time-effective. Fortunately, 3ds Max gives you several different ways to select objects.

The Select icons

The easiest way to select an object is by simply clicking the object in one of the viewports. You can do so with any of four different select icons found on the **Main** toolbar and shown in Table 2-1. If you are in the middle of a command, pressing Esc once or twice or clicking the right mouse icon in the active viewport will end the command and return you to whatever select mode was last active.

Table 2-1. The Select icons

Icon	Name	Keyboard Shortcut
	Select Object	Q
	Select and Move	W
	Select and Rotate	E
	Select and Scale	R

The first icon, which looks like an arrow, is the **Select Object** icon, which can be enabled by pressing Q. This is the only icon of the four that does not allow you to perform a transform with the same click of the mouse used to select the object. The importance of this cannot be overemphasized. The reason it is so important, as you will probably learn many times the hard way, is that it is very easy to inadvertently transform an object when all you intend to do is select the object. In some instances, you may not notice it until it's too late. The undo feature in 3ds Max recycles itself after every 20 commands or actions performed. If the 20th action you performed is an accidental select-and-move command, you won't be able to undo the mistake because the undo queue will be erased and all previous actions will be unavailable for undo. The consequences of this could be very time-consuming to fix. One technique that I recommend when continuously selecting objects without applying a transform is to activate the **Select Object** icon so that you cannot transform an object accidentally. If anything other than the **Select Object** icon is active, you cannot rush the selection of an object without eventually getting burned.

When you do select an object, the selected object turns white and is enclosed in what are called selection brackets. The transform gizmo also appears at the object's pivot point. You can deselect an object by simply clicking anywhere in a viewport where there's not an object.

As a scene becomes crowded, it may become difficult to select the object you want. If two objects lie on top of each other from the perspective of the viewport you're selecting in, clicking the object that's already selected will cause it to be deselected and the other object selected. With many objects lying on top of one another, it may take several clicks of the mouse before you select the object you want.

The Select Objects dialog box

The **Select Objects** dialog box, shown in Figure 2-1, is a great, easy-to-use feature that allows you to select objects in your scene by choosing from a list. I rely heavily on this feature, but find use for only a portion of its capability. The dialog box can be opened by clicking the **Select By Name** icon on the **Main** toolbar, and until closed, no other work in 3ds Max is allowed. An alternative to this is the **Selection** floater, which is identical to the **Select Objects** dialog box, except that it's modeless and therefore can stay open while other work is being performed. The keyboard shortcut for the **Selection** floater is H.

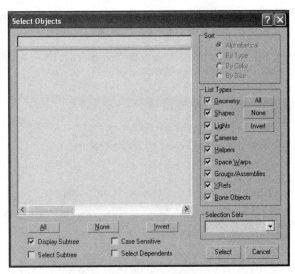

Figure 2-1. The Select Objects dialog box

The **Select Objects** dialog box contains a name list that displays all objects checked in the **List Types** section to the right of the name list. All object types are checked by default and therefore displayed in the name list. By unchecking an object type, you prevent that object type from being displayed in the name list. To highlight an object, simply click the name of the object. Holding down Ctrl allows you to select multiple objects. Holding down Shift allows you to select every object that lies between two objects that you select. Double-clicking any object name closes the dialog box and selects that object.

Above the name list is a field in which you can type. As you type, all of the objects with names that begin with the same letters that you type are highlighted in the name list. For example, if you type the letter **w** in the list, all objects with names that begin with **w** will be highlighted. If you add the letter **a**, then an object with the name **Wall** will remain highlighted, while an object with the name **Window** will no longer be highlighted.

Two wildcard characters can be used within the field to help locate and select objects. The wildcard character * can be used to replace multiple characters, and the character **?** can be used to replace a single character. If you type **Wa***, all objects that begin with **Wa** (such as **Wall** and **Water**) will be highlighted, while objects such as **Window** and **Willow** will not. If you type **?all**, all four-letter object names in which last three letters are **all** will be selected (e.g., **Wall** and **Ball**).

It should be noted that while wildcards are effective for locating objects, you should strive to avoid being in a position that warrants using them. By maintaining a good naming system, you'll save a great deal of time when trying to find objects in large scenes. A good naming system is like a seatbelt—it takes about the same amount of time and can save you a lot of grief. Wildcards are something that I rarely use, as I spend more of my time naming my objects in a way that makes them easy to find and select.

One other feature within the **Select Objects** dialog box that you may find useful on occasion is **Sort**. By default, all objects are listed alphabetically, but you can choose the options of sorting by type, color, or size.

You also have the option of selecting from the **Selection Sets drop-down list, which is a feature that also appears on the Main toolbar and is discussed later in the chapter.**

The remaining options in the dialog box have very limited practicality in architectural visualizations and are not covered in this book.

Selecting an object by name

This exercise demonstrates the use of the Select by Name feature.

1. Reset 3ds Max.
2. Create two spheres, two boxes, and two teapots in any viewport.
3. Click the **Select by Name** icon in the **Main** toolbar, or press H, to open the **Select Objects** dialog box (shown in the following image).

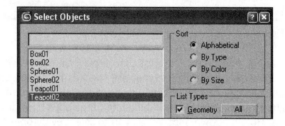

4. In the empty field above the name list, type **S**. All the object names that begin with the letter **S** are highlighted.
5. Click **Select** to select the two sphere objects.
6. Open the **Select Objects** dialog box again and deselect the **Geometry** option under **List Types**. All the **Geometry**-type objects in your scene will disappear from the name list.
7. Reselect the **Geometry** option.
8. Highlight **Box01**, hold the Shift key, and select the **Sphere02** object. The objects between the two names you selected should now be highlighted.
9. Click **Cancel** to end the command.

Select by region

Besides clicking objects directly, you have the option of creating windows with which to define a region of selection. There are two types of window selections: window and crossing. The icon that allows you to toggle between these two options is called the **Window/Crossing** icon (see Figure 2-2); this icon is located on the **Main** toolbar to the left of the **Select and Move** icon.

Figure 2-2. The Window (left) and Crossing (right) selections of the Window/Crossing icon

To make a selection, simply click anywhere in the active viewport away from the object or objects you want to select, drag the mouse, and click somewhere else away from the object(s), so that the drag outline created with the mouse movement either intersects or completely encloses your selection. After the second click of the mouse, the objects will be selected. When the **Window/Crossing** icon is toggled to the **Window** selection option, all objects must be completely enclosed within the selection outline for them to be selected. When toggled to the **Crossing** selection option, an object is selected when any portion of the selection outline touches the object. Let's look at the difference in action.

Notice that in the left image of Figure 2-3, a selection is made that completely encompasses the teapot object and partially crosses the sphere. Since the **Window/Crossing** icon is toggled to **Crossing**, both objects become selected, as shown in the image on the right.

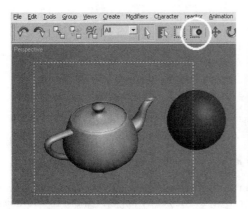 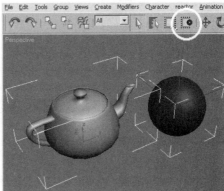

Figure 2-3. A crossing selection

Notice in the images in Figure 2-4 that the **Window/Crossing** icon is toggled to **Window**. Once again, the selection outline in the image on the left completely encompasses the teapot object and partially crosses the sphere object. Since the **Window/Crossing** icon is toggled to **Window**, only the teapot becomes selected, as shown in the image on the right.

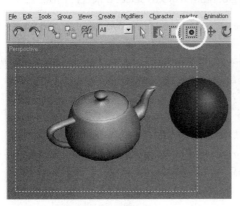 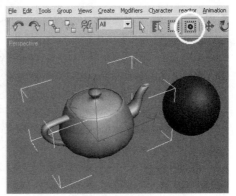

Figure 2-4. A window selection

To the left of the **Window/Crossing** icon is the **Selection Region** icon. This icon is a flyout menu that contains four other shape selection icons that can be used to create other shapes to define selection regions. Figure 2-5 shows the five available shapes. The first icon on the top, **Rectangular Selection Region**, uses a rectangle to define the selection region, and involves two clicks of the mouse—one for each corner of the rectangle. The next icon, **Circular Selection Region**, creates a circular selection region that grows from the center outward. The third icon, **Fence Selection Region**, lets you draw a shape of any kind with multiple clicks of the mouse that define the corners of the shape. The fourth icon, **Lasso Selection Region**, lets you draw a selection region freehand. The last icon, **Paint Selection Region**, lets you select objects by placing the cursor over an object.

Figure 2-5. The Selection Region flyout menu

You can cycle through the five available **Selection Region** icons by pressing Q repeatedly.

In addition to the select-by-region method, you can select many objects at a time by holding Ctrl while clicking all the objects you want individually, or by using the Select By Region feature to add objects to your current selection. To deselect objects individually, hold Alt and select the objects. You can also use the select-by-region method while holding Alt to deselect multiple objects.

Selecting an object by region

This exercise demonstrates use of the Selection Region command to select objects in your scene.

1. Continue from the previous exercise or reset 3ds Max and create two spheres, two boxes, and two teapots in any viewport.

2. Toggle the **Window/Crossing** icon to **Window**. The **Window/Crossing** icon will turn yellow.

3. Click the **Rectangular Selection Region** icon (shown at the top of Figure 2-5).

3. Select either teapot object in your scene by clicking and dragging around the entire object in any viewport.

4. Hold Ctrl and select the other teapot object to add it to the current selection.

5. Hold Alt and select either teapot object to remove it from the current selection. You can also hold Ctrl again to remove an object when you select it.

Selection filters

The **Selection Filter**, shown in Figure 2-6, is a great feature you can use to specify which object types are selectable. If you have a complex scene with hundreds of objects of various types, and all you want to do is modify the lights without hiding all other objects, then applying a filter would be helpful. With a **Light** object selection filter applied, no other object type can be selected, and you can work with the light objects without worrying about inadvertently selecting a different object type.

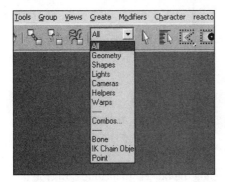

Figure 2-6. The Selection Filter

To enable the **Selection Filter**, select the desired object type from the drop-down list.

Named selection sets

Selecting objects in your scene can be very time-consuming, especially when your scene becomes large and cluttered. If you spend any significant amount of time selecting a group of objects to work on in some way, and you know you're going to need to select the same group of objects again for some other modification, then creating selection sets can save a great deal of time. With just two clicks of the mouse, you can bring back that previously saved selection that took much longer to create the first time. To use the **Named Selection Sets** dialog box (shown in Figure 2-8), click the **Edit Named Selection Sets** icon located on the **Main** toolbar (shown in Figure 2-7).

Figure 2-7. The Edit Named Selection Sets icon

The **Create New Set** icon at the top-left of the dialog box creates a new set that you can name and add objects to or subtract objects from, using the icons that resemble a plus and minus sign. The **Select Objects in Set** icon (third from the right) selects within the dialog and within the scene all of the objects in that set. The **Select Objects** dialog box is also available from here. The **Highlight Selected Objects** icon (far right) highlights within the dialog box all of the objects that are currently highlighted within the scene. You can drag and drop objects from one set to another. You can also drag one set name onto another to combine all of the objects of both sets into the second set name. Double-clicking a set name selects all of the objects within that set. Sub-object selection sets can also be made and selected, but only when in sub-object mode. Sub-object mode is covered in greater detail in Chapter 3.

Figure 2-8. The Named Selection Sets dialog box

An easier way to create a selection set after selecting the objects to include is to type the name of the new set inside the **Named Selection Sets** drop-down list next to the **Edit Named Selection Sets** icon, as shown in Figure 2-9. To recall a selection, click the same drop-down list and select the name.

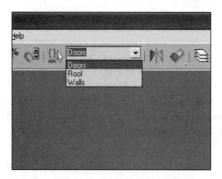

Figure 2-9. The Named Selection Sets drop-down list

Named selection sets highlight the point that I made earlier in the chapter—that you should take whatever time necessary to name the objects in your scene in a way that makes them easy to find and select later on. If you work with others on the same project, this becomes even more important. Someone unfamiliar with your scene can find it extremely difficult to select objects when all the objects are left with the original names, such as **Sphere01**, **Sphere02**, **Cylinder01**, and so on. It becomes very frustrating, for example, to work in a scene with fifty doors that were created as copies of a box and still have the default names **Box01**, **Box02**, **Box03** . . . **Box50**.

Using named selection sets

This exercise demonstrates use of named selection sets with the **Named Selection Sets** dialog box and the **Named Selection Sets** drop-down list.

1. Continue from the previous exercise or reset 3ds Max and create two spheres, two boxes, and two teapots in any viewport.
2. Deselect all the objects in your scene.
3. Select the two teapots in your scene.
4. Click the **Edit Named Selection Sets** icon (shown in Figure 2-7). The **Named Selection Sets** dialog box will open.
5. Click the **Create New Set** icon.

6. Type the name **Teapots** in the field that appears.
7. In any viewport, select one of the sphere objects.
8. In the **Named Selection Sets** dialog box, click the **Add Selected Objects** icon (shown in the following image). The sphere will be added to the named selection set you just created.

9. In the **Named Selection Sets** dialog box, click the **Subtract Selected Objects** icon (shown in the following image). The sphere will be subtracted from named selection set.

10. Close the **Named Selection Sets** dialog box.
11. Deselect all the objects in your scene.
12. Click the down arrow on the **Named Selection Sets** drop-down list, as shown in Figure 2-9. All the named selection sets you created will be displayed.
13. Select the set called **Teapots**. The two teapot objects in your scene will become selected.

Selection lock

A handy feature that lets you quickly lock your selection is the **Selection Lock** toggle icon, shown in Figure 2-10. When this feature is enabled, the current selection cannot be changed. You cannot add objects to or remove objects from the selection no matter where you click. This feature is enabled by clicking the **Selection Lock** toggle icon, an icon that looks like a lock and is located on the Status bar in the Lower Interface bar. You can also use the method I prefer: pressing the space bar. When the feature is enabled, the **Selection Lock** toggle icon turns yellow and stays yellow until the icon is toggled off.

Figure 2-10. The Selection Lock toggle, disabled (left) and enabled (right)

Using the Selection Lock feature

1. Continue from the previous exercise or reset 3ds Max and create two spheres, two boxes, and two teapots in any viewport.
2. Click the **Selection Lock** toggle. The toggle will turn yellow.
3. Try selecting any new objects in your scene (you will be unable to).
4. Click the **Selection Lock** toggle again. The toggle will return to its previous state.

Other ways to select objects

There are a few other interfaces with which to select objects in a scene, such as the **Material Editor**, Track view, and Schematic view. Selecting objects with the **Material Editor** will be covered in Chapter 6, and selecting objects with Track view and Schematic view will be covered in Chapter 12.

Isolate selection

Finally, there is a feature that first appeared in 3ds Max 6 that I would simply find difficult to work without now: Isolate Selection. This feature is available through the **Tools** menu or the keyboard short-cut Alt+Q. Enabling this feature hides all objects except the currently selected object. What's more, it zooms to the extents of the object in the active viewport. In the left image of Figure 2-11, the teapot is selected and the Isolate Selection command is activated. Notice in the image on the right that all other objects disappear and the active viewport is zoomed in to the extent of the teapot object. It also brings up a small dialog box that has a single icon to exit you out of isolation mode.

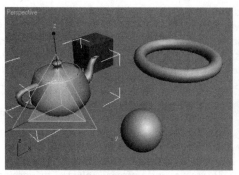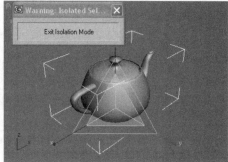

Figure 2-11. Isolating a selection

Using Isolate Selection

This exercise demonstrates use of the Isolate Selection feature.

1. Continue from the previous exercise or reset 3ds Max and create two spheres, two boxes, and two teapots in any viewport.

2. Select the two spheres in your scene.

3. Press Alt+Q. The two spheres will be isolated and all other objects in your scene will be temporarily hidden from view.

4. Click the **Exit Isolation Mode** message that appears. All of the previously hidden objects will return to view.

Displaying objects

3ds Max gives you great flexibility over the display of objects. How you display objects in your scene can greatly affect your speed and efficiency. If you're like me, you hate having to wait on your computer to do anything. Well, if you're not smart about how you display objects in 3ds Max, you can end up doing a lot of waiting.

There are several interfaces that control the display of objects, but as with all areas of the program, you should strive to use the most effective and efficient ones. Undoubtedly, those would have to be the **Display** panel, the **Display** floater, and as usual, the keyboard. The **Display** panel and **Display** floater are very similar in function. In fact, the only features on the panel that don't exist on the floater are the **Display Color** and **Link Display** rollouts, which are of little importance in architectural visualizations and are not discussed in this book.

The two most important and frequently used display features in 3ds Max are located on the **Display** panel and **Display** floater. They are **Hide** and **Freeze**.

Hide simply turns off the display of an object, and **Freeze** locks an object so that it cannot be modified in any way. Objects that you neither need to work on nor see should be hidden. Objects that do not need to be worked on, but still need to be displayed as a reference, should be frozen. Freezing is a great feature when you need to view an object as a reference but don't want to have to worry about inadvertently transforming or modifying it. Frozen objects are displayed in light gray so that they don't stand out and make it difficult to see other objects.

The Display floater

The **Display** floater contains two tabs, **Hide/Freeze** and **Object Level**, which are identical in content to four of the rollouts in the **Display** panel; **Hide**, **Freeze**, **Hide By Category**, and **Display Properties** (see Figure 2-12). Both give you the ability to hide, unhide, freeze, and unfreeze selected or unselected objects. The **By Name** option opens the **Select Objects** dialog box so that you can apply the display change to objects you select by name. The **By Hit** option lets you pick objects in a viewport to apply the display change to. Additionally, the **Display** floater and **Display** panel have a **Hide By Category** option, which lets you quickly hide all scene objects of a certain type (e.g., lights or cameras).

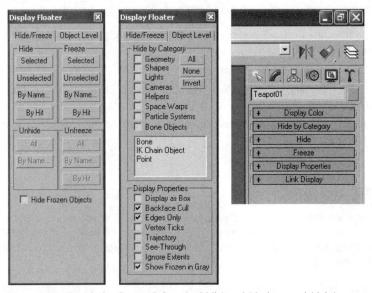

Figure 2-12. The Display floater (left and middle) and Display panel (right)

The **Display** floater and **Display** panel also contain a section that lets you change other display properties. These options, shown in the **Object Level** tab in Figure 2-12, can prove to be invaluable display aids as you work.

- **Display as Box**: This option is disabled by default; enabling it turns any object into a box just large enough to enclose the object. This is used to reduce the display of high polygon models to simple boxes that are easier for your computer to display. In architectural scenes with numerous trees containing tens of thousands of polygons, this can be an invaluable option. Without converting these trees to simple boxes, it wouldn't take many of them to bring your graphics cards to a screeching halt.

- **Backface Cull**: This option is enabled by default; disabling it makes the hidden faces on the backside of an object be displayed.

- **Edges Only**: This option is enabled by default; it causes only the edges of polygons to be displayed. Disabling it causes the shared edge of every face that is not a polygon edge to be displayed.

- **Vertex Ticks**: This option is disabled by default; enabling it causes all vertices in an object to be displayed without having to be in vertex sub-object mode. This can be a nice visual aid at times.

- **Trajectory**: This option is disabled by default; enabling it causes the path that an animated object follows to be displayed as a spline.

- **See-Through**: This option is disabled by default; enabling it causes shaded objects to appear transparent. This does not affect the rendered image, only the viewport display.

- **Ignore Extents**: This option is disabled by default; enabling it causes the object to not affect the zoom extents. If an is object a large distance away from the rest of your scene, such as a light representing the sun, enabling this option will disregard the light and allow the zoom extents to zoom in closer to the extents of the main area of the scene. I use zoom extents constantly and enable this feature whenever I use far-away lights.

- **Show Frozen in Gray**: This option is enabled by default and should be left enabled; disabling it causes frozen objects to appear as if they're not frozen.

As with all areas of 3ds Max, I highly recommend the use of keyboard shortcuts in the display of objects. These shortcuts exist as toggles, so that one press of a key makes the objects disappear and another press makes them reappear. Objects that utilize hide and unhide toggles include cameras (Shift+C), geometry (Shift+G), grids (G), helpers (Shift+H), lights (Shift+L), particle systems (Shift+P), shapes (Shift+S), and space warps (Shift+W).

Finally, the **Object Properties** dialog box is another interface that displays some of the options you just read about and many more. These options are more advanced and will be covered later.

Using the Display floater

This exercise demonstrates use of the **Display** floater.

1. Continue from the previous exercise or reset 3ds Max and create two spheres, two boxes, and two teapots in any viewport.

2. Select the two box objects in your scene.

3. From the **Tools** menu, select **Display Floater**. The **Display** floater will appear, as shown in the left image of Figure 2-12.

4. From the **Display** floater, select **Hide ➤ Selected**. The two boxes will disappear from view.

5. Select **Unhide ➤ All**. The two boxes will reappear.

Layers

When I first started using layers, I remembered the old encyclopedias that showed the anatomy of a frog using pieces of cellophane to show the different layers of the frog. If you want to see just under the skin, turn the page; if you want to see deep under the muscles, turn a few more. Layers in 3ds Max are similar to this kind of display. They provide an easy way to display specific objects or groups of objects.

Using the Layer Manager

Layers are created and managed through the **Layer Manager** dialog box, shown in Figure 2-13. This dialog box is a floater, and thus can remain open while you work. It is accessed through the **Layer** icon on the **Main** toolbar, or the same icon on the **Layers** toolbar. The **Layer Manager** can take up a lot of screen real estate, which for a short period of time is fine. If you're like me and prefer to maximize screen real estate, I suggest turning on the **Layers** toolbar so that you can do many of the same things that you can in the **Layer Manager** without having to open it.

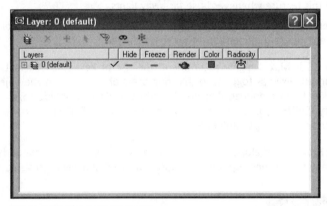

Figure 2-13. The Layer Manager

The **Layer Manager** includes seven icons along the top (as shown in Figure 2-13) that allow you to do the following, respectively, from left to right:

- Create a new layer (containing selected objects)
- Delete highlighted empty layers
- Add selected objects to a highlighted layer
- Select highlighted objects and layers
- Highlight selected objects' layers
- Hide/unhide all layers
- Freeze/unfreeze all layers

Also within the **Layer Manager** are columns for **Hide**, **Freeze**, **Render**, **Color**, and **Radiosity** (covered much later in the book). You can change these options for an individual object; or, by highlighting the layer name, you can make changes to all of the objects on a certain layer. If a property is enabled, an icon is displayed. If the property is disabled, a dashed line is displayed. If you want an object to derive its display options from the layer, then click the appropriate icon until a dot icon is displayed. Objects within a layer can have different display options enabled or disabled. By clicking the column heads, you can sort objects and layers according to the status of the display icons.

The following are some important things to remember about layers:

- Newly created objects are added to the current layer.
- You cannot delete a layer if any objects are assigned to the layer or if it is the current layer.
- Creating a new layer automatically makes it the current layer.
- Each object can be assigned to only one layer.
- All layer names must be unique.
- Layer 0 is the default layer that objects are added to, and this layer cannot be deleted.

Using layers

This exercise demonstrates use of layers in your scene.

1. Continue from the previous exercise or reset 3ds Max and create two spheres, two boxes, and two teapots in any viewport.
2. Select the two teapot objects in your scene.
3. Click the **Layer Manager** icon in the **Main** toolbar. The **Layer Manager** dialog box will open (see Figure 2-13).
4. Click the **Create New Layer** icon.
5. Click the yellow highlighted word **Layer 01** that appears.
6. Type the name **Teapots** and press Enter.
7. Click the plus sign to the left of the new layer named **Teapots**. The two teapots that were selected when you created the layer are now on a layer called **Teapots**. All other objects are on the layer named **0**, by default.

Transforming objects

Transformation is a term used to describe a change in an object's position, size, or orientation in 3D space. Technically, you could argue that you could transform an object with any of the hundreds of available tools in 3ds Max; however, in 3ds Max the term is only actually applied to the use of the Move, Rotate, and Scale commands. These commands are three of the most powerful and critical commands used in 3ds Max. Let's look at each a little more closely to see what they do, before moving on.

Move

The move transform allows you to move any object anywhere in 3D space, along any of the three axes or xy, xz, or yz planes. There are several ways to perform a move transform. In each case, you must first select the object and click the **Select and Move** icon (or press W).

You can click, hold, and drag on the transform gizmo within the active viewport. Placing the mouse over a single axis of the transform gizmo causes that axis to become highlighted in yellow, and restricts transformation to just that axis. Placing the mouse over the area between any two axes causes a rectangle lying in the plane of those two axes to become highlighted and any transformation to become restricted to that plane. Figure 2-14 shows an example of both. In the image on the left, the cursor is placed over the x axis, which becomes highlighted; in the image on the right, the cursor is placed between the x and z axes, which causes the xz plane indicator to become highlighted.

You can use the cursor icons to move an object in small increments, although this is not a preferred method because it is not precise. If you right-click any of the transform icons (**Select and Move, Select and Rotate**, or **Select and Scale**) in the **Main** toolbar, you'll bring up the **Transform Type-In** dialog box, which is discussed in further detail later in this chapter.

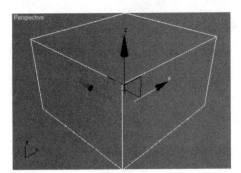 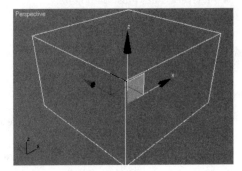

Figure 2-14. The transform gizmo

Scale

The scale transform allows you to increase and decrease the size of an object about its transform gizmo. The scaling of an object's three dimensions, x, y, and z, is uniform by default. You have the option, however, to perform a non-uniform scale, in which one or two dimensions are scaled while the other one or two remain constant. You can also perform a squash scaling operation, in which one dimension is increased in scale and the other two dimensions are decreased in scale.

To access these additional two scaling options, click and hold the **Scale** icon and select either option from the flyout menu, as shown in Figure 2-15. You can also press R repeatedly to cycle through all three scaling options. You can right-click any transform icon to bring up the **Transform Type-In** dialog box.

Figure 2-15. The Scale flyout menu

An example of the non-uniform scale and the squash feature is shown in Figure 2-16, in which the sphere on the left is first scaled non-uniformly along just the vertical axis and then squashed along the same axis.

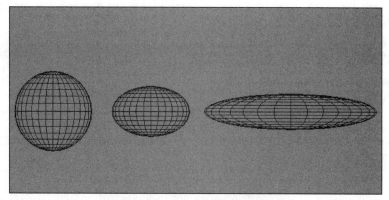

Figure 2-16. Uniform scale, non-uniform scale, and squash scale, shown left to right

Rotate

The rotate transform allows you to spin an object around any axis of its transform gizmo. To perform the rotate transform, select the object, click the **Select and Rotate** icon (or press E) and click, hold, and drag the transform gizmo within the active viewport. You can also right-click any of the transform icons to bring up the **Transform Type-In** dialog box. By placing the transform gizmo in selective locations, you can spin an object any way you want. Rotations are measured in degrees by default; 360 degrees equals a full rotation.

Performing move, scale, and rotate transforms

This exercise demonstrates how to perform move, scale, and rotate transforms.

1. Continue from the previous exercise or reset 3ds Max and create two spheres, two boxes, and two teapots in any viewport.
2. Select one of the objects in your scene.
3. In the **Main** toolbar, click the **Select and Move** icon (or press W).
4. Place your cursor over one of the axes on the transform gizmo that appears. The axis your cursor is over will turn yellow.
5. Click and drag on the highlighted axis. The object will move along the highlighted axis only.
6. Click the **Select and Scale** icon (or press R).
7. Within the Perspective viewport, place your cursor in the middle of the transform gizmo. The center triangle should become highlighted.

8. Click and drag on the transform gizmo. Dragging upward will scale the object up and dragging downward will scale the object down.

9. Click the **Select and Rotate** icon (or press E).

10. Place your cursor over one of the rotation rings and click and drag to rotate the object around the highlighted axis.

The Transform Type-In dialog box

The **Transform Type-In** dialog box, shown in Figure 2-17, is a great tool that can be used to transform objects precisely. This dialog box is available for all three transforms and can be accessed by right-clicking any of the transform icons (or by pressing F12). The dialog box opens to whatever transform icon is enabled, regardless of which icon you right-click. The dialog box is also modeless, which means you can leave it open while you continue to work. You can also switch between the three transforms while you work.

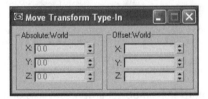

Figure 2-17. The Transform Type-In dialog box

When the dialog box first opens, two columns are displayed: **Absolute:World** and **Offset:World**. The **Absolute:World** column displays the x, y, and z values of the selected object's pivot point position. The pivot point of an object marks the one exact position of the object, even though the pivot may not even lie within the volume of the object, and can in fact be moved far away from the object. By typing a value of **0** for each of the **X:**, **Y:**, and **Z:** boxes while the move transform is active, you are telling 3ds Max to move the object to the world origin (or at least the object's pivot point).

The **Offset:World** column always displays a value of 0 for x, y, and z (unless you are currently typing). This column allows you to transform the object relative to its current position, orientation, or size. For example, when the move transform is active, typing a value of 10 for the z value in the **Offset:World** column will move the object 10 units in the z direction, while typing the same value in the **Absolute:World** column will move the object to a point 10 units from the world origin in the z direction.

Using the Transform Type-In dialog box

This exercise demonstrates use of the **Transform Type-In** dialog box and its effectiveness in transforming objects precise amounts.

1. Continue from the previous exercise or reset 3ds Max and create two spheres, two boxes, and two teapots in any viewport.

2. Select one of the objects in your scene.

3. Right-click the **Move** icon in the **Main** toolbar. The **Move Transform Type-In** dialog box will appear.

4. Double-click the number in the **X:** field under the **Absolute:World** section. The number will become highlighted.

5. Type a new value, slightly larger than the one shown, and press Enter. The object will move to that new x location in the scene.

6. Double-click the **0** inside the **Offset:World (X:)** section of the **Transform Type-In** dialog box. Type the number **1** and press Enter. The object will move exactly 1 unit in the x direction.

Status bar type-in fields

The Status bar type-in, shown in Figure 2-18, allows you to do the same thing as the **Transform Type-In** dialog box: transform an object with absolute or offset values. To transform the object with absolute values, toggle the **Transform Type-In** icon to Absolute mode—for offset, toggle to Offset mode. This icon is located to the left of the **X:** field. The benefit of this tool is that it's docked and out of the way of the viewports. The Status bar is also just that—a bar that shows the status of the object's position, orientation, or scale, depending on which transform is active.

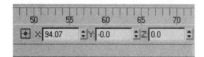 

Figure 2-18. The Status bar type-in fields

Summary

This chapter has covered the essential concepts of selecting, displaying, and transforming objects. If you understand the concepts presented in this chapter, you will be able to work with objects effectively and efficiently.

Now that the essential concepts of working with objects have been covered, it's time to discuss how to create new objects. The next chapter looks at the basics of modeling, and it begins by discussing how to set up 3ds Max for efficient use.

Part 2

MODELING

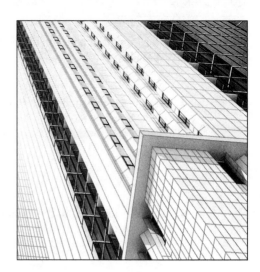

Quick Start 2

GETTING STARTED WITH MODELING

Approximate completion time: 45 minutes

Quick Start 2 builds upon the material covered in Part I, "Getting Around Inside 3ds Max." In this tutorial, you'll jump right into the modeling process by creating the structure of your virtual welcome center. You'll use some of the most powerful modeling features covered in the next three chapters and see how quickly and easily a visualization can be modeled. Although this scene is simplistic in nature, it requires use of many of the same tools as a very large and intricate scene created by a veteran user. For the sake of time and to avoid repetitive features, several of the scene elements have already been created.

1. Open the file you that you saved at the end of Quick Start 1, or open the file 3dsMax8\scenes\Friends_of_Ed\QuickStart02.max.

You'll start by providing some land for the welcome center to rest on.

2. Press H to open the **Select Objects** dialog box and double-click the object named **Site-Grass**. You can also click once on the name and click **OK** to complete the same command.

3. In the Command panel on the right-hand side of the screen, click the **Modify** icon.

4. Click the **Extrude** modifier button. This adds the **Extrude** modifier to the **Site-Grass** object, which changes the spline into a 3D object.

5. In the **Amount** field of the **Parameters** rollout, type **5** and press Enter. This causes the spline that represents the grass to turn into a 3D object with a 5-inch thickness.

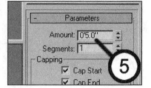

Now you'll create a street for visitors to access your welcome center.

6. Press H to open the **Select Objects** dialog box and double-click the object named **Site-Streets**.

7. Right-click in the active viewport (the one with a yellow line around it), move the cursor over **Convert To:** and select **Convert to Editable Mesh**. The line that represents the street is now a 3D mesh object.

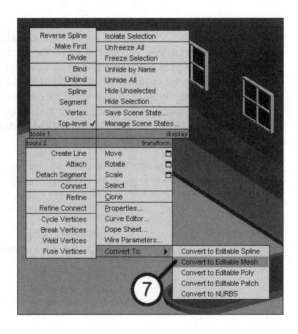

Now that visitors have a way to get to the welcome center, they'll need a place to park.

8. In the **File** menu, select **Import**.

9. Click the **Files of type** drop-down list and select **AutoCAD Drawing (*.DWG,*.DXF)**.

10. Go to the 3dsMax8\scenes\Friends_of_Ed directory and double-click the file **ParkingLines**.

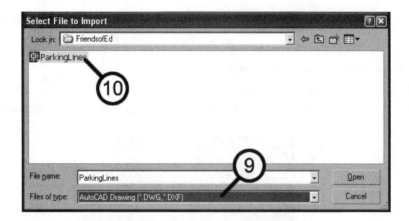

11. In the **AutoCAD DWG/DXF Import Options** dialog box, ensure that the Combine Objects by Layer option is enabled (as shown below). This option tells 3ds Max that all of the line work on the same layer in AutoCAD gets combined into the same object when imported. Click **OK** to exit.

12. Select the **Layer:Site-ParkingLines** object (using the **Select Objects** dialog box), right-click in the active viewport, move the cursor over **Convert To:** and select **Convert to Editable Mesh**. The imported lines can now be seen when rendered. However, since they lie at the same elevation as the street, they need to be raised slightly above the street object.

13. Right-click the **Select and Move** icon in the **Main** toolbar. The **Move Transform Type-In** dialog box appears.

14. In the **Z:** field of the **Absolute:World** column, type **0.5** and press Enter. This raises the parking lines half an inch above the street object—just enough to be rendered properly.

Next, you'll add some mountains behind the welcome center to give your scene a good background.

15. Close the **Move Transform Type-In** dialog box and select the object **Site-Terrain**.

16. In the Command panel, click the **Create** tab.

17. Click the **Geometry** icon (if not already active).

18. Click the drop-down arrow directly below the **Geometry** icon, and select **Compound Objects**.

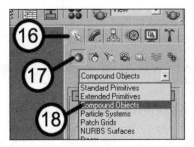

19. Click the **Terrain** button. The lines representing the terrain elevation are used to create mountains. Notice, however, that the mountains have an unnatural, chiseled look, as shown on the right in the following image. Let's smooth out the mountains for a more natural look.

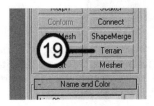
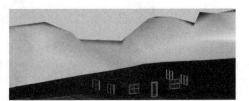

20. In the Command panel, click the **Modify** icon and then click the **TurboSmooth** button. This adds the **TurboSmooth** modifier to the mountains and smoothes their appearance by adding vertices around corners and edges, as shown on the right in the following image.

21. In the **Iterations** field, type **2**. This makes the mountains even smoother by increasing the number of times the modifier is applied to the object. However, this modifier produces more faces than you need. Let's try to reduce the number of faces without reducing the quality of the mountains.

22. Click the **Optimize** button to the left of the **TurboSmooth** button. This dramatically reduces the number of faces from over 2,900 (shown on the left in the following image) to just 850 (shown on the right). You can press F3 to toggle the view from **Smooth + Highlights** to **Wireframe**. If you do, return the view to **Smooth + Highlights** before continuing.

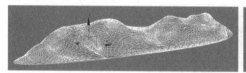 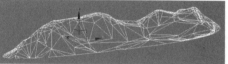

Go ahead and render your scene to see what you've done so far.

23. Press Shift+Q to render the scene. You should see an image similar to the following:

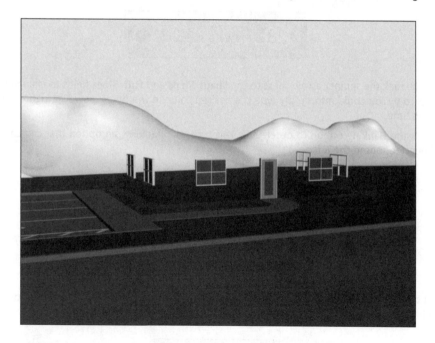

24. Close the render window by clicking the **X** in the upper-right corner.

Now that you have a few site elements in place, it's time to start putting your welcome center together. You already have a foundation in place, so you'll start by erecting some walls.

25. Select the objects named **Bldg-Walls-path** and **Bldg-Walls-profile**. Then press Alt+Q to select and isolate these objects.

26. Deselect both objects and reselect only the **Bldg-Walls-path** object (the larger rectangle).

27. In the Command panel, select **Create ➤ Geometry ➤ Compound Objects**, and click the **Loft** button.

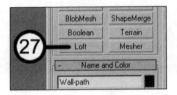

28. Click the **Skin Parameters** rollout to expand the content.

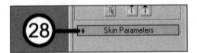

29. Right-click the spinner arrows next to the **Shape Steps** and **Path Steps** fields to change their values to **0**. You could also simply type the desired value in the fields; however, right-clicking will save time.

30. Click the **Banking** option to deselect it. This turns off **Banking**, an option that can cause slight imperfections in the loft.

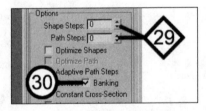

31. In the **Creation Method** rollout, click the **Get Shape** button. 3ds Max now wants you to tell it which shape to loft around the selected path.

32. Click the spline that looks like the cross-section of a wall, named **Bldg-Walls-profile**. A new object is created that will serve as the walls of the office building. Note that the color of the loft you just created is assigned a random color.

33. Click the **Modify** icon, and then click inside the object name field and type **Bldg-Walls**. This renames the loft you just created. You could have also typed the name inside the **Name and Color** rollout within the **Create** panel instead.

34. While still in the **Modify** panel, click the **Smooth** modifier button. This adds the **Smooth** modifier to the loft, which, in lieu of a complex explanation, improves its appearance by changing how the object is shaded.

35. Click the **Exit Isolation Mode** button. This redisplays all the objects that were temporarily hidden.

36. Change the Camera viewport to **Wireframe** mode by pressing the keyboard shortcut F3. In **Wireframe** mode, you can get a sense of the structure under construction. Just to see everything a little more clearly, let's render the scene.

37. Press Shift+Q to render the scene. You should see an image like the one that follows:

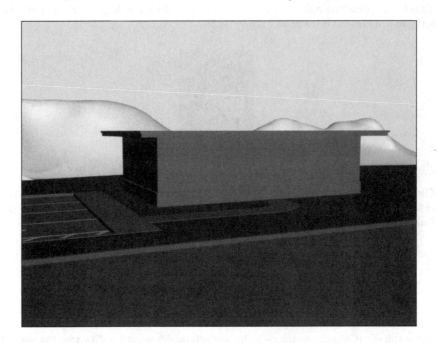

38. Close the render window.

Now it's time to display an object that's been hidden from view until now.

39. In the Command panel, click the **Display** icon.

40. Open the **Hide** rollout (if not already open) and click the **Unhide All** button. The object named **Bldg-Walls-Boolean** is now visible. This is the object you will use to subtract from the walls to create the openings for your windows and door.

41. Select the **Bldg-Walls** and **Bldg-Walls-Boolean** objects. Now you will subtract the volume of the **Bldg-Walls-Boolean** object from the **Bldg-Walls** object to create windows and door openings.

42. Press **Alt+Q** to isolate the objects and then deselect both objects and reselect only the **Bldg-Walls** object.

43. In the Command panel, select **Create ➤ Geometry ➤ Compound Objects** and click the **Boolean** button.

44. Click the **Pick Operand B** button.

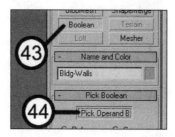

45. In either view, click the **Bldg-Walls-Boolean** object. The volume occupied by the **Bldg-Walls-Boolean** object is now subtracted from the **Bldg-Walls** object, creating openings for the windows and door.

46. Press **Shift+Q** to render the scene again. You should see an image like the one following; however, the color of your walls will probably be different.

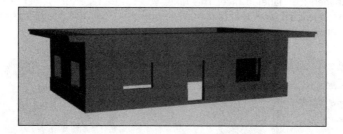

47. Close the render window and click the **Exit Isolation Mode** button.

Now that the walls are up, let's add a roof.

48. Select and isolate the **Bldg-Roof** and **Bldg-Roof-Boolean** objects.

49. Deselect both objects and reselect only the **Bldg-Roof-Boolean** object.

50. In the Command panel, click the **Modify** icon and then click the lightbulb icon to the left of the **Extrude** modifier located in the modifier stack. The icon changes to a lit lightbulb, and the **Extrude** modifier, which was previously off, is now turned on. The **Bldg-Roof-Boolean** object in the viewport now changes into a 3D mesh object.

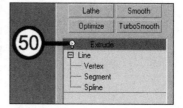

51. Right-click inside the Top view to activate the view and press F3 to change the view to **Smooth + Highlights**. Select the **Bldg-Roof** object, right-click in either viewport, and select **Convert to Editable Mesh** from the quad menu. The roof is converted from splines to a 3D mesh object. Now let's improve the look of the roof by turning it into a standing seam roof.

52. In the Command panel, select **Create ➤ Geometry ➤ Compound Objects**, and click the **Boolean** button.

53. Click the **Cut** option and then click the **Split** option.

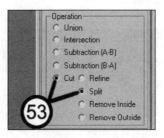

54. Click the **Pick Operand B** button.

55. Click the **Bldg-Roof-Boolean** object in either viewport. You should immediately see the new roof with cuts and splits because it has been split into two separate elements within the one object.

56. Right-click twice in the active viewport and select **Convert to Editable Mesh** from the quad menu.

57. In the Command panel, open the **Selection** rollout (if not already opened) and click the triangle-shaped icon labeled **face**. This takes you to the face sub-object level where you can manipulate individual faces that make up the object. In this case, the faces split by the Boolean operation are automatically selected.

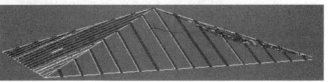

58. Open the **Edit Geometry** rollout in the Command panel (if not already opened), type **2** in the field next to **Extrude**, and then click the **Extrude** button. This extrudes the selected faces 2 inches upwards, creating the appearance of a standing seam roof.

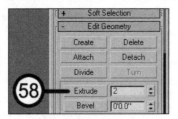

59. Click the text labeled **Editable Mesh** in the modifier stack to close the object's modifier stack.

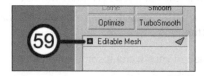

60. Click the **Exit Isolation Mode** button. Activate the **Camera** view (if not already active) and press the keyboard shortcut **P** to change the view to a **Perspective** view.

Next, you'll add a fountain to the front of the welcome center.

61. Select and isolate the **Site-Fountain** object. Use the viewport navigation buttons in the bottom-right corner of the screen to get a better view of the fountain in the **Perspective** viewport.

62. In the Command panel, click the **Modify** icon and then click the **Lathe** button. This turns the spline into a 3D mesh object using the **Lathe** modifier.

Let's try giving the fountain a few different looks before settling on one.

63. In the **Segments** field, type **8** and render the scene. This changes the number of radial segments that make up the fountain, and now the fountain looks octagonal, as shown in the middle image that follows. Press **F3** to change your view to **Smooth+Highlights**. You may want to change your perspective to a more overhead view.

64. Increase the segments to **30** and render the scene. Notice the curved segments of the fountain are much smoother, as shown in the image on the right. With this increase in smoothness, however, comes a large number of vertices. Let's try to reduce the number of faces on the object without changing the fountain's appearance.

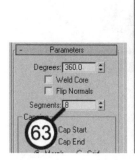

65. Add the **Optimize** modifier. This reduces the number of faces from over 5,000 to only 1,800 (as shown at the bottom of the **Parameters** rollout) without reducing the overall appearance.

66. With the **Perspective** view active, press **C** to change the view back to a **Camera** view. Click the **Exit Isolation Mode** button.

The last thing you're going to add in your scene is some vegetation.

67. Select the **Site-Shrubs** object.

68. While still in the **Modify** panel, type **50000** in the **Duplicates** field. This scatters 50,000 faces around a preselected volume. This is one of numerous ways to create 3D shrubs.

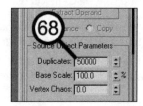

Finally, let's add some trees.

69. In the Command panel, click **Create ➤ Geometry** and select **AEC Extended** from the drop-down list.

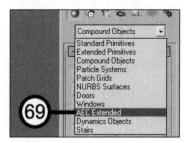

70. Click the **Foliage** button.

71. Scroll down to the bottom of the foliage library and select **Generic Oak**.

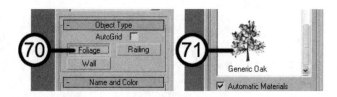

72. In the **Camera** view, place a tree on each of the two circular mulch areas behind the house by clicking in the viewport at these locations. The default tree size is too large for your scene, so let's reduce the height of the trees.

73. With one of the trees selected, click the **Modify** icon, type **20'** in the **Height** field, and repeat with the second tree.

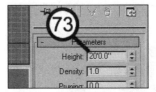

74. Render the scene. Your scene should look similar to the one following:

75. Click the **File** menu, select **Save As**, and name your file MyQuickStart02.max for use in the next Quick Start tutorial.

This concludes Quick Start 2. You have just sampled some of the powerful tools that will be explained in detail in the following chapters on modeling. In Quick Start 3, you'll begin to make the scene come alive by giving the objects real-world materials.

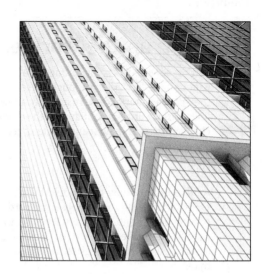

Chapter 3

MODELING BASICS

3ds Max gives you enormous modeling power to create just about anything you can dream up. There are numerous ways to create the same model, and every user seems to have his or her own technique and approach. But in the world of architectural visualizations, there are a few basic modeling types no user can do without: splines, shapes, and meshes. This book does not deal with NURBS, patches, or many of the other powerful modeling types because their usefulness is extremely limited at best.

The building block of any architectural scene is line work. Ideally, an architect or some other professional in the design process will provide this line work in the form of 2D CAD drawings; but occasionally, the 3ds Max user will have to create it from scratch using hand drawings or some other media. Whether the line work is created in 3ds Max or imported from a 2D CAD program, it will end up in the form of a spline or shape, which can be used to create primitives, compound objects, or numerous other object types. All of these object types can then be used to create the editable mesh, which is the powerful and versatile object type prevalent in all architectural scenes.

Before beginning the modeling of any project, however, you should set up 3ds Max for efficient and accurate work. Since 3ds Max was not geared toward any one industry, you should also set up the work environment for architectural work. I'll begin this chapter with scene setup and discuss the many important factors that you should be aware of before beginning any project.

This chapter focuses on how to set up 3ds Max for efficient and accurate architectural work, and how to work with splines, shapes, and meshes.

Setting up the work environment

Setting up your work environment before beginning any project can save you valuable time and prevent unnecessary grief. Although there is an enormous number of settings that control the behavior of the 3ds Max interface, there are only a few important ones that you need to know about. They include units, display drivers, configure path settings, and select preference settings. Some of these need to be changed for each new scene, while others need to be changed only after 3ds Max is installed.

Units

An important setting that should be looked at before you even start setting up a scene is the **System Units** setting. Units are simply a standard of measure, and in 3ds Max they dictate what the true value of any number entered or displayed really means. Since you will be working on architectural visualizations, it only makes sense to use architectural dimensions. Also, since much of your work will originate in AutoCAD with drawings set to architectural dimensions, there's no reason to set your units to anything else.

To change the unit settings, choose **Customize ➤ Units Setup**. The **Units Setup** dialog box (shown in Figure 3-1) opens with a default **Display Unit Scale** of **Generic Units**. Check **US Standard** and ensure the drop-down menu is set to **Feet w/Decimal Inches**. These are display settings, which means any value displayed in 3ds Max is expressed in feet and decimal inches, or ' and ".

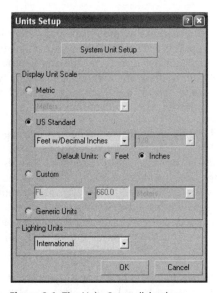

Figure 3-1. The Units Setup dialog box

Next, ensure **Default Units** is set to **Inches**, as shown in Figure 3-1. This means that any number entered into any field will be considered a number expressed in inches if it isn't followed by a unit designation. Therefore, if you change the radius of a sphere to 20 without following it with an apostrophe, the radius becomes 20 inches. But because the display settings are set to **Feet w/Decimal Inches**, the radius will actually change to read 1'8". You can also enter 1'8" yourself; or, even easier, 1'8. An apostrophe (') indicates feet and a double quote mark (") indicates inches.

The reason I suggest changing the **Default Units** to inches is that when you want to enter a certain number of inches into a field, such as 4.5", you won't have to do any math to figure out what the number is expressed in feet (0.375' in this case). It simply saves time. In addition, **AutoCAD** uses inches as its default units, and it can be confusing when working in two programs with two different default unit types.

Last, click the **System Unit Setup** button and ensure that the **System Unit Scale** is set to **1 Unit = 1.0 Inches**, as shown in Figure 3-2. Changing this to read **1 Unit = 1.0 Feet** will cause your entire scene to be scaled up twelvefold. The objects won't actually change in size, they will simply be given new units. A sphere that was expressed as 5 inches will now be expressed as 5 feet.

This also means that when you import an AutoCAD drawing with default units set to inches, all imported objects will remain their original size. If you change your **System Unit Scale** to read **1 Unit = 1.0 Feet**, then a sphere with a radius of 5 inches in AutoCAD will change to a sphere with a radius of 5 feet when imported into 3ds Max.

Figure 3-2. The System Unit Setup dialog box

There are no other settings that need to be altered with the **Units Setup** dialog box; however, I would like to make a note of the bottom half of the **System Unit Setup** dialog box. These values control how accurate 3ds Max is in the use of numerical values. Basically, the closer objects lie to the origin of the World Coordinate System (i.e., 0,0,0), the more accurately objects are displayed and parameters computed. The values in this dialog box indicate that objects would have to be more than 16 million inches away from the origin in order to be inaccurate to an inch. Although this may seem to be more than accurate enough, problems can still arise, as I once learned the hard way. I was once knee-deep in the modeling of a very large project for a golf course community with site elements (streets, lakes, etc.) that I created straight from the line work of an engineering firm's site plan that I imported from AutoCAD. I inserted all my individual objects, such as houses, streetlights, cars, etc. What I didn't realize is that for some reason the drafter had placed all the line work in the AutoCAD file at an incredibly great distance from the origin. So when I inserted all the objects, they too were a long way from the origin and were no longer accurate. I didn't catch it at first, and couldn't figure out why all my modeling operations were messed up. With 3ds Max being 1 inch off at a distance of 16 million inches from the origin, you can't move or modify objects in increments less than one inch. This won't cut it for architectural models. So now the absolute first thing I do with any AutoCAD drawing that I'm going to use is move all line work so that it's centered on the world origin. The moral of the story is to always keep your scene centered on the origin.

One final and very important note about units is that engineering firms typically produce site drawings for architects using engineering scales. In engineering scales, the unit of measure is 1 foot, which means that an object 12 feet long will actually appear only 12 inches long when its line work is imported into 3ds Max. Therefore, you must scale site plans 1200% prior to or immediately after importing.

Setting up 3ds Max with architectural units

This exercise demonstrates how to set up 3ds Max for architectural units.

1. Reset 3ds Max.

2. Click the **Customize** menu and select **Units Setup**. The **Units Setup** dialog box will open, as shown in Figure 3-1.

3. Select **US Standard** and make sure that the drop-down list below is set to **Feet w/Decimal Inches** and **Default Units** is set to **Inches**, as shown in Figure 3-1. Your units will now be set up correctly for architectural work, but for this drawing only. Any new drawing will require the units to be changed again.

Display drivers

When you start 3ds Max for the first time, the **Graphics Driver Setup** dialog box appears (Figure 3-3). This dialog box allows you to either keep the default display driver (by keeping the **Software** option selected) or use other more powerful drivers, such as OpenGL or Direct3D. You can only use OpenGL, Direct3D, or any other driver if your graphics card supports the driver you want to use. To use a customized driver, select **Custom** and choose an installed driver from the drop-down list. If you are unsure of whether your graphics card supports a specific driver, you should use the default software driver. If you change the display driver, you will need to restart 3ds Max.

Figure 3-3. The Graphics Driver Setup dialog box

You can also make display driver changes within the **Viewports** tab of the **Preference Settings** dialog box (Figure 3-4). In the **Display Drivers** section, click **Choose Driver** to change the **Currently Installed Driver**. The **Configure Driver** option opens a dialog box that allows you to make changes to the settings associated with the currently installed driver. One important setting in this dialog box is the **Download Texture Size** setting, which controls the size of the bitmaps displayed in your viewports. Larger maps result in better but slower viewport displays. Each display driver configuration setting represents a trade-off between display quality and display speed, and will require experimentation on your part to optimize for your specific hardware and needs.

Figure 3-4. The Preference Settings dialog box

Configure paths

When 3ds Max is installed, every file is placed in a specific location for future retrieval. Sound files are placed in the Sounds folder, fonts in the Fonts folder, scripts in the Scripts folder, and so on. All of these locations, also known as paths, can be modified within the **Configure User Paths** and **Configure System Paths** dialog boxes of the **Customize** menu, as shown in Figure 3-5. External files are important path types that you may need to update from time to time—they can be found on the **External Files** tab, which is the first tab that appears when you open the **Configure User Paths** dialog box. This is really not one path, but many paths—one for each folder on your computer where you want 3ds Max to search for images that you want to use to texturize your scenes. By default, 3ds Max creates a path for each of the directories within the Maps folder. To add additional folders in which you want 3ds Max to look for images, click the **Add** button within the **External Files** tab. Select **Browse**, locate the directory you want to add, and select **Use Path**.

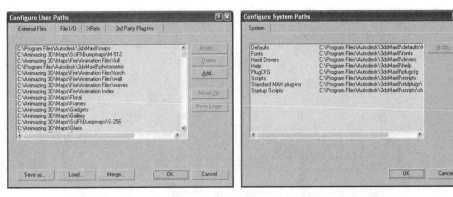

Figure 3-5. The Configure User Paths and Configure System Paths dialog boxes

Once you assign an image to a material, 3ds Max will start all future searches for the image in whatever location you specified when you first assigned the image to the material. If you delete or move the image from the folder to which it was first assigned, during the render process 3ds Max will search for the image in each of the folders (paths) listed in the **External Files** tab of the **Configure User Paths** dialog box. It will start the search in the first folder specified at the top of the list and continue looking in additional folders, in the order the paths are listed. To move a specific path closer to or farther from the top of the paths list, highlight the path and select **Move Up** or **Move Down**. Continue clicking until the path is in the desired location in the list. The result of moving a path higher up on the list is that the path will be searched sooner.

Creating a good directory structure for maps is essential for assigning images efficiently. If you have to spend more than a minute just trying to find where you stored an image on your computer, you're spending too much time and should reorganize your images. Personally, I keep all maps in a separate directory outside of the directory in which 3ds Max was installed. This keeps the maps from being erased or overwritten when 3ds Max is uninstalled or updated. Additionally, I like to create very explicit folder names to make finding a particular image as quick and easy as possible. Figure 3-6 shows a screenshot of what my map directory structure looks like.

Figure 3-6. My personal map directory structure

Configuring paths in 3ds Max

This exercise demonstrates use of the configuring paths feature by changing one of the many folders that 3ds Max searches for a specific file type in.

1. Reset 3ds Max.

2. Click the **Customize** menu and select **Configure User Paths**. The **Configure User Paths** dialog box will open to the **External Files** tab.

3. Click the **File I/O** tab.

4. Scroll down and click **Scenes**, as shown in the following screenshot.

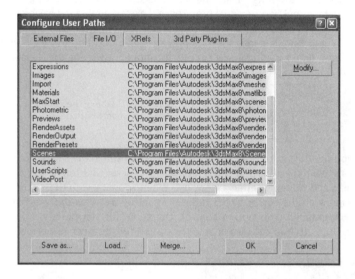

5. Click the **Modify** button.

6. Find another folder in your computer's directory to set as the Scene directory. This will be the folder that 3ds Max starts in when you want to open an existing 3ds Max file.

Preference settings

There are several hundred settings available within the **Preference Settings** dialog box, and for a new user they can be very confusing. Even as an experienced user, I find little need to change the majority of these settings. There are, however, a few important settings that you need to know about. Beyond these, I would discourage you from spending too much time trying to learn as many as you can unless you are an experienced 3ds Max user.

This first critical setting is **Backup Interval (minutes)** in the **Auto Backup** section of the **Files** tab (shown in Figure 3-7). 3ds Max automatically makes a backup file of the file you work in every 5 minutes. When working in 3ds Max, there is nothing I hate more than losing work; even just a few minutes worth. Therefore, I keep this setting at 5 minutes as much as possible. However, the larger a scene becomes, the longer it takes for these automatic backups to complete. When 3ds Max runs the auto backup, you cannot do anything with the program and must wait until the backup is complete. When your scenes become so large that you are waiting longer than you like on these backups, change this setting so that the backups occur at greater intervals.

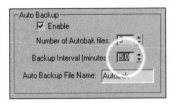

Figure 3-7. The Auto Backup settings

Also within the **Files** tab is a setting called **Zoom Extents on Import**, as shown in Figure 3-8. This setting is enabled by default, but as a personal preference, I always disable it. Leaving this option enabled means that every time you import an object into your scene from another file, 3ds Max will automatically perform the **Zoom Extents** command within every viewport. I find this very annoying, especially when I have just spent time zooming into a specific location in my scene that I want to focus on.

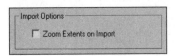

Figure 3-8. Disabling the Zoom Extents on Import option

The last setting you should ensure is set properly is **Middle Button** in the **Mouse Control** section of the **Viewports** tab, as shown in Figure 3-9. The middle mouse (scroll) button is best utilized when set to control the panning and zooming within a viewport. When zooming with the mouse, it is ideal to have the zooming centered on the cursor of the mouse. To set up 3ds Max this way, enable **Zoom About Mouse Point (Orthographic)**. This option controls the zoom for viewports with orthographic views, such as Top, Left, User, etc. You can also enable the option for perspective viewports.

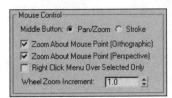

Figure 3-9. Options controlling the zooming and panning capabilities of the mouse

These three settings I have mentioned are the only ones I make a point to change whenever I install 3ds Max. I would never discourage exploring and experimentation within 3ds Max, as that is often the only means some users have to learn, but I do not think new users should attempt to learn every setting, as it may only confuse and frustrate. The 3ds Max programmers have done an excellent job optimizing the default Preference settings for the majority of users; for the most part, the settings are optimal for those of us in the visualization industry. Generally, if you get to the rare point at which you decide there has to be a better setting for a particular feature being used, you will probably know enough to be able to figure out where to find the setting and how to change it.

This exercise demonstrates the changing of three critical settings found in the **Preference Settings** dialog box.

1. Reset 3ds Max.

2. Click the **Customize** menu and select **Preference Settings**.

3. Click the **Files** tab.

4. In the **Auto Backup** section, change **Backup Interval (minutes)** to **10.0**. This will cause 3ds Max to create a backup file of your current scene every 10 minutes. The file will be found in the AutoBak directory within 3ds Max.

5. Deselect **Zoom Extents on Import**, as shown in Figure 3-8. This will prevent 3ds Max from performing the **Zoom Extents** command every time a file is imported.

6. Click the **Viewports** tab.

7. In the **Mouse Control** section, enable the **Zoom About Mouse Point** option for both orthographic and perspective views, as shown in Figure 3-9. This will allow you to zoom in and out of a scene wherever the mouse is placed.

Customization

Experienced 3ds Max users often find it helpful to customize the 3ds Max interface to their specific style of work, and 3ds Max contains very powerful customization features that make this possible. However, customization can be a complex endeavor, and placing a discussion of the subject at the beginning of a book would be inappropriate because new users aren't familiar enough with the capability and power of a program like 3ds Max to know the best way to customize. Trying to customize 3ds Max before learning at least some of the program is putting the cart before the horse, as the saying goes. Because of this, I have placed an explanation of customization in Appendix C, near the end of the book.

Working with shapes and splines

When creating architectural visualizations, you will almost always work with drawings that originate in a 2D CAD program such as AutoCAD (see Figure 3-10). Why is this? Because someone will undoubtedly want to build the project you create in 3ds Max, and to do so, someone must submit construction drawings to their respective local governments in order to obtain the required building permits. These days, almost all architectural construction drawings are created with CAD software, and unlike other applications for 3ds Max—such as character animation, which incorporates more creativity and artistic interpretation—architectural modeling is very precise, and what you see is what you need to create.

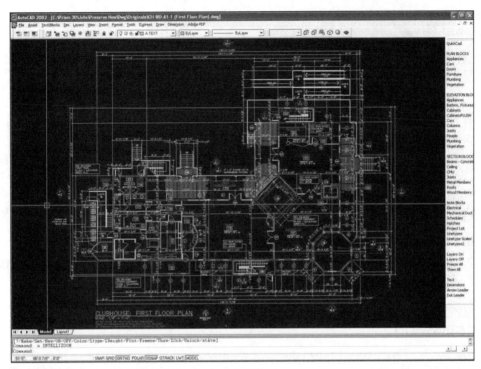

Figure 3-10. Example of a floor plan drawing in AutoCAD

That being said, unless someone hands you a few sketches and says "Show me what this looks like in 3D," you will usually be at the mercy of the drafter that put the drawings together. In fact, with the exception of one project in which the client said exactly that, every one of the 100-plus 3D projects I have worked on began with AutoCAD drawings. Knowing how to interpret architectural drawings is a must, and knowing how to work with them in AutoCAD is equally important.

If you ask a 3ds Max user in any field other than architecture what the building blocks of 3D are, chances are he or she will tell you primitive solids (i.e., spheres, boxes, cylinders, etc.). With architectural visualizations, however, the building blocks are shapes and splines. Primitive solids are a great supplement, but your work will truly begin with a mass of shapes and splines.

Shapes and splines defined

So what are shapes and splines? Essentially, they are both made up of the same ingredient: lines with curves defined by mathematical equations. Shapes are simply tools to facilitate the arrangement of line work into a certain pattern, such as text. How laborious would it be to write your name in 3ds Max with individual lines that have to be curved, bent, and shaped just right? With the text shape, writing your name can take just a few seconds. Figure 3-11 shows several examples of shapes.

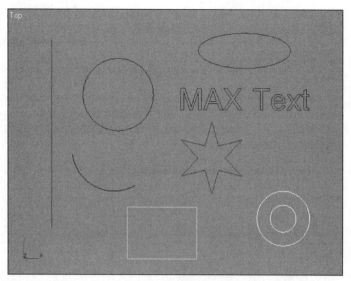

Figure 3-11. Examples of shapes in 3ds Max

Splines are different from shapes in that splines are not created from scratch; they are converted from other objects—most commonly shapes. Take, for example, the simple circle. The circle is a shape with one basic parameter, the radius value. You can't do very much with a simple circle; but convert it to a spline and you can suddenly turn that circle into almost any type of line imaginable. Since splines usually begin with shapes, I will first discuss shapes, and then cover how to manipulate those shapes once converted to splines.

Shape basics

Figure 3-12 shows an example of each of the shapes available for creation. In creating 3D architectural structures, you will probably find only an occasional use for such shapes as the star, donut, or NGon—but four shapes that you won't be able to do without are the line, circle, arc, and text.

Figure 3-12. Available shapes in 3ds Max

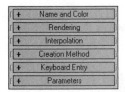

Figure 3-13. Typical shape rollouts

Most of the shapes have several common rollouts: **Name and Color**, **Rendering**, **Interpolation**, **Creation Method**, **Keyboard Entry**, and **Parameters** (as shown in Figure 3-13). They are very similar for all shapes.

Within the **Object Type** rollout (see Figure 3-12) are the **AutoGrid** and **Start New Shape** options. By checking the **AutoGrid** option, you can set the creation point for a shape on the surface of an existing object. When you do so, the new shape's normal is aligned with the normal of the face your cursor is over when the shape is created. This causes the new shape to be aligned with the surface of the object.

Figure 3-14 shows an excellent example of the **AutoGrid** feature. With one click of the mouse, you can place a text shape of the word **YIELD** on the surface of a triangle-shaped street sign without having to create the shape and execute the move and rotate commands several times.

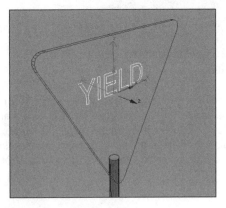

Figure 3-14. Using AutoGrid to place a shape on the surface of an object

Using the AutoGrid feature

This exercise demonstrates use of the **AutoGrid** feature by placing text on the surface of a box.

1. Reset 3ds Max.
2. In the Perspective view, create a box with a length, width, and height of 500.
3. Click the **Shapes** icon within the **Create** panel.
4. Enable the **AutoGrid** feature.
5. Click the **Text** button and move the cursor over one of the sides of the newly created box. A reference gizmo appears, with the z axis aligned with the normal of the face the gizmo is over.
6. Click one of the sides of the box to place the text object on the surface of the box. Repeat the process for the two other sides visible in the Perspective view, as shown in the following image:

The **Start New Shape** option is checked by default; it makes every newly created shape a separate object. When not checked, each additional shape created becomes another part of a single object.

The **Creation Method**, **Keyboard Entry**, and **Parameters** rollouts need no real explanation. Personally, I can't recall a time that I've ever used anything other than the default creation method, and I can't recall ever using the **Keyboard Entry** feature because it's simply too slow. The two rollouts that warrant discussion are **Rendering** and **Interpolation**, and we'll look at these next.

The **Name and Color** rollout simply gives you a place to change the default name and color that is used upon creation.

The Rendering rollout

Shapes by default are not rendered, but by selecting the **Enable In Renderer** option in the **Rendering** rollout (see Figure 3-15), the shape will be included in the rendering. The lines that make up the shape will appear tubular, with a thickness and number of sides that you specify. The minimum number of sides possible is three, which creates a triangular cross-section. This feature has limited use in architecture, but there are times when you may find its use invaluable, such as creating the branches of a tree. The benefit of this feature is that while the shapes appear to be solids when rendered, and thus can significantly increase render times, they are still displayed as lines within the viewports and do not significantly increase viewport refresh rates. You can, however, show the shapes in the viewports as they will appear when rendered. To do so, select the **Enable In Viewport** option.

Figure 3-15.
The Rendering rollout

Creating renderable shapes and splines

This exercise demonstrates how to make shapes and splines renderable.

1. Reset 3ds Max.

2. Create a circle in the Perspective view with a radius of 100.

3. In the **Rendering** rollout, check the **Enable in Renderer** and **Enable in Viewport** options, as shown on the left in the following image.

4. Change **Radial Thickness** to **10.0**. The circle is now renderable and can be seen in the viewport the same way it will be when rendered, as shown on the right in the following image:

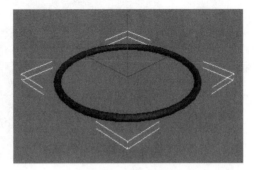

5. Save your work for use in the next exercise.

The Interpolation rollout

In the next rollout, **Interpolation** (Figure 3-16), you can control the smoothness of curves within a shape. By definition, interpolation means inserting or introducing between other elements or parts.

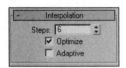

Figure 3-16. The Interpolation rollout

Increasing the number of steps increases the number of vertices and makes the curves in the shape appear smoother. Different shapes require a different minimum number of vertices and segments to be defined.

Take, for example, the circle shown in Figure 3-17. The circle is defined by four initial vertices and thus has four initial segments. Without any additional steps to define its curve, the circle resembles a diamond, as in the image on the left. If the number of steps is increased to 1, one additional vertex (or step) is inserted in each of the original four segments, as shown in the middle image. If the number of steps is increased to 2, two additional vertices are inserted in each of the original four segments, as shown in the image on the right. As the step value is increased, the curves in the path become smoother. The default value of 6 provides a fairly smooth curve, but in many cases you will need to increase this number significantly.

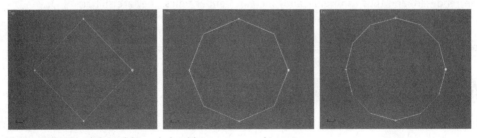

Figure 3-17. From left to right, a circle with zero, one, and two steps

The **Optimize** option removes any unnecessary vertices in a shape, such as multiple vertices in a straight section of a shape. Figure 3-18 shows the effect of using **Optimize** on a simple extruded spline with two straight segments and a curved segment. With **Optimize** disabled, the straight segments receive just as many additional steps as the curved segments. The **Optimize** option should always remain enabled, except in some specialized circumstances.

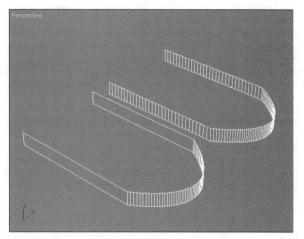

Figure 3-18. A spline with Optimize enabled (left), and the same spline with Optimize disabled (right)

The **Adaptive** option automatically places vertices in the locations necessary to produce a smooth look at all curved sections of a shape. When the **Adaptive** option is enabled, the **Optimize** option becomes disabled—it is no longer necessary since 3ds Max determines the correct number of vertices to use for each segment. Figure 3-19 shows the effect of using the **Adaptive** option on the extruded letter "S." Notice that the straight segments receive no unnecessary steps, while the more curved areas receive as many steps as needed to produce decent curves. The **Adaptive** option can be very handy when you work on large splines that would be too time-consuming to manage segment by segment.

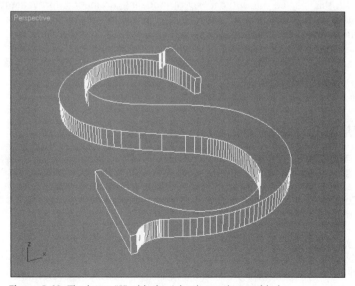

Figure 3-19. The letter "S" with the Adaptive option enabled

87

Using Interpolation with Shapes and Splines

This exercise demonstrates how to use interpolation to make curved segments of shapes and splines smoother.

1. Continue from the previous exercise.

2. Open the **Interpolation** rollout and type **0** in the **Steps** field. This causes the circle to be square-shaped because it has no steps to define the curved segments between the original four vertices.

3. Increase the **Steps** value to **12**. The circle now becomes smooth.

4. Decrease the **Steps** value to **0** once again.

5. Enable the **Adaptive** option in the **Interpolation** rollout. This option causes 3ds Max to automatically place vertices in the locations necessary to produce a smooth look at all curved sections of the shape. The circle is now smooth again.

Spline basics

Once a shape is converted into a spline, a wealth of features are made available that give you tremendous modeling power. With the tools provided, you can manipulate the individual segments or vertices of a spline with great precision and versatility. Many of the critical tools in the spline rollouts are similar to those explained in the next section of this chapter, "Working with meshes and polys," and are also used in the next two modeling chapters. Therefore, you will gain a solid understanding of splines throughout the course of the remaining discussion on modeling.

It wasn't long ago, pre-3ds Max, that users were forced to create many architectural elements, such as walls, roofs, and doors, from scratch using primitive solids. I remember creating walls by extruding shapes or stacking one shape on top of another, much like working with LEGOs. While there are still situations in which this may be the optimal way of modeling, dramatic improvements in shapes and splines have enabled users to achieve the same result in a fraction of the time with far more flexibility in making modifications as their work progresses. If you want to create architectural visualizations at warp speed, then a good understanding of how to work with shapes and splines (also known as 2D modeling) cannot be overemphasized. For now, let's take a look at the next important step in the modeling process: 3D modeling.

Working with meshes and polys

Mesh and poly objects will comprise the vast majority of objects you will create in architectural visualizations. In large, complex scenes, you may have (and should strive to include) such finer details as particle systems, environment effects, or even third-party plug-in objects, such as RPCs (Rich Photorealistic Content, www.archvision.com). The meat and potatoes of your scenes, however, will be mesh and poly objects.

Meshes and polys have several advantages over other modeling types. They are easy to work with and manipulate, they lend themselves to more exact and precise modeling, and they are perhaps the most common modeling type, supported by a large number of 3D packages.

Editable mesh and editable poly objects are very similar, yet they have many distinct differences. **Editable Poly** provides several unique features unavailable with **Editable Mesh**, and is generally more advanced. Learning the characteristics and capabilities of the poly object becomes much easier with an understanding of the mesh object. Because of this, and to avoid the confusion that can arise with their many similarities, this book only covers the editable mesh. Once you develop an understanding of the mesh object, I recommend investigating some of the great features that give the poly object such strong support from users in the 3D world.

Creating mesh objects

Mesh objects cannot be created from scratch. They can only be converted from other objects. The **Create** panel allows for the creation of various types of models, such as primitives, shapes, compound objects, patches, and NURBS. Nowhere, however, is there a create button for mesh objects. On the other hand, all of the objects discussed in this chapter could be converted to meshes.

There are several ways to convert an object to a mesh (see Figure 3-20). One way is to right-click the object in the active viewport and select **Convert To: Editable Mesh** from the pop-up quad menu. Another way is to right-click the object within the **Modifier Stack**. You can also add the **Edit Mesh** modifier to an object, and finally, you can collapse an object by selecting **Collapse** from the **Utilities** menu.

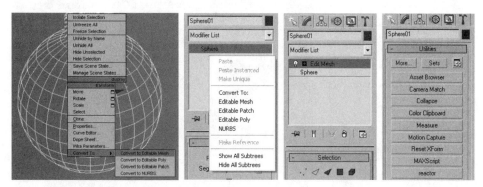

Figure 3-20. Various methods of converting objects to a mesh

Creating mesh objects

This exercise demonstrates a few of the ways to create mesh objects.

1. Reset 3ds Max.

2. Create a sphere in the Perspective view.

3. Right-click in the Perspective view to bring up the quad menu.

4. Move the cursor over the **Convert To** option and select **Convert To: Editable Mesh**. The sphere is now a mesh object.

5. Click the **Undo** icon to return the object to a sphere.

6. In the **Modify** panel, click the **Modifier List** drop-down list and select **Edit Mesh**. This adds the **Edit Mesh** modifier to the sphere. The object is now a mesh again.

7. Save your work for use in the next exercise.

Editing mesh objects

You can change the structural appearance of an object in several ways: with transforms, modifiers, utilities, controllers, and even materials. But no method of changing an object's structure is as powerful and versatile as the **Edit Mesh** feature. All mesh editing occurs at one of the five sub-object levels: vertex, edge, face, polygon, or element. Sub-objects are the components that make up a mesh. Once you convert an object to an editable mesh, you can enter sub-object mode in a few different ways, as shown in Figure 3-21. For example, you can select **Edit Mesh** in the **Modifier Stack**, click the small plus sign to its left to show the five sub-object levels, and then click the sub-object you wish to work on. Another way is to click one of the sub-object icons listed in the **Selection** rollout directly below the **Modifier Stack**. You can also right-click an object in the active viewport and select a sub-object level from the quad menu. Yet another way is to press a number key from 1 to 5 when **Edit Mesh** is listed at the top of the **Modifier Stack** (as shown in Figure 3-21). Press 1 for the **Vertex** sub-object level, 2 for **Edge**, 3 for **Face**, 4 for **Polygon**, and 5 for **Element**.

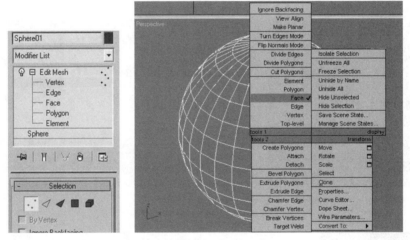

Figure 3-21. Various methods of entering sub-object mode

When you enter a sub-object level, the sub-object icon in the **Selection** rollout and the sub-object name for the level that you enter both turn yellow. To exit sub-object mode, you can click the same icon or the name of the level again. Clicking other features in 3ds Max, such as a different panel within the **Control** panel, can cause the sub-object mode to close automatically. Until sub-object mode closes, you cannot select any other object in your scene.

Once in sub-object mode, you can select individual sub-objects by clicking them, or multiple sub-objects by holding down Ctrl while clicking them, as shown in the left image of Figure 3-22. Notice the plus sign that appears below the cursor when holding down the Ctrl key, indicating the next selection will be added to the current selection. Holding down Ctrl while clicking already selected sub-objects will cause them to be deselected. Holding down Alt while clicking selected sub-objects will also cause the sub-objects to be deselected, as shown in the right image in Figure 3-22. Notice the minus sign that appears below the cursor when holding down the Alt key, indicating the next selection will be subtracted from the current selection. Window selections can also be used in sub-object mode to select or deselect more than one sub-object.

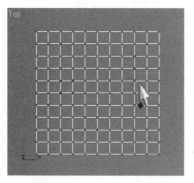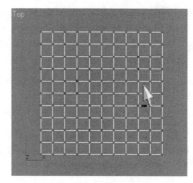

Figure 3-22. Hold down Ctrl to add selections (left); hold down Alt to subtract selections (right)

Sub-objects that you select turn red in viewports. Once sub-objects are selected, they can be transformed just like any other object. Sub-objects can also be cloned like any other object. Holding down the Shift key while applying a transform (move, rotate, or scale) causes the selected sub-objects to be cloned. After applying the transform, the **Clone Part of Mesh** dialog box appears and prompts you to choose **Clone To Object** or **Clone To Element** (Figure 3-23). The **Clone To Object** option makes the cloned selection an entirely new object with a name of your choosing. **Clone To Element** causes the cloned selection to remain part of the existing object but become a new element within that object.

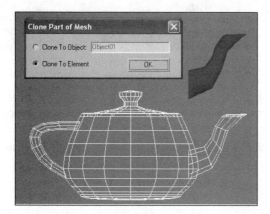

Figure 3-23. Using Shift to copy a sub-object selection

When working with editable mesh objects in the **Modify** panel, you are provided four rollouts: **Selection, Soft Selection, Edit Geometry**, and **Surface Properties**. Each rollout contains powerful features that take quite some time to master. The remainder of this chapter focuses on the most important features of these rollouts.

Editing mesh objects

This exercise demonstrates a few of the ways to edit mesh objects.

1. Continue from the previous exercise.

2. In the **Modify** panel, click the **Vertex** sub-object level in the **Selection** rollout, as shown in the left image of Figure 3-21. The **Vertex** icon will turn yellow.

3. In the Front view, select a few vertices using a selection window. The selected vertices turn red. You can now perform a transform on the selected vertices.

4. Right-click in the active viewport and select the **Face** sub-object level from the quad menu, as shown in the right image of Figure 3-21.

5. In the Front view, select a few of the faces in the top half of the sphere using a window selection.

6. Hold down the Ctrl key and select all of the faces in the bottom half of the sphere, as shown on the left in the following image:

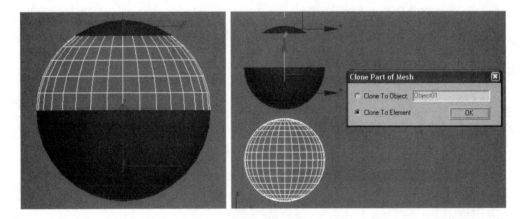

7. Hold down the Shift key, move the cursor over the y axis of the transform gizmo, and click and drag upward. A copy of the selection is made.

8. Move the copy above the original sphere and release the mouse. The **Clone Part of Mesh** dialog box appears.

9. Click **OK** and click the highlighted **Faces** icon in the **Selection** rollout. The **Edit Mesh** modifier is now closed.

The Selection rollout

The **Selection** rollout (shown in Figure 3-24) focuses on providing efficient methods for selecting sub-objects. Depending on the object you're working on, this can be a challenge at times. A good understanding of all the options in the **Selection** rollout can greatly facilitate the process of making a sub-object selection.

Figure 3-24. The Selection rollout

- **By Vertex**: This option allows you to click a vertex in order to select all edges, faces, polygons, or elements connected to the vertex. In Figure 3-25, all four polygons are selected just by clicking the one vertex connected to each of them.

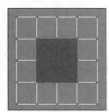

Figure 3-25. The By Vertex option enabled

- **Ignore Backfacing**: This option allows you to select only those sub-objects with normals facing toward your perspective in the active viewport. If you make a window selection of a teapot, as shown in the right image of Figure 3-26, only those faces on the side closest to your perspective will be selected, as shown in the left image. This option is tremendously helpful when you want to select the faces on just one side of a wall.

Figure 3-26. The Ignore Backfacing option enabled

- **Ignore Visible Edges**: This is a powerful option that really has little practical value in architectural visualizations. It allows you to select all polygons that lie within the same plane. Normally, when you click a single polygon, only that polygon is selected. This option ignores the edges of the polygon you select and selects all polygons that lie on the same plane (or close enough to the same plane, as determined by the planar threshold). I tried to but could not find a single situation in which this option would benefit the selection process.

- **Show Normals**: This option causes all face normals to be displayed, which can be a visual aid when trying to determine why materials, lighting, shading, or individual faces of a model appear flawed or missing altogether. A face normal determines which way a face is oriented, and greatly affects all of the aforementioned characteristics. For example, if you apply a material that is only one-sided (i.e., viewable from one side) to a sphere, and all of the face normals are oriented inward and away from your perspective, then you won't see the half of the sphere closest to you. All you would see would be the inside of the back half of the sphere. You won't need this option very often if you do good modeling, but when you do need it, you'll be very thankful you have it. The **Scale** option lets you change the length of the line that represents a normal. Figure 3-27 shows a sphere with all faces selected and the **Show Normals** option enabled.

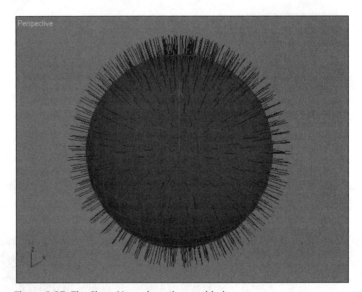

Figure 3-27. The Show Normals option enabled

- **Hide**: It should be no surprise that this option simply hides selected sub-objects, while **Unhide All** makes them visible again.

- **Named Selections**: Once you select a group of sub-objects, you can assign a name to the selection by typing the name in the **Named Selection Sets** drop-down list on the **Main** toolbar. By clicking **Copy and Paste** under the **Named Selections** section of the **Selection** rollout, you can copy and paste your selection to other objects later.

Using Selection rollout options

This exercise demonstrates use of a few of the **Selection** rollout options.

1. Reset 3ds Max.

2. In the Perspective view, create a cylinder with a radius of 25 and a height of 50.

3. In the **Display Properties** rollout of the **Display** panel, enable **Vertex Ticks**. This will make the exercise easier to visualize.

4. In the **Modify** panel, add an **Edit Mesh** modifier and enter the **Face** sub-object level.

5. Enable the **By Vertex** option and select the center vertex on the top of the cylinder. All of the faces on the top of the cylinder are selected, as shown in the following image:

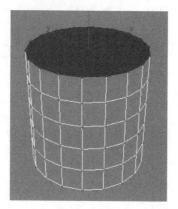

6. Enable the **Ignore Backfacing** option.

7. In the Front view, create a window selection around the entire cylinder to select all the faces. Click the **Arc Rotate SubObject** icon in the viewport navigation controls, and rotate the view in the Perspective view. You can see that because of the **Ignore Backfacing** option, none of the faces on the back of the cylinder were selected.

8. Enable the **Show Normals** option. The normals of all the selected faces appear.

The Soft Selection rollout

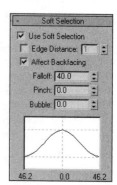

The **Soft Selection** feature, shown in Figure 3-28, is one of my favorites in 3ds Max. I have found its use limited almost entirely to the manipulation of terrain features, but in this way it is simply invaluable. When you select a sub-object or a group of sub-objects and apply a transform, only those sub-objects are moved. When you enable **Soft Selection**, however, other sub-objects in the vicinity of those selected are also affected by the transformation of the selected sub-objects. The degree to which those other sub-objects are affected depends on their proximity to the selected sub-objects and the settings in the **Soft Selection** rollout. The purpose of this feature is to soften the effect of a transformation.

Figure 3-28. The Soft Selection rollout

95

Notice in the left image of Figure 3-29 that a group of vertices is moved upward without soft selection enabled. There is a distinct cliff-like look to this transformation. In the image on the right, soft selection is enabled before the transformation. Notice that the vertices in the vicinity of those selected are highlighted to some degree, and the transformation appears more like a rolling hill than a cliff.

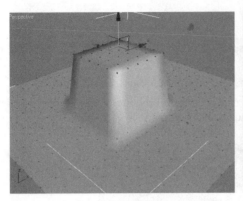

Figure 3-29. Soft selection enabled

As I mentioned, soft selection works great for terrain features, but architectural elements such as buildings, light poles, or tennis courts can't benefit much from soft selection because these elements must be precisely crafted and don't usually involve curved surfaces.

The following is a description of the relevant options available within the **Soft Selection** rollout:

- **Use Soft Selection**: This option simply enables the **Soft Selection** feature.
- **Affect Backfacing**: This option is enabled by default and causes a window selection to select not only those sub-objects in the foreground with normals facing your perspective, but also those sub-objects on the backside of the objects with normals facing away from your perspective. Disable this option when you want your window selection to only select those sub-objects on the side closest to your perspective.
- **Soft Selection Curve**: The **Soft Selection Curve**, as shown in the bottom of Figure 3-28, is a graphical representation of how the transformation of selected sub-objects affects transformation of surrounding sub-objects within a given range. The curve is controlled by three parameters: **Falloff**, **Pinch**, and **Bubble**.
- **Falloff**: This parameter defines the greatest distance from the selection at which sub-objects will still be affected. Any sub-object at a distance greater than this value will not be affected. The value entered in the **Falloff** field is displayed on the left and right ends of the **Soft Selection Curve**. Notice that the far left image in Figure 3-30 shows a single vertex selected and moved upward without soft selection enabled. The middle image shows the same transformation with the default **Falloff** value of **20**, and the image on the right shows the same transformation with a **Falloff** value of **40**.

Figure 3-30. The effects of using Falloff

- **Pinch**: This parameter controls how much the affected sub-objects will appear to be pinched at the point where selected sub-objects meet unselected sub-objects. The left image in Figure 3-31 shows the same vertex transformation as described previously, this time with a **Pinch** value of **1.0**. Notice that the apex of the transformation is pinched, but the resulting falloff appears to have been diminished. This isn't the case, however—changing the **Pinch** value simply changes the shape of the **Soft Selection Curve**, which is a reflection of how much the surrounding sub-objects will be transformed. In this case, the pinch of the curve is achieved by allowing sub-objects to be affected only if they're very close to the selected sub-objects. Increasing the falloff at this point simply has the effect of reducing the steepness of the curve.

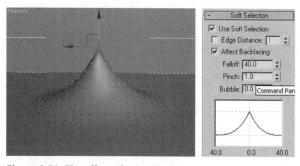

Figure 3-31. The effect of using Pinch

- **Bubble**: This parameter has the opposite effect of pinch in that it gives a bubble-like appearance to those sub-objects halfway between the selected sub-objects and the sub-objects at the limit of the falloff. Figure 3-32 shows the effect of a **Falloff** value of **40.0**, a **Pinch** value of **0.0**, and a **Bubble** value of **1.0**.

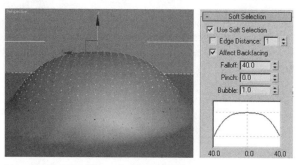

Figure 3-32. The effect of using Bubble

97

■ **Edge Distance**: This option is explained last because an understanding of the previous **Soft Selection** parameters is necessary. The **Edge Distance** value sets a limit on the number of edges away from the selection that will be affected by the **Falloff**, **Pinch**, and **Bubble** values. When enabled, it doesn't matter how high your falloff distance is set. By default, only sub-objects within one edge of the selected sub-objects will be affected. Changing this value to **2** will allow sub-objects two edges away from the selection to be affected, and so on.

Using soft selections

This exercise demonstrates the use of soft selections when applying transforms.

1. Reset 3ds Max.
2. In the Perspective view, create a plane with a length and width of 100, and set the number of length and width segments to 40.
3. Right-click in the Perspective view and use the quad menu to convert the plane to an editable mesh.
4. In the **Selection** rollout, click the **Vertex** sub-object level.
5. Open the **Soft Selection** rollout, as shown in the right image of Figure 3-32, and select **Use Soft Selection**.
6. Click a vertex near the center of the mesh.
7. Click and drag the spinner to the right of the **Falloff** field. Drag upward to increase the **Falloff** value. Notice that the vertices in the mesh surrounding the selected vertex change colors as the falloff changes.
8. Select the move transform, place the cursor over the z axis of the transform gizmo, and click and drag the soft selection upward. Your view should look similar to the right-hand image in Figure 3-30.

The Edit Geometry rollout

To cover the features within the **Edit Geometry** rollout (Figure 3-33) to their full potential and capability, one would need an entire chapter. Much of this rollout, however, provides no benefit to those of us working in the field of architecture. Therefore, I will cover those features that you should concentrate your efforts on, and point out features that you can ignore. Many features of the **Edit Geometry** rollout are only available in certain sub-object modes. When not available, those features are grayed out and not selectable.

Some features within this rollout are available both in and out of sub-object mode, while others are available only in select sub-object modes. To eliminate redundancy, I will first discuss the important features available both in and out of sub-object mode, and then discuss those that are available only in certain sub-object modes.

Figure 3-33. The Edit Geometry rollout

Important features available anywhere

This section explains the important features available in and out of sub-object mode: **Attach**, **Explode**, **Remove Isolated Vertices**, **View**, and **Grid Align**.

Attach

You can use the **Attach** button to attach objects to the currently selected editable mesh object. Object types that can be attached include primitives, patches, compound objects, and any other object types that can be converted to an editable mesh. Many objects cannot be attached. These include lights, cameras, helpers, third-party plug-in objects (such as RPCs), and basically any object that cannot be collapsed to a mesh. Certain objects, such as particle systems, which can be collapsed to a mesh, shouldn't be collapsed because doing so removes any unique features the object holds, which in the case of particles is motion.

Objects that are attached to other objects are automatically converted to editable meshes and inherit the properties of the object to which they are attached. When you attach an object to another, and both objects have different materials applied, a dialog box appears giving you three options: **Match Material IDs to Material**, **Match Material to Material IDs**, and **Do Not Modify Material IDs or Material**. These options will be discussed in Part 3 of this book.

To attach an object to another, select a mesh object, such as the teapot in Figure 3-34 (which was first converted to a mesh object), click the **Attach** button (which turns yellow), move the cursor over the other object you want to attach (the cursor changes when it's over acceptable objects), and pick the object (such as the torus shown in Figure 3-34). To exit the Attach command, you must either right-click in the current viewport, hit Esc on the keyboard, or click the **Attach** button.

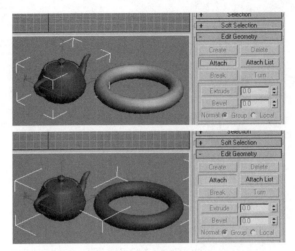

Figure 3-34. One object being attached to another

Instead of picking each individual object you want to attach, you can select from a list. To do so, click the **Attach List** button, which opens the **Attach List** dialog box shown in Figure 3-35. This dialog box looks similar to the **Select Objects** dialog box, and it allows you to select objects in the same way. Only acceptable objects are listed in this dialog box.

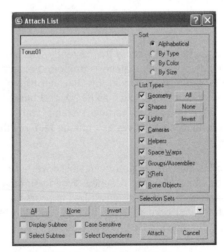

Figure 3-35. The Attach List dialog box

In sub-object mode, the **Attach List** button changes to the **Detach** button. This is because the only things that can be attached in sub-object mode are sub-objects, which aren't named. Additionally, the only thing that can be detached from an object is a sub-object.

Although any sub-object type can be detached, objects that are attached become new elements within the object they are attached to, and therefore can be selected in their entirety with one click of the mouse, using the Element sub-object mode.

One of the things that can bring even a fast computer to a halt when rendering is a scene with too many objects. Every time 3ds Max renders a scene, it must prepare all scene objects. Preparing objects involves several steps; and the more objects a scene contains, the more steps 3ds Max must repeat. If you have two objects and attach one to the other, 3ds Max only has to perform the steps once instead of twice.

So what constitutes too many objects? For a typical workstation, such as one with a 3.8 GHz processor and 2 GB of RAM, I would never allow my scenes to contain more than 1,000 objects, and I usually try to keep it to a few hundred unless absolutely necessary. Before I was wise to this, I often rendered scenes of over 1,000 objects; and preparing the objects took up to 90% if the rendering time. The bottom line is, if you have two or more objects with the same material applied, and have no specific need to keep them as separate entities, then you should attach and collapse the objects. Besides the benefit of reduced rendering times, attaching objects makes finding and organizing objects much easier.

Attaching Objects

This exercise demonstrates the use of the **Attach** feature in the **Edit Geometry** rollout.

1. Reset 3ds Max.
2. Create two spheres in the Perspective view.
3. Select one of the spheres and convert to an editable mesh.
4. In the **Edit Geometry** rollout, select **Attach**.
5. Select the other sphere and right-click to end the Attach command.
6. Both spheres are now elements of the same object.
7. Save your work for use in the next exercise.

Explode

Occasionally, you may have the need to blow objects up. The **Explode** feature (shown in Figure 3-36) gives you this ability outside of sub-object mode, and within the Face, Polygon, and Element sub-object modes. This feature is like the opposite of **Attach**, allowing you to separate selected faces into individual objects or elements within the same object. The value to the right of the **Explode** button determines which faces are exploded. If the angle between the normals of selected faces exceeds the value shown, then those selected faces with the exceeding angles are exploded. If the **Objects** option is selected, then all exploded faces become individual objects. If **Elements** is selected, all exploded faces become elements within the object.

Figure 3-36. The Explode feature

Remove Isolated Vertices

This feature is not needed very often, but occasionally it can come in handy. It allows you to remove vertices within an object that are not part of any face, and thus serve no function or purpose. Vertices can become isolated as a result of certain modeling techniques, such as deleting vertices in vertex sub-object mode or performing Boolean operations.

The left image in Figure 3-37 shows a simple plane with **Vertex Ticks** turned on for ease of display. The middle image shows the same plane after select vertices have been deleted, leaving an isolated vertex on each of the four corners. By clicking **Remove Isolated Vertices**, the four vertices are deleted. With some features, such as **Boolean**, 3ds Max usually detects such an occurrence and asks you if you wish to remove the isolated vertices. It's also worth mentioning that, by default, 3ds Max will automatically remove any vertices that become isolated when you delete faces in sub-object mode. Nonetheless, when they exist, they can prevent you from applying certain modifiers. Some of my past coworkers swear that isolated vertices are the cause of occasional 3ds Max program crashes.

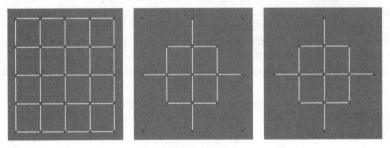

Figure 3-37. Removing isolated vertices

View Align and Grid Align

The **View Align** and **Grid Align** features allow you to move selected objects or sub-objects so that all the vertices that make up the objects or sub-objects you select lie in a plane perpendicular to the active viewport's perspective. In the top-left image of Figure 3-38, a group of vertices are selected, and in the perspective view to the right, those vertices are raised up a small amount. If at any time you want to bring all or some of the vertices back to a single plane (as shown in the bottom images), select the vertices you want to move (or any other sub-object type), right-click in the Top viewport (since it's the view you want to align to), and click the **View Align** icon. All selected vertices will become aligned in the same plane, and that plane will exist at the averaged location of all moved vertices.

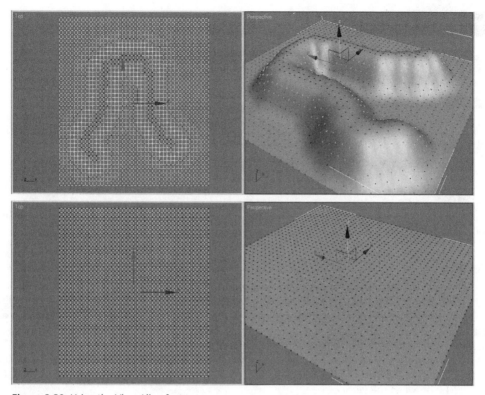

Figure 3-38. Using the View Align feature

Important features available only in sub-object modes

This section covers the important features available only in sub-object modes: **Detach**, **Delete**, and **Weld**.

Detach

This feature, available in all but the Edge sub-object mode, simply separates selected sub-objects from the rest of the main object. To detach sub-objects, make a sub-object selection, click the **Detach** button, and give the new object a name. When prompted to name the new object, you are given the options **Detach to Element** and **Detach as Clone**. The **Detach to Element** option makes the sub-object selection an element within the object. The **Detach as Clone** feature makes a copy of the detachment so that the original can be left intact and unchanged.

Detaching Objects

This exercise demonstrates the use of the **Detach** feature in the **Edit Geometry** rollout.

1. Continue from the previous exercise.
2. Click the **Element** sub-object level.
3. Select one of the sphere elements and click **Detach** in the **Edit Geometry** rollout.
4. Click **OK** to detach the selected sub-object as a new object in the scene.
5. Click the **Element** sub-object level to exit sub-object mode.

Delete

This feature deletes any sub-object selection. When you delete a vertex, any face using the deleted vertex will also be deleted.

Weld

This feature, available only in Vertex sub-object mode, works in the editing of meshes much like it does in the editing of splines. The **Weld** command simply welds all selected vertices that lie within the distance specified in the **Selected** field. In Figure 3-39, a simple plane is created with a width and length of 4 units, and containing 4 length and width segments (as shown in the top two images). Therefore, the distance between each vertex is exactly 1.0. The bottom-left image shows two vertices selected, which are then welded together, as shown in the bottom-center image. They are welded because the value entered into the **Selected** field is **1.01** (see Figure 3-39)—just greater than the distance of 1.0 between the vertices.

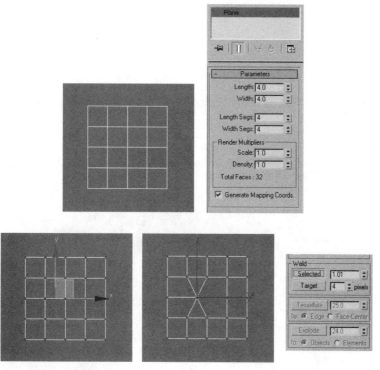

Figure 3-39. Welding vertices

Summary

Hopefully, you now understand the basics of modeling an architectural scene and how important it is to set up 3ds Max properly before beginning any project. It can be heartbreaking to fall victim to some of the perils that can come from not properly setting up the 3ds Max environment, such as losing hours of work or learning months later that you've been using the wrong graphics driver.

This chapter has covered the most important concepts in scene setup, as well as the important basic features of splines, shapes, and meshes. The concepts in this chapter will give you the foundations of efficient architectural modeling.

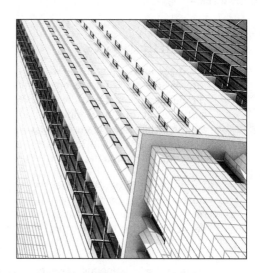

Chapter 4

THE CRITICAL COMPOUND OBJECTS TYPES (LOFT, BOOLEAN, TERRAIN, AND SCATTER)

Now that the basics of modeling have been covered, it's time to discuss some of the truly powerful modeling tools for architectural visualizations. Within the **Geometry** tab of the **Create** panel is a drop-down list (discussed in Chapter 1) that provides access to numerous object-creation tools for every different industry. Many of these groups of tools provide little or no help to visualizations, however, as they are geared more toward other industries. In fact, of the 11 groups listed, only 3 are discussed in this book. The first group, **Standard Primitives**, is obviously a must for all 3ds Max users. Another group, **Particle Systems**, is a must for anyone needing to show flowing water, snow, or other types of systems comprised of small particles. The third group of tools covered in this book, **Compound Objects**, provides four critical modeling tools for the visualization industry.

Compound objects, as the name implies, are object types created from two or more objects. Compound objects can be created from two splines, two primitives, or any number of object types. What makes compound objects so critical is that they each perform at least one specific task far better and faster than any other tool in 3ds Max. As I say throughout this book, there are usually numerous means to the same end. Sometimes, however, there is clearly a fastest means, and the compound objects discussed in this chapter constitute four such examples.

Creating Lofts

If somebody were to ask me what the most powerful and versatile feature of 3ds Max is for creating architectural visualizations, I would say without hesitation: the Loft feature. Whether you're creating walls, street curbs, rain gutters, or window sills, no other feature in 3ds Max can create the architectural features you will need as quickly and with as much flexibility as lofts can. In 3ds Max, there are so many ways to do the same thing, but when it comes to lofts, there's clearly a fastest way.

The term "loft" has many definitions, but the one that applies most closely here is "to propel into space." The Loft feature in 3ds Max requires two splines or shapes: one that defines a path, and one that defines the shape that gets "propelled into space" along the path.

To access the Loft command, select a shape or spline and click **Create ➤ Geometry ➤ Compound Objects ➤ Loft**. When you do, five rollouts appear, as shown in Figure 4-1. The remainder of this section explores the contents of these rollouts.

Figure 4-1. The Loft feature

The Creation Method rollout

This rollout simply gives you the option of lofting a shape along a path, with the loft being created at the shape's location or the path's location. Personally, I cannot think of a single architectural application for which the **Get Path** creation method would be more beneficial. Figure 4-2 shows the difference between the two options. The image on the left shows two rectangles, the larger representing the wall outline of a building and the smaller representing a typical wall section. The middle image shows a loft created at the path location, and the right image shows a loft created at the shape location. The difference should be clear.

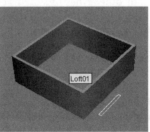

Figure 4-2. Creating lofts with Get Path (center) and Get Shape (right)

Lofts in visualizations should be created using the **Get Shape** option, in which the user creates the paths in the locations where the lofts will exist, and then creates the shapes off to the side in some arbitrary location. To create a loft using this method, select a single path (a shape or spline that represents the location of the loft), click **Get Shape**, and then select the shape. The path must be a continuous, unbroken shape or spline for the **Get Shape** option to be selectable.

The other option available in the **Creation Method** rollout allows the user to move or copy the shape or path during creation or keep the default method of instance. The instance method allows you to update the loft by updating either the path or shape after creation. The **Move** and **Copy** methods do not offer this flexibility of modification, and I therefore recommend always leaving the **Instance** option selected. As long as the object remains a loft, a direct link is maintained with the path and profile. This aspect of lofts is illustrated in a crude but easy-to-understand example in Figure 4-3, which depicts a loft used to represent the walls and fascia of a simple structure.

The top-left image in Figure 4-3 shows a path representing the perimeter walls of the structure and a small shape representing the wall section. The top-middle image shows the loft created from the two. In the top-right image, you can see that the height of the loft is increased, which was done by simply moving individual vertices of the shape. The loft changes its structure accordingly. In the bottom-left image, two vertices of the path are moved, and again the loft changes accordingly, as shown in the bottom-right image. This link that the loft maintains with the shape and path makes the loft a powerful and versatile tool.

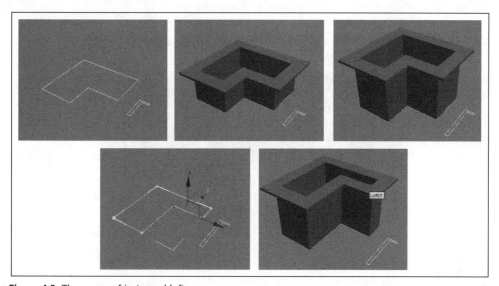

Figure 4-3. The power of instanced lofts

Creating a loft

This exercise demonstrates how to create a simple loft that represents the walls of a building using two shapes to represent a loft path and a loft shape.

1. Reset 3ds Max.

2. Change the units to **US Standard**.

3. In the Top view, create a rectangle with a length and width of 30'. This shape will represent the loft path.

4. In the Top view, create a second rectangle, with a length of 10' and a width of 8". This shape will represent the loft shape.

5. Select the smaller rectangle (representing the loft shape) and click the **Hierarchy** tab.

6. Click **Affect Pivot Only**.

7. Click the **Align** icon, and in the Top view, click the smaller rectangle. The **Align Selection** dialog box appears.

8. Under **Current Object**, select **Pivot Point**, and under **Target Object**, select **Minimum**, as shown in the following screenshot. Select the **X** and **Y** positions, and deselect the **Z** position. Click **OK** to end the command. This command moves the pivot point to one of the bottom corners of the shape.

9. Select the large rectangle representing the loft path.

10. In the Command panel, click **Create ➤ Geometry ➤ Compound Objects ➤ Loft**.

11. Click **Get Shape**. The loft will be created, as shown in the following illustration:

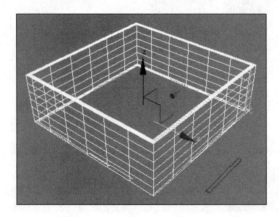

12. Select the small rectangle (representing the loft shape) and add the **Edit Spline** modifier.

13. Enter Vertex sub-object mode, and highlight the top two vertices of the loft shape.

14. In the Top view, move the selected vertices 2' upward along the y axis. The loft representing the walls of a building should increase in height by the same 2'.

The Surface Parameters rollout

The next rollout, **Surface Parameters** (see Figure 4-4), contains several useful features that help the loft stand out as one of the most versatile and powerful modeling tools. Fortunately, most lofts will not require these settings to be adjusted. **Smoothing Length** and **Smoothing Width** should be left enabled because they remove any shading imperfections, which can otherwise be quite noticeable. **Apply Mapping** allows you to apply materials to a loft in a way no other tool can: along the length of a loft. If you want the image of tree bark, for example, to be repeated along the branch of a tree that twists and turns, this option makes that possible with minimal distortion to the map. Otherwise, you are left to create mapping with tools that would make this much more difficult and probably lead to significant distortion of the map. The **Length Repeat** and **Width Repeat** parameters control how often the maps are tiled in their respective directions.

Under the **Materials** section is an option you may find useful: **Generate Material IDs**. This option applies material IDs to a loft in the same way they're assigned to the loft's shape. For example, in Figure 4-4, a multi/sub-object material composed of two sub-materials is applied to the wall loft. Notice the bottom of the wall has a brick material applied, and the top is painted a light tan color. This is because the bottom segment of the shape is assigned a sub-material ID of **1** (brick) and the top segment of the shape is assigned a sub-material ID of **2** (paint); and those two materials are occupying the material 1 and material 2 slots within the multi-object material defined in the **Material Editor**.

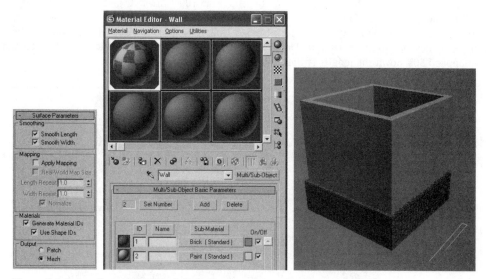

Figure 4-4. Generating material IDs for lofts

Once you select **Use Shape IDs** and apply a multi/sub-object material to the loft, the loft uses the material IDs of the shape to determine which parts of the loft get which sub-material. As a matter of practice, I do not use this feature much because there are usually better ways to apply materials to lofts, which will be discussed in Chapter 6. Nonetheless, it is a feature that many veteran users like and is worth some experimentation.

The **Output** section gives you the option to create the loft as a patch or a mesh. The default **Mesh** option should be kept because meshes allow for better editing, and your lofts will eventually be collapsed to a mesh anyway.

The Path Parameters rollout

The next rollout, **Path Parameters** (see Figure 4-5), allows you to apply multiple shapes along the same path. You can specify where in the path each shape begins its effect on the loft in one of three ways: percentage down the length of the path, distance down the length of the path, and the path steps (i.e., vertices) down the length, starting with vertex 1.

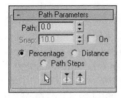

Figure 4-5. The Path Parameters rollout

The top-left image in Figure 4-6 shows a loft created with the circle shape, and the top-middle image shows the same loft modified by adding a star shape at 100% down the length of the path (i.e., the other end of the loft). To do this, type **100** in the **Path** field (as shown in the top-right image of Figure 4-6), click **Get Shape** again, and pick the star shape. Notice that 3ds Max transitions the loft from the circle shape to the star shape. The bottom-left image shows the same loft with the star shape being applied 50% down the length of the path.

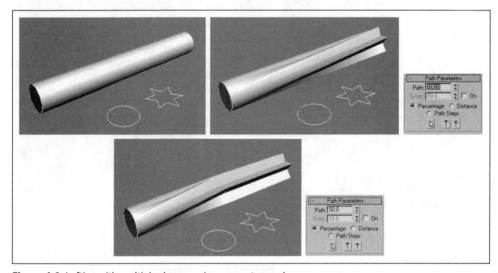

Figure 4-6. Lofting with multiple shapes, using percentage values

Another way to loft multiple shapes along the same path is using the loft's steps to determine the location of each shape's effect on the loft. The top-left image in Figure 4-7 shows the same loft in the previous example with two steps added along the loft (as shown in the **Path Steps** field of the top-right image). The bottom-left image shows the result of checking **Path Steps** (bottom-right image), entering **1** into the **Path** field, reexecuting the **Get Shape** command for step 1, and repeating this process for steps 2 and 3. In short, steps 0 and 3 (the ends of the loft) get the circular shape, while steps 1 and 2 (the middle of the loft) get the star shape.

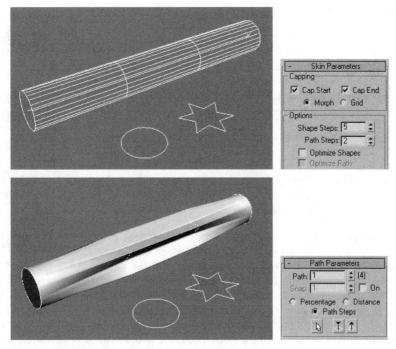

Figure 4-7. Lofting with multiple shapes using Path Steps

The final way to loft multiple shapes along the same loft is by using a specific distance to determine the location of each shape's effect on the loft. The loft in the preceding example is exactly 150 units long, and therefore, with the **Distance** option enabled, you can achieve the same result by reapplying the star shape to the loft at a distance of 50 and 100. In short, the distances of 0 and 150 units (the ends of the loft) get the circular shape, while the distances of 50 and 100 (the middle of the loft) get the star shape. The images in Figure 4-8 show the four distances for which the two shapes must be applied.

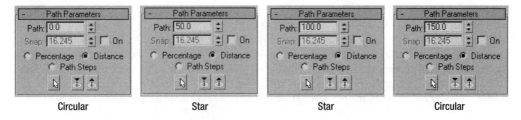

Figure 4-8. Lofting with multiple shapes using Distance values

The Skin Parameters rollout

The next rollout, **Skin Parameters** (see Figure 4-9), begins with options to cap the start and end of the loft. A cap simply closes or fills in the ends of the loft with faces so that the loft doesn't appear hollow. The **Cap Start** and **Cap End** options are selected by default, along with the **Morph** option, and should not be changed unless there is a specific reason to justify doing otherwise. I have never found such a reason.

Figure 4-9. The Skin Parameters rollout

Under the **Options** section is the most critical portion of the loft rollouts, which was discussed briefly in the previous example. The **Shape Steps** parameter lets you increase or decrease the number of additional vertices added between the original vertices that make up the shape. The **Path Steps** parameter allows you to do the same thing for the path. Both have a default of 5, but they will almost always need to be based on the situation.

Figure 4-10 shows an example of modifying both the shape steps and path steps. The image on the left shows a small circle, which represents the shape, lofted along a larger circle that represents the path. The loft is created using all of the default values for each rollout, to include five path and shape steps. Notice in the middle image what happens when only **Shape Steps** is reduced to **0**, thus retaining only the original four vertices to define the look of the shape. The result is a loft with a diamond-shaped cross-section. In the image on the right, **Shape Steps** is put back to its default value of **5**, and this time **Path Steps** is reduced to **0**, leaving only the original four vertices to define the path. The result is a diamond-shaped path with a circular cross-section.

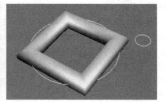

Figure 4-10. Using Shape Steps and Path Steps

The **Optimize Shapes** and **Optimize Path** options remove any unnecessary vertices in the shape or path, such as multiple vertices in a straight section of the shape. The **Adaptive Path Steps** option automatically places vertices in the location necessary to produce a smooth look to all curved sections of the shape. Figure 4-11 shows one example of these options, in which a loft representing a street curb is lofted with and without the **Optimize Path** option enabled. Notice that when enabled (as in the left image), all unnecessary steps are removed from the straight segments of the path.

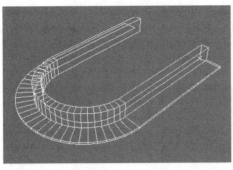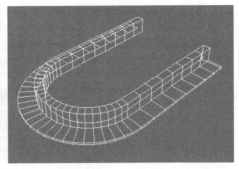

Figure 4-11. The Optimize Path option enabled (left) and disabled (right)

There are several other options in this rollout, but the only others you will likely have to modify within architectural projects are the **Banking** and **Flip Normals** options. I highly recommend turning off **Banking** unless you specifically need it to correctly model something like a roller coaster, for which you want the shape to be banked at curves in the path. Leaving **Banking** checked often causes slight but often noticeable imperfections in the modeling process where corners exist in the path. Additionally, you may encounter rare occasions when your loft appears to be inside out. This occurs when, for whatever reason, the program doesn't know which way the loft should be viewed. When this happens, try selecting the **Flip Normals** option to correct the problem.

Additionally, you may find it visually helpful to disable the **Transform Degrade** option so that you can see changes to the loft while you are applying transforms. Otherwise, you have to finish applying the transform before you get to see what the result is.

The last section within the **Skin Parameters** rollout, **Display**, needs no modification.

Modifying the shape steps and path steps of a loft

This exercise demonstrates how to modify the shape steps and path steps of a loft to provide an adequate number of vertices for smooth curves.

1. Reset 3ds Max.
2. Change the units to **US Standard**.
3. In the Top view, create a circle with a radius of 10', and a second circle with a radius of 2'.
4. Select the larger circle.
5. In the Command panel, click **Create ➤ Geometry ➤ Compound Objects ➤ Loft ➤ Get Shape**.
6. Click the smaller circle. The loft is created with default settings, as shown in the left image in the following illustration.
7. In the Command panel, click the **Modify** tab.

8. Open the **Skin Parameters** rollout and change **Path Steps** to **0**. The loft becomes diamond-shaped because there are no longer any path steps, as shown in the middle image.

9. Change **Path Steps** back to its default value of **5**, and then change **Shape Steps** to **0**. The loft is now circular again but has a diamond-shaped cross-section, as shown in the right image.

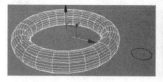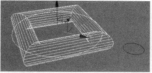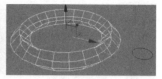

The Deformations rollout

The last rollout for lofts, **Deformations**, appears only within the **Modify** panel. It contains some powerful tools, but their practicality is very limited in architectural visualizations. I do not use them at all because I simply never have the need to deform lofts in these ways. In other fields of work, however, these tools can be invaluable. I will not cover deformations in this book.

Creating Booleans

The Boolean feature in 3ds Max is another immensely powerful tool in the creation of architectural visualizations, and in my opinion, second only to the Loft feature in terms of usefulness. A Boolean is an object created from the combination of two separate objects. How the objects combine to form a Boolean depends on the type of Boolean operation performed. Some examples include adding the geometry of one object to another, or using one object's volume to subtract from another object's volume. With Booleans, you can easily create window and door openings within a wall; you can create streets, parking symbols, and sidewalks out of a terrain surface; you can cut ornate designs out of simple primitives; and much more. One of the best things about Booleans is how simple they are to create. Now we'll focus on the procedures used to create each of the different types of Booleans.

To access the Boolean feature (shown in Figure 4-12), select **Create ➤ Compound Objects ➤ Boolean**. Each type of Boolean operation requires two objects; the first object is operand A and the second object is operand B. There are four rollouts that make up the Boolean feature. The first, **Name and Color**, requires no explanation, and the last rollout, **Display/Update**, is of little importance, and a rollout I have never found necessary. With the **Pick Boolean** rollout, the only feature you will probably ever use is the **Pick Operand** button, which actually executes the Boolean command. The point is, the Boolean feature is a very simple feature with only a few important options.

Figure 4-12. The Boolean feature

Union

The **Union** operation (Figure 4-13) combines two objects into one, regardless of whether they overlap. To perform a union, select an object (A), select **Boolean ➤ Union**, and then select a second object (B), which you'll add to A. Which object is A and which is B is irrelevant.

 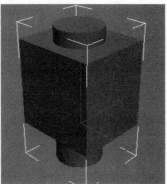

Figure 4-13. An example of a union

Subtraction

The **Subtraction** operation (see Figure 4-14) subtracts one object's volume from another. To perform the operation, select the object that you want to subtract from (A), and then select the second object whose volume you want subtract from the first (B). The result is that object B's volume is subtracted from object A. With the **Subtraction** operation, you have the option of subtracting B from A (default) or A from B. It makes no difference which method you use as long as you select the objects in the order required to achieve the result you need. This is one of countless examples in 3ds Max where there are more ways than one to accomplish a task.

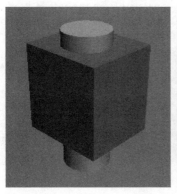 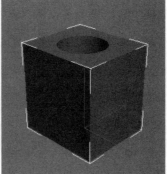

Figure 4-14. An example of a subtraction

117

Intersection

The **Intersection** operation (Figure 4-15) creates an object from only the overlapping part of two objects. As with the **Union** operation, which object is A and which is B is irrelevant. This operation has only rare use in architecture.

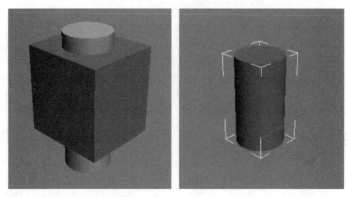

Figure 4-15. An example of an intersection

Cut

The **Cut** operation (Figure 4-16) is a very important tool in my repertoire. This operation uses the volume of one object to split another object into two parts, or to change another object's structure by adding vertices.

For example, the left image in Figure 4-16 shows an extruded star intersecting a plane. The middle image shows the result of using the **Refine** option, which creates new edges in the plane where it's intersected by the star. The third image shows the result of the **Split** operation, a personal favorite. This operation lets you perform a cookie-cutter type of action, in which the volume of an object that lies within the volume of an intersecting object is separated from the rest of itself. To complete the separation, you must select Face sub-object mode, click detach, and name the new object.

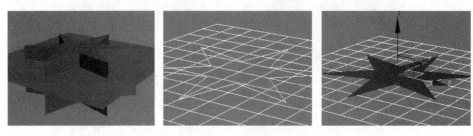

Figure 4-16. Example of the Cut operation

Creating a Boolean

This exercise demonstrates how to create the various Boolean types.

1. Reset 3ds Max.

2. In the Perspective view, create two equally sized spheres that overlap each other, as shown in the left image of the following illustration.

3. With one of the spheres selected, in the Command panel, click **Create ➤ Geometry ➤ Compound Objects ➤ Boolean ➤ Pick Operand B**. The Boolean is created with the default **Subtraction** method.

4. Click each of the various operation types to see the result of each Boolean. Compare your results to the following illustration, which shows two original spheres (left), and from left to right, an example of a union, an intersection, and a subtraction.

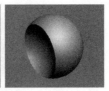

Suggestions for creating Booleans

Booleans can seem temperamental and uncooperative when conditions for their creation are not ideal. Here are a few things to keep in mind when performing Boolean operations:

- Make sure that the objects you're subtracting from other volumes are closed surfaces. When I first started creating Booleans, I would import what I thought were closed splines from AutoCAD, extrude those splines to create a solid, and subtract those solids from my wall loft to create window and door openings. Many times the Boolean operation would be erratic or not work at all. For the longest time, I didn't realize that the problem was that during import, the start and end vertices of the splines didn't automatically weld. 3ds Max treated them as open surfaces, even though when extruded they appeared to be solids. The easy fix is to manually weld the vertices before extruding.

- Boolean operations do not always work well when some of the object faces are long and skinny. If an operation does not work right the first time, try adding more vertices to the mesh through object parameters, or even with certain modifiers such as the **Tessellate**.

- Objects that have modifiers in their modifier stack can sometimes cause problems with the Boolean operation. One thing to try, and something I always do anyway when creating Boolean objects, is to collapse each object to a mesh prior to the operation. Collapsing after the operation is also a good practice in that it makes future Booleans work better and helps to reduce file size.

- Boolean operations can be erratic when face normals are not consistent. Make sure each object's face normals are unified and facing the proper direction. The normal modifier can accomplish this.

- Never perform a Boolean on linked objects. Booleans will not work on linked objects, and one of the operands will most likely disappear.

Creating terrain

The Terrain modeling tool is a great way to create terrain from elevation contour lines. Drawings containing elevation contour lines are usually created by surveyors or landscape architects with a program such as AutoCAD. Whether these lines are created in 3ds Max or imported from other programs, they must be closed to be used in the Terrain feature.

To create terrain, place the contour splines at varying elevations, select all the splines, and click the **Terrain** button in the **Compound Objects** drop-down menu. When you do, several rollouts appear with numerous options, as shown in Figure 4-17. You can add additional splines at any time by clicking the **Pick Operand** button in the **Pick Operand** rollout. All of the splines that make up the terrain object are listed as operands in the **Operands** list. The top three images in Figure 4-18 show several splines positioned at various elevations, and the bottom two images show the result of applying the Terrain command with different options found in the **Form** section of the **Parameters** rollout.

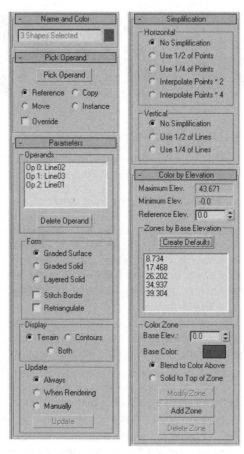

Figure 4-17. The Terrain rollouts

The **Form** section includes options for how the terrain is formed. The **Graded Surface** and **Graded Solid** options, both shown in the bottom-left image of Figure 4-18, will almost always be the most applicable to architectural visualizations because they depict natural terrain. Both options provide the same result, except that **Graded Solid** puts a bottom and a skirt on the surface, making the surface viewable from any direction. The **Layered Solid** option, shown in the bottom-right image of Figure 4-18, provides a tiered terrain, which may be beneficial in certain situations. The other options within the **Parameters** rollout do not need to be discussed for architectural work.

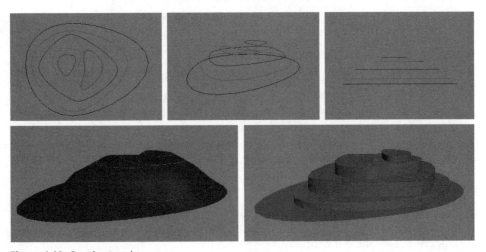

Figure 4-18. Creating terrain

The **Simplification** rollout contains some very important options to understand. If it is not necessary to have highly detailed or accurate terrain, you may want to try the **Use 1/2 of Points** or **Use 1/4 of Points** options. These options simply reduce the number of vertices used to model the terrain, which reduces the total number of polygons and the strain on your computer. If the number of polygons is not a factor, and you intend to have the best looking terrain you can, I recommend using the **Interpolate Points *4** option. This option provides the best terrain by interpolating the spaces in between the lines, thus providing smooth, realistic curves. Under the **Vertical** section, use the **No Simplification** option for best results, or the **Use 1/2 of Lines** or **Use 1/4 of Lines** options if you are trying to reduce polygons.

Although not a favorite of mine, you may want to try coloring your terrain with features in the **Color by Elevation** rollout. There are much better ways to apply materials to your terrain, which will be discussed in Chapter 6, but if you want a simple and quick method to give your terrain color, this may suffice. Simply click the **Create Defaults** button to apply default colors to default elevations. To make a change, highlight one of the elevation values that now appears in the elevations windows, and use the color swatch to change the color of each zone. You must click the **Modify Zone** button before the changes take effect.

Creating a terrain object

This exercise demonstrates how to create a terrain object using splines that represent contour lines.

1. Reset 3ds Max.

2. In the Top view, create a series of five circles that do not overlap, as shown in image 1 of the following illustration. These lines will represent contour lines.

3. Select each spline individually, and using the **Transform Type-In** dialog box or the transform gizmo, move each spline (except the outer spline) upward along the z axis. Move the smaller splines that are closer to the center farther upward (as shown in image 2), as they represent higher elevations.

4. Select all of the splines, and in the Command panel, click **Create ➤ Geometry ➤ Compound Objects ➤ Terrain**. A terrain object is created, as shown in image 3. Notice, however, that the terrain is jagged around the base. This is because there are not enough vertices to define the perimeter.

5. Select the bottom outer circle, enter Segment sub-object mode, and select the four segments that define the circle (as shown in image 4).

6. Scroll down to the bottom of the **Geometry** rollout under the **Edit Spline** modifier and type **10** in the **Divide** field.

7. Click **Divide**. The original four segments are divided into ten additional segments each, and the base of the terrain object is now smooth, as shown in image 5 and 6. You can repeat this process for each spline if necessary.

8. Undo steps 5 through 7 to return the terrain to its original form with the jagged bottom.

9. Select the terrain object and click the **Modify** tab in the **Command** panel.

10. In the **Simplification** rollout, click **Interpolate Points * 4**. This also increases the number of points used to define the elevation lines; however, unlike dividing the line segments as described in steps 5 through 7, this method does not provide the same flexibility for defining the number of additional vertices used.

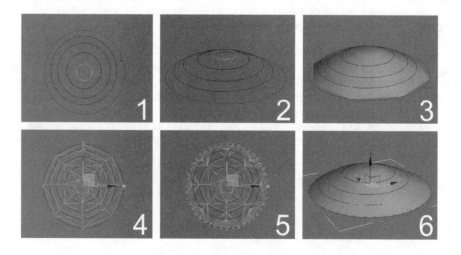

Creating scatter objects

The Scatter feature arranges copies of a selected object over the surface or within the volume of another object. The object that is scattered is the source object, and the object that the source is scattered on or within is known as the distribution object. In architectural visualizations, the Scatter feature's usefulness is limited primarily to the creation of vegetation. In this way, it's a great tool for scattering leaves around the branches of a tree or blades of grass around the surface of a lawn.

Figure 4-19 shows an example of the scatter routine by scattering a palm tree around the surface of a simple plane object. The top-left image shows the plane and a tree off to the side. To scatter the tree, select the source object (palm tree) and select **Create ➤ Compound Objects ➤ Scatter**. Complete the scatter routine by clicking the **Pick Distribution Object** button (first rollout) and then clicking the distribution object, which in this scene is the plane. The top-right image shows the result. By default, 3ds Max only places one object, and requires you to specify the number of duplicates desired. Also, notice that the plane appears to be a different color. This is because, by default, a copy of the distribution object is created with a new color and exists in the same space. The first thing to do is to turn off this distribution object. Scroll down to the **Display** rollout, open the rollout, and select **Hide Distribution Object**, as shown in Figure 4-19.

Figure 4-19. The Scatter feature

Within the **Scatter Objects** rollout is a section called **Objects**, which contains the source and distribution operands (palm tree and plane objects, respectively). In the **Source Object Parameters** section (see Figure 4-20), you can change the number of duplicates, but caution should be taken to ensure that you don't lock up your computer by entering too large a number for the particular object you want to scatter. Many operations in 3ds Max (such as this one) can consume a lot of RAM if you enter too large a value for the parameter. If you make too many duplicates of an object with a large number of polygons, the computer may run out of memory and crash. The right image in Figure 4-20 shows the result of increasing the **Duplicates** value to **20**.

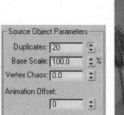

Figure 4-20. Increasing the Duplicates value to 20

The remaining three options in this section do not require any modifications, but I will explain them in the event that a rare exception arises. **Base Scale** specifies how much the distribution object is scaled before being scattered, with 100% signifying no change in size. The **Vertex Chaos** value specifies how much randomness to apply to the positioning of vertices. This option can distort the appearance of the object being scattered, but can sometimes add a nice touch of realism in certain situations. The **Animation Offset** value specifies the number of frames that must go by before another duplicate is created.

Distribution object parameters

The first option in this section, **Perpendicular**, aligns each duplicate so that the duplicate's normal is aligned with the normal of the face it's closest to. Without **Perpendicular** enabled, all duplicates would remain oriented in the direction of the initial object. The left-hand image in Figure 4-21 has **Perpendicular** enabled, and the image on the right shows the same object with **Perpendicular** disabled.

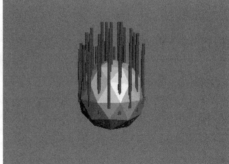

Figure 4-21. The Perpendicular option enabled (left) and disabled (right)

The **Use Selected Faces Only** option allows you to select specific faces on which to distribute the duplicates. The next variable, **Distribute Using**, determines how the duplicates are to be scattered over the distribution object.

The Transform rollout

The **Transform** rollout specifies the maximum amount of transformation randomly applied to each object. The duplicates can be randomly rotated, moved, or scaled about any or all three axes. The top-right image in Figure 4-22 shows the palm trees again, this time with a **Z Rotation** value of **90** applied. This means that all objects are randomly rotated around their z axis +/– 90 degrees. The bottom-right image has a **Z Scaling** value of 50% applied. This means that all objects are randomly scaled along the z axis between +/– 50% (i.e., some trees are 50% taller, some are 50% shorter, and some are anywhere in between). These two settings are particularly useful when scattering vegetation, which, as I stated before, is probably the most practical application of the Scatter command.

Figure 4-22. z axis rotation and scaling

Creating a scatter object

This exercise demonstrates how to create a scatter object, using a teapot as the object to be scattered and a plane as the distribution object.

1. Reset 3ds Max.

2. In the Top view, create a plane with a width and length of 100, and a teapot with a radius of 10, as shown in image 1 of the following illustration.

3. Select the teapot, and in the Command panel, click **Create ➤ Geometry ➤ Compound Objects ➤ Scatter**.

4. Click **Pick Distribution Object** and click the plane in any viewport. The scatter object is created with only one object (by default), as shown in image 2. Notice also that a duplicate plane object is created, which becomes the real distribution object. This object, however, is not desired and should be hidden from view.

5. In the **Display** rollout, enable the **Hide Distribution Object** option. The duplicate plane disappears.

6. Within the **Source Object Parameters** section of the **Scatter Objects** rollout, type **12** in the field next to **Duplicates**, and press Enter. There are now a total of 12 teapots that make up the scatter object, as shown in image 3. Notice, however, that all of the teapots are oriented along the same axis.

7. Within the **Rotation** section of the **Transforms** rollout, type **90** in the field next to **Z:**. This will randomly rotate each teapot around the z axis somewhere between 0 and 90 degrees, as shown in image 4.

8. Within the **Distribution Object Parameters** section of the **Scatter Objects** rollout, change the **Distribute Using** option from **Even** to **Area**. This changes how the objects are distributed about the distribution object, as shown in image 5. You should test the **Even**, **Area**, and **Volume** options to see which produces the best look.

9. Within the **Scale** section of the **Transforms** rollout, type **50** in the field next to **Z:**. This will randomly scale each teapot along the z axis somewhere between +/− 50%, as shown in image 6.

Summary

The four compound objects discussed in this chapter provide tremendous modeling power for 3ds Max users in the visualization industry. Whether you are trying to create terrain from an engineering drawing of contour lines, scatter leaves along the branches of a tree, or erect complex walls capable of easy modification, compound objects can do the job.

This chapter has covered four powerful modeling tools that begin the creation process of certain scene elements. More often than not, however, the compound objects you create in your scenes will still need further manipulation before they are complete. Whether your objects are created as compound objects or standard primitives, the next chapter discusses the critical modeling modifiers that will help you finish the modeling process for your scene.

Chapter 5

THE CRITICAL MODELING MODIFIERS

Modifiers are powerful features in Max that no modeler could do without. But with over 90 different modifiers for the typical primitive, you can quickly become overwhelmed trying to learn too many of them. Like most areas of Max, you should attempt to master just the important features that will allow you to work effectively and efficiently in your line of work. This chapter covers the modifiers that are most critical to modelers working on architectural visualizations. This list is by no means all you need to know or should strive to learn, as there are many other less utilized, but very effective, modifiers. However, this list consists of what I consider the critical, must-know modifiers, and for me, comprises the vast majority of the modifiers I use on a regular basis.

This chapter does not include a discussion of the **Edit Mesh** and **Edit Spline** modifiers, probably the two most frequently used modifiers for visualizations. These modifiers are discussed in Chapter 3.

The Extrude modifier

The **Extrude** modifier, shown in Figure 5-1, is one of the simplest and most often used modifiers for visualizations. The modifier simply makes a copy of itself along the local Z axis a given distance away from the original, and connects the two splines or shapes to form a mesh. The **Amount** value is the extrusion distance, and the **Segments** value defines how many segments will be created evenly along the length of the extrusion. The **Capping** options, which are automatically enabled, create faces to cover the ends of the extrusion. Only closed splines or shapes that are extruded can be capped. Mapping coordinates and material IDs are also generated automatically. The **Smooth** option, which is also automatically enabled, smoothes the extrusion.

Figure 5-1. The Extrude modifier

Using the Extrude modifier

This exercise demonstrates use of the **Extrude** modifier by creating a tube from a circle.

1. Reset 3ds Max.

2. In the Perspective viewport, create a circle with a radius of 10, as shown in the left image of the following illustration.

3. Apply the **Extrude** modifier with the default settings.

4. In the **Amount** field, type **10**, and in the **Segments** field, type **3**. This creates a column ten units tall, divided into three equal segments. These extra segments would be necessary if you later wanted to apply certain modifiers, such as the **Bend** modifier. Without the extra vertices, these types of modifiers will not work.

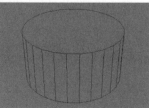
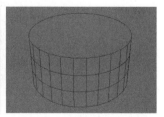

The Smooth modifier

The **Smooth** modifier, shown in Figure 5-2, is a critical component in the creation of many architectural models. This modifier simply gives the surface of an object a smoother appearance; not by adding vertices, but by changing the way surfaces are shaded. Smoothing eliminates the appearance of facets by grouping faces into smoothing groups. Adjacent faces are grouped into the same smoothing group when the angle between their normals is not greater than the specified threshold. Adjacent faces that lie in the same smoothing group are shaded to appear to be part of the same smooth surface.

All objects have smoothing automatically applied upon their creation. By default, when you apply the **Smooth** modifier to an object, Max assumes you wish to assign smoothing manually and disables the **Auto Smooth** feature in the modifier. So the initial result of applying the **Smooth** modifier is that the object will have no smoothing. The left image in Figure 5-3 shows a sphere with the **Smooth** modifier applied (and the **Auto Smooth** feature disabled). Notice that every face is visible because there is no smoothing applied. The right image shows the result of enabling the **Auto Smooth** option, in which the sphere receives its original smoothing again (assuming that angle between adjacent faces does not exceed the **Threshold** value). Once the **Smooth** modifier is applied, you can control precisely which faces receive smoothing by changing the **Threshold** value.

Figure 5-2.
The Smooth modifier

Figure 5-3. Smoothing a sphere

The images in Figure 5-4 show the effect of smoothing on a simple box. The image on the left shows a simple box without the **Smooth** modifier applied. When the **Smooth** modifier is first applied, the box remains the same; however, when the **Auto Smooth** feature is enabled and the threshold (the angle between the adjacent sides of the box) is increased to 90 or greater, Max places all the sides into the same smoothing group, resulting in the image on the right. Max applies the same smoothing group to all faces, assuming that you want the object to appear smooth even though it contains a 90-degree angle. The result, obviously, is a strange looking object.

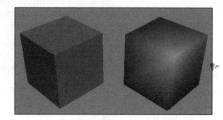

Figure 5-4. Smoothing a box

The Noise modifier

Here's a handy modifier that gives you the power to create everything from moving water to wind blowing through trees. The **Noise** modifier, shown in Figure 5-5, randomly moves the vertices of an object along selected axes. The **Strength** value sets the amount of displacement in the direction of the selected axis. The **Seed** value is a variable that assigns a new orientation for each numerical value entered. Two objects with the same value will look identical—but changing the value of either to any other value will make the two objects look completely different. There is also a **Fractal** option, which in conjunction with the **Roughness** and **Iterations** settings, can give an object a more jagged appearance. **Roughness** defines the amount of variation, and **Iterations** defines the number of times the variation is made. More iterations means a more chaotic look and longer computation times. If you select the **Animate Noise** option, the vertices will move back and forth throughout the duration of frames specified. **Frequency** determines the speed of noise changes, and **Phase** determines where the noise wave starts and ends. As with any modifier, animating the **Phase** value is a simple and easy way to animate the effects of the modifier.

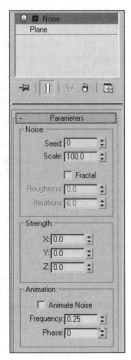

Figure 5-5. The Noise modifier

Figure 5-6 shows an example of the **Noise** modifier at work. The top-left image shows a high-density plane with a width and length of 150 units before the modifier is applied. The bottom-left image shows the same plane with the modifier applied and a **Z Strength** value of 50. In the top-right image, the **Z Strength** value is doubled to **100**. In the bottom-right image, the **Fractal** option is enabled.

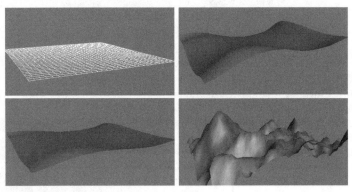

Figure 5-6. An example of the Noise modifier

Using the Noise modifier

This exercise demonstrates use of the **Noise** modifier to create relief in a mesh.

1. Reset 3ds Max.
2. In the Perspective viewport, create a plane with a length and width of 10, and four length and width segments, as shown in the left image of the following illustration.
3. Apply the **Noise** modifier. There should be no change to the plane.
4. Within the **Noise** section of the **Parameters** rollout, change the **Scale** value to **10**.
5. Within the **Strength** section, change the **Z** value to **5**. The plane appears to take on a wavy appearance, as shown in the middle image.
6. Change the **Z** value to **10**. The displacement of the vertices doubles because the strength of the noise is doubled.

 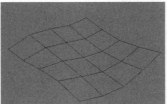 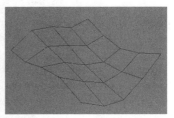

The Optimize modifier

The **Optimize** modifier, shown in Figure 5-7, is an extremely useful modifier that can help you reduce the total number of polygons in a model without significantly degrading its appearance. After you apply the modifier, you should analyze the last value in the rollout: **Before/After**. This tells you how many faces make up the object with and without the modifier applied. In most cases, you will probably find that the default settings are optimal for reducing faces without significantly degrading appearance. If after applying the modifier you decide that the impact is negligible, you can try adjusting some of the parameters within the modifier.

The **Face Thresh** parameter is the best parameter to experiment with. This value is the minimum angle that can exist between the normals of any two faces. If the angle between any adjacent normals is less than this value, Max removes as many faces as it can and creates new faces as necessary, while not allowing the angle between any adjacent normals to be less than the **Face Thresh** value. Figure 5-8 shows the model of a volcano to illustrate the benefits of using the **Optimize** modifier. The top-left image shows a high-density wireframe model comprised of 3,200 faces. Although this results in smooth curves and looks great when shaded, as shown in the top-right image, this is a large number of faces. If the viewer's perspective does not warrant such detail, you can use the **Optimize** modifier to reduce the overall number of faces. The bottom images in Figure 5-8 show the result of applying the **Optimize** modifier with all of the default values. The number of faces is reduced from 3,200 to 760 without any perceptible loss of detail (at least from this distance).

Figure 5-7. The Optimize modifier

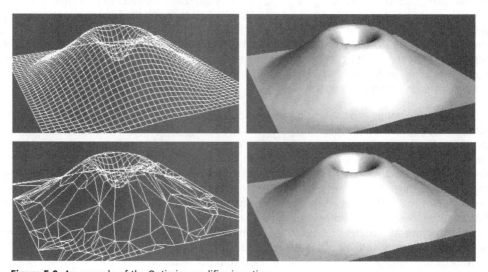

Figure 5-8. An example of the Optimize modifier in action

The TurboSmooth modifier

The **TurboSmooth** modifier, shown in Figure 5-9, is a fast and memory-efficient modifier that smoothes an object by adding vertices around corners and edges. The sharper the corner or edge, the greater the effect of this modifier. Although this modifier has less applicability in architectural modeling than other modifiers discussed thus far, it comes in handy when you want to smooth certain object types that appear too chiseled. These object types can include terrain, statues, fountains, or furniture, to name a few.

In the **Main** section of the rollout, you can specify how many iterations to run (i.e., how many times to apply the modifier action). This essentially makes the object smoother with each additional iteration. Since the **TurboSmooth** modifier can significantly slow down viewport refresh rates, you can specify one **Iteration** value for the viewport, and another for rendering. When you enable the **Render Iters** feature, the **Iterations** value determines the number of iterations shown in the viewport, and the **Render Iters** value determines the number of iterations for the rendering.

Figure 5-10 shows the previous volcano example with the original plane object containing far fewer initial vertices. Despite having a mesh with only a fraction of the vertices, applying the **TurboSmooth** modifier yields almost the same result as starting with a high-density mesh.

Figure 5-9.
The TurboSmooth
modifier

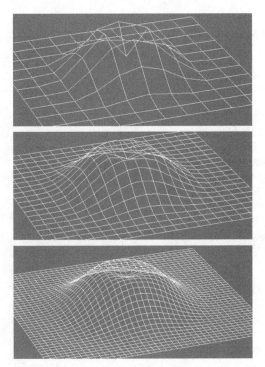

Figure 5-10. The TurboSmooth modifier in action, with zero, one, and two iterations, from top to bottom

This exercise demonstrates use of the **TurboSmooth** modifier to subdivide the polygons on a mesh.

1. Reset 3ds Max.

2. In the Perspective viewport, create a plane with a length and width of 10, and four length and width segments, as shown in the left image of the following illustration.

3. Apply the **TurboSmooth** modifier to the plane, using the default settings. Notice that each polygon on the plane is divided into four equally sized polygons. Applying this modifier to an object representing jagged terrain would cause the terrain to be smoothed.

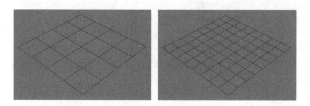

The Displace modifier

The **Displace** modifier, shown in Figure 5-11, changes the geometry of an object through the use of a map or a bitmap image. When a map is applied to an object, the areas of the object on which darker parts of the map exist are recessed (pushed down) and areas of the object on which brighter areas of the map exist are elevated (pushed up).

In the **Parameters** rollout is a section called **Displacement**, which contains a **Strength** value that directly controls the amount of displacement. In the **Image** section are buttons for loading and unloading bitmaps and maps. The **Blur** value controls the blur applied to the image, which in the case of the skater shown in Figure 5-12, can smooth out the rough edges. In the **Map** section, you can control the alignment of the bitmap or map; options include **Planar**, **Cylindrical**, and **Spherical**.

Figure 5-12 shows an example of the **Displace** modifier in action. The image on the left is used to create an impression in a high-density plane, as shown in the image on the right. In order for the **Displace** modifier to work properly in this type of situation, you must create a high-density mesh to work with, because without enough vertices, the **Displace** modifier can't create detail.

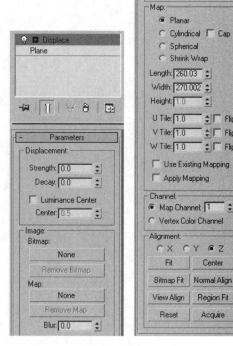

Figure 5-11. The Displace modifier

Figure 5-12. An example of the Displace modifier in action

The images in Figure 5-13 show another example of the **Displace** modifier, this time in the creation of a volcano. The image on the left shows a high-density mesh prior to displacement. The middle image shows the map used for the displacement. The right image shows the result of the **Displace** modifier (with the map) applied to the plane object, using a **Strength** of **80**. If the **Strength** value were **40**, then the volcano would be half as tall.

Figure 5-13. A volcano created with the Displace modifier

Using the Displace modifier

This exercise demonstrates use of the **Displace** modifier to model terrain.

1. Reset 3ds Max.
2. In the Perspective viewport, create a plane object with a width and length of 100 units, and with 30 length and width segments, as shown in the top-left image of the following illustration.
3. Apply the **Displace** modifier.
4. Within the **Image** section of the **Parameters** rollout, click the button that says **None** directly below **Map**, as shown in the top-middle image. The **Material/Map Browser** appears. (This tool won't be discussed until Chapter 6, but don't worry—for now you'll only have to do one simple thing with it.)

5. In the **Material/Map Browser**, select **Noise** from the list of map types, as shown in the top-right image. Select **OK** to close the **Material/Map Browser**.

6. Within the **Displacement** section of the **Parameters** rollout, type **20** in the **Strength** field (bottom-left image), and press Enter. The vertices that make up the plane object are now displaced along the z axis, as shown in the bottom-right image. The amount of displacement for each vertex depends on where the black and white portions of the noise map exist. (Maps will be covered in much greater detail in Chapters 7 and 8.)

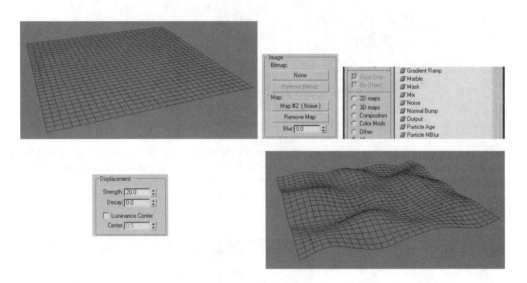

The Lathe modifier

This is a seldom-used but sometimes critically important modifier that enables you to create a 3D object by rotating a shape or spline along an axis. The **Lathe** modifier, shown in Figure 5-14, is named after the machine tool that spins a block of material while a cutting or forming tool is applied to the block, allowing it to be shaped into an object with symmetry about an axis of rotation. One of the most common uses of the **Lathe** modifier in architectural visualizations is in the creation of columns and balusters, as shown in Figure 5-15. Other possible uses include lamps, fountains, door knobs, and any other types of objects that have rotational symmetry along one axis.

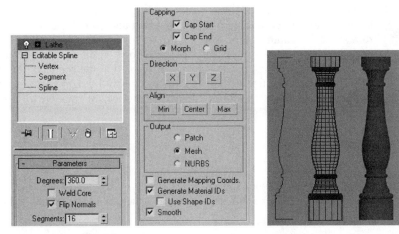

Figure 5-14. The Lathe modifier

When you first apply the **Lathe** modifier, Max rotates the shape 360 degrees using 16 segments during the course of the rotation. In most cases, 16 segments are sufficient to provide smooth curves about the axis of rotation; however, for close-ups, this value may need to be increased. Figure 5-15 shows balusters with a varying number of segments. The first baluster on the left contains the minimum required 3 segments, and the remaining balusters contain 4, 5, 8, and 16 segments, respectively. Although the first few examples contain far fewer segments than what is necessary for a smooth rotation, using 3, 4, or 5 segments provide a unique and often desirable look for balusters or columns.

Figure 5-15. The Lathe modifier with 3, 4, 5, 8, and 16 segments, from left to right

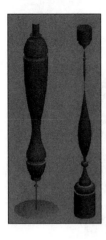

In the **Align** section of the **Lathe** modifier, you can align the axis of revolution to the minimum, center, or maximum extents of the shape. By default, the **Lathe** modifier rotates a shape about its pivot point, which for many shapes is its center. This is often not desirable and can result in very strange models. In the case of the balusters just discussed, the pivot point of the shape was located at the center of the shape, and when the **Lathe** modifier was applied, the result was the right image in Figure 5-16. The left image shows the result of aligning the axis of rotation to the minimum extent of the shape.

Figure 5-16. The Lathe modifier with a Min rotation (left) and a Cen rotation (right)

The STL Check modifier

This modifier checks an object to ensure it can be exported to the StereoLithography (STL) format. Exporting to STL format, or similar formats such as VRML, is something you are sure to be doing in the next few years with the explosion of a new technology known as 3D printing. 3D printing allows you to print your models directly to a 3D printer, with or without materials applied. In order to do this, the model must have good integrity. The STL format requires the object to have a closed surface (i.e., a surface with no holes or gaps). When you apply the modifier, all problems are listed in the **Status** section of the **Parameters** rollout. The modifier checks for such errors as open edges, multiple edges, double faces, and spikes. Spikes are faces that are connected at only one edge. You can select one or all of these options. Once found, the modifier can select the problem edges or faces.

The left image in Figure 5-17 shows a simple plane with selected faces missing. The right image shows same plane after applying the **STL Check** modifier. Notice the highlighted areas, which indicate problems with the model's integrity. For more information on 3D printing, check out the leading company on this new technology, EMS, at www.ems-north.com.

Figure 5-17. An example of the STL Check modifier

The Cap Holes modifier

Sometimes in the course of modeling or importing 3D models from other programs, faces can go missing. The **Cap Holes** modifier, shown in Figure 5-18, detects and fills these holes by creating faces along open edges. **Cap Holes** is also an option that is automatically enabled during the creation of a loft. If disabled, the loft would have openings at each end. Although this modifier is not needed as frequently as most others discussed in this chapter, when it is needed, it comes in very handy.

Figure 5-18. The Cap Holes modifier

Figure 5-19 shows an example of a plane with a hole that is easily filled using the **Cap Holes** modifier.

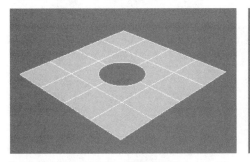 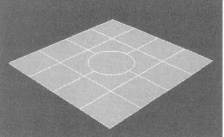

Figure 5-19. An example of the Cap Holes modifier

Using the Cap Holes modifier

This exercise demonstrates use of the **Cap Holes** modifier to fill in missing faces of a box.

1. Reset 3ds Max.

2. In the Perspective viewport, create a box of any size, with four length, width, and height segments, as shown in the left image of the following illustration.

3. Apply the **Edit Mesh** modifier (discussed in Chapter 3), enter Face sub-object mode, and delete a few faces from the box, as shown in the middle and right images.

4. Apply the **Cap Holes** modifier. All of the missing faces are filled in, and the box returns to its initial condition.

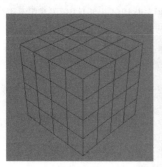 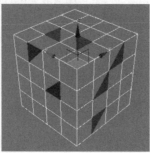 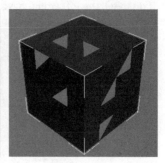

Summary

This chapter has covered a number of powerful modifiers for use in architectural visualizations. As I stated at the beginning of the chapter, this list is by no means all you should know. The use you find for some modifiers are limited only by your imagination. Many of the tips and tricks you come across in the 3D community involve innovative ways of using modifiers to perform a specific function in record time. With nearly 100 different modifiers available for some objects, just about anything that can be dreamed-up can be modeled. The only questions are "How will it be modeled?" and "How long will it take?"

Part 3

MATERIALS

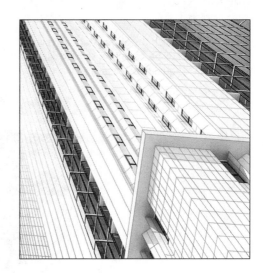

Quick Start 3

GETTING STARTED WITH MATERIALS

> *Approximate completion time: 45 minutes*

Quick Start 3 continues where the end of Quick Start 2 left off. In this tutorial, you'll begin applying premade materials to some objects, and you'll create other materials from scratch to be applied to the remaining objects. You'll quickly see how materials can breathe life into a scene and help you begin to achieve realism. As mentioned in the previous tutorial, this scene is simplistic in nature—but nonetheless, it requires use of the same tools a veteran user would use to create a very large and intricate scene.

1. Open the file that you saved at the end of Quick Start 2, or open the file 3dsMax8\scenes\Friends_of_Ed\QuickStart03.max.

Let's start by applying the grass material to the scene.

2. Press H to open the **Select Objects** dialog box.

3. Select the **Site-Grass** object and click **Select**.

4. Press M to open the **Material Editor**. This is the main interface with which materials are applied to a scene.

5. Click the top-left sample slot with the green grass material, if not already selected. When a sample slot is selected, a white border appears around it.

6. Click the **Assign Material to Selection** icon found directly below the six sample slots. This assigns the material to the **Site-Grass** object you just selected.

7. Click the **Show Map in Viewport** icon. This allows the image of the grass, also known as a map, to be seen in a shaded viewport. The quality of the viewport display depends heavily on the quality of your graphics card.

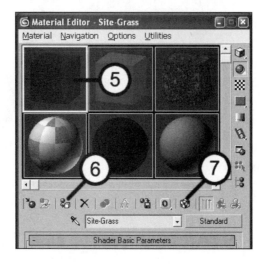

8. Press F9 to render the scene (close the render window when you've finished viewing). The map on the grass is stretched too far over too much area. Let's reduce it in size. To do so, you need to add the **UVW Map** modifier.

9. In the Command panel, click the **Modify** tab.

10. Click the **UVW Map** modifier (or add the modifier from the drop-down list).

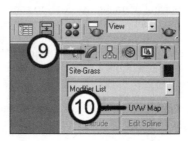

11. In the **Parameters** rollout, type **20'** in the **Length** and **Width** fields. This tells 3ds Max that you want the map (grass image) to be 20' × 20', so that when placed on an object, it covers 20 feet in the X direction and 20 feet in the Y direction.

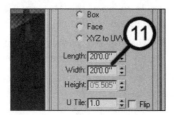

Now that the map is placed on the grass object correctly, let's do the same with the street object, but this time taking a shortcut.

12. Select the **Site-Street** object.

13. In the **Material Editor**, click the top-middle sample slot. The slot changes to show the white border around it, indicating that it's the active slot.

14. Change the name of the material from **02 – Default** to **Site-Street**. Each sample slot represents a different material, and each material is given a generic name. For simplicity and ease of use, most of the materials in your scene match the names of the objects in the scene. The only exception is when a material is applied to multiple objects.

15. Click the **Assign Material to Selection** icon. You've now just applied the Site-Street material to the Site-Street object.

16. Click the **Show Map in Viewport** icon. You can not see the map of the street in the viewport as you did with the grass because there were no mapping coordinates created automatically when the street object was created. Certain object types allow for automatic mapping coordinates, but this was not one of them.

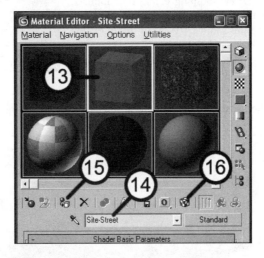

17. In the Command panel, click the **Modify** tab, if it's not already open.

18. Click the **UVW Map** modifier.

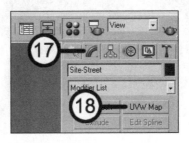

19. Scroll to the bottom of the **Parameters** rollout and click the **Acquire** button.

20. Click the Site-Grass object in the viewport (or select **Site-Grass** from the **Select Objects** dialog box). Notice that when you move your cursor over various objects in the viewport, the cursor symbol changes only when placed over objects that you can borrow UVW mapping coordinates from (i.e., objects with the **UVW Map** modifier applied).

21. When the **Acquire UVW Mapping** dialog box appears, click **OK** to accept the default option. You have just told 3ds Max to acquire the same **UVW Map** modifier settings as the Site-Grass object—therefore, the map applied to the street also represents an area of 20 feet by 20 feet.

22. Let's see how your scene looks so far. Press F9 to render the scene (close the render window when you've finished viewing). It should look similar to the following image:

Now let's apply a material to the mulch in your scene.

23. Select the Site-Mulch and Site-Grass objects, and isolate them by pressing Alt+Q.

24. Deselect both objects and reselect only the Site-Mulch object.

25. In the **Material Editor**, click the top-right sample slot.

26. Click the **Assign Material to Selection** icon. You've now just applied the Site-Mulch material to the Site-Mulch object.

27. Click the **Show Map in Viewport** icon. Just like the previous material you applied, you can't see the map of the mulch in the viewport. The reason for this is that the mulch object was created as an editable mesh. If you had extruded the lines representing the mulch, generic mapping coordinates would have been created automatically. Instead, you simply collapsed the lines to an editable mesh, and mapping coordinates were not created. Since the object has no mapping coordinates, you can't see the map.

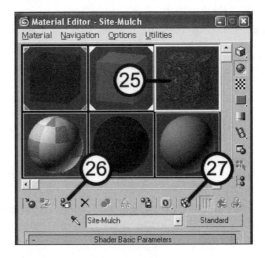

28. In the Command panel, click the **Modify** tab.

29. Click the **UVW Map** modifier.

30. Scroll to the bottom of the **Parameters** rollout and click the **Acquire** button.

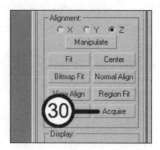

31. Click the Site-Grass object in the viewport (or select **Site-Grass** from the **Select Objects** dialog box).

32. When the **Acquire UVW Mapping** dialog box appears, click **OK** to accept the default option. You have just borrowed the mapping coordinates from the grass object and applied them to the mulch object.

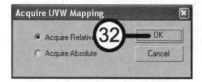

33. Press F9 to render the scene. The mulch material is clearly visible, but the map appears slightly large. Let's reduce it in size.

34. In the **Parameters** rollout of the **UVW Mapping** modifier you just applied, change the **Length** and **Width** values to **10'**. This changes the map size from the acquired 20-by-20-foot area to the new 10-by-10-foot area.

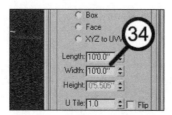

35. Press F9 to render the scene again (close the render window when you've finished viewing). Now the map of the mulch appears to be a reasonable size.

36. Click the **Exit Isolation Mode** button.

37. Select the Bldg-Walls object.

38. In the **Material Editor**, click the Bldg-Walls material (the bottom-left sample slot). Notice that this material contains three separate sub-materials. Let's see what happens when you apply it to the walls.

39. Click the **Apply Material to Selection** icon to apply the material. You just applied a multi/sub-object to the walls in your scene; however, the object only displays one color. The reason for this is that you haven't told 3ds Max which faces get which sub-materials.

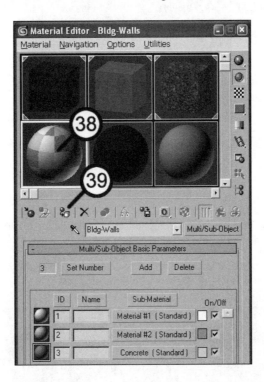

40. Activate the Front view by right-clicking in it. The view should be in wireframe (if it's not, press F3).

41. Isolate the walls by pressing Alt+Q.

42. Right-click inside the viewport, select **Convert To:** from the quad menu, and select **Convert to Editable Mesh**.

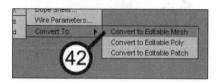

43. Right-click inside the viewport again and select **Face** from the quad menu.

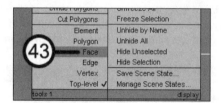

44. Click the **Window/Crossing** icon (if necessary) so that the toggle is set to the **Window** selection, as shown in the following image:

To perform the next step, you may need to move the Material Editor off to the side of your view so that it does not block your view of the walls, as shown below.

45. In the Front view, use a **Window** selection to select the top of the Bldg-Walls object that represents the soffit and fascia, as shown in the following image:

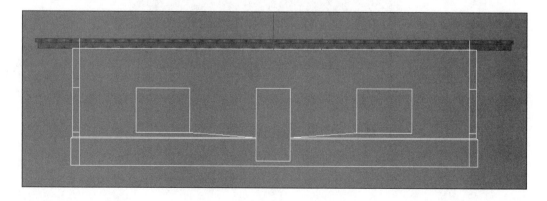

46. In the Command panel, scroll down to the **Surface Properties** rollout, type **1** in the **Set ID** field, and press Enter. The selected faces have just been assigned material ID 1. When you deselect the faces, you'll be able to see in a shaded view that they now display the same white sub-material listed in material ID 1 of the applied material (in the **Material Editor**).

47. In the Front view, use a window selection to select the trim that runs along the bottom of the wall, as shown in the following image. Be sure not to select the bottom of the window openings.

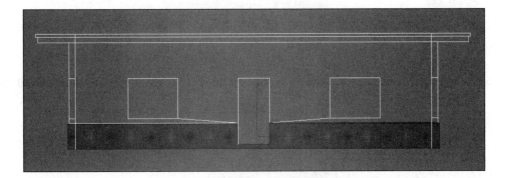

48. In the Command panel, type **2** in the **Set ID** field and press Enter. You have just changed the selected faces to material ID 2, and you will be able to see in a shaded view that the faces display the sub-material in material ID 2 of the applied material. You don't need to assign material ID 3 because all the faces were assigned that ID by default.

49. In the Command panel, click the yellow **Editable Mesh** in the modifier stack. This closes the modifier stack.

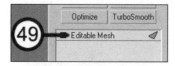

50. Activate the Camera view.

51. Click the **Exit Isolation Mode** button and press F9 to render the scene again. The **Missing Map Coordinates** error message appears because the material you just applied has a map within it, and the objects don't contain mapping coordinates (the **UVW Map** modifier).

52. Click Cancel to close the error message, and then close the render window.

53. In the Command panel, click the **UVW Map** modifier to add this modifier to the walls.

54. In the **Parameters** rollout of the **UVW Map** modifier, select the **Box** option, and type **10'** in each of the **Length**, **Width**, and **Height** fields. You've now applied the **UVW Map** modifier and told 3ds Max that the map represents an area of 10 feet by 10 feet. Also, by using the box method and a **Height** value of **10'**, you've told 3ds Max to apply the map to vertical sides of the object in 10-foot increments.

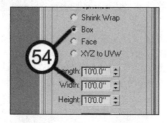

55. Press F9 to render the scene again. The scene is starting to come together. Notice that the walls now have a textured appearance, which is due to a bump map applied to the material and the **UVW Map** modifier applied to the object.

56. Select the Site-ParkingLines object.

57. Click the bottom-middle sample slot, which represents a material named Scene-White. This will be the material you apply to the parking lines in your scene.

58. Click the **Assign Material to Selection** icon. Notice the parking lines are now bright blue. This is obviously not going to work, so let's change the color.

59. In the **Blinn Basic Parameters** rollout, click the **Diffuse** color swatch. This opens the color selector.

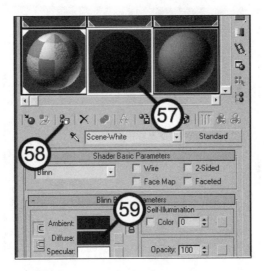

60. Drag the **Whiteness** slider downward so that the color changes to white. You can also change the color to white by typing a value of **255** into the **Red**, **Green**, and **Blue** fields. Now your parking lines should appear white in the viewport.

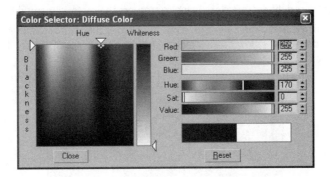

Since this material is white, and several other objects in your scene can use this same color, let's apply it to a few more objects.

61. Press H and select the following objects from the **Select Objects** dialog box: **Bldg-Door**, **Bldg-Floor**, **Bldg-Frames**, **Site-Curbs**, **Site-Fountain**, and **Site-Sidewalks**. Click **Select** when finished (remember to hold down Ctrl to select multiple objects).

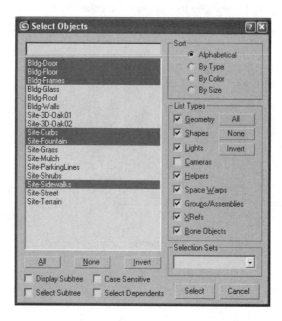

62. In the **Material Editor**, click the **Assign Material to Selection** icon. Now the material used for the parking lines has been applied to six other objects in the scene.

63. Select the Bldg-Glass object.

64. Click the bottom-right sample slot, which represents the material named Bldg-Glass.

65. Click the **Assign Material to Selection** icon and render the scene. Notice that the glass in the building is now a gray color, but it's lacking reflection and transparency. Let's add these two characteristics.

66. Click the **Maps** rollout to open it.

67. Click the Reflection map channel.

68. Select **Raytrace** from the **Material/Map Browser** and click **OK**. This step adds a Raytrace map to the Reflection map channel and will cause the glass to reflect.

69. Render the scene (close the render window when you're finished viewing). Notice that the rendering took much longer to complete. This is because of the extra work 3ds Max has to perform to calculate the reflections. The reflections are a little too strong, so let's reduce them slightly.

70. In the **Material Editor**, click the **Go to Parent** icon. This takes you out of the Reflection channel and back into the Parent (the base material).

71. In the **Reflection Amount** field, type **50**. This reduces the reflection strength to 50%.

72. Scroll up to the **Blinn Basic Parameters** rollout, change the **Opacity** from **100** (representing 100%) to **70**. Opacity is the opposite of transparency, so by making this material 70% opaque, you're making it 30% transparent.

73. Render the scene again. Unfortunately, there are not many objects for the glass to reflect, and since there are no objects inside the building, the effect of transparency is not as clear as it could be. Regardless, as you add objects to your scenes, these two characteristics will enhance the appearance of your glass.

74. Right-click the active material slot and select **5 X 3 Sample Windows** from the menu that appears. This changes the array of sample slots so that you can see more than the default six.

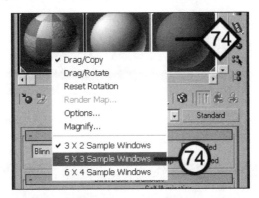

75. Click any new sample slot (i.e., with a gray sphere).

76. Click the **Pick Material from Object** icon. Notice that when you move your cursor into the viewport area, the cursor symbol changes to an eyedropper, like the icon you just selected. Notice also that when your cursor is over an object in your scene, the symbol changes slightly to an eyedropper that's filled with fluid. This means that your cursor is over an object with a material applied.

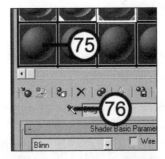

77. Place your cursor over either of the two trees in your scene and click the mouse. Notice that the sample slot changes to show you the multi/sub-object material that was applied to the tree. This is the default material applied to the 3ds Max tree you created in the previous tutorial; however, the leaves are not green, so let's change their color.

159

78. In the **Material Editor**, click the fourth sub-material ID color swatch. This is the sub-material color that is applied to the leaves.

79. Change the color to a dark green and render the scene again. Notice that the trees are now green.

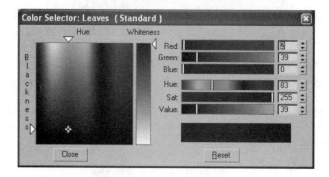

80. Select the Site-Terrain object.

81. Click the sample slot for the material named Site-Terrain (the fourth material on the top row).

82. Click the **Assign Material to Selection** icon.

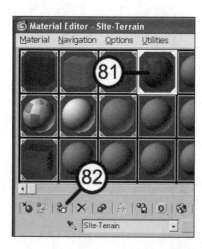

If you render the scene now, you will get an error message saying **The following objects require map coordinates and may not render correctly**. As the message states, the **Site-Terrain** object needs mapping coordinates. Let's see if you can apply mapping coordinates with minimal help.

83. In the **Modify** panel, add the **UVW Map** modifier to Site-Terrain, and apply box mapping with a length, width, and height of 15 feet.

Since the colored roof is still the unnatural-looking default orange color that 3ds Max gave it upon creation, you should try giving it a new color.

84. Create a new material in one of the empty sample slots, call it **Bldg-Roof**, and give it a blue-green color.

85. Select the Bldg-Roof object and apply the material you just created.

86. Render the completed scene. Your image should look similar to the following:

87. Save your file as MyQuickStart03.max for use in the next Quick Start tutorial.

This concludes Quick Start 3. You have just sampled some of the powerful tools that will be explained in detail in the following chapters on materials. During the next tutorial, you will see how adding just a few lights can, in just a few minutes, transform your scene into a truly realistic work of art.

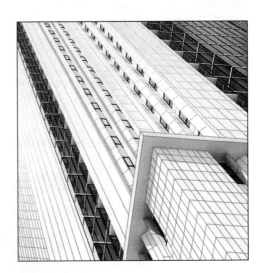

Chapter 6

MATERIAL BASICS

The word "material," as generally defined in dictionaries, is simply the substance out of which a thing is or can be made. In 3ds Max, the meaning is not much different—it is a characteristic that defines the appearance of an object. Within each material are numerous properties that determine the appearance. Thanks to the power of the **Material Editor** in 3ds Max, we can realistically simulate any material on Earth by controlling all the visual properties a material possesses.

This chapter focuses almost entirely on the **Material Editor** and, more specifically, those features that you would incorporate with your work on visualizations. In the next two chapters, I'll cover the critical map channels and map types, and discuss UVW mapping in great detail. But for now, a good understanding of the **Material Editor** interface is crucial to working efficiently with materials.

The Material Editor

The **Material Editor** is an immense interface with which materials are defined and applied. It can be accessed by selecting **Rendering ➤ Material Editor**, by clicking on the **Material Editor** icon on the **Main** toolbar, or by pressing M. Just like all features in 3ds Max, the **Material Editor** contains far more power and functionality than is typically needed for architectural visualizations. Likewise, there are some features that are significantly more critical to know than others. As usual, I will place greater emphasis on those features that are critical in the creation of architectural visualizations.

Sample slots

The sample slots in 3ds Max are the windows in which materials are displayed on sample objects both before and after they are applied to objects in your scene. The sample slots can display either a map or material. Select the slot in which you want to work by simply clicking anywhere inside the slot. Only 1 slot can be selected at a time, and the selected (or active) slot is indicated by a white border, as shown in Figure 6-1. 24 slots are available, but by default, 6 slots are displayed in a 2 × 3 grid. To access the remaining 18, use the slider below the slots.

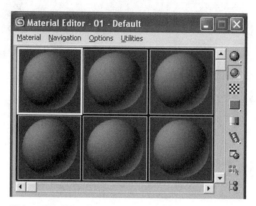

Figure 6-1. Material Editor sample slots

Clicking the **Options** icon (shown in the following image) opens the **Material Editor Options** dialog box, which gives you the option to change the slot layout to a 5 × 3 or 6 × 4 array, as shown in Figure 6-2. Right-clicking inside a sample slot also brings up a menu that allows you to change the layout.

The **Material Editor Options** dialog box contains many other options that can change the appearance of the sample slots—but personally, I like the slots the way they appear by default, and will leave these options for you to explore.

Figure 6-2. Available sample slot layouts

Changing the sample slot background

The **Background** icon provides an important feature that allows you to change the background of the slots. Sometimes the default gray background is not conducive to displaying transparent materials such as glass. In these instances, you can click the **Background** icon (shown in the following image) to change the background to a multicolored checkered image (or any other image you want).

Changing the sample slot object type

You also have the option to change the object type displayed in the sample slots from the default sphere to a box, cylinder, or any other object type you want. To do so, click and hold the **Sample Type** flyout icon (shown in the following image) and select the object type.

To create a custom object, create a .max file with the lone object in it and make sure that the object can fit inside a 100-unit cube. Click the **Options** icon, which opens the **Material Editor Options** dialog box, and under **Custom Sample Object**, click the **File Name** button to find the file that contains the object you want to load (see Figure 6-3).

Figure 6-3. Choosing a custom sample slot object type

Magnifying a sample slot

You will probably find it difficult at times to see the details of your materials within the sample slots, especially if you use the 6 X 4 layout. To see a larger display of a sample slot, double-click the sample slot and resize it to your liking by clicking and dragging on any corner (see Figure 6-4). You should leave the **Auto** option enabled so that any changes made to your material are updated in the sample slot.

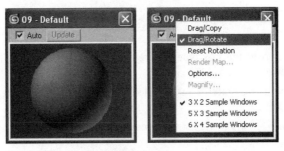

Figure 6-4. Magnifying a sample slot

If you want to see the sample object from a different perspective, you can rotate the view just like in a viewport. To do so, right-click inside the sample slot, select **Drag/Rotate**, and drag on the object. Holding down Shift constrains the rotation around a single axis. Reset the view by selecting **Reset Rotation** from the **Material** menu.

Working with sample slots

This exercise demonstrates some of the ways you can work with sample slots.

1. Reset 3ds Max.

2. Press M to open the **Material Editor**.

3. Click the **Options** icon (shown in the following image).
   The **Material Editor Options** dialog box opens.

4. In the **Slots** section, select the 6 × 4 option (see the following illustration) and select **OK**. The sample slot layout changes from the default 3 × 2 to a 6 × 4 layout.

5. In the **Blinn Basic Parameters** rollout, type 75 in the **Opacity** field, as shown in the following illustration. This makes the material slightly transparent.

6. Click the **Background** icon (shown in the following images). The background of the sample slot changes to a checkerboard display, making the transparent material easier to work with.

7. Click and hold the **Sample Type** icon. A flyout menu appears with three possible sample types (shown in the following image).

8. Move the cursor over the box type and release the mouse button. The object in the active sample slot changes to a box.

9. Double-click the active material sample slot. The sample slot is made into a larger separate window.

10. Place the cursor over any corner of the window. Sizing arrows appear.

11. Click and drag to resize the window.

12. Right-click inside the resized sample slot and select **Drag/Rotate**.

13. Click and drag inside the sample slot to rotate the view of the box sample type.

14. Right-click inside the sample slot again and select **Drag/Copy** to return the click/drag option to its default setting.

15. Click the **X** button in the top-right corner of the resized sample slot to close the sample slot.

Naming materials

The importance of a good naming convention for your materials cannot be overemphasized. Just like the objects in your scene, the materials you use should be named in a manner that allows you to find them quickly and easily, and immediately recognize which objects in your scene those materials are applied to. It would be very time-consuming to find the material you're looking for if it looks like other materials and is named something like "23-Default," especially if the material is not loaded in a sample slot and you have to search for it in the **Material/Map Browser**.

The best way that works for me is to give each material the same name as the object it is applied to in the scene. As an example, in my scenes, I would name an object that represents sidewalks **Site-Sidewalks**, and use this same name for the material that is applied to the sidewalk object (see Figure 6-5). If I want to apply this same material to the object that represents the curbs, I will change the name of the material to **Site-Sidewalks/Curbs**. This way, I know immediately upon looking at the material name what object or objects this material is applied to.

Figure 6-5. The Material drop-down list and the Material Editor's title bar

All materials are given a default name, which is listed in the **Material** drop-down list, located below the sample slots (as shown in the left image of Figure 6-5). In this case, the name has been changed to **Site-Sidewalks**. Notice that this name also appears in the **Material Editor**'s title bar. You can rename a material by typing a new name in the drop-down list.

Creating new materials

To create a new material, drag a material from one sample slot to another, and change the name of the new copy.

You can also create a copy of a material by clicking the **Make Material Copy** icon (shown in the following image). If you apply the new copy to your scene without changing the name, a dialog box appears stating that a material with the same name already exists in the scene. You are then given the option to replace or rename the material.

Assigning materials to objects

Once you load a material into a sample slot, you can assign it to an object in your scene. There are two main methods to do so.

One way is to simply drag and drop the material from the sample slot directly onto an object in a viewport. This method does not usually work too well if there are several objects near the cursor at the point of release inside the viewport, because 3ds Max won't know to which object you want it to apply. If you pause the cursor momentarily over the object, you will see the object's name appear next to the cursor, indicating the object to which you're about to apply the material.

A more reliable way to assign materials, the **Assign Material to Selection** icon (shown in the following image), requires you to select the object or objects you want to apply the material to, and then select the icon.

Whenever the material of a selected object is shown in a sample slot, the sample slot will display small white triangles in each of its corners, as shown in the right image in Figure 6-6. This indicates that the material is applied to the selected object and that the material is "hot." "Hot" materials are connected to the objects in the scene; and changing the material in the **Material Editor** causes the scene to be updated automatically. Usually, this is what you want anyway, but on occasion, you may want to work on a copy of a material without affecting the scene in any way. To "cool" an object in this way, simply make a copy of the material without changing the name or reassigning the material from the new sample slot copy. Any changes you make will no longer affect your scene.

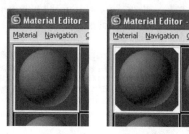

Figure 6-6. A cool material (left) and a hot material (right)

Whenever you apply a material to an object in your scene, the material is added to the scene library, regardless of whether the material is displayed in a sample slot. A library is simply a collection of materials stored within a file, whether that be a .max scene file or a standard .mat material library file, which will be discussed in greater detail later. In this case, when a material is applied to an object, that material becomes part of the scene library; but once all objects that hold that material are deleted, the material is removed from the scene library.

By clicking the **Put Material to Scene** icon (shown in the following image), however, you can put a material in the scene library without having to worry about it being removed.

Creating, naming, and assigning new materials

This exercise demonstrates how to create, name, and assign new materials within the **Material Editor**.

1. Reset 3ds Max.
2. Press M to open the **Material Editor**, if it's not already open.
3. Click inside the **Material** drop-down list, and change the name to **Building-Walls**, as shown in the following illustration.

4. Click and hold inside the active sample slot of the material you just renamed, drag the sample slot to an adjacent slot, and release the mouse button. The material is duplicated inside the sample slot you copied to.

5. Change the name of the material copy to **Building-Doors**. You've just created a new material, but you haven't assigned it to an object yet.

6. Create a simple box in any viewport.

7. Inside the **Material Editor**, click the **Assign Material to Selection** icon (shown in the following image). The material named **Building-Doors** is now assigned to the box you just created.

8. Click the **Make Material Copy** icon (shown in the following image) and, inside the **Material** drop-down list, change the material name to **Building-Windows**. This creates and names a new material without deleting an already existing material. Had you just changed the name without using the **Make Material Copy** command, the material named **Building-Doors** would no longer exist.

9. Click and hold the material named **Building-Walls**, and drag the material onto the box in any viewport. Notice the corners of the material sample slot have white triangles. This indicates that the selected object contains this material.

10. Deselect the box object in the scene. Notice now that the white triangles in the sample slot have changed to gray triangles, indicating that this material is on an object in the scene, but not on an object that is currently selected.

11. Save your work for use in the next exercise.

Loading materials in the sample slots

At times, you may want to create a new material from an existing material in your scene that is not loaded in a sample slot, or create a new material from one found in another 3ds Max scene. There are two main methods to load materials into sample slots.

The first way to load a material is by using the **Pick Material from Object** icon (shown in the following image). Simply select the sample slot you want to load the material into, click the **Pick Material from Object** icon, and click the object in your scene that contains the material you want to load.

The second method is by clicking the **Get Material** icon (shown in the following image), which opens the **Material/Map Browser**. Once you find the material you're looking for, you can load it into the sample slot by double-clicking the material or dragging and dropping the material into the sample slot. (The **Material/Map Browser** will be covered later in this chapter.)

Removing materials and maps

Click the **Reset Material/Maps to Default Settings** icon (shown in the following image) to reset the material or map to its default settings. The two reasons you may want to do this is to free up a used sample slot, or to remove an unwanted material or map from an object.

When you click this icon without the active material being assigned to an object in your scene, the message box in Figure 6-7 appears. If you select **Yes**, the sample slot is returned to its initial state, and you can start the material creation process from scratch.

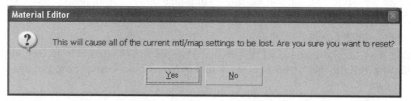

Figure 6-7. Resetting the material/map settings of an unassigned material

When you click the **Reset Material/Maps to Default Settings** icon with the active material already assigned to an object in your scene, a different dialog box appears, cautioning you that the material you want to reset is currently assigned to at least one object in the scene (shown in Figure 6-8). If you select the default option, **Affect only mtl/map in the editor slot**, the material remains unchanged, and the sample slot is simply reset to its initial state. Essentially, this erases the sample slot but not the material applied to the object.

If you select the other option, **Affect mtl/map in both the scene and in the editor slot**, the material is reset to its default settings, not just the sample slot. The material will remain with the same name and will still be applied to the same object(s)—but because the material settings are reset, this option achieves basically the same thing as deleting the material from the scene.

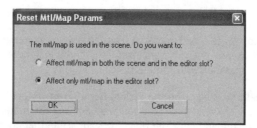

Figure 6-8. Resetting the material/map settings of an assigned material

Loading and removing materials and maps

This exercise demonstrates how to load and remove materials and maps within the **Material Editor**.

1. Continue from the last exercise.

2. Press M to open the **Material Editor**, if it's not already open.

3. Click a new sample slot without an assigned material.

4. Click the **Pick Material from Object** icon (shown in the following image).

5. Move the cursor, which is now displayed as an eyedropper, over the box in any viewport. The eyedropper changes from appearing empty to appearing full when placed over an object with a material assigned.

6. Click the box in any viewport. The material assigned to the box is now loaded into the active sample slot. This material should be named **Building-Walls**.

7. For visual purposes, change the color of this material by clicking the color swatch next to **Diffuse** in the **Blinn Basic Parameters** rollout, as shown in the following illustration:

8. The **Color Selector** dialog box opens, as shown in the following image. Move the cursor over the color selector, click to select a color, and click **Close**.

9. Click the **Reset Material/Maps to Default Settings** icon (shown in the following image), select the default option (**Affect only mtl/map in the editor slot**), and select **OK** to close the command. Notice that the box stills contains the material, but the material in the sample slot is no longer that material.

10. Reload the material on the box back into the active sample slot using the **Pick Material from Object** icon.

11. Click the **Reset Material/Maps to Default Settings** icon again, this time selecting the other option, **Affect mtl/map both in the scene and in the editor slot**. Select **OK** to close the command. Notice this time the material name doesn't change but the material returns to its default settings and the box receives those new settings.

Selecting objects by material

The **Material Editor** features a great tool that allows you to select objects in your scene that have the selected material applied to them. When you click the **Select by Material** icon (shown in the following image), the **Select Objects** dialog box opens with all the objects selected that have the selected material applied. Click the **Select** icon to select these objects.

Showing maps in a viewport

When a viewport is in shaded mode, you can display the maps contained within materials by clicking the **Show Map in Viewport** icon (shown in the following image). This feature allows you to easily distinguish one object from another within the viewports and quickly determine which objects have what materials applied.

The quality of the maps displayed and the speed at which the viewports can refresh the views depends heavily on the quality of the graphics card. Figure 6-9 shows an example of the **Show Map in Viewport** feature. Both boxes contain the same material, but the box on the right has the **Show Map in Viewport** feature enabled, whereas the box on the left does not. In a scene with many different architectural elements and many different materials, having this option enabled can be a great visual help.

Figure 6-9. Example of the Show Map in Viewport feature disabled (left) and enabled (right)

Material Editor icons

Table 6-1 provides a quick reference for each of the icons that surround the **Material Editor** sample slots. Some of these icons have just been discussed, and others will be discussed in the next chapter.

Table 6-1. Material Editor icons

Icon	Name	Description
Site-Sidewalks	**Material** drop-down list	Displays the name of the material, which can be changed by typing a new one in this field. The drop-down list lists the names of the sub-materials that make up the material.
Standard	**Material Type** button	Displays the current material or map type. Opens the **Material/Map Browser** and allows you to assign a new material or map type.

Icon	Name	Description
	**Pick Material from Object** icon	Selects a material from an object in the scene and loads it into the selected sample slot.
	**Get Material** icon	Opens the **Material/Map Browser**.
	**Put Material to Scene** icon	Updates any materials in the scene that have changed.
	**Assign Material to Selection** icon	Places the selected material on the selected object.
	**Reset Map/Mtl to Default Settings** icon	Resets all map and material settings to their original configurations.
	**Make Material Copy** icon	Makes a copy of the selected material in a different sample slot.
	**Make Unique** icon	Makes the selected instanced material a completely new and unconnected material.
	**Put to Library** icon	Opens a dialog box that allows you to rename the material and save it to the current library.
	**Material Effects Channel** icon	Assigns a material effect ID to the material. The ID can tell 3ds Max what video post or rendering effects are assigned to what materials.
	**Show Map in Viewport** icon	Shows the material's map on an object in a shaded viewport.
	**Show End Result** icon	Toggles between showing a sub-material or sub-map and showing the end result of the material or map.
	**Go to Parent** icon	Moves up one level within the current material.
	**Go Forward to Sibling** icon	Moves to the next map channel with a map loaded.
	**Sample Type** icon	Changes the sample type object from one solid type to another. The default type is a sphere; other options include a cylinder, cube, and a custom object that you select.
	**Backlight** icon	Toggles the backlighting in the selected sample slot on and off.

Continued

Table 6-1. *Continued*

Icon	Name	Description
	Background icon	Toggles a multicolored checkered background behind the selected material on and off. This is a visual aid for viewing certain materials, such as transparent ones.
	Sample UV Tiling icon	Changes the UV tiling for the map in the sample slot. The default is 1 × 1; other options include 2 × 2, 3 × 3, and 4 × 4. These settings change only the display in the sample slot and have no effect on the material.
	Video Color Check icon	Checks the selected material to see if it contains any colors not supported by the NTSC and PAL formats.
	Make, Play, Save Preview icon	Lets you make, play, and save an animated material preview.
	Options icon	Opens a dialog box that includes options defining the number of sample slots, sample slot light intensity, custom slot backgrounds, and much more.
	Select by Material icon	Lets you select all objects in your scene that use the current material by opening the **Select Objects** dialog box with those objects selected.
	Material Map Navigator icon	Opens the **Material/Map Navigator** dialog box, which displays all the sub-materials and utilized maps of the current material.

The Material/Map Browser

The **Material/Map Browser**, shown in Figure 6-10, is an interface that lets you browse for materials in the current scene you are working in, in the library of another scene, or in a library stored in a special Max-created file with the .mat extension. In addition to loading materials from a library, you can use the **Material/Map Browser** to create or update material libraries yourself.

The **Material/Map Browser** opens when you click the **Get Material** icon, the **Material Type** icon, or a map icon. If you are currently browsing a library, the material library name is shown across the top of the browser. Directly below, on the right-hand side, is the material name, followed by icons that provide different viewing options. To the right of these are icons that let you clear and delete materials from a library, as well as update the current scene you're working in with the materials from a library. These icons are only available when a library is open. Below these icons is a window that displays the materials and maps in the currently open library. Materials have a blue sphere to the left of the material name, while maps have a green parallelogram. If materials or maps have the **Show Map in Viewport** option enabled, these icons will be displayed in red.

At the top-left of the browser is a text field in which you can type the material name to search and select the material you're looking for. Below this are radio buttons that allow you to change the location in which to browse for materials.

If you want to search for materials in a separate library file saved on your computer, click the **Mtl Library** button. Doing so activates the **File** section on the bottom-left of the browser, in which you can open, merge, or save libraries through an explorer window.

Other options for browsing include searching the **Material Editor**'s 24 sample slots, or searching within the scene in which you are working. The option I use most often is the **Selected** option. Along with the **Pick Object From Material** icon (which looks like an eyedropper), I use this option to load a material from an object I've selected in my scene.

To load a selected material from the **Material/Map Browser** into the selected sample slot, you can either drag and drop the material name or double-click it.

Material libraries

Material libraries provide a great way to manage, load, and save materials and maps for current or future use. When I'm working in architectural scenes that can often contain several dozens of materials, I don't like to waste time recreating the same materials over and over again, or searching through old project files to find the scene that contains the materials that I used before. Instead, with a couple of clicks of the mouse, I can have all of my typical materials available for viewing and loading into the **Material Editor** sample slots.

Figure 6-10. The Material/Map Browser

To create a library of your favorite materials, you can edit an existing library or create a new one from scratch, as shown in Figure 6-11. In either case, you will need to open the **Material/Map Browser** and click the **Save As** button to save the library to a certain location with a certain name.

If you start with an already created library, you should delete the materials you don't want and add the materials in your scene that you do want. To add the materials you want, highlight the sample slot with the desired material and click the **Put to Library** icon.

If you are starting a new library from scratch, you should merge all the objects from the various scenes that contain the desired materials and click the **Scene** option under the **Browse From** section of the **Material/Map Browser**. When you click the **Scene** radio button, all of the materials loaded in your scene will appear in the **Material List** window on the right side of the browser. If you want, you can delete individual materials from the scene library, and then save the scene library as a completely separate material library elsewhere on your computer.

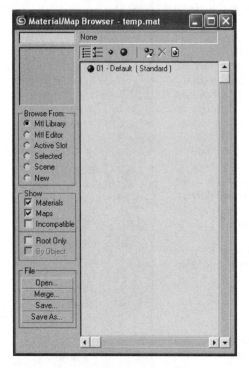

Figure 6-11. The temp.mat material library

Creating and editing material libraries

This exercise demonstrates how to use the **Material/Map Browser** to create and edit material libraries.

1. Reset 3ds Max.

2. Press M to open the **Material Editor**.

3. Click the **Get Material** icon (shown in the following image) to open the **Material/Map Browser**.

4. Under the **Browse From** section of the **Material/Map Browser**, select **Mtl Library**.

5. In the **File** section, select **Open**. This opens the **Open Material Library** window to the Autodesk\3dsMax8\matlibs directory. This directory contains a number of existing libraries that shipped with Max.

6. Select the Wood.mat file, and select **Open** to open this library. The contents of this library are now shown in the **Material/Map Browser**.

7. Double-click the material labeled **Word_Bark**. The material is now loaded into the active sample slot. You can also drag and drop the material into the sample slot.

8. Inside the **Material/Map Browser**, highlight the material labeled **Wood_Driftwood**.

9. Click the **Delete from Library** icon (shown in the following image). The material is now deleted from the Wood.mat library. Next, you'll save this library under a new name.

10. Under the **File** section, click **Save As**, and name the library **Wood_New**. You've just created a new library that contains one fewer material than the library named Wood.mat.

The Material/Map Navigator

The **Material/Map Navigator** icon (shown in the following image) opens the **Material/Map Navigator** (Figure 6-12), a feature in the **Material Editor** that displays the entire material hierarchy of the selected sample slot.

This feature is handy when you want to explore the layers of just the selected sample slot and not have to sift through dozens of materials in the **Material/Map Browser**. In the browser, all materials and maps are displayed, unlike the navigator, which displays only the contents of the selected sample slot.

Figure 6-12. The Material/Map Navigator

Material Editor rollouts

While the **Material Editor** sample slots and the icons that surround them manage materials and their display, they don't affect the actual appearance of the materials (with the exception of the **Material Type** button). A material is fashioned by the tools and features found in the rollouts below the sample slots. Although these rollouts can appear quite complicated and intimidating, they are in fact quite easy to conquer.

The **Material Editor** contains seven initial rollouts for the standard material (Figure 6-13), most of which will require little or no use for foundation-level readers in the visualization industry. The standard material type is the default type, and provides a single, uniform color distribution based on the settings of the **Ambient**, **Diffuse**, and **Specular** color swatches. Other material types will be discussed in the next chapter, but for right now, you'll explore the rollouts for the most commonly used material type, the standard material.

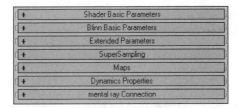

Figure 6-13. The seven standard rollouts

177

The Shader Basic Parameters rollout

The first rollout, **Shader Basic Parameters** (Figure 6-14), specifies the shading type, which will be explained in greater detail in the next chapter. To the right of the shader type are four options: **Wire**, **2-Sided**, **Face Map**, and **Faceted**.

Figure 6-14. The Shader Basic Parameters rollout

The Wire option

The **Wire** option makes a model appear as a wireframe object, with the wires running along the edges of the individual polygons of the model. This option is a great way to create fences, window mullions, and a few other architectural features, because it requires only a fraction of the number of faces required to model the same looking object. The left image in Figure 6-15 shows the sample slot of a material with the **Wire** option enabled. In the right-hand image, a simple plane with four length and width segments is used to simulate a small wire fence by applying a material with the **Wire** option enabled. The number of faces needed to produce the object is only 32, but modeling the same object requires 356 faces. This disparity is multiplied when you create larger models. A fence that runs 100 yards could easily require tens of thousands of faces, yet the simple plane with a material applied that uses the **Wire** option would only require about a tenth of the number of faces.

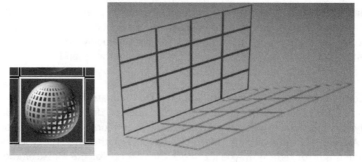

Figure 6-15. An example of a material with the Wire option enabled

Using the Wire option to create a fence

This exercise demonstrates one of the many uses of the **Wire** option in visualizations.

1. Reset 3ds Max.

2. In the Front viewport, create a plane with a width of 100 units, a length of 20 units, 20 width segments, and 4 length segments.

3. Click the **Zoom Extents** icon to maximize the view of the plane.

4. Press M to open the **Material Editor**.

5. In the **Shader Basic Parameters** rollout, enable the **Wire** option and click the **Assign Material to Selection** icon. The plane now looks like a wire fence with the wires running along the edges of each polygon.

6. Click the **Quick Render** icon (shown in the following image) to see the results of applying the **Wire** option to the material.

7. Open the **Extended Parameters** rollout, and in the **Wire** section, increase the **Size** to **2**.

8. Render the object again with the new wire size. The viewport will not show changes to the wire size, so you must render the object to see the effects of the change.

9. Save your work for use in the next exercise.

The 2-Sided option

The **2-Sided** option is a great feature that can be beneficial to you in many situations. It simply makes the faces of an object viewable from both sides, regardless of which side the face normals are oriented toward. This option comes in handy when, for whatever reason, some of the face normals of an object are oriented in the wrong direction and your usual remedies are not fixing the problem. As shown in the left image in Figure 6-16, some of the faces of the wall are oriented inward. Although a simple **Unify Normals** routine will fix this particular situation, it may not help for more complex models. In those situations, making the material two-sided will fix the problem, as shown in Figure 6-16's right-hand image.

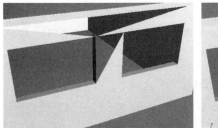 

Figure 6-16. A one-sided object (left) and a two-sided object (right)

Another situation in which this feature works great is when you want to give the appearance of increasing the number of faces in your scene without having to do so, and without increasing the strain on your computer. Modeling blades of grass, for example, can be quite a demand on your computer since you need so many faces for even the smallest of areas. Both images in Figure 6-17 show an object that contains the same number of faces, yet the image on the right appears to contain twice as many blades of grass as the left image because the object in the right image uses a two-sided version of the same material.

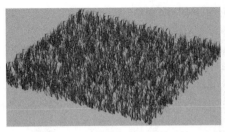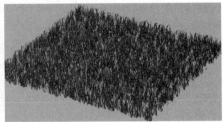

Figure 6-17. An example of grass without the 2-Sided option (left) and with the 2-Sided option (right)

The other two options in the **Shader Basic Parameters** rollout, **Face Map** and **Faceted**, are simply unnecessary in architectural visualizations. **Face Map** applies maps to each polygon of an object, and **Faceted** ignores smoothing between faces. Neither of these options will benefit your work. It should be noted that if you use Direct3D drivers, there is a high probability that the **2-Sided** option will not work.

Enabling the 2-Sided feature

This exercise demonstrates the use of the **2-Sided** option in visualizations.

1. Continue from the previous exercise.
2. In the Perspective viewport, rotate the view so that you can see the backside of the plane object. Notice that you cannot see the plane from the backside because the material is one-sided.
3. Press M to open the **Material Editor**, if it's not already open.
4. In the **Shader Basic Parameters** rollout, enable the **2-Sided** option. Notice the plane is now visible from the backside.

The Blinn Basic Parameters rollout

Within the **Blinn Basic Parameters** rollout (shown in Figure 6-18) is a drop-down list that contains all of the available shading options (for the standard material, 3ds Max gives you eight). Shaders are mathematical algorithms that determine the way light illuminates a surface. The default shader is the Blinn shader, which works well for most materials you will want to represent, especially exterior scenes in which you're not close enough to the objects to see the benefit of using other shaders. For now, I would suggest sticking with the Blinn shader even in cases in which other shaders would be better. This is mainly because the use of other shaders requires knowledge of a much larger number of settings, many of which can be confusing if you don't have an advanced level of understanding about 3ds Max.

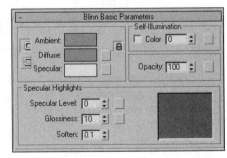

Figure 6-18. The Blinn Basic Parameters rollout

The Ambient, Diffuse, and Specular Color swatches

The next section of this rollout contains three color swatches that control the ambient, diffuse, and specular components of an object's illumination. To the left of the color swatches are two small squares that you can click to lock the ambient and diffuse colors so that they stay the same. By default, 3ds Max has locked the **Ambient** and **Diffuse** swatches. Except for situations when you want to take advantage of advanced lighting techniques such as radiosity, it is not necessary to unlock these two components. The two small squares to the right of the **Diffuse** and **Specular** color swatches are shortcut buttons for adding maps in lieu of or in conjunction with the diffuse or specular portions (also referred to as channels) of an illuminated surface. When a map is loaded, the buttons show an uppercase **M**, and when the loaded map is inactive, a lowercase **m** is displayed. Just as the **Ambient** and **Diffuse** color swatches are locked by default, so too are their channels, as indicated by the lock symbol to the right of the color swatches. This lock should be left in place because disabling it would only be needed when advanced lighting and material techniques are used.

The Specular Highlights section

Below the color swatches is the **Specular Highlights** section. The **Specular Level** option controls the intensity of the specular highlights, and the **Glossiness** option controls the size of the highlights. The **Soften** value spreads the highlight across the area controlled by the **Glossiness** value, but its impact is all but negligible. The graph on the right-hand side of the **Specular Highlights** shows a representation of the **Specular Level** and **Glossiness** values across an object's surface, measured from the center point of the greatest specular highlight. The greater the **Specular Level** value, the greater the intensity of the highlight. The greater the **Glossiness** value, the smaller the area of specular highlight. The spinners to the right of the input fields provide a quick and easy way to change these values, and the graph provides a great way to see how the values affect the overall surface. Although the **Specular Level** value can go as high as 999, in creating architectural visualizations I have never needed a **Specular Level** greater than 100, which represents maximum specular reflection. Figure 6-19 shows several different sample slots with their corresponding **Specular Level** and **Glossiness** values.

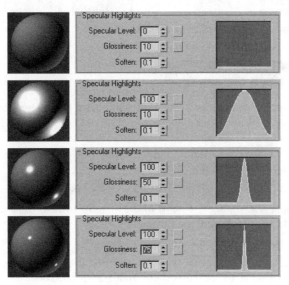

Figure 6-19. Various specular highlights

181

The Self-Illumination section

In the **Self-Illumination** section of this rollout, you can specify how much illumination a material creates for itself, and how much effect shadows and highlights have.

By changing the value in the field to the right of the word **Color**, you can control how much diffuse color illumination an object receives. A value of **0** results in no self-illumination, whereas a value of **100** results in the entire surface of the object receiving the same diffuse color illumination and no shadows or highlights. The three left-hand images in Figure 6-20 illustrate the range from 100 to 0.

If you click the **Color** option, the value field and spinners are replaced with a swatch that allows you to set the amount of glow a material creates for itself. A color setting of pure black results in no glow, whereas a setting of pure white results in the object appearing completely white over the entire surface and receiving no shadows or highlights. Any color in this swatch other than pure white results in a mix of the selected color and some degree of highlights and shadows. The three right-hand images in Figure 6-20 illustrate this.

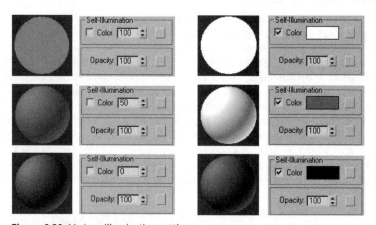

Figure 6-20. Various Illumination settings

Using the Blinn Basic Parameters rollout

This exercise demonstrates the characteristics of the **Blinn Basic Parameters** rollout.

1. Reset 3ds Max.

2. In the Perspective viewport, create a sphere of any size, and click the **Zoom Extents** icon to maximize the view of the sphere.

3. Press M to open the **Material Editor**, if it's not already opened.

4. In the first sample slot, change the name of the material to **Test**. You'll use this material to test the characteristics of the **Blinn Basic Parameters** rollout.

5. Apply the material (in its default state) to the sphere.

6. Click on the Background icon (looks like a checkerboard) to change the background. This will make the material easier to see when we make it transparent.

7. Click the color swatch next to **Diffuse**, and select a greenish color. Notice the sphere in the viewport changes to this color, as shown in image 1 of the following illustration.

8. In the **Specular Highlights** section, increase the **Specular Level** to **100**. Notice the intensity of the specular highlights increases dramatically, as shown in image 2.

9. Increase the **Glossiness** to **50**. This reduces the size of the specular area, as shown in image 3.

10. Next, decrease the **Opacity** to **50**. The sphere now becomes 50% transparent, as shown in image 4.

11. Increase the **Self-Illumination** value to **100**. Notice the sphere receives no shadows, as shown in image 5.

12. Lastly, enable the **Color** option under **Self-Illumination**, click the color swatch that appears next to it, and select a gray value halfway between pure black and pure white. Notice the sphere is now partially glowing, as shown in image 6.

The Extended Parameters rollout

The **Extended Parameters** rollout (see Figure 6-21) contains three sections: **Advanced Transparency**, **Reflection Dimming**, and **Wire**. Reflection dimming produces very subtle changes to reflections that exist in shadows. Because it is an advanced feature, it will not be covered in this book.

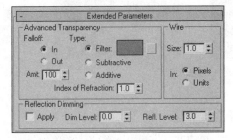

Figure 6-21. The Extended Parameters rollout

The Advanced Transparency section

The **Advanced Transparency** section can be used to add transparency to illuminated objects, such as a light bulb. Figure 6-22 illustrates the effect of various **Amount** and **Falloff** settings in conjunction with increased self-illumination and specular highlights (both within the **Blinn Basic Parameters** rollout).

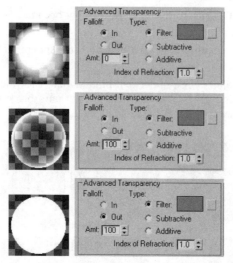

Figure 6-22. Various Advanced Transparency settings

The Wire section

The **Wire** section's only function is to control materials with the **Wire** option enabled. As discussed earlier, the **Wire** option is a handy feature for simulating fences and window mullions at a fraction of the processing power required for their 3D counterparts. The **Size** value controls the thickness of the wire, and the **In** setting determines whether the size is expressed in units or screen pixels. Figure 6-23 shows examples of wire **Size** settings of **1.0**, **2.0**, and **3.0**.

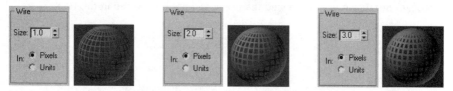

Figure 6-23. Various wire size settings

The SuperSampling rollout

The only purpose of the **SuperSampling** rollout (shown in Figure 6-24) is to improve the quality of animations by decreasing the effect of aliasing. Aliasing is a term to describe imperfections in the rendering process caused by color changes that are too drastic, and that occur over too small an area of screen space to be adequately depicted by the pixels that define that space. In a single still image, aliasing is certainly noticeable and can reduce realism; and if the same scene is set in motion, it can produce a very distracting effect and ruin the animation. Two examples of this are flickering and texture crawling.

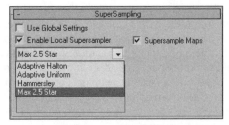

Figure 6-24. The SuperSampling rollout

Flickering occurs during animations when materials (such as the grass in Figure 6-25) have a speckled appearance with drastic changes in color occurring over a small number of pixels. In these cases, the computer cannot accurately determine which color to assign a given pixel, because the edge of two colors exists in the middle of a pixel. In the top image of each of the following sets (Figures 6-25 and 6-26), supersampling is disabled, and the contrast in adjacent pixels is harsher than in the bottom images, in which supersampling is enabled. When scenes with these textures are animated, the difference between the two can be dramatic.

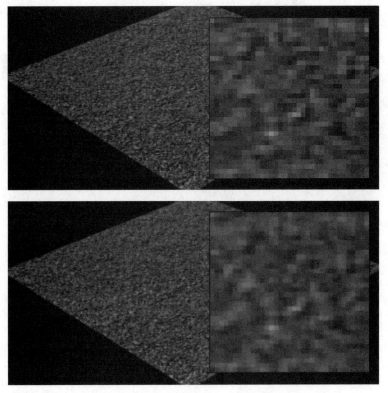

Figure 6-25. Supersampling disabled (top) and enabled (bottom)

Texture crawling occurs in animation in areas along the edges of lines and polygons. This undesirable effect happens because there are not enough pixels available on a typical monitor to properly display mathematically smooth lines and polygon edges. When a 3D scene is transposed onto a monitor's pixel grid, or raster, each pixel is colored according to whether or not it is covered by an object in the scene. Aliasing occurs because the raster system does not properly handle the case in which a pixel is only partially covered. Partially covered pixels occur along the edges of objects and are referred to as edge pixels or fragment pixels. The mishandling of fragment pixels results in harsh, jagged color transitions between an object's edge and the background. Examples of materials in which texture crawling is prevalent are bricks in a wall, pavers in a walkway, and fascia on a roof. In the top image in Figure 6-26, anti-aliasing is disabled and the edges are much more jagged than in the bottom image, in which anti-aliasing is enabled. In animations, these edges appear to crawl whether they are the edges of an object or the edges within a material applied to an object.

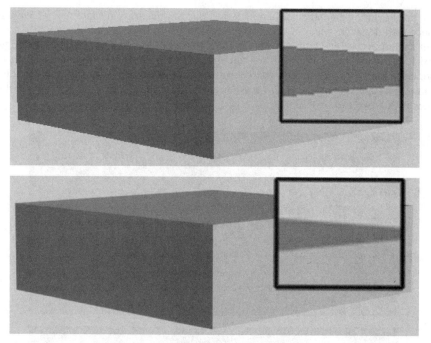

Figure 6-26. Anti-aliasing disabled (top) and enabled (bottom)

Anti-aliasing techniques attempt to smooth jagged edges by properly handling fragment pixels (i.e., adjusting the pixel color according to the amount of pixel coverage). 3ds Max incorporates anti-aliasing filters in the rendering process by default, and although they greatly improve renderings and animations, in some scenes the standard filters aren't enough. Supersampling is an additional anti-aliasing process that samples the colors around a pixel and uses that information to determine the final color of the pixel. Supersampling can be initiated for specific materials or for the entire scene.

This rollout, shown in Figure 6-24, initiates supersampling specifically for the selected material. Four supersampling methods are available with 3ds Max, but each one slows the rendering process to some degree. My advice for supersampling is to not enable it until you see that you need it, and then to test each of the four methods on a small sample sequence with the problematic material isolated.

If you decide that you must use supersampling for an entire scene, go to the **Renderer** tab of the **Render Scene** dialog box and enable **Global SuperSampling**.

Another entirely different way to perform supersampling, which I like to use myself, is to render the scene at a higher resolution than what the final output is actually going to be, and then scale down to that final output. This is, in effect, a way of supersampling for yourself.

The Maps rollout

This rollout is the heart of material creation and is covered in great detail in the next chapter.

The Dynamic Properties rollout

This rollout is used in animations involving collisions and is not needed in architectural visualizations.

The Mental Ray Connection rollout

This rollout is used for mental ray materials, which are not covered in this book.

Summary

This chapter has covered the essential features of the **Material Editor** in great detail. The **Material Editor** itself is a fairly simple interface, especially when you only focus on those features that would be of use to those of us in the visualization field. What makes the **Material Editor** seem so complex is not the number of features that make up the interface, but rather the degree to which you can make individual materials complex. You can create great looking materials in very little time, or even use existing material libraries—but either way, the time you spend navigating the **Material Editor** can be made minor. On the other hand, you can add tremendous complexity to your work by incorporating the seemingly endless features that affect your individual materials. Nonetheless, the **Material Editor** is just the first step in working with materials. You cannot create a great visualization without incorporating the process known as mapping. The next two chapters cover the critical map channels and map types, and UVW mapping. After reading these chapters, you should know everything you need to create great-looking materials.

Chapter 7

THE CRITICAL MAP CHANNELS

As mentioned in the previous chapter, the **Maps** rollout is the heart of material creation. In this rollout, maps are applied to specific areas of a material, known as channels. A standard material contains each of the twelve map channels listed in Figure 7-1. Some of these channels can have a tremendous impact on architectural visualizations, while others have less importance. This chapter focuses on the critical map channels and how to use them to create realistic materials for use in visualizations.

Beginning with this chapter and continuing throughout the rest of this book, you will need select files to complete the tutorials. These files, along with the instructions of how to them load into 3ds Max, can be downloaded from the book's web page at www.friendsofed.com. You will also need to add the Friends_of_Ed folder to the **External Files** list within the **Configure Paths** dialog box.

Figure 7-1. The Maps rollout

The Maps rollout

The **Maps** rollout (shown in Figure 7-1) consists of four columns. The second column from the left indicates the name of the channel. The first column on the left is the enable/disable switch for the map that is loaded into that channel. When a map is loaded into a channel, its name appears in place of the channel button labeled **None** adjacent to the name of the channel. The column labeled **Amount** (third from left) specifies the percentage of the map that will be displayed, if one is loaded and enabled. With an amount of **100**, only the map will be displayed in the corresponding channel. With an amount of **50**, 50% of what is displayed for the channel will come from the map and 50% will come from the settings in the **Basic Parameters** rollouts. With an amount of **0**, the loaded map will not have any effect on the material. If the switch in the first column is set to disable the map, then the map will have no effect on the material, regardless of the value in the **Amount** column.

Now, let's take a look at those critical map channels at work. The examples in this chapter will make this interface very clear.

The Diffuse Color channel

The Diffuse Color channel—probably the most frequently used map channel—allows you to replace the diffuse color specified in the **Blinn Basic Parameters** rollout with a map. Since the diffuse color is usually the main component of an object's appearance, placing a map in the Diffuse Color channel will make the material appear just like the map. The Diffuse Color channel can completely replace the diffuse color if the amount is set to 100. Alternatively, it can exist in conjunction with the diffuse color by any percentage specified in the **Amount** field. Figure 7-2 shows a map applied to the Diffuse Color channel in varying amounts.

Figure 7-2. The Diffuse map mixed with the Diffuse Color using an Amount value of 100, 75, 50 and 25, from left to right

Using the Diffuse Color channel

This exercise demonstrates use of the Diffuse Color channel by loading into it a simple bitmap.

1. Reset 3ds Max.

2. Press M to open the **Material Editor**.

3. Click any sample slot, open the **Maps** rollout, and click the channel button labeled **None** to the right of the words **Diffuse Color**, as shown in the following illustration. The **Material/Map Browser** opens.

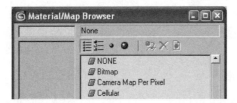

4. Double-click the word **Bitmap** in the **Material/Map Browser**, as shown in the following illustration.

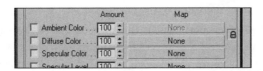

5. Go to the directory 3dsMax8\Images\Friends_of_Ed, select the file Tile01.jpg, and select **Open**. The image is now loaded in the Diffuse Color channel.

6. Click the **Go to Parent** button (shown in the following image) to return to the **Maps** rollout.

7. Click the Diffuse Color map shortcut button, shown in the following illustration (located to the right of the Diffuse color swatch). Notice the shortcut now has a capitalized **M** on it, indicating an active map is loaded into the Diffuse Color channel. A lowercase **m** would indicate that a map is loaded but has been deactivated. Since a map is already loaded, clicking this shortcut takes you directly to the **Bitmap Parameters** rollout, from which you can change the map. If a map is not loaded, clicking this shortcut takes you to the **Material/Map Browser**.

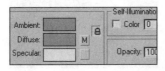

8. In the **Bitmap Parameters** rollout, click the channel button next to the word **Bitmap**, as shown in the following illustration. This opens a file explorer window from which you can load a new map.

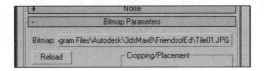

9. Press Esc to cancel this process, and click the **Go to Parent** button to return to the **Maps** roll-out again.

10. In the Perspective viewport, create a box width a length, width, and height of 100.

11. Apply the material you just created to the box.

12. Click the **Show Map in Viewport** option. The image of the tile can now be seen in a shaded viewport.

13. In the **Maps** rollout, disable the map loaded in the Diffuse Color channel by clicking the check box next to the words **Diffuse Color**, as shown in the following illustration:

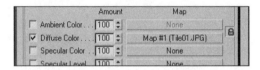

The Opacity channel

The Opacity channel enables you to produce materials that are visible in certain parts and transparent in other parts. The left image in Figure 7-3 shows an image of a plant that can be applied to the Diffuse Color channel. The middle image shows a black-and-white version that can be applied to the Opacity channel. The image in the Opacity channel tells Max which parts of the Diffuse Color map to show and which parts to make transparent. Pure white areas of the Opacity map will allow the corresponding areas of the Diffuse Color map to be visible, while pure black areas cause the corresponding areas of the Diffuse Color map to be transparent. In the example below, the opacity map (middle image) allows the plant to be cut out of the photograph and displayed without the background, as shown in the image on the right.

Figure 7-3. Using the Opacity channel to mask portions of a photograph

In addition to using a black-and-white image for the Opacity map, such as a .jpg or .bmp, you can use the alpha channel of a .tga file to serve as the Opacity map. The result of using a .tga file for both the Diffuse Color and Opacity channels is the same as using two separate images; but when using a .tga file, you must tell 3ds Max to use the alpha channel in the Opacity channel. To use a .tga file, load the file in both the Diffuse Color channel and the Opacity channel. In the Opacity channel, go to the

Bitmap Parameters rollout, and under the **Mono Channel Output** section, click the **Alpha** option, as shown in Figure 7-4. Then exit the Opacity channel, and in the **Blinn Basic Parameters** rollout, change all three color swatches to pure black, and set the **Specular Level** and **Glossiness** values to **0**. Not changing the color swatches to pure black and not reducing the specular highlights will produce undesirable results. In the sample slot, you should see the image with the background cut out.

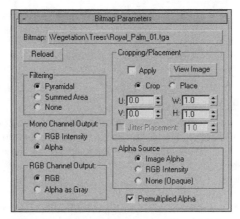

Figure 7-4. A .tga file used in the Diffuse Color and Opacity channels

Some examples of things that Opacity maps can benefit in architectural visualizations include vegetation, people, street signs, lampposts, animals, cars, and boats.

Using the Opacity channel

This exercise demonstrates use of the Opacity channel by loading an image into the Diffuse Color channel and copying it into the Opacity channel.

1. Reset 3ds Max.

2. Open the **Material Editor**.

3. Click any sample slot, open the **Maps** rollout, and click the channel button labeled **None** to the right of the words **Diffuse Color**, as shown in the following illustration:

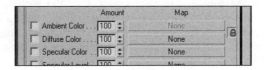

4. Double-click the word **Bitmap** in the **Material/Map Browser**, as shown in the following illustration:

5. Go to the directory 3dsMax8\Images\Friends_of_Ed, select the file Tree01.tga, and click **Open**. The image is now loaded in the Diffuse Color channel.

6. Change the sample slot object type from the default sphere to a cube to better see the resulting appearance of the material. Notice the entire image appears on each side of the cube. You will now load the alpha channel embedded in this .tga file to show only the tree and to mask everything else in the image.

7. Click the **Go to Parent** button to return to the **Maps** rollout.

8. Click and hold on the map loaded in the Diffuse Color channel, as shown in the following illustration. Drag and release on top of the **Opacity** channel button.

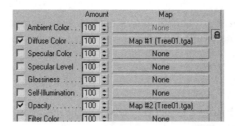

9. You will be prompted to either make an instance of, copy, or swap the map loaded into the Diffuse Color channel, as shown in the right image of the preceding illustration. Select **Copy**, and click **OK**.

10. Click the **Opacity** channel button into which you just loaded the map. The **Bitmap Parameters** rollout opens.

11. Scroll down within the **Bitmap Parameters** rollout to the section labeled **Mono Channel Output**, and click the **Alpha** option, as shown in the following illustration. This tells 3ds Max to load the alpha map embedded in the .tga file into the Opacity channel. Notice now in the sample slot that only the tree is shown on the sides of the cube, while the rest of the image is cut out.

12. Within the **Cropping/Placement** section of the **Bitmap Parameters** rollout, click the **View Image** button, as shown in the following illustration. The .tga image is displayed.

13. Click the **Display Alpha Channel** icon (the first icon to the right of the red, green, and blue channel buttons). This shows the alpha map (shown on the right in the following image) embedded in the .tga file, and why portions of the image are hidden. Any portion of the alpha map shown in black will hide the corresponding portion of the overall image. You can adjust an image's alpha map in programs like Adobe Photoshop by working with its channels within the program.

14. Now, to see the results of this new material in action, try applying the material to a simple plane object.

The Bump channel

The Bump channel is a powerful feature in 3ds Max that can give materials a realistic 3D appearance. The Bump channel uses the brighter areas of an image to make the material appear raised, while darker areas of the image make the material appear to be recessed. The ideal bump map is a purely grayscale image; however, a full color image will also work. The Bump channel amount can range from 0 to 999, although values over 300 usually result in so much relief that the material doesn't look realistic. The left image in Figure 7-5 shows a box object simulating stucco. The only map applied to the material is the black-and-white image to the right of the box, which was applied to the Bump channel with an **Amount** value of **50**.

Figure 7-5. Applying a grayscale image to the Bump channel to produce a textured appearance

Bump maps can be used in a wide variety of material types, including walls, grass, water, concrete, tile, wood, and many others. Bump maps are also very handy when you want to produce objects with engravings or impressions.

Using the Bump channel

This exercise demonstrates use of the Bump channel by loading into it the grayscale image shown on the right in Figure 7-5.

1. Reset 3ds Max.
2. Open the **Material Editor**.
3. Click any sample slot, open the **Maps** rollout, and click the channel button labeled **None** to the right of the word **Bump**.
4. Go to the directory 3dsMax8\Images\Friends_of_Ed, select the file Stucco01.jpg, and click **Open**. The image is now loaded in the **Bump** channel.
5. In the Perspective viewport, create a box with a length, width, and height of 100.
6. Apply the material to the box.
7. Click the **Quick Render** icon to see the result of applying the map to the Bump channel of this material. Notice that the box appears to be made of stucco, as shown in the images in the following illustration.
8. In the **Maps** rollout of the stucco material you just created, increase the effect of the map in the Bump channel by increasing the **Amount** from the default value of **30** to **100**. The image on the right in the following illustration shows the result of increasing the Bump channel **Amount** to **100**.

9. Render the box again to see the effect of increasing the Bump channel **Amount**.

The Reflection channel

Reflections can add a tremendous amount of realism to any scene. Depending on the lighting in your scenes, reflections might be found on such objects as windows, water, or even polished teapots (as shown in Figure 7-6). If not used wisely and in moderation, however, reflections can impose a heavy burden on your processor and slow your rendering speed to a crawl.

Figure 7-6. Using an image to simulate an artificial reflection

The easiest and least processor-needy way to use reflections is to load a map into the Reflections channel. This makes the material appear to reflect objects in your scene. For example, in Figure 7-6, the image of the lake was loaded into the Reflection channel of a material applied to the teapot. This was the only change made to the material to make it appear this way.

The reflection amount can range from 0 to 100, where 0 results in no reflection and 100 results in a near mirror-like reflection, depending on the other rollouts and map channel settings. Figure 7-7 shows reflection amounts ranging from 100 to 25.

Figure 7-7. Reflection amounts of 100, 75, 50, and 25, from left to right

More realistic but processor-hungry ways of producing reflections include using the Flat Mirror and Raytrace maps, as shown in Figure 7-8.

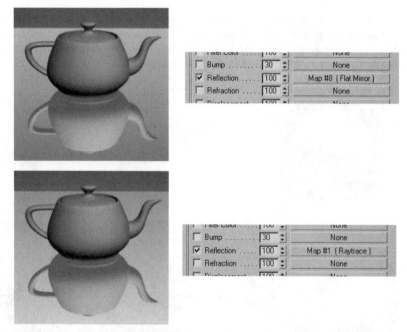

Figure 7-8. Reflections using a Flat Mirror map (top) and a Raytrace map (bottom)

To create Flat Mirror **reflections**, simply add the Flat Mirror map type to the Reflection channel. Flat Mirror maps render much quicker than Raytrace maps; however, more caution must be taken in their use. Notice that in the **Note** section of the **Flat Mirror Parameters** rollout, it states, **Unless 'Apply Faces with ID' is checked, this material must be applied as a sub-material to a set of coplanar faces**. This means that if you choose to use the Flat Mirror map, you must ensure that the material is applied only to objects that lie in the same plane. Not doing so can result in the material causing erratic reflections or no reflections at all. Figure 7-9 illustrates this with the same material applied to two reflective objects. On the left side of the image is a simple flat plane object, which creates proper reflections. On the right side is a curved mesh whose reflections are incorrect because not all the faces in the object are coplanar.

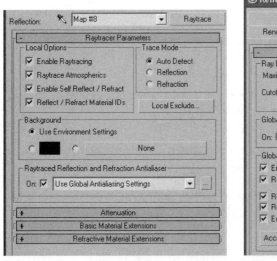

Figure 7-9. Flat mirror reflections on coplanar faces (left) and non-coplanar faces (right)

Raytrace maps provide the most powerful and realistic reflections of all the standard map types. To create Raytrace map reflections, simply add the Raytrace map type to the **Reflection** channel. The Raytrace map contains four rollouts (shown in the left image of Figure 7-10) with numerous settings that can take a long time to master. Although only advanced users will find it necessary to adjust many of these settings, there are a few important settings that anyone using raytracing should understand.

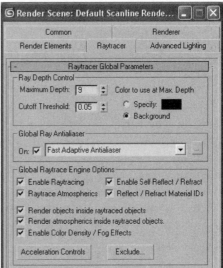

Figure 7-10. The Raytracer Parameters rollout (left) and the Render Scene dialog box (right)

In the **Local Options** settings, enable **Raytrace Atmospherics** if you want to include atmospheric effects such as fog or volume light. Atmospheric effects (covered in Chapter 18) can significantly increase your rendering times, and when included in reflections, this effect is multiplied. If it is not necessary to include atmospherics, you should disable this option.

199

At the bottom of the **Raytracer Parameters** rollout is a setting that controls anti-aliasing for the material. This option is disabled until it is enabled globally in the **Render Scene** dialog box. By default, all reflections lack anti-aliasing because in most cases it is not necessary; also, enabling this option can significantly increase rendering times. When you're close enough to objects using raytraced materials that you can see the impact of not using anti-aliasing, you may decide to enable this option. Before you can enable this option for a specific material, however, you must enable the **Global Ray Antialiaser** option found in the **Raytracer** tab of the **Render Scene** dialog box (see the right image of Figure 7-10). When you do, the **Raytrace Reflection and Refraction Antialiaser** option will be selectable for specific materials. The button to the right of this setting is a shortcut that will take you to the **Render Scene** dialog box. If you decide to use this option, make sure you create a material specifically for those objects that you want to use anti-aliasing for, and have the option disabled for all other raytraced materials.

The last option that bears covering is the **Local Exclude** option found in the **Raytracer Parameters** rollout. Use this feature to exclude objects that you don't want to be reflected. For some complex objects that would significantly burden the computer if they included reflections, you might want to exclude reflections if doing so would not be noticeable.

Using the Reflection channel

This exercise demonstrates use of the Reflection channel by loading into it a Raytrace map.

1. Reset 3ds Max.
2. Open the **Material Editor**.
3. Click any sample slot, open the **Maps** rollout, and click the channel button labeled **None** to the right of the word **Reflection**.
4. Load a Raytrace map into the Reflection channel.
5. In the Perspective viewport, create a plane of any size and a teapot centered on the plane, as shown in the left image of the following illustration.
6. Select the plane and apply the raytrace material.
7. Render the scene to see the results of the raytrace material. The plane now reflects the teapot, as shown in the right image.

The Displacement channel

The next critical map channel that you should have in your arsenal is the Displacement channel. Unlike the Bump map, the Displacement map actually displaces the geometry of a surface according to light and dark areas of a map or image loaded into the Displacement channel. Use of this channel is similar to using the **Displace** modifier. In order to use this map type for mesh objects, the **Displacement Approx.** modifier must be applied.

Figure 7-11 illustrates an example of how displacement mapping can be used to simulate terrain or water. To apply the Displacement map as shown in this example, create a plane object with just one length and width segment. Load a Noise map (described in more detail in the next chapter) into the Displacement channel with an amount of 100, and apply the map to the plane object. Last, apply a **Displacement Approx.** modifier to the object. The result will look like the plane object shown in Figure 7-11. To achieve smoother curves in the object, start with a plane object with more length and width segments, or change the **Subdivision Presets** from the default **Medium** setting to **High**. You can explore other settings in the modifier to achieve higher-quality displacements, but caution should be taken in these settings, as they can easily result in meshes with an astronomical number of faces.

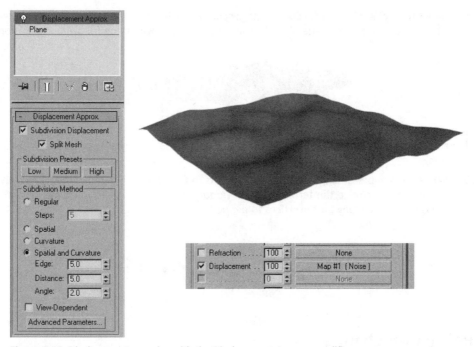

Figure 7-11. Displacement mapping with the Displacement Approx. modifier

Using the Displacement channel

This exercise demonstrates use of the Displacement channel by loading into it a Noise map to simulate mountainous terrain.

1. Reset 3ds Max.
2. Create a plane with a length and width of 100, and one length and width segment.
3. Open the **Material Editor**.

4. Load a Noise map into the Displacement channel.

5. Apply the material to the plane.

6. Select the plane and add a **Displace Approx.** modifier. In the viewport, you will see no change to the plane.

7. Render the scene to see the result of the material and modifier applied to the plane, as shown in the following illustration:

8. Double the default **Amount** value of the displacement to **200**, and render the scene again. Notice the displacement in the plane is twice as great, as shown in the following illustration:

9. Return to the modifier stack for the plane and select the base object in the stack (i.e., the plane).

10. Change the number of length and width segments to ten, leave the modifier stack, and render the scene again. Notice the terrain is much smoother, as shown in the following illustration, because there are many more vertices to define the curves:

The Refraction channel

Refraction is the bending of light as it passes through one medium into another. Like reflections, refractions can significantly improve the quality and realism of your scenes; but also like reflections, this improvement comes at a price. Refractions are also a more advanced feature that should only be used when all of the other channels discussed in this chapter are understood.

You can create refractions using a bitmap or a procedural map. The most important variable controlling refraction is the index of refraction (IOR), found in the **Extended Parameters** rollout of the standard material (Figure 7-12). The IOR simply controls how much the material refracts transmitted light. At an IOR of 1.0 (the IOR of air) objects do not distort. At 1.5 (the IOR of glass), objects will distort a large amount. Table 7-1 shows some typical objects and their IOR values.

Table 7-1. Some typical objects and their IOR values

Object	IOR Value
Vacuum	1.0
Air	1.0003
Water	1.333
Glass	1.5 to 1.7

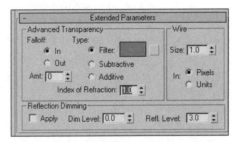

Figure 7-12. The Index of Refraction setting, found in the Extended Parameters rollout

To create refractions using a Thin Wall Refraction map type, load the Thin Wall refraction into the Refraction channel, click the Go to Parent icon, and in the Extended Parameters rollout, change the Index of Refraction value. Try some of the values shown in Table 7-1. The Reflect/Refract map type can be used as a procedural map to create automatic refractions. However, for more accurate refractions of an object in a refractive medium (such as an object in water), you should use the Thin Wall Refraction material. Figure 7-13 shows an object refracted at various values.

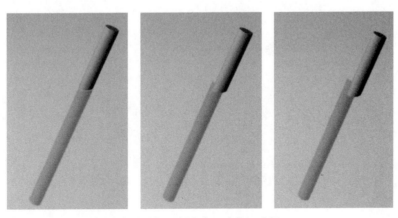

Figure 7-13. IOR values of 1.0, 1.5, and 2.0, from left to right

Summary

This chapter has delved into the heart of material creation for the standard material: the **Maps** rollout. Although there are numerous types of materials, the standard material is the most commonly used, and for foundation level users, the one that should be concentrated on. Within this chapter, you applied the Bitmap map type to the most critical map channels: those channels that will afford you the widest range of material creation for visualizations. There are many other channels, which you can use to add even greater depth and realism to your scenes, but the uses for those channels are not as extensive as the ones covered in this chapter. Additionally, the skills needed to utilize those channels are far greater than the skills needed to learn the critical channels covered in this chapter.

For the sake of simplicity, this chapter focused primarily on the Bitmap map type. The next chapter describes the other critical map types that can be applied to the map channels you've just learned about. After learning these map types, you will begin to see that there isn't much in the way of materials that you can't create.

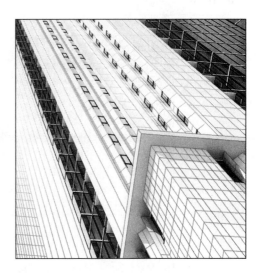

Chapter 8

THE CRITICAL MAP TYPES

The number of uses for maps in the various map channels of a material is about as limitless as your imagination. They can be applied to objects as simply as you would apply wallpaper to a wall, or they can be used in complex ways to control very specifically the parameters of other maps. Just as in other areas of 3ds Max, there are usually numerous ways to accomplish the same thing when creating materials; likewise, when creating materials, there are many features that, while great for other industries, serve little purpose in architectural visualizations. I will not cover these features. Instead, I will explain the map types that are critical for the visualization industry, and show you how to get the most out of them to create stunning materials that will help bring your work to life.

The Bitmap map

The Bitmap map type (shown in Figure 8-1) is the most commonly used map type in architectural visualizations and, fortunately, one of the easiest. When you load this map type into a map channel, five rollouts appear. With the exception of the **Bitmap Parameters** rollout, each of these rollouts appears with many of the other map types.

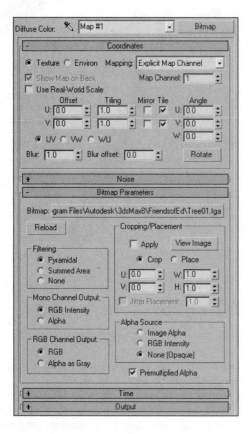

Figure 8-1. The Bitmap Parameters rollout

The Coordinates rollout

The **Coordinates** rollout, shown in Figure 8-2, controls how a map is positioned and oriented on an object, and how it is repeated (tiled) over the object's surface. Before this rollout can be adequately explained, you must understand UVW coordinates. UVW coordinates are the material version of the XYZ coordinates. Just as an object's position in 3D space is defined in XYZ coordinates, a material's position on an object is defined in UVW coordinates. These coordinates are required for every object to which a map is applied. The difference in the letters used is simply to avoid confusion between transformation coordinates.

Figure 8-2. A bitmap applied to a simple box with default coordinate values

The first option I want to point out is the option to create the map as a texture or environment map. Environment maps are images applied to the background of a viewport. I highly discourage anyone from using them, because they're always fixed, regardless of how the view changes; and they're usually not realistic. I recommend leaving this option on **Texture**, as shown in Figure 8-2.

Offset and tiling

Below this option are the **Offset** and **Tiling** parameters, which control where the center of the image falls on an object's surface, and how many times the image will be copied over the length of an object's surface. To see how these parameters really work, lets look at an example.

The images in Figure 8-3 show a material with a bitmap image of a leaf applied to a box. In the top-left image, the **Tiling** value is kept at its default value of **1.0**. Because of this, the leaf appears only once on each side of the box, rather than being repeated. The **Offset** value is also kept at its default value of **0.0**, which causes the leaf to be centered on each side of the box, rather than being offset from the center.

In the top-right image, the **Tiling** value is changed to **2.0**, which causes 3ds Max to try to place the same image of the leaf twice on each side of the box. To do so, 3ds Max must reduce the image to half its original size. However, since the image is scaled down from its center, it's cut in half along each edge of the box. To change the position of the tiled leaf images, you must use the **Offset** feature.

The bottom-right image shows the effect of a U Offset value of **0.25**, for which the image is moved 25% along the u axis. This offset causes the two images of the leaf to be centered and fit perfectly within each side of the box, but only along the u axis of each side. The bottom-right image shows the effect of a **V Offset** value of **0.25**, for which the image is moved 25% along the v axis. This offset causes the two images of the leaf to be centered and fit perfectly within each side of the box along the v axis.

Figure 8-3. Examples of the Tiling and Offset features

Angle

To the right of this **Tile** option are three parameters that allow you to rotate the bitmap along the u, v, or w axes. You will probably never need to change the **U** and **V** values; however, you may often find it necessary to change the **W** value to something like **45.0**, which essentially turns the bitmap 45 degrees about the w axis, as shown in Figure 8-4.

Figure 8-4. Rotating a bitmap +/– 45 degrees along the w axis

Blur and blur offset

If you find that a particular material in your scene is producing an undesirable amount of aliasing, despite whatever anti-aliasing filters you might be using, you might want to try increasing the **Blur** value, located in the bottom-left of the rollout. Rather than using other methods, such as supersampling, which can significantly increase your rendering times, increasing the **Blur** value can reduce jagged edges without affecting rendering times. Try increasing the default value of **1.0** to **1.5**, **2.0**, or **2.5**, until the aliasing effect is removed. Figure 8-5 shows examples of different **Blur** settings.

Figure 8-5. Blur settings of 1.0 (default setting), 2.0, and 3.0, from left to right

You can also increase the blur offset of an individual material to simulate objects in a scene that are out of focus due to their distance from the camera. Unlike **Blur**, which applies a greater blur to objects the farther away they are from the view, **Blur offset** applies the same blur amount regardless of distance.

The last parameter worth mentioning in the **Coordinates** rollout, **Map Channel**, will be left until the next chapter, because its use is tied directly to the discussion of UVW Mapping.

Using the Coordinates rollout of a Bitmap map

This exercise demonstrates some of the key features within the **Coordinates** rollout of a Bitmap map.

1. Reset 3ds Max.

2. Create a box with a length, width, and height of 100.

3. Open the **Material Editor**.

4. In the Diffuse Color channel of any material, load a Bitmap map using the image Tile01.jpg in the 3dsMax8\Images\Friends_of_Ed folder.

5. Apply the material to the box. The result should look like image 1 in the example figure at the end of this exercise.

6. Go to the **Coordinates** rollout of the material you just created and change the **Tiling** amount to **2.0**, as shown in the following illustration. The result should look like image 2 in the example figure.

7. Change the **W** angle value to **45.0**, as shown in the following illustration. This rotates the map 45 degrees along the w axis of the material. The result should look like image 3 in the example figure.

8. Disable the **Tile** option, as shown in the following illustration. This prevents the map from being copied across the surface of the box. The result should look like image 4 in the example figure.

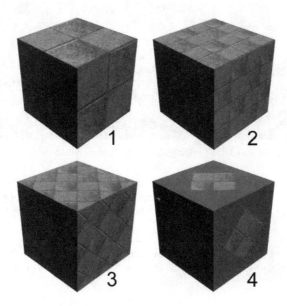

The Noise rollout

The **Noise** rollout (see Figure 8-6) is a personal favorite of mine because it does something that nothing else in 3ds Max seems to be able to do: it can make certain map types appear to not lose their resolution, regardless of how close the maps are to the camera.

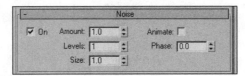

Figure 8-6. The Noise rollout

Figure 8-7 shows the result of the camera coming close to the street and grass objects in a scene. In the top-left image, the maps appear normal, but in the top-right image, the maps appear pixilated because the resolution of the maps is not high enough to support such close views. The bottom image shows the same map with noise enabled. Notice the **Amount** is set to the maximum possible value of **100.0** and the **Size** is set to the minimum possible value of **0.001**. The grass texture is no longer pixilated, regardless of how close you get. Furthermore, the grass will never appear bland, regardless of how far away it is.

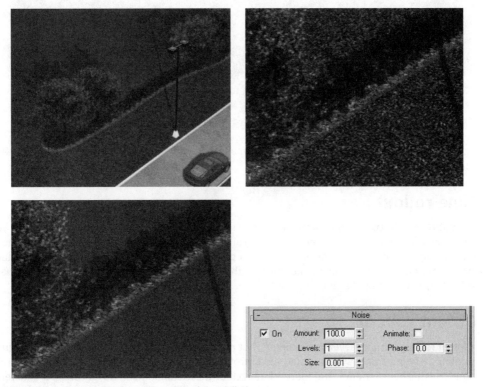

Figure 8-7. Using the Noise settings to reduce pixilation

These settings can also reduce the need for tiling a bitmap. The top image in Figure 8-8 shows a street texture that appears to be tiled, even though it's seamless. The bottom image shows the same Bitmap map with noise applied, using the same settings as the last example. Notice the tiled effect is no longer visible, yet there is still a decided texture.

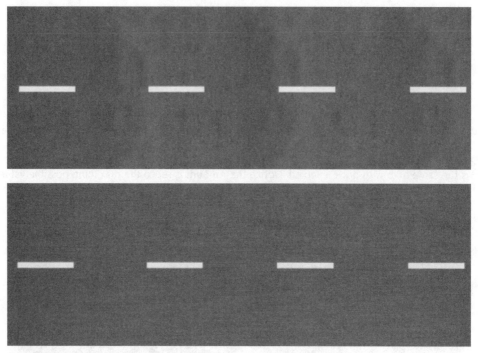

Figure 8-8. Using the Noise setting to reduce the tiled effect of bitmaps

Though the need should be rare, you can even animate the noise by enabling the Animate **option** and changing the **Phase** value over time.

The Time rollout

This rollout is used to control the playing of video clips that are applied as maps. For example, if you want to show a TV playing in your interior scene, you can set the **Start Frame** to a particular frame in your animation so that the TV turns on at a certain point along the animation. Other options include **Playback Rate**, which changes the playing speed of the video clip, and **End Condition**, which can make the video play over and over again.

The Output rollout

The **Output** rollout contains several parameters, but none that I find particularly useful in architectural visualizations. The parameters can be used to control the final output of a map's saturation, contrast, brightness, highlights, midtones, and more—but each of these should need no adjusting. If a material needs adjustments in any of these areas, the chances are that either the scene has poor lighting or the material is poorly constructed and should be adjusted with other parameters.

The Gradient map

The Gradient map produces a change from one color or map to another. It can be used in practical ways with just about every map channel, or in conjunction with another map type. It uses two or three colors or maps to produce a gradient in a linear or radial direction. Its only unique rollout is the **Gradient Parameters** rollout, which contains three color swatches and map icons for loading maps into its color channels. Color #1, or its representative map, is placed at one end of the gradient, Color #3 is placed at the other end, and the position of Color #2 is determined by the **Color 2 Position** parameter, located below the color swatches. A **Color 2 Position** value of **0.5** places Color #2 halfway between #1 and #3, a value of **0.9** places Color #2 near Color #1, and a value of **0.1** places it near Color #3.

The Gradient map will probably not be one of your more frequently used maps, but it can come in handy in certain situations. One common use is in background images representing the sky, for which you can specify two or three colors at some point in the sky, and have 3ds Max interpolate all of the colors in between, as shown in Figure 8-9. The gradient is applied to the Diffuse Color channel of a material, which is applied to a cylindrical object representing the sky.

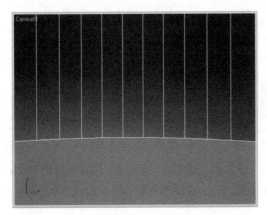 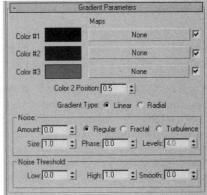

Figure 8-9. Applying a gradient to the Diffuse Color channel

Another way I like to use Gradient maps is to represent the mulched areas around trees, as shown in Figure 8-10. The image on the left shows the boundary between grass and mulch as a harsh abrupt change, which is not as realistic as the image on the right, in which a radial gradient is applied to the Opacity channel of the mulch material. When used in this method, the areas of the Opacity channel that receive pure black are transparent, and the areas that receive pure white are completely opaque. This causes the simple square-shaped mesh to disappear around the edges, giving it an apparent round shape that fades into the grass object. Note, however, that the mulch object must be moved slightly above the grass object so that the two objects don't occupy the same space. You can do the same thing by using the Gradient map in the Diffuse Color channel, with Color #1 being the same as the surrounding grass, and Colors #2 and #3 being the mulch.

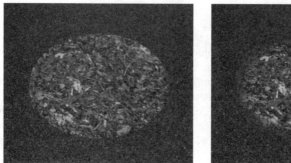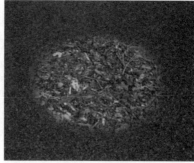

Figure 8-10. Using a gradient to soften the edge between grass and mulch

These are just two examples in which the Gradient map can come in handy to represent architectural elements. Your imagination can help you use this map type to benefit many other elements.

The Gradient Ramp map

The Gradient Ramp map (shown in Figure 8-11) is a more powerful and versatile version of the Gradient map. The Gradient Ramp map produces any number of changes from one color or map to another, and a variety of controls make this map type useful in many different situations.

The Gradient Ramp map contains only one unique rollout: **Gradient Ramp Parameters**. Along the top of the rollout is the Gradient bar, which presents a linear representation of the color changes from the start point on the left to the end point on the right. By default, three flags that control color or maps appear along the bottom edge of the Gradient bar. When one of the flags is selected, the flag turns green and its RGB value appears above the Gradient bar, along with its position on the gradient. The position is represented as a percentage, with 0% and 100% representing the left and right edges of the bar, respectively. The Gradient bar can contain an unlimited number of flags, and therefore an unlimited number of colors or maps.

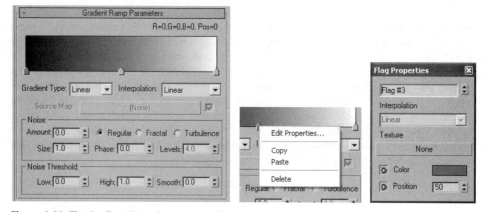

Figure 8-11. The Gradient Ramp Parameters rollout

To change the color of a flag or add a map to it, right-click the flag and select **Edit Properties** (as in the middle image of Figure 8-11). A dialog box appears with a field at the top displaying the flag name, as shown in the right image. You can change the flag name and switch to a different flag using the spinner. Load a map by clicking the **Texture** icon, or change the color by clicking the color swatch. Change the flag's position by typing a new value, using the spinner, or closing the dialog box and dragging the flag along the Gradient bar. Create a new flag by simply clicking anywhere in the Gradient bar.

Below the Gradient bar are two drop-down lists that allow you to specify the shape of the gradient, as well as the interpolation, which controls the transition from one flag to another. Below these drop-down lists are controls for adding noise to the final output. With all of these features, the Gradient map can produce an enormous variety of looks to a map. Like some other map types, the number of ways you can use the Gradient Ramp map is limitless.

Using the Gradient Ramp map

This exercise demonstrates use of the Gradient Ramp map.

1. Reset 3ds Max.
2. Create a box with a length, width, and height of 100.
3. Open the **Material Editor**.
4. In the Diffuse Color channel of any material, load a Gradient Ramp map.
5. Apply the material to the box. The result should look like image 1 in the four-box example illustration at the end of this exercise.
6. In the **Gradient Ramp Parameters** rollout, right-click the flag at the bottom-left corner of the Gradient bar and select **Edit Properties**, as shown in the following illustration. The flag will turn green when selected.

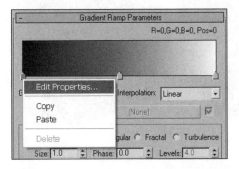

7. Click the color swatch in the **Flag Properties** dialog box that appears, and select the color red from the color selector, as shown in the following illustration. Close the color selector and the **Flag Properties** dialog box.

217

8. Render the scene again. The result should look like image 2 in the following example illustration.

9. Right-click the flag at the bottom-right corner of the Gradient bar, and select a green color for this flag using the same process as in steps 6 and 7.

10. Render the scene again; the result should look like image 3 in the example illustration.

11. Click, hold, and drag the middle flag under the Gradient bar to a location near the right flag, as shown in the following illustration. This simply changes the location at which the three colors merge.

12. Render the scene again; the result should look like image 4 in the following illustration.

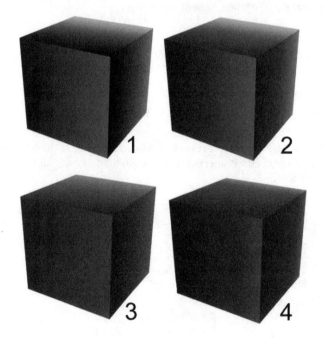

The Mix map

The Mix map, shown in Figure 8-12, combines two colors or maps in specified amounts to produce a blended result. This map type contains only one unique rollout: **Mix Parameters**. At the top of the rollout are two color swatches and map icons. Use the color swatches to choose two different colors to mix, and use their adjacent map icons to load maps in place of the colors. Below the color swatches is a **Mix Amount** parameter and its adjacent map icon.

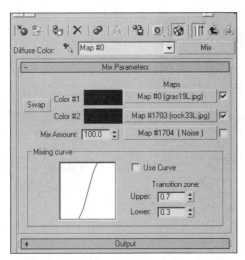

Figure 8-12. The Mix Parameters rollout

The **Mix Amount** controls how much of each color or map is used in the blend. A **Mix Amount** of **0.0** results in 100% of Color #1 being shown and 0% of Color #2 being shown. A **Mix Amount** of **100.0** produces the opposite result. A **Mix Amount** of **50.0** results in 50% of each color or map being displayed. Figure 8-13 illustrates how two bitmaps can be mixed together with a range of mix amounts. Color #2 (grass image 2) is mixed with Color #1 (grass image 1) using a mix amounts of 0, 25, 50, 75, and 100.

Figure 8-13. Two separate grass images mixed with amounts of 0, 25, 50, 75, and 100, from left to right

The **Mix Amount** map icon can be used to produce a randomized blend between both colors or maps, in which Color #1 is displayed in random locations and Color #2 is displayed in all other locations. Figure 8-14 shows a material with a Mix map applied to the Diffuse Color channel. If you make Color #1 red and Color #2 yellow, and load a Noise map into the **Mix Amount** slot, the result is a material with a randomized mixture of both colors. Changing the **Size** value within the **Noise Parameters** rollout changes the size of the red and yellow parts. To have more of Color #1, use more black in both color slots in the **Noise Parameters** rollout. To have more of Color #2, use more white.

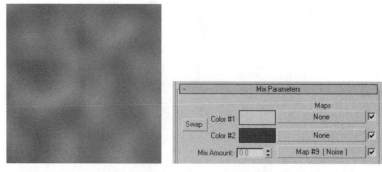

Figure 8-14. Example of mixing red and yellow, using a Noise map in the Mix Amount slot

The Noise map

The Noise map is a map type that is probably most useful in controlling the appearance of other map types, as just explained in the discussion of the Mix map type. By loading a Noise map into the Bump channel, for example, you can randomly apply bumps to an object in a noise pattern.

The Noise map contains three rollouts. The **Coordinates** rollout for noise is built much like the **Coordinates** rollout for other map types (explained previously), and adjusting this rollout is usually not necessary. The only unique rollout for this map type is the **Noise Parameters** rollout. Along the top of the rollout are the **Noise Type** options of **Regular**, **Fractal**, and **Turbulence**. Which option you select depends on the look you're trying to achieve. **Fractal** is a favorite of mine when I'm trying to depict aged surfaces, such as rusted metal. Figure 8-15 displays an example of each.

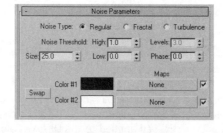

Figure 8-15. An example of mixing red and yellow with a Noise map, using (from left to right) Regular, Fractal, and Turbulence noise types.

In the middle of the rollout is the **Size** parameter. Smaller values make the mixture appear grainier, while larger values make the mixture appear more marbleized. The images in Figure 8-15 use the default **Size** of **25.0**, but because the scale of the map is dependent on object size, you will almost always have to experiment with various size values to achieve the correct scale. By animating the **Phase** value, you can make the material appear to move like a fluid.

The two color swatches provide a way to control the characteristics of the parent material. When applying a Noise map to the Bump channel, for example, the two colors indicate which part of the object shows elevated areas and which part shows recessed areas. Pure white areas of a noise map will cause the object to show elevated areas while pure black areas will cause the object to show recessed areas.

The Noise map has many applications. One of my favorites is using it in the Bump channel of a material simulating water. By adding the Noise map, some areas of the water material appear to be elevated and other areas appear to be recessed. The effect is a water material that appears to have rolling waves.

Using the Noise map

This exercise demonstrates use of the Noise map in the Bump channel to create some relief to terrain.

1. Reset 3ds Max.
2. Create a plane with a length and width of 100.
3. Open the **Material Editor**.
4. In the Bump channel of any material, load a Noise map.
5. Apply the material to the plane and render the scene. The plane appears to have some relief, as shown in the left image of the following illustration.
6. In the **Noise Parameters** rollout, reduce the **Size** value from the default value of **25.0** to a new value of **10.0**. The scale of the relief is reduced accordingly, as shown in the right image of the following illustration:

The Smoke map

The Smoke map is very similar to the Noise map, both in its features and its application. The **Smoke Parameters** rollout works in nearly the same way as in the **Noise Parameters** rollout, and like the Noise map, the Smoke map is great for producing random areas of opacity, bump, and diffuse color. Figure 8-16 shows one example of the Smoke map using the default settings. It should be noted that, as with other maps, the final appearance of an image like the one in Figure 8-16 depends not only on some of the map settings, but also the size of the object to which the material is applied. For example, using the default **Size** value of **40.0** will not work for an object that is only 1 unit long and 1 unit wide.

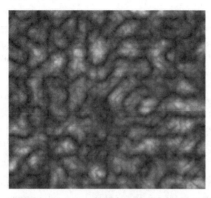

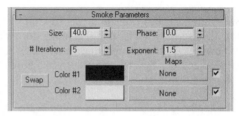

Figure 8-16. A Smoke map applied to the Diffuse Color channel

The Waves map

The Waves map is a nice feature that does a pretty good job simulating the wave action of water. By adjusting the parameters of this rollout, you can simulate everything from calm water with very little wave action to large, choppy waves moving at high speed. To achieve the exact result you're looking for, you'll probably have the best luck changing each parameter to extreme values so that you can see their individual effects on the result. To illustrate the effect of each setting, Figure 8-17 shows several different images and the settings used for each. The default black color is replaced with a dark blue color to better simulate water. It is important to note that in this case, the material is applied to a simple plane with a width and length of 100 units. Using different sized objects will require these settings to be scaled appropriately.

The **Amplitude** controls the apparent height of the waves by setting the contrast between the two different wave colors. Lighter areas represent the ridges, or higher parts in the waves, and darker areas represent the troughs, or lower parts in the waves.

The **Wave Radius** controls the curvature of the waves, with small numbers simulating small ripples that originate nearby, and large numbers simulating waves originating from a great distance.

The **Wave Len Max** value controls the thickness of Color #1, which since set to white by default, controls the wave thickness.

The **Wave Len Min** value controls the thickness of Color #2, which since set to black by default, controls the trough thickness.

The **Num Wave Sets** value specifies how many wave sets are used in the pattern. Wave sets are groups of radially symmetrical waves that originate from randomly selected points. To simulate a stone dropped in water, you would have one origin for the ripples, so **Num Wave Sets** would be set to 1. Setting this value to a higher number, such as 5, could simulate water in a swimming pool, with wave action originating from no specific location.

You can load maps into the color channels; however, achieving realism while doing so can be more difficult than just using colors.

Finally, by animating the **Phase** value, you can simulate wave movement.

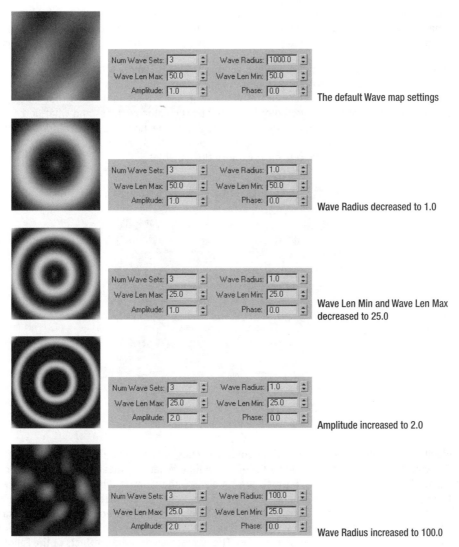

The default Wave map settings

Wave Radius decreased to 1.0

Wave Len Min and Wave Len Max decreased to 25.0

Amplitude increased to 2.0

Wave Radius increased to 100.0

Figure 8-17. A Wave map applied to a 100-square-unit plane object

The Falloff map

Here's another one of those 3ds Max features that's so useful and so large in application, an entire chapter could be devoted to its use. Like other map types, the uses of the Falloff map are limited only by one's imagination, and with a little imagination one can produce some amazing materials. In short, the Falloff map creates a gradient of two colors or maps in specific intensity and in a specific direction. It uses an object's face normals and viewing direction to determine where to place the colors. Faces perpendicular to the viewing direction receive the **Front** color (black by default) and faces parallel to the viewing direction receive the **Side** color (white by default). All other faces are shaded somewhere between the two colors, depending on the angle.

This gradient can benefit any map channel by accentuating certain map characteristics and toning down others. It can be used to ease the transition from one map characteristic to another, or to accelerate it. It functions as a little bit of many different map types, including Mix, Gradient, and Composite.

The Falloff map type contains only one unique rollout: **Falloff Parameters** (shown in Figure 8-18). In the first section of this rollout, **Front:Side**, you define the two colors that are used with the map and how the falloff is applied. To the right of the color swatches are amount fields (not labeled) that dictate what percentage of the diffuse color is defined by the color swatches and what percentage is defined by a map. **Falloff Type** and **Falloff Direction** determine how the two colors or maps are applied. Because the number of combinations is too enormous to cover, I will just cover a few. To see the true potential of this map type, one must explore the variables.

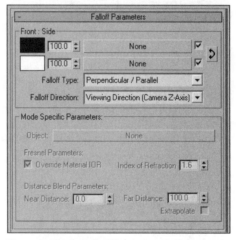

Figure 8-18. The Falloff Parameters rollout

The default settings include black-and-white color swatches, a **Perpendicular / Parallel Falloff Type**, and a **Viewing Direction (Camera Z-Axis) Falloff Direction**. What this means is that the color black will be placed everywhere the face normals are parallel to the viewing direction, and white will be placed everywhere the normals are perpendicular. You can change the placement of the two colors and the direction they fall off by changing the **Falloff Type** and **Falloff Direction** values. For example, if you change the **Falloff Direction** to **Camera X-Axis**, the white appears on the front and back of an object and falls off to the black areas on the sides. The easiest way to see the effects of the Falloff map is to apply it to the Diffuse Color or Opacity channel of a material.

Figure 8-19 shows how adding a Falloff map to the Diffuse Color channel affects a material. The image on the left shows the default settings of the Falloff map when the material is applied to a simple cylinder. Since the Front color is black, the faces that are parallel to the view receive black, and the faces perpendicular to the view receive the Side color (white). The image on the right shows the effects of swapping the two colors.

Figure 8-19. The effect of adding a Falloff map to the Diffuse Color channel

Figure 8-20 shows how adding a Falloff map to the Opacity channel affects a material. The image on the left shows the default settings of the Falloff map when the material is again applied to a simple cylinder. Notice in the image on the left that the front of the cylinder is transparent. This is because the front of the cylinder receives the black color—and in the Opacity channel, black means transparent and white means opaque. The image on the right shows the result of swapping the colors.

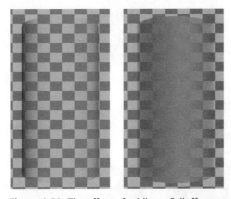

Figure 8-20. The effect of adding a Falloff map to the Opacity channel

Figure 8-21 shows another good example of the Falloff map at work. In this example, the Falloff map is applied again to the Opacity channel, and the only setting that is changed from the default value is the **Falloff Type**. By changing the **Falloff Type** to **Distance Blend**, you can make a material become transparent as it gets farther from the viewing direction. The top image shows a road with a length of 1,000 units and no Falloff map applied. Below this is an image of the same road and material with a **Distance Blend Falloff Type** applied to the Opacity channel. Notice at the bottom of the **Falloff Parameters** that the **Near Distance** value is **0.0**, and the **Far Distance** value is **1000.0**. This means that the material begins to become transparent at a distance of 0 and becomes completely transparent at a distance of 1,000 units from the view. In the bottom image, the **Near Distance** is set to **500.0** so that the road begins its transparency at 500 units away.

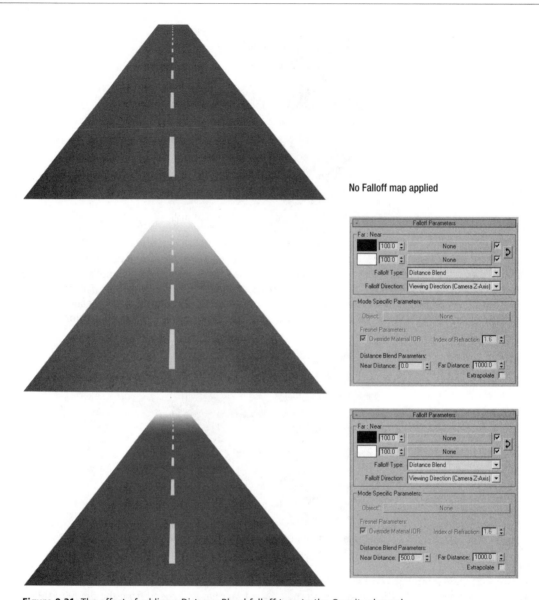

Figure 8-21. The effect of adding a Distance Blend falloff type to the Opacity channel

Using the Falloff map

This exercise demonstrates use of the Falloff map in the Opacity channel to give some unique looks to materials.

1. Reset 3ds Max.
2. In the Perspective viewport, create a teapot of any size.
3. Open the **Material Editor**.
4. In the Opacity channel of any material, load a Falloff map.
5. Apply the material to the teapot and render the scene with the default settings. The rendered image looks like an x-ray of the teapot (as shown in the left image of the illustration at the end of this exercise).
6. In the **Falloff Parameters** rollout, click the **Swap Colors/Maps** button to the right of the color swatches, as shown in the following illustration.
7. Render the scene again. The teapot now has a different but equally unique look (shown in the right image of the following illustration). Try experimenting with all the variables discussed in this chapter.

Summary

Creating maps is much like creating a recipe. Many times you don't know what you want for the end result, and you find yourself stumbling onto a great product. Other times you may know exactly what you want, but you don't know what ingredients or quantities to use. In either case, it will probably require a good amount of trial and error. There is simply no limit to the number and types of materials you can create, even with just the map types covered in this chapter. There is also no limit to the complexity with which materials can be created. One thing to keep in mind, however, is that simple is sometimes better. Great materials don't have to mean complex materials. Furthermore, you should utilize an existing material whenever possible rather than recreating one. Good use of material libraries can go a long way to increasing efficiency and productivity.

The final process in working with materials is UVW mapping. In the next chapter, you will learn how to precisely control the location and orientation of a map on an object and how to shape it to the specific type of object you apply it to. After learning this process, you will know everything you need to know to create and apply powerful and life-breathing materials to your scenes.

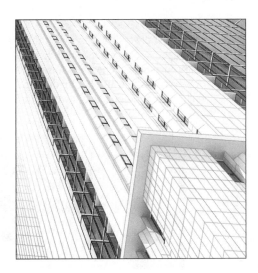

Chapter 9

UVW MAPPING

The last step in the process of applying materials in 3ds Max is UVW mapping. UVW coordinates were covered briefly in Chapter 8, but now it's time to discuss the process of mapping in greater detail. UVW mapping is the process by which materials are positioned, scaled, and oriented on objects in a scene. The UVW coordinate system is the same as the XYZ coordinate system, but uses the next three sequential letters to differentiate mapping from modeling. The u, v, and w directions correspond to the x, y, and z directions, respectively.

In 3ds Max, there are two types of maps: 2D and 3D. Since 2D maps are by definition two-dimensional, they require specific instructions, known as mapping, on how to be applied to a three-dimensional object. You control how 2D maps are applied to objects by controlling their mapping. 3D maps, also referred to as procedural maps, use mathematical calculations to determine how materials are placed on objects. Because of this, 3D maps do not require the same instructions 2D maps do (i.e., they do not require mapping). This chapter focuses on how to control the mapping of 2D maps.

Generating mapping coordinates

Whether a material contains an image or a 2D map, the material will require mapping to be applied properly to an object. Most primitive objects you create in 3ds Max will generate their own mapping coordinates, as will shapes when you apply certain modifiers, such as **Extrude**. What this means is that when mapping coordinates are created for an object, 3ds Max makes its best guess as to how the map is supposed to be applied to the object. Unfortunately, this best guess is rarely going to suffice, and you will almost always want to tweak the way a map is applied to an object. The left image in Figure 9-1 is an image of a brick wall, which is applied to the box objects to its right. The box on the left had mapping coordinates generated automatically, which placed the brick wall image on each side of the box. However, this may not be the desired look. If you want, for example, the brick wall image enlarged on each side of the box, as shown in the box on the right, you can apply a **UVW Map** modifier.

Figure 9-1. A simple box with two different mappings

The UVW Map modifier

The **UVW Map** modifier (shown in Figure 9-2) is the primary tool to control the mapping of an individual object. Two identical objects with the same material applied can look completely different if they receive different **UVW Map** modifiers.

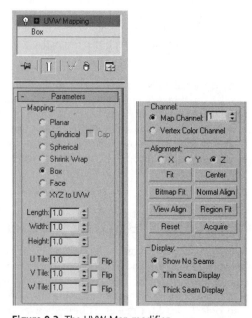

Figure 9-2. The UVW Map modifier

The modifier contains only one rollout: **Parameters**. At the top of this rollout are options for seven different mapping coordinates. Each one employs a unique method for placing the map on an object. Figure 9-3 illustrates a few of the more practical coordinate types.

Planar: The first image on the left shows a box with planar coordinates. Only the top side of the box receives the map properly because the map is applied in only one plane (hence the term "planar"). Notice that the other sides contain streaks that begin at the edge of the image that's applied on the top side. I rarely use this map coordinate because in most cases the box method will produce better results.

Cylindrical: The map is wrapped around the cylinder without any distortion; however, the top receives improper mapping. If the top and bottom of the cylinder were detached from the rest of the object, you could apply planar or box coordinates to finish the mapping. As an example, this would be the optimal coordinate type for mapping the trunk of a tree.

Spherical: The map is wrapped around a sphere. Although there is some distortion of the map across the surface of the sphere, this is the best coordinate type for a sphere. As an example, this would be the optimal coordinate type for mapping a spherical sky.

Box: This is the most practical coordinate type, comprising the vast majority of all mapping I perform. For objects shaped any other way than spherical and cylindrical, this will probably be the coordinate type that yields the best results.

Figure 9-3. The planar, cylindrical, spherical, and box coordinate types, from left to right

Working with the UVW gizmo

3ds Max allows you to use a modifier gizmo in much the same way you use a transform gizmo. The modifier gizmo is shaped to resemble the way the map is applied to or wrapped around an object. Figure 9-4 displays each of the gizmos for the map coordinate types displayed in Figure 9-3. With the modifier gizmo, you can further control the location and orientation of the map.

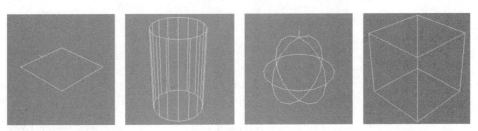

Figure 9-4. UVW Map gizmos

231

Sizing and tiling

The size of the gizmo controls the size of the map as it is applied to the object. When the UVW map is first applied to the object, its size is scaled to the length, width, and height extents of the object. If the object is a box with a height, width, and length of 100 units, then the gizmo will have a length, width, and height of 100 units, as shown in Figure 9-5.

Figure 9-5. Gizmo size and tiling options

To make the gizmo half this size, enter a value of **50.0** for each dimension, or tile the map twice over the same distance. Entering a value of **2.0** in each of the **UVW Tile** fields will produce the same result as reducing the gizmo size from 100 units in each dimension to 50 units.

To apply a map with correct scale, you must first determine the dimensions of the image being mapped. As an example, if you are trying to apply the image of the brick wall shown in Figure 9-6 to an object representing a wall, you should determine what size of brick wall the image represents in real life. In this case, the image of the brick wall is three bricks long and six bricks tall. Knowing that a standard brick is 8 inches long and 2.66 inches tall, you can conclude that the image shows a brick wall that is 2'0" long and 1'4" tall. Therefore, if you want your object to be mapped to an accurate scale, you should use the box mapping option with a **Length** and **Width** of 2'0.0" and a **Height** of 1'4.0", as shown in Figure 9-6.

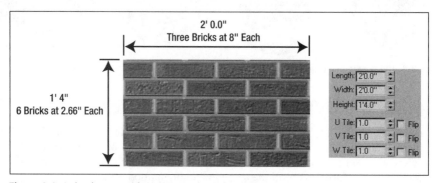

Figure 9-6. A simple map with UVW mapping information

Alignment

When you first apply the **UVW Map** modifier, the gizmo is centered on the object and sized to the extents of the object. These two characteristics are set by default whenever the **UVW Map** modifier is applied, and are represented by two separate options: **Fit** and **Center**. These options, along with several others, can be found in the **Alignment** section of the **Parameters** rollout, as shown in Figure 9-2. After manipulating the UVW gizmo, you may find the need to return the gizmo to its original state, in which case you can select the **Reset** option or even reapply the **Fit** option. You may need only to adjust the gizmo so that it becomes centered on the object, in which case **Center** is the option you want.

The only other option I use regularly, and the one I find most useful, is the **Acquire** option. **Acquire** allows you to copy the UVW map parameters from one object and apply them to another, which can save a great deal of time when creating mapping coordinates for a large number of objects.

To use the **Acquire** option, select the object you want to copy the mapping to, apply the **UVW Map** modifier to the object, select **Acquire**, and select the object to which you want to copy the mapping. The **Acquire UVW Mapping** dialog box will appear, as shown in Figure 9-7, prompting you to select either **Acquire Absolute** or **Acquire Relative**. For most architectural elements you apply mapping to, the option you select won't matter. Most objects will have a map that is tiled over and over again throughout the surface area of the object, and the exact starting location of the mapping is almost always insignificant. This is especially the case when you deal with seamless maps, which are maps that show no easily discernible border when tiled over and over again.

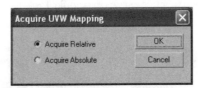

Figure 9-7. The Acquire UVW Mapping dialog box

The **Acquire Relative** option places the map on the object in the same location as the object from which the mapping is borrowed. The **Acquire Absolute** option places the map on the object as if it were being tiled from the borrowed object.

Working with the UVW Map gizmo

This exercise demonstrates how to use the UVW Map gizmo to accurately map an image onto an object.

1. Reset 3ds Max.
2. Change the units to architectural units.
3. Create a box with a length of 20'0", a width of 8", and a height of 6'0".
4. Open the **Material Editor**, and in the Diffuse Color channel of any material, load a bitmap using the image Rockwall01.jpg in the 3dsmax8\Images\Friends_of_Ed folder, as shown in the following illustration:

5. Apply the material to the box and select the **Show Map in Viewport** option. In the Perspective viewport, the result should look like the top-left image in the following illustration. Notice how distorted the image is when stretched to fit the length of the wall to which it's applied.

6. Apply the **UVW Map** modifier using the **Box** option.

7. Make a guess at how large the portion of the rock wall you see in the image would be in real life. (In order to place the image correctly on your object, you will have to tell 3ds Max how big or small to make the image in your scene.) If your object is 100 yards long, and you stretched this image over it, the image would look unrealistic in your scene because it clearly represents a much smaller wall. For the purpose of this exercise, let's assume that the rock wall in the image (at least the part you can see) is 5'0" long and 4'0" tall in real life.

8. In the **UVW Map** modifier, set the **Length** and **Width** to 5'0" and the **Height** to 4'0".

9. The wall object in the Perspective viewport should look like the bottom-left image of the following illustration:

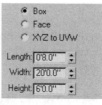

Map channels and multi/sub-objects

If you ever decide to apply a multi/sub-object material to an object, and require each sub-material to have its own UVW map (i.e., not require each sub-material to be mapped by the same UVW coordinate values), you must use map channels. Let's say you create a box and want to apply the left image in Figure 9-8 to each side of the box, and the middle image to the top of the box, as shown in the right image of Figure 9-8.

Figure 9-8. Two different maps of a multi/sub-object material applied to the same object (using map channels)

The first thing you will have to do is create a multi/sub-object material with both of these sub-materials. Since multi/sub-objects have not yet been discussed, the method to do so will be explained here. If you want to follow along with the following demonstration, you can use the two images shown in Figure 9-8. They are named Wallpaper01.jpg and Wallpaper02.jpg and can be found in the 3dsMax8\Images\Friends_of_Ed folder.

To create a multi/sub-object material, click a new material slot, click the **Material Type** icon, and select the multi/sub-object. Click the empty sub-material map slot for material ID 1 (see Figure 9-9), and assign the left image in Figure 9-8 (Wallpaper01.jpg) to the Diffuse Color channel. Assign the middle image (Wallpaper02.jpg) to the Diffuse Color channel of material ID 2.

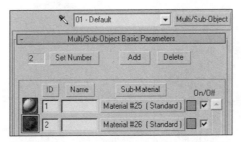

Figure 9-9. A multi/sub-object material with two sub-materials

Select the box in one of the viewports and add the **Edit Mesh** modifier. Go to the **Polygon** sub-object level, and select all of the side polygons in one of the viewports. Go to the **Surface Properties** rollout, and assign the side polygons to material ID 1, as shown in Figure 9-10. Select the top polygon and assign it to material ID 2.

Figure 9-10. Assigning material IDs to sub-objects

Apply the material to the box and enable the Show Map in Viewport option. Your result should look like Figure 9-11. You have just applied a multi/sub-object material to an object.

Figure 9-11. A multi/sub-object box

But how do you tile the image on the top of the box two times in each direction, as shown in Figure 9-12? You could always tile the image in the **Material Editor**, but that would affect all the objects in your scene with this material. If you only want to affect this one object, you must use the **UVW Map** modifier. The problem is then that the **UVW Map** modifier affects all the sub-materials on a single object. To apply the **UVW Map** modifier to only one sub-material, you must use map channels. By assigning a unique map channel to each sub-object material, you can limit specific **UVW Map** modifiers to specific sub-object materials.

Figure 9-12. An example of changing the map channel in the Material Editor

Let's see how it works. Go back to the **Coordinates** rollout of the map applied to the Diffuse Color channel of material ID 2. Change the **Map Channel** value to **2**, as shown in Figure 9-13.

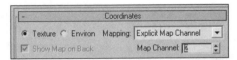

Figure 9-13. Changing the Map Channel value in the Material Editor

Render the image now, and you should get the **Missing Map Coordinates** error message. This is because the box doesn't have a UVW map applied to material ID 2. You must apply a second **UVW Map** modifier to the box and change its **Map Channel** value to **2**, as shown in Figure 9-14.

Figure 9-14. Changing the Map Channel value in the UVW Map modifier

Now, you can finally tile the image on the top of the box by changing the **U Tile** and **V Tile** values to **2.0**, as shown in Figure 9-15, to achieve the desired result.

Figure 9-15. Changing the U and V Tile values in the UVW Map modifier

Working with map channels

This exercise demonstrates how to use map channels to apply multiple **UVW Map** modifiers to a single object with a multi/sub-object material.

1. Reset 3ds Max.
2. In the Perspective viewport, create a box with a length of 10'0", a width of 8", a height of 8'0", and 2 height segments. This box will represent a wall that will receive a multi/sub-object material.

3. Add an **Edit Mesh** modifier to the box, enter Face sub-object mode, and highlight the faces in the top half of the wall, as shown in the left image of the following illustration:

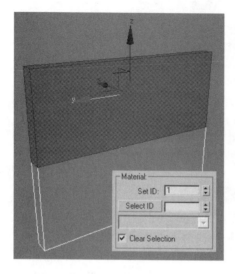 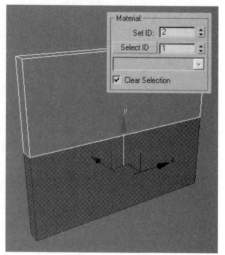

4. Scroll down to the bottom of the **Edit Mesh** modifier, and in the **Material** section of the **Surface Properties** rollout, enter a value of **1** in the **Set ID** field. This assigns a material ID of 1 to the highlighted faces.

5. Highlight the faces in the bottom half of the wall and assign a material ID of 2 to these faces, as shown in the right image of the preceding illustration.

6. Open the **Material Editor**, and in any material, select the **Material Type** button.

7. Select **Multi/Sub-Object** and select **OK** to close the **Material/Map Browser**. This changes the material type from **Standard** to **Multi/Sub-Object** and opens the **Replace Material** dialog box.

8. Select **Discard old material**, and select **OK** to close.

9. In the **Multi/Sub-Object Basic Parameters** rollout, select **Set Number**, as shown in the following illustration:

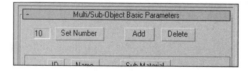

10. Change the **Number of Materials** value to **2** and click **OK** to close. This changes the number of sub-materials to 2.

11. Click the **Material Type** button for material 1. This reopens the standard rollouts that you would see for any standard material.

12. In the Bump channel, load a bitmap using the Siding01.jpg image in the 3dsmax8\Images\ Friends_of_Ed folder, as shown in the following illustration, and enable the Show Map in Viewport option. Increase the Bump **Amount** to **300** to accentuate the effect of the Bump map. This will create the appearance of 3D siding on the material.

13. Change the diffuse color of material 1 to something other than the default gray.

14. Click the **Go to Parent** icon twice to return to the root of the multi/sub-object.

15. Click the **Material Type** button for material 2.

16. In the Diffuse Color channel, load a bitmap using the image Brick01.jpg.

17. Enable the **Show Map in Viewport** option and apply the material to the box representing the wall in your scene.

18. Apply the **UVW Map** modifier to the wall, change the mapping type to **Box**, and render the scene. The wall should look like image 1 in the illustration at the end of this exercise.

19. Change the length, width, and height of the UVW mapping to 5'0", and render the scene again. The wall should now look like image 2. Notice that the brick portion looks OK, but the siding portion has improper UVW mapping.

20. Add a second **UVW Map** modifier to the wall, as shown in the following illustration, and change the mapping type to Box. Change the length, width, and height of the UVW mapping to 4" (inches); and render the scene again. Now the siding portion of the wall looks OK and the brick portion has poor mapping, as shown in image 3.

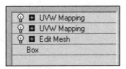

21. In the **Modifier Stack**, select the first UVW map (the bottom one), and in the **Channel** section of the **Parameters** rollout, change the **Map Channel** to 2. This makes the first UVW map apply only to sub-maps in channel 2. Now you must tell 3ds Max which sub-map will be in channel 2.

22. Return to the Diffuse Color channel of the brick material, and in the **Coordinates** rollout, change the **Map Channel** to 2. This assigns the brick sub-material to channel 2 and makes the UVW map assigned to channel 2 apply only to the brick sub-material.

23. Render the scene a final time, and it should look like image 4 in the following illustration. Now both materials of the wall have proper mapping because they each have their own UVW map applied to their individual map channels.

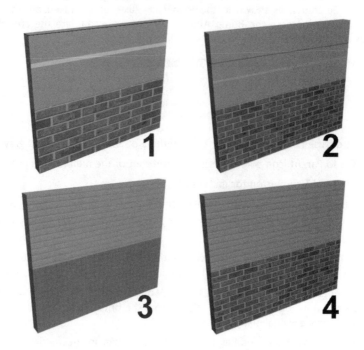

Summary

This chapter has focused on the last step in the material application process: UVW mapping. UVW mapping controls the position, scale, and orientation of maps on objects in a scene. Although there are several different mapping tools in 3ds Max for the various different industries, the **UVW Map** modifier is the main tool that controls mapping for architectural scenes.

Also covered were map channels, which allow you to apply multiple **UVW Map** modifiers to a single object that uses a multi/sub-object material. Although I'm not a huge fan of the multi/sub-object material, I find there are times when it becomes useful, and knowing how to apply different **UVW Map** modifiers to each of the different sub-maps of a single object is important. Doing so would not be possible without assigning each sub-map an individual map channel and applying a separate **UVW Map** modifier to each map channel.

There are many other powerful material features that can add a great deal of depth to your scenes, but at this point, the foundations of materials have been covered and it's time to move on to the next major step in the 3D creation process: lighting!

Part 4

LIGHTING

Quick Start 4

GETTING STARTED WITH LIGHTS

> *Approximate completion time: 45 minutes*

In this tutorial, you'll tackle what is considered by most veteran 3ds Max users as the most critical component of any 3D scene—lighting. Although the topic of lighting is enormous, here you will see just how easy it is to achieve great lighting results in just a few minutes. In this tutorial, you'll begin immediately by placing several light sources in your scene to simulate **global illumination**—a term used to describe the bouncing of light from one surface to another. You'll then try lighting the same scene with lights that display real-world characteristics and energy values and that create global illumination automatically. By the end of this tutorial, you'll have a good idea of what it takes to create realistic lighting for a 3D visualization.

1. Open the file that you saved at the end of Quick Start 3, or open the file 3dsMax8\scenes\Friends_of_Ed\QuickStart04.max, found in the download page available from www.friendsofed.com.

Let's start by changing the viewport configuration and then inserting some basic light types.

2. Right-click the Camera viewport name.

3. Select **Configure** from the menu that appears. The **Viewport Configuration** dialog box appears.

4. Click the **Layout** tab.

5. Select the configuration with four evenly sized viewports, and click **OK** to complete the command.

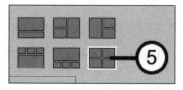

6. Click the **Zoom Extents All** icon in the bottom-right corner of the screen. This maximizes each viewport display. (Make sure you click the Zoom Extents All icon rather than the **Zoom Extents All Selected** icon—they are in the same flyout.)

7. Make the top-left viewport a Front view (keyboard shortcut F), make the top-right a Camera view (shortcut C), make the bottom-left a Left view (shortcut L), and make the bottom-right a Top view (shortcut T), as shown in the following image. Some of these views may already be configured this way. Also, make sure the Camera view is a shaded view (using **Smooth + Highlights**) and that all other views are wireframe.

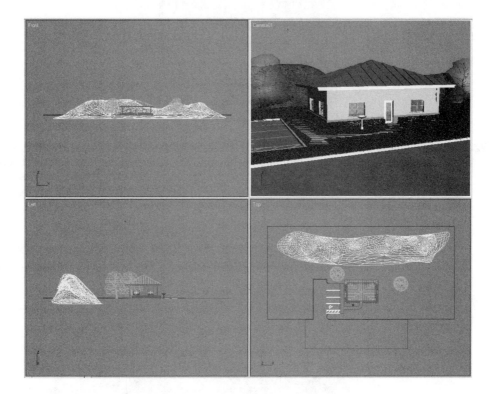

8. Click the **Zoom Extents All** icon.

9. In the Command panel, click the **Create** tab, if not already active.

10. Click the **Lights** icon. The standard light types are displayed.

11. Click the **Omni** button.

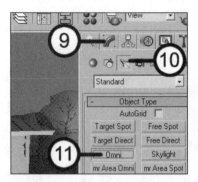

12. In the Top viewport, click once in the bottom-left corner of the viewport to place the first omni light in your scene, as shown in the following image. Notice that your scene becomes darker. This is because the light you just created has just replaced the two default lights that 3ds Max uses to initially light your scene. Since the light you created exists at an elevation of 0 feet, it must be elevated to cast light on your scene.

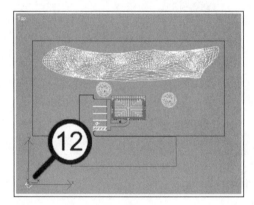

13. Click the **Zoom Extents All** icon again to ensure that the entire scene is visible in the wireframe viewports, including the light you just created.

14. In the Left view, move the light upward until it makes a 45-degree angle with ground, as shown in the following image. Notice in the Camera view that the scene becomes more brightly lit.

15. In the Command panel, give the light object the name **Sun**. This light will serve as the Sun in your scene.

16. Render the Camera view (close the render window when finished viewing). Notice that the scene is clearly illuminated; however, the light is not casting shadows. When lights are created, they are set to not cast shadows by default. Let's enable shadows for the light you created.

17. Right-click inside the active viewport and select **Cast Shadows** from the quad menu.

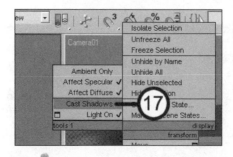

18. Render the Camera view. Shadows are now clearly evident; however, they don't look very good at the moment—you'll rectify this next.

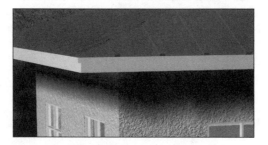

19. In the Command panel, click the **Modify** icon.

20. Click the **Shadow Map Params** rollout to open it.

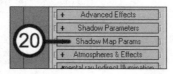

21. In the **Size** field, type **2000**. In lieu of a complicated explanation, this effectively increases the resolution of the shadows, giving them a crisper and more defined edge.

22. Render the Camera view. Now the shadows look much sharper. Make note of how long the scene took to render, because before you add more lights to simulate global illumination (bounced light), you're going to take a look at some other shadow types and see not only how they look, but also how long they take to render. Look in the bottom-left corner of the 3ds Max interface to see the last frame-rendering time.

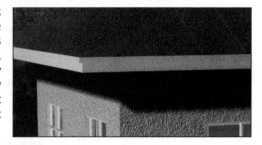

23. In the **Shadows** section of the **General Parameters** rollout, use the drop-down list to change the shadow type from **Shadow Map** to **Adv. Ray Traced**.

24. Render the Camera view. Notice the shadows are more distinct and generally higher quality; however, the scene takes about twice as long to render using **Adv. Ray Traced**. Next, you'll look at a more commonly used shadow type.

25. In the drop-down list, select **Ray Traced Shadows**.

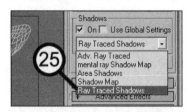

26. Render the Camera view. Notice that this shadow type provides an even cleaner edge than advanced ray traced shadows, although at a hefty price. Using the default settings, the ray traced shadows take approximately five times longer to render than advanced ray traced shadows, and ten times longer than the shadow map. However, you can remedy this quite easily—there is one important setting for ray traced shadows that you should always experiment with: **Max Quadtree Depth**.

27. Click the **Ray Traced Shadow Params** rollout.

28. Change the **Max Quadtree Depth** from the default value of 7 to **8**.

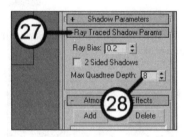

29. Render the Camera view. Once again, in lieu of a complicated explanation at this point, changing this value will significantly reduce render times. In this scene, it cuts the rendering time approximately in half. However, experimentation is required to determine which value (between 8 and 10) will result in the fastest rendering time. If you wish to investigate the explanation of **Max Quadtree Depth** and why it affects rendering times so much, please see the 3ds Max help files on this subject.

30. Change the **Max Quadtree Depth** value to **9** and render the Camera view again. Notice that the rendering time is almost cut in half again. Let's try the highest available value.

31. Change the **Max Quadtree Depth** value to **10** and render the Camera view again.

32. Once again, the rendering time is significantly reduced, approximately 25% more. In the end, ray traced shadows actually render slightly faster than advanced ray traced shadows after optimizing this setting. Regardless of which shadow type you choose, experimentation should always be made with some of the more important settings. Each shadow type has unique advantages and a unique look. For now, though, you'll stick with the **Ray Traced Shadows** option.

Now let's add a few more lights around the corners of the scene to simulate global illumination (bounced light). These lights are often referred to as fill lights.

33. In the Top view, while holding Shift, drag the light to the right edge of the screen to clone it.

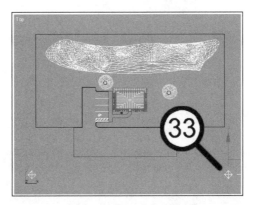

34. Rename the light **Fill01**, leave the cloning method on **Copy**, and click **OK** to complete the Clone command. Make sure the light is positioned in the bottom-right corner of the Top view. The intent here and in the next few steps is to place a light in each corner of the scene so that the scene is illuminated on all sides (as it would be with bounced light).

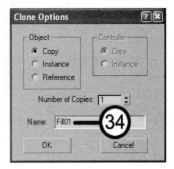

35. In the Top view, hold Shift again, and drag the light you just created to the top-right corner of the screen, as shown in the following image.

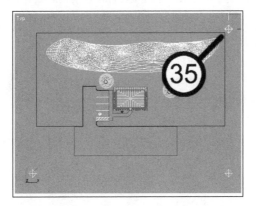

36. Make sure that the light is named **Fill02**, and this time select the **Instance** cloning method.

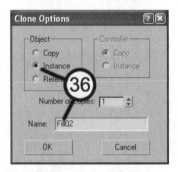

37. In the Top view, hold Shift again, and drag the light you just created to the top-left corner of the screen, as shown in the following image.

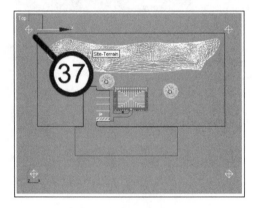

38. Make sure the light is named **Fill03**, and once again select the **Instance** cloning method and click **OK** to complete the command. The last three lights you created will serve as fill lights. Since the cloning method used was **Instance**, changing one light will cause all three to change. Notice also that the four lights are positioned in the four corners of the viewport. This is generally a good place to start your lighting, although the exact number and placement of lights in your scene is just as much an art as it is a science. Once again, experimentation is usually required to achieve the desired results.

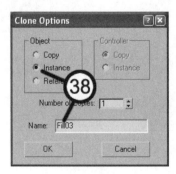

39. In the **General Parameters** rollout, disable the **Shadows** option. This turns off shadows for all the fill lights.

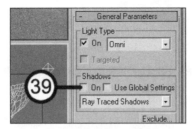

40. Click the **Intensity/Color/Attenuation** rollout to open it.

41. Change the **Multiplier** value from **1.0** to **0.33**. This value simply scales the intensity of the light. A good rule of thumb is to have the sum of the **Multiplier** values for your fill lights equal the value for the main shadow casting light. Again, since all three fill lights are instances, changing one will cause all three to change, so realistically it doesn't matter which fill light you make the change to. So the main light in your scene (**Sun**) uses a multiplier value of **1.0** while the other three fill lights in the scene use a value of **0.33**.

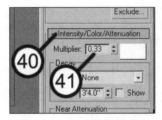

42. Render the Camera view. The rendering should look similar to following figure; however, every monitor is unique, and your rendering may have different brightness and contrast settings.

The standard lights have given you decent lighting, but let's see if you can improve the look by using real global illumination. To do so, you'll need to use a completely different type of light, known as a **photometric light**.

43. Select and delete the four lights in your scene.

44. In the Command panel, click the **Create** icon.

45. Click the **Lights** icon, if not already active.

46. Click the drop-down list and select **Photometric**.

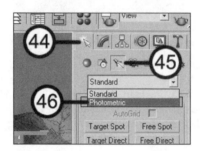

47. Click the **IES Sun** button. This will allow you to create a light type that simulates the Sun. (By the way, IES simply means Illuminating Engineering Society, the governing body that establishes light specifications for engineers to use in calculating illumination).

48. In the Top view, click and hold in the bottom-left corner of the viewport, drag to the center of the viewport, and release the mouse button. This places the light in the corner of the viewport, and a target object for the light to point to in the center of the viewport. When you add this light, your scene will appear extremely bright. However, this is OK. I will discuss it further in a moment.

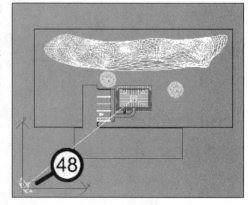

49. In the Left view, with only the light selected (not its target), move the light upward in your scene so that it makes an approximate 45-degree angle with the ground.

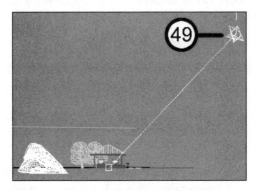

50. In the Command panel, click the **Modify** icon.

51. In the **Sun Parameters** rollout, enable the **Shadows** option.

52. In the shadow type drop-down list, change the shadow type to **Ray Traced Shadows**.

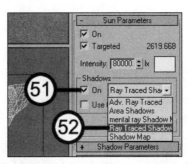

53. Click the **Ray Traced Shadow Params** rollout to open it.

54. Make sure that the **Max Quadtree Depth** is set to **10**; however, when you render your scene in the next step, you may find that your rendering takes an excessively long time to complete. If this happens, you should cancel the rendering process and experiment with a different Max Quadtree Depth setting (7, 8, or 9).

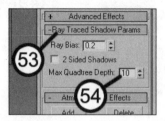

55. Render the Camera view. The image will look extremely overexposed. The IES Sun is a photometric light, and like all photometric lights, it needs exposure control to prevent renderings like this. Even standard lights can benefit from the use of exposure control.

56. Press 8 to open the **Environment and Effects** dialog box.

57. In the **Exposure Control** rollout, click the drop-down list and select **Automatic Exposure Control**. This setting does not provide the most control over your exposure, but it does provide sufficient quality at this point. If you want to see a quick preview of your scene, you can press the **Render Preview** button (located in the **Exposure Control** rollout).

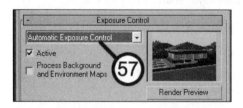

58. Close the **Environment and Effects** dialog box.

59. Render the Camera view. The rendering should look much better now. Notice, however, the high contrast between sunlight and shade. This is because light is not bouncing around from surface to surface as it does in the real world. Since the only source of light is the IES Sun, light can't reach the areas in shadow. To fix this, you could fake radiosity (bounced light) by adding fill lights as you did earlier in the tutorial, or you could use a feature called IES Sky to fake sky-light bouncing around the atmosphere.

60. In the Command panel, click the **Create** icon.

61. Click the **IES Sky** button. This is a photometric light source that simulates atmospheric skylight (light bouncing around the atmosphere). In any scene with such harsh shadows as this, adding an IES Sky light will decrease the effect of light from a single source, and add ambient light to areas in shadow.

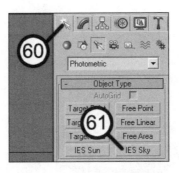

62. In the Top view, click and hold in the bottom-right corner of the viewport, drag to the center of the viewport, and release the mouse button. This places the light in the corner of the viewport, and a target object for the light to point to in the center of the viewport (just like when you created the IES Sun).

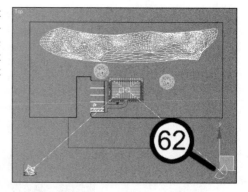

63. In the Left or Front view, with only the light selected (and not its target), move the light upward in your scene so that it makes an approximate 45-degree angle with the ground (just like you did with the IES Sun).

64. Render the Camera view. The rendering should have improved drastically with the addition of the skylight. Now that you've used this method to simulate bounced light, you'll actually include radiosity in your scene. First, turn off the IES Sky light so that the effect of radiosity is easy to see.

65. Right-click inside the active viewport, and turn off the light by clicking **Light On**.

66. Press F10 to open the **Render Scene** dialog box.

67. Click the **Advanced Lighting** tab.

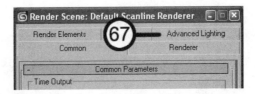

68. In the **Select Advanced Lighting** rollout, click the drop-down list and select **Radiosity**. This tells 3ds Max to calculate radiosity (bounced light) in your rendering.

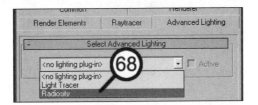

69. In the **Radiosity Processing Parameters** rollout, type **50** in the **Initial Quality** field. The default value of 85% is a good setting for final production renderings; however, 50% is sufficient for test renders, and takes much less time to calculate. You could even go as low as 30% and achieve reasonable test renders.

70. Click the **Start** button. This begins the process of calculating radiosity. It will take a minute or two for 3ds Max to complete the calculations.

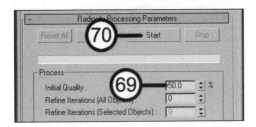

71. When the radiosity solution is complete (the blue radiosity-processing bar will stop, and the Camera viewport will show a change in illumination), render the scene. Notice that radiosity illuminates areas of shadow above the windows; however, there are shadows in the scene that didn't receive as much illumination—for example, the shadows of the trees. In addition, there is very little color bouncing from one surface to another (a significant benefit of good radiosity solutions). Notice also the irregularities on the left side of the roof. There are numerous settings that can significantly change and drastically improve the quality of the rendering, which will be discussed in the following chapters. Good solutions, however, can take a long time to calculate (several hours for very large scenes). Fortunately, a solution only needs to be calculated once, not for each individual frame of an animation.

For now, though, you'll disable radiosity and turn on the skylight in your scene (which was previously off).

72. In the **Select Advanced Lighting** rollout, discard the radiosity solution by clicking the drop-down list and selecting **<no lighting plug-in>**. The Camera viewport shows a change in illumination. If you want to disable radiosity but keep the solution you calculated for later use, deselect the **Active** option; however, keeping the solution will cause the file size to increase dramatically.

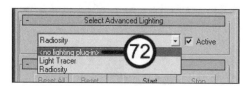

73. Select the IES Sky object (**Sky01**).

74. Right-click in the active viewport and click **Light On** in the quad menu. The skylight object is now turned on again.

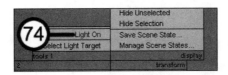

75. Save your file as MyQuickStart04.max for use in the next Quick Start tutorial.

This concludes Quick Start 4. This tutorial has shown you a small sampling of the incredible power of lighting in 3ds Max, and how important good lighting is to your final rendering. With standard lights, you can fake global illumination and achieve fairly good renderings. With photometric lights, you can add greater realism and achieve real-world light characteristics, but when combined with radiosity, you can achieve a level of realism that is otherwise not possible. In the next tutorial, you'll finally put things in motion and prepare an animation for rendering.

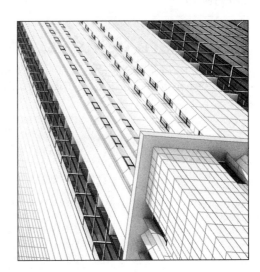

Chapter 10

BASIC LIGHTING

If you ask any veteran 3ds Max user what the most important element of a good 3D scene is, you'll always get the same answer—lighting. Good lighting can make a scene with bad modeling or materials look good. Likewise, poor lighting can make a scene with good modeling and materials look bad. Lighting can have a dramatic effect on the composition of your scene. It can convey a specific mood or inspire the viewer to feel a particular way. In fact, many competitions in the 3D world are won or lost by the application of lighting.

This chapter deals with the principles and procedures of standard lights, which are lights that are not based on real-world light properties. Although standard lights do not incorporate the properties of real-world lights, it is possible to set up standard lights in your scenes so well that they simulate real-world lights and give your scenes a photorealistic look.

Chapter 11 covers photometric lights, which are lights that simulate real-world properties. With photometric lighting, you can see what your interior scene looks like illuminated by a single 100-watt lightbulb, multiple 4-foot cove fluorescent lights, or any number of real-world light types. The last chapter on lighting, Chapter 12, provides an introduction to global illumination, which is a system that uses physically based lighting to accurately depict the way light bounces off objects, and cumulatively affects the lighting and shading of surrounding objects. By the end of these three chapters on lighting, you will have the ability to light your scenes in a photorealistic manner.

Standard lights vs. photometric lights

3ds Max provides two types of lights, which can be accessed through the drop-down list of the **Lights** section in the **Create** panel (Figure 10-1): standard lights and photometric lights.

Figure 10-1. The two light types: standard and photometric

Standard lights are not physically based, and therefore do not exhibit real-world lighting properties. With standard lights, you can control attenuation, which is a term used to describe how light fades as it moves away from its source. You can specify with great precision where a light begins and ends its attenuation, or whether or not a light attenuates at all. In addition, standard lights use a multiplier value of 1.0 to represent a fully bright light, and a color swatch to determine the light's color.

Photometric lights, on the other hand, are physically based, and therefore exhibit real-world lighting properties. Attenuation and color in photometric lights are automatically calculated and are based on the type of real-world light source used. Because photometric lights are physically based, a scene must be built at the proper scale for the lighting to be accurate. In the real world, a single 100-watt light-bulb could light a small 10-by-10-foot room, but if that room was built out of scale and was as big as a stadium, that same light might be unnoticeable.

Which type of light you decide to use in your 3D scenes depends on several different things. If you can successfully use standard lights to accurately create the realism your project calls for, then standard lights might be the best option. However, if you are trying to simulate very accurately what a scene looks like with a particular type of real-world light, then photometric lights are the way to go. If you want to maintain precise control over the attenuation of a light to achieve a unique effect, then you need to use standard lights. If you want to incorporate some advanced lighting procedures such as global illumination, then again photometric lights will be the best option. Whatever your project calls for, 3ds Max provides the power and versatility to meet any type of lighting need.

The standard light source types

There are three standard light source types in 3ds Max: **direct lights**, **omni lights**, and **spotlights**, as shown in Figure 10-2. Each source type has unique characteristics and is suited for different uses. Depending on the scene type, any one of these source types may be best suited to serve as the primary light source.

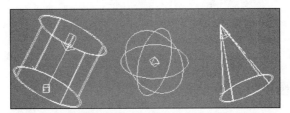

Figure 10-2. The standard light source types: direct (left), omni (center), and spotlight (right)

There is an additional source type known as **skylight**, indicated in Figure 10-1; however, skylight is designed for use specifically with Light Tracer, which is not covered in this book. Light Tracer is a global illumination system that offers good rendering results but is little used in a production environment because of its long rendering times.

Figure 10-1 also shows the availability of two other standard light source types: **mR Area Omni** and **mR Area Spot**. These two types are for use with the mental ray renderer, which is not covered in this book. These two types are likewise not covered.

Omni lights

Omni lights cast light in all directions from a single point. They are probably most widely used in all types of lamps, from street lamps to desk lamps; but under the right controls, they can even be used to effectively simulate sunlight. Placed far enough away from the objects in a scene, an omni light's rays can appear to be parallel, as shown in the left image of Figure 10-3. In this way, it can simulate sunlight, which strikes the Earth with parallel rays, since the Sun is so far away from Earth. However, since the light of an omni light source emanates from a singe infinitely small point, an omni light placed close to the objects in a scene will casts shadows in all directions, as shown in the right image. The sphere in the center of the right image is not the light itself, but rather an object simulating a light source.

Figure 10-3. An omni light creating parallel shadows (left) and non-parallel shadows (right)

Spotlights

Spotlights cast light in a specific direction from a single point, as shown in Figure 10-4. They are probably the most versatile of the three light source types. They can be used in numerous ways, from the headlights of a car to the track lights found on the ceiling of a residence; from the light shaped by a lamp shade to the spotlight that illuminates a tree from below at night.

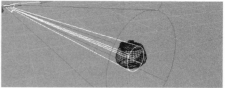

Figure 10-4. The spotlight

Direct lights

Direct lights cast parallel light rays in a single direction, and are therefore most widely used in simulating sunlight. Likewise, the shadows cast by direct lights are always parallel; they will not spread, regardless of how close the lights are to the objects. Unlike omni lights and spotlights, direct lights do not emanate from a single point, but rather from a flat circular area defined by the user, as shown in Figure 10-5.

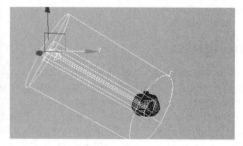

Figure 10-5. The direct light

Creating lights

Before you place your first light in a scene, 3ds Max places two default lights to provide light to any objects that you create. Otherwise, you wouldn't see anything you create until placing your first light. One default light is positioned above and to the left, and another is placed below and to the left. As soon as you create your first light, 3ds Max removes these two default lights. If you delete all your lights from a scene, the two default lights return.

There are three ways to create, position, and orient lights in 3ds Max. Omni lights require a single click of the mouse in a viewport to create and place. They do not require any other steps to be oriented because omni lights cast light in all directions. **Free** and **target lights**, which can be used for spotlights or direct lights, require a specific orientation because their light is cast in a specific direction. Both types are identical except for one major characteristic. **Free lights** have only one component: the light; whereas **target lights** have two components: the light and the target. Target lights are always oriented to face the target, and because the target can move independently from the light, the target can be animated. The left image in Figure 10-6 shows a target spotlight and the right image shows a free spotlight. Notice that both images are the same except for the small box (target) near the center of the left image. Target lights always face their targets, so moving this target changes the direction that the light faces. To change the direction of a stationary free light, you can apply the rotate transform or use one of the viewport navigation control icons listed in Table 10-1.

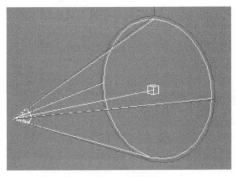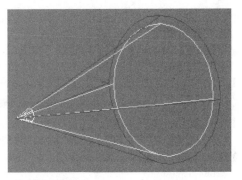

Figure 10-6. The target spotlight (left) and the free spotlight (right)

Free lights and target lights are both light types that can be used in the creation of spotlights and direct lights. The creation process for free lights is the same whether you want to create a spotlight or a direct light. Likewise, the creation process for target lights is the same regardless of which light type you want to create.

To create a free light using the Command panel, click **Create ➤ Lights ➤ Free Spot** or **Free Direct**, and click once in any viewport. The light will face the direction of the view unless the viewport is displaying a User, Perspective, Camera, or Target Light view, in which case the light will face in the negative z direction.

To create a target light, click **Target Spot** or **Target Direct**, click and hold inside a viewport, and drag the mouse to position the target. Release the mouse button to place the target.

Sometimes, you might find it helpful to see a view of your scene from the perspective of one of your lights. Once a light is created, you can easily switch a viewport to the view through the light's perspective by right-clicking the viewport name, selecting **Views** from the menu, and selecting the light's name from the next menu. Seeing the view from a light is only possible with a direct light or spotlight.

Creating lights

This exercise demonstrates how to create free and target lights.

1. Reset 3ds Max.
2. In Perspective view, create a teapot of any size.
3. Within the **Create** panel, click the **Lights** icon. The **Object Type** rollout appears with eight buttons available.
4. Click the **Free Spot** button.
5. In Front view, click, hold, and drag to create the light, and move it into a position centered on the teapot. Release the mouse button to place the light.
6. Right-click within the active view to end the light-creation command.
7. Using the move and rotate transforms, position and orient the light so that it's above and away from the teapot, and pointing down at it. Notice the highlights move around on the teapot as the light is moved.

8. Right-click the Perspective view name, select **Views** from the menu, and select **Fspot01** from the next menu.

9. In any other view, apply a couple of transforms to the free spotlight to see their effects on the newly created light view.

10. Press Delete to delete the light. Notice that the light view changes back to Perspective view.

11. In the Command panel, click the **Target Spot** button.

12. In the Top view, click, hold, and drag to create the light, and move the light target into a position centered on the teapot. Release the mouse button to place the light target.

13. Right-click the Perspective view name, select **Views** from the menu, and select **Spot01** from the next menu.

14. In any other view, apply a couple of transforms to the target spotlight and the target to see their effects on the newly created light view.

Viewport navigation controls

When you create a light view, the viewport navigation controls in the bottom-right corner of the screen change to account for the source of the new view. Table 10-1 shows each of the new icons available when a light view is active.

Table 10-1. Light view icons in the viewport navigation controls

Icon	Name	Description
	Dolly Light	Moves the light along the axis in which the light is pointing
	Dolly Target	Moves the target along the axis in which the light is pointing
	Dolly Light+Target	Moves light and target along the axis in which the camera is pointing
	Light Hotspot	Changes the light's **Hotspot/Beam** diameter value (discussed later in this chapter)
	Light Falloff	Changes the light's **Falloff/Field** diameter value (discussed later in this chapter)
	Roll Light	Spins the light along its local z axis
	Orbit Light	Rotates the light around the target
	Pan Light	Rotates the target around the light

Some additional notes about the viewport navigation controls are as follows:

- By holding down the mouse scroll wheel, you can execute the Truck Light command without having to click the icon. The Truck Light command works just like the pan command and can even be accessed through the same viewport navigation icon.

- By holding down the Shift key, you can constrain light movement to a single axis.

- By holding down the Ctrl key, you can magnify the effects of the viewport navigation controls.

Light placement

In addition to the ability to place lights using transforms and viewport navigation controls, 3ds Max gives you the opportunity to place lights precisely using two other helpful features: Align Camera and Place Highlight.

Align Camera

The Align Camera feature aligns a camera, or in this case a light, to the normal of a specific face on a specific object. This allows you to precisely position and orient an existing light so that it is directly in front of and facing a particular object.

To use this feature, select a light as shown in the top-left image of Figure 10-7. Click and hold the **Align** icon in the **Main** toolbar, and select the **Align Camera** icon from the flyout. Click and hold on top of any face inside the active viewport. A blue normal arrow will appear on the face that your mouse is over, as shown in the top-right image. Once you let go, the selected light will move directly in front of and aligned with the normal of the face you choose, as shown in the bottom-left image. The image on the bottom-right shows the new view from the selected light.

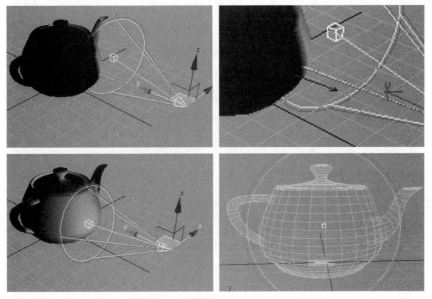

Figure 10-7. The Align Camera feature used to align a light

Place Highlight

Another tool that you can use to position lights in your scene is the Place Highlight command. This feature is similar to the Align Camera feature, except that Place Highlight moves the selected light to a position that causes a highlight to appear in the current viewport. This does not align the light to a face normal as does the Align Camera feature; it simply moves the light so that it provides the maximum possible highlight in the area of the object that you move your cursor over. Also, instead of showing you just a blue arrow to align the camera with, the Place Highlight command displays the light in its new position as you move your cursor from one face to another.

The icon for the Place Highlight command is located directly above the **Align Camera** icon within the **Align** flyout. To use this command, click the **Place Highlight** icon and click and hold the left mouse button on top of any face inside the active viewport. A blue normal arrow will appear on the face that your mouse is over, and the light will move into position. If you move the cursor over other faces, the light will follow along and update its position. To finish the command, release the left mouse button and the light will remain in position, aligned with the normal of the last face your mouse was over.

Positioning lights

This exercise demonstrates how to use the Align Camera and Place Highlight features to position lights effectively within your scenes.

1. Reset 3ds Max.

2. Create a sphere of any size within the Perspective view.

3. Create a free spotlight anywhere in your scene.

4. Click and hold the **Align** icon to reveal the flyout icons, and click the **Align Camera** icon.

5. Click and hold the left mouse button on top of any face of the sphere inside the active viewport. A blue normal arrow will appear on the face that your mouse is over. Release the mouse button and the light will move into position.

6. Click and hold the **Align** icon again to reveal the flyout icons, and click the **Place Highlight** icon.

7. Click and hold the left mouse button on top of any face of the sphere inside the active viewport. A blue normal arrow will appear on the face that your mouse is over, and the selected light will align itself with this normal and be positioned in the location that maximizes the highlight. Release the mouse button and the light will move into position.

Light parameters

When an omni light is created, five new rollouts appear (as shown in Figure 10-8), with the last one specifically geared toward the type of shadows used. When a spotlight or direct light is created, the same rollouts appear, as well as an additional rollout geared toward the type of light source used. This section of the chapter covers each of these parameters, highlighting those parameters that should receive special attention.

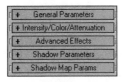

Figure 10-8. The common standard light rollouts

When you switch to the **Modify** panel, three additional rollouts appear; one for atmospheric effects, which is covered in Chapter 18, and two for mental ray, which is not covered in this book.

The General Parameters rollout

When a light is created, it is automatically turned on. At the top of the **General Parameters** rollout (shown in the left image of Figure 10-9) is an option to turn the light off, which can be used at any time. This same option can be found in the **Object Properties** menu or in the quad menu of the light. A light that is turned off will show as black in the viewports.

To the right of the **On/Off** option is a drop-down list that can be used to change a light from one source type to another. If a spotlight or directional light is used, an option to enable or disable a target becomes selectable, along with the distance in scene units from the light to the target. This distance has no effect on the lighting in your scene; it serves only as a guide.

Figure 10-9. The General Parameters rollout

In the **Shadows** section is an option to enable shadows for the selected light, which is disabled by default. Another option allows you to use global settings to determine the characteristics of the light. This is a great option when you want to maintain consistent settings across several lights without having to instance the lights. This option applies the same settings to all the lights, so that changing a setting for one changes the same settings for all the lights that have this option enabled.

The **Exclude** button at the bottom of the rollout gives you the ability to exclude select objects from a light's effect. When you click this button, the **Exclude/Include** dialog box appears, as shown on the left in Figure 10-10. By default, objects are included in a light's effect—however, you can also selectively keep objects from being illuminated by the light, or you can keep them from casting shadows caused by the light, or both. In Figure 10-10, **Torus Knot01** is excluded from the shadow casting caused by the light, and the result is that the object doesn't cast shadows.

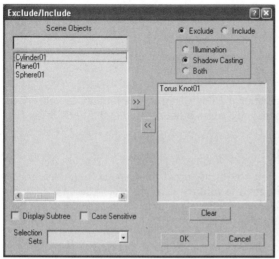

Figure 10-10. Excluding an object from shadow casting

Also in the **Shadows** section of the rollout is one of the most important settings involving lights. The shadow type drop-down list, shown in the right image of Figure 10-9, provides all the available shadow types that can be used with the selected light. Knowing which shadow type to use for any given light is critically important. The different shadow types provide a wide range in quality, use, appearance, rendering time, and RAM used.

Shadow map

Shadow map is the default shadow type. It is not a true shadow, but rather a faked shadow created by mapping an image onto the objects behind the object casting the shadow. The resolution of the applied map, which is set in the **Shadow Map Params** rollout, determines how accurate the shadows are. Because it is a faked shadow and not as accurate as other shadow types, the shadow map produces soft shadows rather than crisp, hard shadows. These edges become more erratic and degraded as the light is moved farther away from the object casting shadows, or as the resolution of the map is decreased. The left image in Figure 10-11 shows a teapot casting decent shadows with a light positioned very close by. In the right image, the light is moved far away from the teapot, resulting in poor shadows. Later in the chapter, you will learn how to correct for this degraded quality.

Figure 10-11. A shadow map with a light source close by (left) and far away (right)

The greatest advantage of this shadow type is that it is often faster than any other type. Some disadvantages are that this shadow type uses a large amount of RAM and it doesn't respect transparency. An object with transparency applied, such as glass, will cast the same shadow as a fully opaque object, as shown in Figure 10-12.

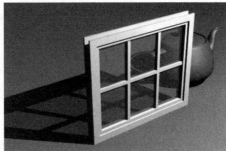

Figure 10-12. Transparent objects not supported by shadow maps (left) and those supported by other shadow types (right)

Using shadow map lights and the various light source types

This exercise demonstrates some of the characteristics of shadow map lights and the three different light source types.

1. Reset 3ds Max.

2. In the Perspective view, create a plane with a length and width of 10'.

3. In the Perspective view, create a teapot with a radius of 1' and center the teapot on the plane.

4. Click the **Zoom Extents Selected** icon.

5. In the Command panel, select **Create ➤ Geometry ➤ Lights ➤ Omni**.

6. In the Top view, click near the bottom-right corner of the plane to place the light.

7. Raise the light 10' above the plane. This places the light in a good location to cast a shadow that can be easily seen.

8. Right-click inside the Perspective view (to make it active) and click the **Quick Render** button in the **Main** toolbar. The teapot renders without any shadows.

9. Click the **Modify** tab, and in the **General Parameters** rollout, enable the **Shadows On** option. This enables shadows with the default shadow map type.

10. Click the **Quick Render** button again. Now the teapot casts shadows; however, notice how poor the shadows appear to be.

11. Move the light to about twice the distance from the teapot, and render the Perspective view. Notice that the shadows are now even lower quality. Later in the chapter, you'll use the available shadow parameters to improve the quality of the shadows.

12. Use the **Undo** icon to return the light to its original location.

13. In the **General Parameters** rollout, click the **Light Type** drop-down list and select **Spot**. Notice that the omni light changes to a spotlight with a cone pointing in the negative z direction.

14. In the **Main** toolbar, click and hold the **Align** flyout and select the **Place Highlight** icon.

15. Click and hold on the teapot and move the cursor around the surface of the teapot. Release the mouse button when you are happy with the placement of the highlight. Notice that the light is moved into a position where it places a highlight on the teapot in the location you selected.

16. Render the scene again. The spotlight is now casting light on the teapot.

17. Click the **Light Type** drop-down list and change the light type to **Directional**.

18. Render the scene again.

19. Keep this scene open or save it for use in the next tutorial.

Area shadows

This shadow type can be applied to any light type and is often used to simulate shadows cast by large light sources, such as stadium lights or long rows of track ceiling lights. It produces area shadows using a virtual light of a specific size and shape defined by the user. In the **Area Shadows** rollout that appears when this shadow type is used, you specify the size, shape, and quality of the shadow, as well as how the shadow is dispersed. The areas shadow type produces soft edges that become softer as the light is moved farther away from the objects casting shadows. When used properly, this shadow type can produce a unique and very realistic look; however, it often takes a great deal of time and experimentation with the many settings to produce the desired look. Figure 10-13 shows an example of the unique shadow effects capable with area shadows.

Figure 10-13. An example of area shadows

Some advantages of this type of shadow are that it supports transparency and opacity mapping, and uses very little RAM. A major disadvantage, however, is that it can take a very long time to render—even more so with higher-quality settings.

Raytraced shadows

As the name implies, raytraced shadows are generated by tracing a sample of rays as they leave a light source and interact with the object casting the shadow. Raytraced shadows are much more accurate and usually more realistic than shadow maps or area shadows, and always produce a hard edge. When used improperly, however, the hard edge that comes with raytraced shadows can produce an unrealistic look. Since raytraced shadows are not generated using a map, you do not have to adjust resolution as you do for shadow maps and area maps. Figure 10-14 shows an example of the hard edges that result from using raytraced shadows.

Figure 10-14. An example of raytraced shadows

Some advantages of raytraced shadows are that they support transparency and opacity maps, and they are extremely accurate. The two biggest disadvantages are that raytraced shadows can significantly increase render times and they do not allow for soft shadows.

Advanced raytraced shadows

Advanced raytraced shadows are a personal favorite of mine for many scene types, especially those with an extremely large polygon count, or for long animations with a short production deadline. They combine the best characteristics of all the available shadow types. Like raytraced shadows, they are very accurate and physically realistic, meaning that they take into account an object's physical and material attributes. They support transparency and opacity maps, and unlike raytraced maps, can be modified to produce soft edges. They also use a small amount of RAM and are usually much faster to render than raytraced shadows. They can even be used to produce a look similar to area shadows if you use some of the antialiasing options found in the **Adv. Ray Traced Params** rollout. In Figure 10-15, you can see that advanced raytraced shadows can be made to look similar, and sometimes indiscernible from raytraced shadows.

Figure 10-15. An example of advanced raytraced shadows producing results identical to raytraced shadows

Using area, raytraced, and advanced raytraced shadows

This exercise demonstrates some of the differences between the different shadow types.

1. Continue from the last tutorial or go to the 3dsMax8\Scenes\Friends_of_Ed directory and open the file Ch10-01.max.

2. Select the directional light.

3. Click the **Modify** icon.

4. In the **General Parameters** rollout, click the **Shadow Type** drop-down list and change the shadow type from **Shadow Map** to **Area Shadows**.

5. Render the Perspective view. Notice the soft-and-speckled appearance to the shadows.

6. Repeat step 4 using the **Ray Traced Shadows** and **Adv. Ray Traced Shadows** options.

7. Keep this scene open, or save it for use in the next tutorial.

The Intensity/Color/Attenuation rollout

This rollout provides direct control over a light's intensity, color, and attenuation (see Figure 10-16).

Figure 10-16. The Intensity/Color/Attenuation rollout

Intensity

The intensity of a light is a measure of the light's strength, or ability to illuminate a scene. It is directly controlled by the **Multiplier** setting, which by default is set to **1.0**. Doubling this value doubles the intensity of the light, as shown in Figure 10-17.

 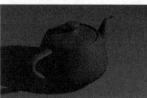 

Figure 10-17. Multiplier settings of 1.0 (left), 0.5 (middle), and 2.0 (right)

Color

You can change the color a light produces using the color swatch in this rollout, much like adding a colored filter to a light. The color of the light in your scene can have a dramatic impact on the mood that your scene inspires. Adjusting the color slightly can also add a great deal of realism. For example, bright sunlight has a yellow hue to it, so adding a small amount of yellow light to a scene can make a daytime exterior rendering look more realistic. For a scene that occurs during a sunset or sunrise, you might try changing the color of your light to incorporate a small amount of red or orange.

Decay

In this section of the rollout, you can specify the rate at which the intensity of your light decays, or diminishes, with distance. In the real world, light decays the farther away it gets from its source. It does so at a specific rate, which is equal to the inverse square of the distance. In the **Type** drop-down list are options for setting decay at the real-world setting of **Inverse Square**, at a more subtle setting of **Inverse**, or at the default setting of **None**. If you are trying to simulate sunlight, you shouldn't allow your light to decay because the light that strikes the earth is constant over the small amount of area that your scenes occupy. On most other light sources, decay is a good option to use, although you will probably find that setting a light to **Inverse Decay** will cause too much decay and not allow your scene to be illuminated enough. This is because in the real world, there is so much more ambient light and radiosity. For most lights, I have found the **Inverse** setting to produce a more realistic look.

You can also specify a start distance for the decay of light. By setting a value of 120 units, or 10', your light won't start decaying until a distance of 10 feet from the light. By enabling the **Show** option, you can see this distance pictorially in the viewport.

Attenuation

Attenuation is another term to describe the diminishing of light with distance, and in 3ds Max, attenuation settings give you another way to control the intensity of light with distance.

The **Near Attenuation Start** value specifies the distance at which the light begins to produce illumination. The **End** value specifies the distance at which light reaches full brightness after fading in from zero illumination at the **Start** distance.

The **Far Attenuation Start** value specifies the distance at which light begins to fade out from full illumination, and the **End** value specifies the distance at which the light is completely diminished.

Figure 10-18 shows an example of near and far attenuation. In this example, a direct light is set up to cast light in the direction of five teapots that are lined up in a row. As the settings in the rollout indicate, **Near Attenuation** and **Far Attenuation** have been enabled. The **Near Attenuation Start** value is set to **20.0**, which means the light doesn't begin until 20 units away from the source. The top-left image shows that the first teapot on the far right is positioned before the **Near Attenuation Start** distance and is therefore not illuminated at all. The **Near Attenuation End** value is set to **40.0**, which means that the light reaches full intensity at 40 units from the source. The second teapot from the right is positioned between the **Near Attenuation Start** and **Near Attenuation End** distances, and is therefore only partially illuminated. The **Far Attenuation Start** value is set to **60.0**, which means that the light begins to diminish at 60 units from the source. The third teapot is positioned between the **Near Attenuation End** and **Far Attenuation Start** distances, and is therefore fully illuminated. The **Far Attenuation End** value is set to **80.0**, which means that the light is completely diminished at a distance of 80 units from the source. The fourth teapot is positioned between the **Far Attenuation Start** and **Far Attenuation End** distances, which means it is partially illuminated. The fifth teapot is positioned after the **Far Attenuation End** distance, and is therefore not illuminated at all.

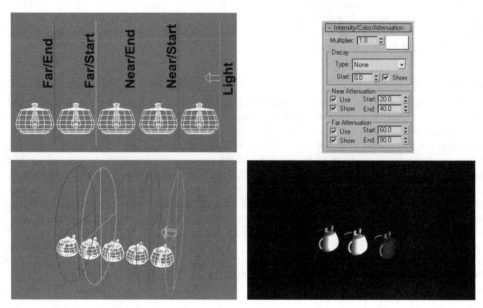

Figure 10-18. An example of near and far attenuation

To enable **Near Attenuation** or **Far Attenuation**, enable the **Use** option for either one. You can enable the **Show** option to graphically see in the viewports where the attenuation distances lie in relation to other objects in your scene.

Working with intensity, color, and attenuation settings

This exercise demonstrates the effect of changing the intensity, color, and attenuation settings of a light.

1. Continue from the last tutorial or go to the 3dsMax8\Scenes\Friends_of_Ed directory and open the file Ch10-02.max.

2. Select the directional light.

3. Render the Perspective view.

4. Click the **Modify** tab, if it's not already active.

5. Open the **Intensity/Color/Attenuation** rollout and change the intensity from **1.0** to **2.0**. Notice the shaded view reflects the change of the light's intensity.

6. Render the Perspective view again. Notice the light is twice as intense.

7. Click the color swatch next to the **Intensity** setting and select any color from the color selector. Notice the shaded view reflects the change again. Close the color selector.

8. Render the Perspective view again. Notice the objects in the scene take on the color of the light.

9. In the **Far Attenuation** section, enable the **Use** option for far attenuation.

10. Right-click the slider arrows next to the **End** field of **Far Attenuation**. Notice both the **Start** and **End** settings are changed to **0**.

11. Render the Perspective view. There is nothing visible because the light is set to diminish completely at a distance of 0' from the light.

12. Increase the **Start** setting of **Far Attenuation** until the visual guide in the viewport passes the teapot.

13. Render the Perspective view again, and you should be able to see the teapot again. If not, increase the **Start** value until the guide is clearly past the teapot's position.

14. Keep this scene open or save it for use in the next tutorial.

The Advanced Effects rollout

In the **Affect Surfaces** section of this rollout (Figure 10-19) are a couple of options that allow you to adjust the contrast and soften the edge between diffuse and ambient areas of the surface. I have never found a use for these features and have always left them at their default value of 0.0.

Figure 10-19. The Advanced Effects rollout

In the **Projector Map** section of this rollout is an extremely useful feature for architectural visualizations. With the Projector Map feature, you can use a light as a projector to project the image of a map or animation onto the surface of objects in your scene, as shown in Figure 10-20. The projector feature works the same way as a projector you would find in a movie theater, in which an image or animation is placed in front of a light and is projected onto a surface.

To load a map into a light, simply click the button labeled **None** and select a map type from the Material / Map Browser. Doing so will enable the Project Map feature automatically so that you don't have to enable the **Map** option. Once you load a map, you can drag and drop it into a material sample slot in the **Material Editor**. When you drag and drop a map to or from the **Material Editor**, you are asked if you would like to make a copy or instance of the map. You should always choose the Instance option so that changes you make to the map in the **Material Editor** cause the projector map to change as well. You can also drag and drop an image directly from the **Asset Browser** or a map from the Material / Map Browser.

Figure 10-20. Using a projector light to simulate a real-life projector

Another practical example of the use of a projector map is in the simulation of shadows. The left two images of Figure 10-21 show a scene with a simple plane that is mapped with the image of a tree. Since the tree is just an image and not a 3D object, the shadow cast by the tree would just be the shadow of the plane. To remedy this, the **Cast Shadows** option is disabled for the plane (tree), and the black-and-white image of the tree canopy (far-right image) is loaded into the projector map slot of the light, which is positioned just above the image of the tree. The multiplier of the projector light is then changed to –0.5, which causes light to be taken out of the area defined by the white portion of the tree canopy image. Negative multiplier values cause light to be removed from the objects hit by the light. The more negative the value, the darker the shadows.

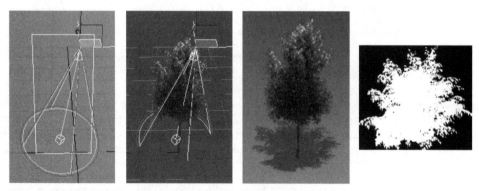

Figure 10-21. Using a projector map to simulate the shadow of a tree

The Shadow Parameters rollout

The **Shadow Parameters** rollout, shown in Figure 10-22, provides settings that control the look of shadows.

Figure 10-22. The Shadow Parameters rollout

You can use the color swatch to change the color of the shadows or simply change the strength of the shadows. The left image in Figure 10-23 shows a teapot casting a shadow created with the default shadow parameters. In the middle image, the color swatch is set to a gray color, which lightens the shadows significantly. The right image shows even lighter shadows created with a pure white color.

Figure 10-23. Using the color swatch to change shadow strength

The **Dens.** field to the right of the color swatch changes the density of the shadow, which is simply another way to lighten or darken shadows. Changing the density from its default value of 1.0 to 0.5 will cause the shadows to be half as dark.

The strength, or darkness, of shadows is a very important setting for the main shadow casting light in your scene. Very dark shadows imply a bright, sunny day; however, if other elements in your scene don't support a bright sunny day, then your scene's realism will suffer.

Below the **Dens.** field is a button you can use to load a map into the shadow of an object. In Figure 10-24, the image of a tile floor is loaded into the shadow of the teapot, producing a strange but unique effect. The practicality of this feature may be limited, but it's a good one to keep in your bag of tricks.

Figure 10-24. Loading a map into the shadow of a teapot

The **Light Affects Shadow Color** feature blends the light's color with the shadow color, which usually produces results that can be achieved by changing the other shadow parameters discussed.

The **Atmospheric Shadows** section of the **Shadow Parameters** rollout deals with atmospheric effects, which are covered in Chapter 18.

> ### Changing the color and strength of shadows

This exercise demonstrates how to change the color and strength of shadows using the settings in the **Shadow Parameters** rollout.

1. Continue from the last tutorial or go to the 3dsMax8\Scenes\Friends_of_Ed directory and open the file Ch10-03.max.
2. Select the directional light.
3. Render the Perspective view.
4. In the Command panel, click the **Modify** icon.
5. Open the **Shadow Parameters** rollout.
6. In the **Object Shadows** section, click the color swatch, select any color from the color selector, and click Close.
7. Render the Perspective view. Notice that the shadow takes on the color you selected.
8. Use the **Undo** icon to return the color to black.
9. Change the **Dens.** setting to **0.5**.
10. Render the Perspective view. Notice that the shadow is now only as half as strong as it was.
11. Use the **Undo** icon to return the shadow to full strength.
12. Keep this scene open or save it for use in the next tutorial.

Rollouts for specific shadow types

The following sections will describe the various rollouts for using the different shadow types.

The Shadow Map Params rollout

The **Shadow Map Params** rollout, shown in Figure 10-25, appears whenever the selected light uses shadow maps. A shadow map is simply an image of a shadow mapped onto objects that receive shadows. The size or resolution of the mapped image, in pixels, is a major factor in the accuracy and look of the shadow.

Figure 10-25. The Shadow Map Params rollout

The top image in Figure 10-26 shows a column with a shadow created with a shadow map. 3ds Max computes this shadow by creating a mapped image of the object from the perspective of the light. The **Size** value in the **Shadow Map Params** rollout specifies how many pixels squared the image will be. A larger **Size** value results in greater resolution and accuracy of the mapped image. The bottom three images show the effect of increasing the **Size** value. As the **Size** increases, the number of pixels used to make up the shadow increases, thereby allowing more accurate shadow edges.

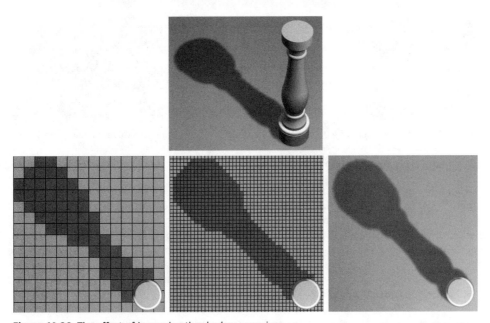

Figure 10-26. The effect of increasing the shadow map size

It is important to note that when using shadow maps, the quality of the shadows depends directly on not only the size of the shadow map, but the distance of the light to the objects receiving the shadows. Moving your light farther away from the objects in your scene will cause the shadow map to be less accurate.

Although shadow maps are not my favorite shadow types, when I do use them I always set the **Size** value to at least **2000**. This usually produces good results and a fairly clean-edged shadow, even when the light is at a reasonable distance. You could use higher values, but shadow maps consume a large amount of RAM. At some point, you will be using too much RAM, and you may even run out. If your light fails to produce any shadows at all, you will know that you've set the **Size** value too high.

Also within the **Shadow Map Params** rollout is a setting for map bias, which moves the shadow toward or away from shadow-casting objects. The **Bias** setting is used to prevent shadow-bleeding and to correct problems when objects cast shadows on themselves. These problems are usually minimal or insignificant, and this setting can usually be left at its default value of **1.0**.

Sample Range specifies how much area within the shadow is sampled, or averaged. This directly affects how soft the shadow's edge is. The left image of Figure 10-27 shows the column's shadow with the **Sample Range** set to its default value of **4.0**. In the middle image, the **Sample Range** is reduced to its minimum value of **0.1** to emphasize the effect of the setting. The right image shows the effect of doubling the **Sample Range** value to **8.0**. The **Sample Range** can be a very critical setting when you are trying to soften the edge of your shadows, which become harder when you increase the shadow map's **Size** value. As a side note, notice in the middle image that there are a few places where the column casts a shadow on itself, and the result is poor. However, this is only noticeable because the **Sample Range** is set to its minimum value. When the **Sample Range** is set to a reasonable value, the effect is unnoticeable.

Figure 10-27. Sample ranges of 4.0, the default value (left); 0.1, the minimum value (middle); and 8.0 (right)

Absolute Map Bias is not an option you should ever have to worry about, and it will not be covered in this book.

Use the **2 Sided Shadows** option whenever you are trying to correct problems in your shadows that exist due to certain faces on your objects not casting shadows. This occurs when the normal of a face is oriented away from the light and not visible from the light's perspective. The example in Figure 10-28 shows the typical teapot in its default state, in which light passes through the area surrounding the lid without detecting a surface. Because of this, shadows are not cast and the effect is very noticeable. To correct this problem, enable the **2 Sided Shadows** option, and shadows will be cast for faces that are oriented away from the light, as shown in the right image.

Figure 10-28. The 2 Sided Shadows option disabled (left) and enabled (right)

Changing the quality of a shadow map

This exercise demonstrates how to change the resolution of a map to improve a shadow's quality.

1. Continue from the last tutorial or go to the 3dsMax8\Scenes\Friends_of_Ed directory and open the file Ch10-04.max.

2. Select the directional light.

3. Go to the Modify panel, and in the **General Parameters** rollout, click the drop-down list and change the shadow type to **Shadow Map** (if not already set).

4. Render the Perspective view.

5. Open the **Shadow Map Params** rollout.

6. Change the **Size** to **100** and render the Perspective view. Notice that the shadows have blurred significantly.

7. Change the **Size** to **1000** and render the Perspective view. Notice that the shadows become much sharper.

8. Keep this scene open or save it for use in the next tutorial.

The Area Shadows rollout

The **Area Shadows** rollout, shown in Figure 10-29, includes a **Basic Options** section to change the shape of the light and enable the **2 Sided Shadows** option. Below this is a section that controls antialiasing options, which primarily affect the edge of the shadow. By experimenting with these options, particularly **Sample Spread** and **Jitter Amount**, you can achieve some fascinating results. Area shadows are not as practical as other shadow types, but they can produce unique results that may come in handy some day. If you decide to use area shadows to achieve a particular effect or look, try to keep the **Shadow Integrity** and **Shadow Quality** settings as low as possible to reduce excessive rendering times. The **Area Light Dimensions** section controls the length, width, and height of the light source.

Figure 10-29. The Area Shadows rollout

The Ray Traced Shadow Params rollout

The **Ray Traced Shadow Params** rollout, shown in Figure 10-30, is a small rollout with just a few settings. The **Ray Bias** and **2 Sided Shadows** options work the same for raytraced shadows as they do for shadow maps.

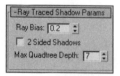

Figure 10-30. The Ray Traced Shadow Params rollout

The only unique setting is **Max Quadtree Depth**. The definition and concept of a quadtree can be difficult to grasp. Suffice to say that when using raytraced shadows, you should keep the **Max Quadtree Depth** value set to at least 7. Increasing the value up to a maximum of **10** may reduce rendering times at the cost of memory, but it may be worth a try.

Whenever possible, avoid using omni lights with raytraced shadows for reasons directly related to quadtrees. Omni lights used with raytraced shadows will require more memory and could take significantly longer to render than raytraced shadows used with spotlights or directional lights.

The Adv. Ray Traced Params rollout

The **Adv. Ray Traced Params** rollout, shown in Figure 10-31, contains only one unique option not already discussed with other shadow types. The mode option, set to **2-Pass Antialias** by default, should be kept at this setting, as it provides the best results at a negligible increase in rendering time.

The **Antialiasing Options** section of the rollout is identical to the same section that appears with area shadows. Again, these settings affect the edge of the shadows and allow you to produce a wide array of shadow affects. By experimenting with the shadow spread and the jitter amount, you can make some very unique and unusual shadow types that might come in handy for some future project.

Figure 10-31. The Adv. Ray Traced Params rollout

The Optimizations rollout

The **Transparent Shadows On** option in the **Optimizations** rollout (shown in Figure 10-32) gives you the ability to use opacity maps with advanced raytraced shadows.

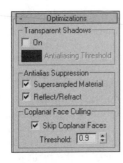

Figure 10-32. The Optimizations rollout

If you do not enable this option, objects with transparent areas derived from opacity maps will not render correctly. The left image in Figure 10-33 has the **On** option enabled, and the right image has it disabled.

Figure 10-33. The Transparent Shadow On option enabled (left) and disabled (right)

The remainder of this rollout contains several settings that are best left at their default values.

The Spotlight and Directional Parameters rollouts

The **Spotlight Parameters** and **Directional Parameters** rollouts, shown in Figure 10-34, are identical rollouts that perform the same function. They control the shape and size of hotspots and falloff areas of a light.

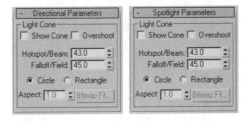

Figure 10-34. The identical Directional and Spotlight Parameters rollouts

The first option enables the **Show Cone** feature, which causes the cone to be visible when the light is not selected. Without this option enabled, a light's cone disappears when the light is deselected.

The next option, **Overshoot**, causes the light to cast light in all directions; however, projections and shadows will only occur within its cone. I recommend not using this feature.

The **Hotspot/Beam** parameter controls the size of a light's hotspot in units. In conjunction with the **Falloff/Field** parameter, it controls the look of hotspots and falloff areas. The actual size used may be irrelevant, depending on the distance of the light to the objects being illuminated. The hotspot area of an illuminated object receives a light's full intensity and the falloff area receives a diminished amount of the light. Proper use of these two parameters is usually crucial to the realism of the lights in your scene.

The left image in Figure 10-35 shows a teapot illuminated with a **Falloff/Field** setting almost identical to the **Hotspot/Beam** setting. In the right image, the **Hotspot/Beam** value is reduced to almost zero. Notice the transition from hotspot to falloff in each image. In the left image, there is virtually no falloff because the hotspot size is almost the same as the falloff size. Note that the **Falloff/Field** setting cannot be set lower than the **Hotspot/Beam** setting.

Figure 10-35. A high Hotspot/Beam value (left) and a low Hotspot/Beam value (right)

Changing the quality of a shadow map

This exercise demonstrates how to change the resolution of a map to improve a shadow's quality.

1. Continue from the last tutorial or go to the 3dsMax8\Scenes\Friends_of_Ed directory and open the file Ch10-05.max.
2. Select the directional light.
3. Render the Perspective view.
4. Go to the Modify panel and open the **Directional Parameters** rollout.
5. Right-click the slider arrows next to the **Falloff/Field** parameter to reduce the value to 0.5. Notice the scene becomes dark in the view.
6. Render the Perspective view. Notice the scene is completely dark.

7. Click a few times on the upward **Hotspot/Beam** arrow until the entire teapot is illuminated in the viewport.

8. Render the Perspective view. Notice the teapot is now illuminated.

9. Click several times on the upward **Falloff/Field** arrow until the entire plane is illuminated in the viewport.

10. Render the Perspective view. Notice the scene is much more illuminated now.

Summary

This chapter has covered a large amount of information concerning the most critical component of a 3D scene—lighting. Lighting is part science and part art. If an architect gives two 3ds Max users the same set of architectural drawings and asks for an architectural visualization, the modeling by both users should look nearly identical. The materials applied to the scene should also be similar based on the guidance and input given by the architect. The lighting, however, may vary drastically based on the types of lights used and the artistic skills of the user.

This chapter focused on the basics of lighting, and the discussion was limited to standard lights. Chapter 11 will cover photometric lights and briefly explore their integration with advanced lighting features. Chapter 12 will focus closely on one of the most ubiquitous procedures of advanced lighting—global illumination. Although global illumination is considered an advanced lighting feature, my coverage will be limited to the critical components of this feature, and the discussion will be understandable at the foundations level.

By the end of these three chapters on lighting, you will have the foundation skills required to produce photorealistic visualizations.

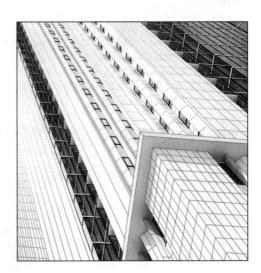

Chapter 11

PHOTOMETRIC LIGHTING

Standard lights give you the ability to create great lighting for architectural scenes with minimal effort. With photometric lights, however, you can take your visualizations to a new level. Photometric lights are based on real-world light characteristics and enable you to create physically accurate lighting. You can simulate everything from the common 100W light bulb to the sun.

Photometric lights achieve the best results when used in combination with global illumination, which is covered in the next chapter. As a foundation for discussion on global illumination, this chapter covers each of the five types of photometric lights and two lighting systems which allow you to simulate sunlight. With a good understanding of the concepts in this chapter, the advantages of the realism that photometric lighting has to offer will be clear.

Exposure control

Before beginning a discussion on photometric lighting, we need to discuss a feature in 3ds Max that is critical to its use—exposure control. Exposure control corrects the output level and color range of a rendering to better match what your eyes would see in real life. Exposure control can improve the lighting of any scene, even when standard lights are used. When photometric lighting is used, exposure control becomes more critical. When you use attenuation in a scene, which is automatic with photometric lights, your lights tend to have a high dynamic range, because some parts of your scene with a light close by may be brightly lit, while other parts may be dimly lit.

The exposure control settings, shown in Figure 11-1, are found in the **Environment and Effects** dialog box, which you can access through the **Rendering** menu or open by pressing the keyboard shortcut "8." The **Exposure Control** rollout is located in the **Environment** tab, and when a selection is made from the drop-down list, an additional rollout appears directly below, providing settings for the exposure control selection.

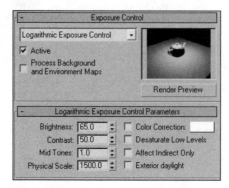

Figure 11-1. The exposure control settings

Types of exposure control

There are four types of exposure control in 3ds Max: Automatic, Linear, Logarithmic, and Pseudo. Deciding which one to use will probably take some experimentation, but some general guidelines are as follows:

- **Automatic**: This type of exposure control is good for still images or images where subtle effects are used. Effects are covered in Chapter 18.

- **Linear**: This type is best used for scenes with a low dynamic range, for example, dark or nighttime scenes where the range of brightness is very low from one area of the scene to another.

- **Logarithmic**: This type is best used for scenes with a high dynamic range, for example, exterior scenes where the range of brightness is very high from one area of the scene to another. This type also works best for scenes where a standard light is the primary light source in your scene. In addition, the logarithmic exposure control should be used for animations, because the automatic and linear options can cause flickering.

- **Pseudo**: This exposure control type is simply a tool that displays illumination levels in your scene using colors. When you render your scene with this type of exposure control, an additional render window opens that displays your scene with a rainbow of colors and a scale at the bottom signifying the illumination levels for each color. This feature serves nicely for performing advanced light studies in your scenes.

Exposure control parameters

The **Exposure Control Parameters** rollout changes depending on the type of exposure control selected. The Pseudo exposure control contains a completely unique rollout; however, the other three types contain exactly the same settings, though Logarithmic contains two additional options: **Affect Indirect Only** and **Exterior daylight** (as shown in Figure 11-1). The **Affect Indirect Only** option should be used when standard lights are the primary lights, and the **Exterior daylight** option should be used when the IES Sun, IES Sky, or Daylight systems are used. The remainder of this chapter focuses on an explanation of these features.

If any adjustments to the settings in the **Exposure Control Parameters** rollout are warranted, they will be small. For example, if you're using logarithmic exposure control and you need to change the default brightness level of 65 to 80 or higher, you probably have more fundamental problems with your lighting that should be corrected elsewhere. Large adjustments can harm the realism of your scene more than no adjustments at all. The **Render Preview** button lets you create a small preview of your scene with the selected exposure control without having to render the scene.

Photometric light types

There are five types of photometric lights, as shown in Figure 11-2: **Point**, **Linear**, **Area**, **IES Sun**, and **IES Sky**. The controls for point, linear, and area lights are similar in many ways to the controls for standard lights. IES Sun and IES Sky, however, are very unique lights with very difficult controls that will be discussed later in this chapter. **IES** stands for Illuminating Engineering Society, which is recognized as the technical authority on illumination.

Figure 11-2.
The photometric light types

Point, linear, and area lights

As their names imply, the point, linear, and area lights emit light from different geometries. A point light emits light from a single point in space, a linear light from a line of definable length, and an area light from a definable area. Unique icons distinguish one type from another, as shown in Figure 11-3.

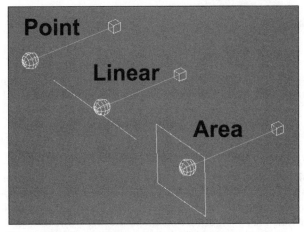

Figure 11-3. The point, linear, and area light types

293

When either a linear or area light is created, a unique rollout is used for each. The **Linear Light Parameters** rollout specifies the length of the line that will emit light, and the **Area Light Parameters** rollout specifies the area that will emit light. Both rollouts are shown in Figure 11-4.

Figure 11-4. The Linear and Area Light Parameters rollouts, respectively

All other rollouts for the point, linear, and area light types are the same as the rollouts available with standard lights, with the exception of one: the **Intensity/Color/Distribution** rollout, described next.

Intensity/Color/Attenuation rollout

This rollout, shown in Figure 11-5, is similar in function to the **Intensity/Color/Attenuation** rollout used with standard lights; however, attenuation is calculated automatically with photometric lights, so the attenuation settings are replaced with a distribution setting.

Figure 11-5.
The Intensity/Color/Distribution rollout

Distribution The Distribution drop-down list allows you to specify light distribution in four different ways: Isotropic, Spotlight, Diffuse, or Web. The type of distribution available will vary among the different light types.

An isotropic distribution casts light equally in all directions. This distribution is available only with a point light type.

A photometric **spotlight** casts a focused beam of light similar to the spotlight of a standard light. However, a photometric spotlight diminishes the light to 50% at the hotspot/beam angle. Standard light is at 100% at the hotspot/beam angle. With both standard and photometric lights, the intensity falls off to zero by the time the light reaches the falloff/field angle. The hotspot/beam and falloff/field angles are set in the **Spotlight Parameters** rollout, as shown in Figure 11-6.

Figure 11-6.
The Spotlight Parameters rollout

A **diffuse** distribution emits light from a virtual surface, with more intense light leaving the surface at perpendicular (90 degree) angles and less intense light leaving the surface at angles parallel to the virtual surface. This distribution is available only with area and linear light types.

A **web** distribution casts light according to a 3D definition specified in an external file. These files are often available from lighting manufacturers and from the Internet. When a web distribution is selected, one more unique rollout appears—the **Web Parameters** rollout, as shown in Figure 11-7. This distribution is available with each of the three light types.

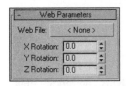

Figure 11-7.
The Web Parameters rollout

Color In the **Color** section of the rollout, you can set the color of your photometric light in one of two ways. You can use the drop-down list to select the color based on the real-world color characteristics of a particular type of light, as shown in the left image of Figure 11-8, or you can enable the Kelvin option and use the temperature setting to specify particular color, as shown in the right image.

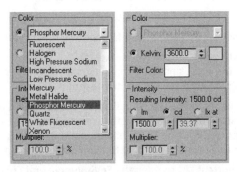

Figure 11-8. Specifying a light's color with a light type (left) and with a temperature setting (right)

When you select a light type from the drop-down list, the color swatch next to the Kelvin parameter is updated to reflect the light you select. For example, incandescent light typically has a very faint beige color, and phosphor mercury light has a light green color.

When you select the Kelvin option, the color swatch also updates to reflect the change in color.

You can also adjust the color of the light by using the **Filter Color** swatch directly below the Kelvin temperature setting. Adjusting a color with this swatch simulates the effect of using a colored filter in front of the light.

Intensity The intensity settings specify the strength or brightness of the light in physically based quantities. There are three different real-world units used to specify the intensity of a light: lm (lumens), cd (candela), and lx (lux).

- The **lumen** value is a measure of the overall output of a light and is usually listed on a package of light bulbs right next to the watts used.
- **Candela** is a measure of light energy per unit of time emitted by a point source in a particular direction; you should just remember it as another way to measure intensity of a light.
- The **lux** value specifies intensity at a particular distance away from the light source.

The **Multiplier** setting simply multiplies the intensity of the photometric light the same way it does for standard lights.

Creating photometric lights

This exercise demonstrates how to create photometric lights and modify their characteristics.

1. Reset 3ds Max.
2. In the Perspective view, create a plane with a width and length of 20'.
3. In the **Name and Color** rollout, click the color swatch and select a pure white color for the plane. Using white allows you to see the light's color better.
4. In the Top view, create a teapot with a radius of 2' and center the teapot on the plane.
5. In the Command panel, click **Create ➤ Lights**, and from the drop-down list, select **Photometric**.
6. Click the **Target Point** button. In the Top view, click and hold near the bottom-right corner of the plane to create the light, and drag the cursor to the center of the teapot. Release the mouse button to set the light's target near the teapot.
7. Without moving the target, move the light 5' above the plane and render the Perspective view. Notice that the illumination is barely perceptible, if at all, because you are using a photometric light without any exposure control. The light automatically creates an inverse squared attenuation, and it is too far away from the teapot to illuminate it without exposure control.
8. Press the keyboard shortcut "8" to open the **Environment and Effects** dialog box.
9. In the **Exposure Control** rollout, click the drop-down list and select **Logarithmic Exposure Control**.
10. Render the Perspective view. Notice that the scene is brighter now.
11. In the Top view, move the light toward the center of the scene until it's directly above the teapot and render the Perspective view again. Notice that the teapot is much brighter now, because the light is closer. Also, the light is white, because the default color is set to a D65White light.
12. Go to the **Modify** panel, click the **Multiplier** option, and change the multiplier value to 200%. This makes the light twice as intense.

13. Click the **Color** drop-down list and change the light to a **Phosphor Mercury** type. Notice the green hue shown in the view.

14. Click the **Distribution** drop-down list, select **Spotlight**, and render the Perspective view. Notice that the light falls off to zero intensity when it reaches the falloff/field angle.

Preset Lights

One of my favorite features in 3ds Max is the set of available **Preset Lights**—a group of preset photometric lights that load specific light settings based on their real-world characteristics. For example, when you load the typical 100W light bulb, the settings in the **Intensity/Color/Distribution** rollout automatically change to the settings required to reproduce the real-world characteristics of a 100W light bulb, as shown in Figure 11-9.

Figure 11-9. The real-world settings of a preset 100W light bulb

To create a preset light, click the **Create** menu and select **Lights ➤ Photometric Lights ➤ Presets**; then select the type of light you want to create, as shown in Figure 11-10.

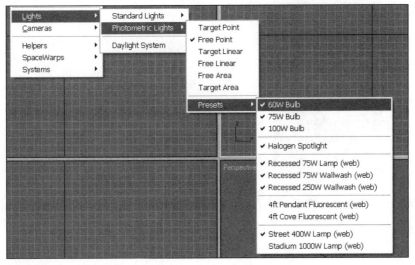

Figure 11-10. The available preset lights

Fortunately, 3ds Max has provided us with some of the most common light types found in the real world. If you want to create others not included in this list, determine the intensity value for the light you want to create using one of the three unit types mentioned. Then select the light type from the drop-down list in the **Color** section of the rollout. You can also make adjustments to the preset lights in order to create new lights.

IES Sun

IES Sun is a physically based light that simulates the bright light of the sun. It consists of a single light and target. When you create an IES Sun, five rollouts appear (not including the two mental ray rollouts that we will disregard). Four of the five rollouts are nearly identical to rollouts that appear for other light types. The most unique rollout, **Sun Parameters** (Figure 11-11), gives you control over the intensity of sunlight, the types of shadows it casts, and the objects to exclude from its affect.

By default, 3ds Max creates the IES Sun with an intensity of 80,000 lx. Notice, that no distance is associated with this unit of measure, as in other photometric light types, because the intensity that reaches the objects in your scene will be the specified value regardless of how far away the light is placed from the objects in your scene. In other words, objects in your scene are illuminated the same regardless of how high above your scene you place the IES Sun. Because of this, there is no attenuation for this light.

As with other light types, I recommend using advanced raytraced shadows with many of your scenes, depending on your exact needs. In the **Sun Parameters** rollout, you can specify the types of shadows to be used with the sunlight.

Notice the **Shadow Parameters** rollout is very similar to the same rollout with other light types. The only thing missing is the color swatch that allows you to change the color of the shadows and the feature that allows you to assign a map to the shadows. Instead of the color swatch, use the **Density** setting to directly specify how dark you want your shadows to be.

Figure 11-11. The Sun Parameters and Shadow Parameters rollouts

IES Sky

IES Sky is a physically based light that simulates the atmospheric effects of skylight. Skylight is the ambient, indirect light that results from the scattering of sunlight through the atmosphere.

The **IES Sky Parameters** rollout (Figure 11-12) is very simplistic, consisting partly of a multiplier, a color swatch, and a switch for the light and shadows. It also contains a setting for the cloud coverage that impacts how much light is scattered through the sky. In the **Render** section is the setting **Rays per Sample**. This is the number of rays 3ds Max uses to calculate skylight as it reaches a given point in space. Increasing this value can improve your renderings but also increases rendering times. When used in animations, flickering can result when this value is too low. Make sure you increase the default value to about 30 to prevent flickering.

Remember that the IES Sky will work correctly only when the sky object is pointing in the negative direction of the Z axis, or downward when viewed from the Top view.

Figure 11-12. The IES Sky Parameters rollout

Creating sunlight and skylight photometric lights

This exercise demonstrates how to use the sunlight and skylight features to simulate real-world direct and indirect illumination from the sun.

1. In the 3dsMax8\Scenes\Friends_of_Ed folder, open the file Ch11-01.max.
2. In the Command panel, select **Create ➤ Lights**, and from the drop-down list, select **Photometric**.
3. Click the IES Sun button and in the Sun Parameters rollout change the shadow type to Adv. Ray Traced and enable the Shadows option.
4. In the Top view, click and hold near the top-left corner of the plane to create the light, and drag the cursor to the center of the building. Release the mouse button to set the light's target near the building, as shown in the following left image.
5. In the Front view, move the IES Sun approximately 45 degrees up, as shown in the following right image.

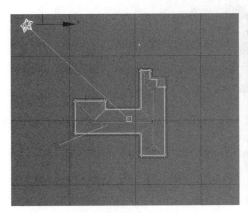
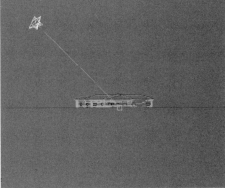

6. Render the Camera view. Notice that portions of the building in the direct path of the sunlight are completely white and all other portions are completely back, as shown in the following illustration. To improve the lighting in this scene, add exposure control.

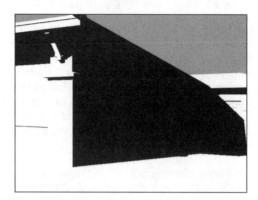

7. Press the keyboard shortcut "8" to open the **Environment and Effects** dialog box.

8. In the **Exposure Control** rollout, click the drop-down list and select **Logarithmic Exposure Control**.

9. In the **Logarithmic Exposure Control Parameters** rollout, enable **Exterior daylight**.

10. In the **Exposure Control** rollout, click **Render Preview**. You see a small sample of what the rendered image will look like.

11. Render the Camera view. Notice that the scene looks better, but there is still no illumination in areas not in the direct path of the sunlight, as shown in the following illustration. The next step is to create the effect of bounced atmospheric light.

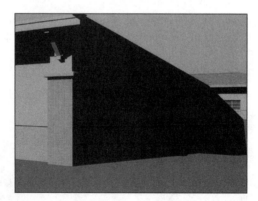

12. In the Command panel, with **Photometric** still selected as the light type, click the **IES Sky** button.

13. Place the IES Sky in the same location and in the same manner as you placed the IES Sun. Remember to elevate the IES Sky approximately 45 degrees into the sky.

14. Render the Camera view. Notice now that there is an appearance of indirect illumination in areas that were previously dark. In the next chapter, you'll learn methods to improve lighting even more in scenes such as this using global illumination.

Daylight

The combination of direct sunlight and indirect skylight is a system that 3ds Max refers to as Daylight. Although you can create daylight manually by creating the IES Sun and IES Sky lights separately, you can use the Daylight feature in 3ds Max to do the work for you. The Daylight system uses a light that simulates the sun and mimics its movement over the earth at a specific location. With the Daylight system you can simulate sunlight in Paris at 4:02 p.m. on January 14 or in Rome at 9:31 a.m. on October 14. You can also animate the sunlight to see the sun's movement at a specific location and use the system to perform shadow studies for proposed or existing structures.

The Daylight feature is located in the **Systems** section of the **Create** panel, as shown in Figure 11-13.

Figure 11-13.
The Sunlight and Daylight features

When you click the **Daylight** button, the **Control Parameters** rollout appears, as shown in Figure 11-14. The rollout provides controls for specifying a location on earth, a time of day, and a year for the position of the sun. The Orbital Scale has no effect on the quality or accuracy of the light; it simply moves the sun higher up above the objects in your scene. The **North Direction** setting specifies the direction of north in your scene, as assigned by a compass rose that is created when the daylight is created, as shown in Figure 11-15. By default, north is 0 and points in the positive direction of the Y axis. East is 90 degrees and points in the positive direction of the x axis. You must correctly specify north in your scene to accurately depict the position and movement of the sun. Changing the direction of north will cause the compass rose to update, and rotating the compass rose will cause the North Direction parameter to update.

Figure 11-14.
The Control Parameters rollout

To create daylight, click the **Daylight** button in the Systems section of the **Create** panel. Click and drag inside the Top or Perspective view to place the compass rose. Release the mouse button when the compass rose is to your liking, remembering that the size of the compass rose has no bearing on the affect of the light. After releasing the mouse button, drag the mouse again to elevate the sun upward along the positive direction of the z axis.

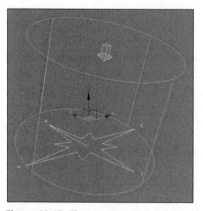

Figure 11-15. The compass rose and directional light of the Daylight feature

Once a daylight system is created, the system is modified primarily in two different places. Since the **Control Parameter** rollout, shown in Figure 11-14, deals with the movement of the sun over time, the rollout is accessed through the **Motion** panel once the system is created. The remaining rollouts are accessed through the **Modify** panel.

Standard lights vs. IES Sun and IES Sky

The first rollout in the **Modify** panel is the **Daylight Parameters** rollout, shown in Figure 11-16. In this rollout, you specify which type of light serves as the sunlight and which type of light serves as the sky-light. By default, 3ds Max creates a standard directional light for the daylight system; however, you can use the IES Sun in its place to take advantage of its photometric qualities. Using the daylight system even with a standard directional light is beneficial, because you can simulate the correct position of the sun. By changing the light type to IES Sun, you can also achieve photometric quality and add a great deal of realism to your scene. To change the type of light used, click the **Sunlight** drop-down list and select IES Sun, as shown in Figure 11-16.

The same concept applies when using the light type that simulates skylight. By changing the **Skylight** setting to IES Sky, you can take advantage of the photometric quality of the IES Sky. As mentioned in the last chapter, the Skylight object is designed to work directly with the Light Tracer global illumination rendering solution. Since Light Tracer is rarely used in a production environment because of its lengthy rendering times, the Skylight is also rarely used. For that reason, this book does not cover the Light Tracer and Skylight features. When you do change the skylight to IES Sky, the **IES Sky Parameters** rollout appears along with the other rollouts in the **Modify** panel.

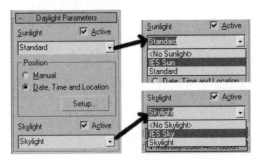

Figure 11-16. The Daylight Parameters rollout

The **Position** section of the rollout contains the **Manual** control that allows you to adjust the location of the light in your scene rather than setting the location based on date, time, and location settings. You can also adjust the intensity value of the sunlight in manual mode. The **Setup** button is a shortcut button that takes you to the **Motion** panel where you can modify the date, time, and location settings.

It is important to remember that the IES Sun and IES Sky lights are photometric lights, and to gain the most out of their use when using the scanline renderer, you need to use the advanced lighting feature radiosity along with exposure control, both of which are discussed in the next chapter. Light Tracer can be used in lieu of radiosity to achieve good results; however, I do not recommend Light Tracer in a production environment.

Sunlight

The Sunlight feature is found next to the Daylight feature in the **Systems** section of the **Create** panel. The Sunlight feature in 3ds Max is the same as the Daylight feature, except it lacks the added benefit of skylight and the option to utilize the IES Sun. When you create a sunlight system, a free directional light is created with raytraced shadows. The light is the same as the lights created through the **Lights** section of **Create** panel, except that this light is tied directly to the feature that simulates the position and motion of the sun. After creating the sunlight system, you can access this feature through the **Motion** panel. This feature exists primarily as a legacy tool, for when you load older files that were created before the Daylight system was developed.

Summary

Photometric lighting enhances any architectural scene and provides several benefits over standard lighting. With photometric lights, you can produce stunning realism and physically accurate lighting with minimal effort. This chapter covered each of the photometric light types and the two systems that are used to simulate sunlight. By combining the concepts covered in this chapter with the concepts covered in the next chapter, you can take your lighting to an even higher level.

Whether aware of it or not, a viewer will usually grade the quality of an architectural visualization by the quality of the lighting. Lighting is without a doubt one area in scene creation that will make or break a visualization. If any additional time can be spent improving the quality of your work, lighting should be the first area you consider.

Chapter 12

GLOBAL ILLUMINATION

As any veteran 3ds Max user will tell you, lighting is the most critical element in a visualization. No other phase of scene creation depends so heavily on experience and requires as much artistic talent. When used correctly, good lighting can make even the poorest designs look beautiful. Likewise, incorrect lighting can ruin a quality design and negate great work in all other phases of scene creation.

The previous two chapters dealt with lighting techniques for local illumination, which only takes into account the light that takes a direct path from the light source (also known as direct illumination). While local illumination provides fairly good results in a relatively short amount of time, it can never achieve the quality and realism that global illumination can provide. **Global illumination** is a lighting process that takes into account not only the light taking a direct path from the light source, but also the light that has bounced from other surrounding surfaces (also known as indirect illumination).

This chapter describes the process of using global illumination in your scenes to achieve photorealistic quality. True global illumination requires the use of photometric lights. Combined with the features discussed in the previous chapter on photometric lights, this chapter will describe how to achieve true global illumination with lights that you should be familiar with.

Principles of global illumination

Creating convincing lighting in 3ds Max is a complicated process, which reflects the complex nature of light behavior in the real world. To understand how 3ds Max calculates global illumination, you must first understand how light behaves in the real world and why the world appears to us the way it does. Why are our surroundings still illuminated when the sun is below the horizon? Why is the sky blue or a sunset red? Why is absolute darkness a rarity? The best examples are all around you. Let's start answering these questions by looking at some of our images from "Quick Start 4." In the left image of Figure 12-1, the scene receives only direct illumination, which causes the areas in shadow to be completely black. In contrast, the image on the right shows both direct and indirect illumination, and the areas of shadow are slightly illuminated. In reality, the source of all light in both images is the sun. The shadows in the image on the right are not completely black, because sunlight is bouncing all around the scene. Light not only bounces from object to object, it also bounces off particles in the air that redirect it in all directions.

Figure 12-1. Direct illumination (left) and global illumination (right)

Shaders

In 3ds Max, lighting is calculated with algorithms known as **shaders**. These algorithms predict the intensity and color of light being reflected off the surface of objects in a scene. Shaders also control the shape, size, and overall appearance of specular highlights of objects. By doing so, they help define for the viewer what kind of material makes up an object. For example, on smooth surfaces, the specular highlights are smaller and more pronounced, as shown in the left image of Figure 12-2. On rough surfaces, the specular highlights are spread out over a greater area and are not as pronounced, as shown in the right image. By controlling the shape of a specular highlight, you can give even more indication of an object's material type. 3ds Max contains numerous shaders that enable you to simulate any type of surface material; however, using a wide variety of shaders and their many settings can be very confusing and is not necessary for inexperienced 3ds Max users. Once you have a solid foundation of global illumination, you should try experimenting with other shader types beside the default

Blinn shader. The Blinn shader is used as the default shader because it has very soft and round highlights. This quality gives you the flexibility to simulate a wide range of materials rather than restricting you to just those materials that have harder and less round highlights.

Figure 12-2. Small specular highlights (left) and large specular highlights (right)

Radiosity

Radiosity is a term used to describe the effect of light bouncing around in a scene. When light bounces from one object to another, it not only illuminates other objects, it transmits reflected color. This color bleeding effect is perhaps the single most critical component in making visualizations appear photorealistic. Notice that in several of the rendered images in this book's colored gallery, a great deal of color reflects from one object to adjacent objects. These subtle effects of color reflection are critical to the overall believability and realism of the rendering. While radiosity can dramatically effect the realism of a scene, its use can have an equally dramatic effect on the time needed to render.

To calculate radiosity, 3ds Max creates an invisible duplicate of a scene and breaks down each duplicate into a mesh of small polygons with a size of your choosing, as shown in Figure 12-3. As we will discuss further in this chapter, the size of the invisible polygons is critical to the accuracy of global illumination and equally critical to the time needed to calculate radiosity. When 3ds Max determines that light strikes one of these invisible polygons, it calculates where that reflected light goes next and with what intensity, color, and diffusion it strikes the next surface. This information is stored in the vertices of the polygon that the light strikes and contributes to the overall illumination of the polygon. The cumulative effect of all the bounced light in a scene, after attenuation eventually stops the bouncing process, is the **radiosity solution**. Calculating a radiosity solution can take hours, depending on the quality you specify for the solution and the size of the invisible polygons. Fortunately, however, the radiosity solution only needs to be created once for any given scene, and is valid until light settings are changed or scene objects are manipulated in any way. In other words, you can create an animation of any length while only calculating the radiosity once.

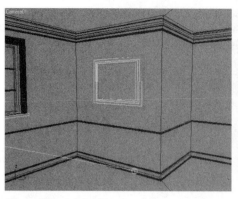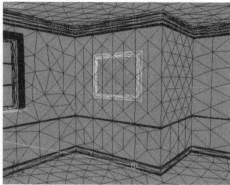

Figure 12-3. Subdividing a mesh

To use radiosity in a scene, click the keyboard shortcut F10 to open the **Render Scene** dialog box, click the drop-down list in the **Select Advanced Lighting** rollout and select **Radiosity** (as shown in Figure 12-4). A number of rollouts will appear giving you precise control over radiosity calculation.

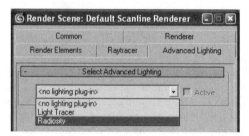

Figure 12-4. Enabling advanced lighting in 3ds Max

Radiosity Processing Parameters rollout

Within the **Radiosity Processing Parameters** rollout are numerous basic parameters that require your attention for any job.

Initial Quality

As its name implies, this value sets the overall quality of the radiosity process. The default of 85% is sufficient for calculating **Radiosity** during the final production rendering but is much higher than necessary for test renders. When experimenting with **Radiosity**, try using **Initial Quality** values as low as 30%. These values will suffice for test renders and are calculated in a fraction of the time needed to calculate the default value of 85%.

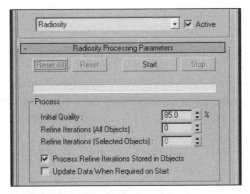

Figure 12-5. Basic radiosity parameters

During the initial quality stage of the rendering process, the lights in your scene shoot virtual rays containing a certain energy value (dictated by the light settings). This energy is distributed over the individual faces of each object in the scene and is stored in the vertices of each face. But because of the arrangement, size, and orientation of the faces in an object, adjacent faces may have widely varying energy values. This variation can lead to unrealistic illumination and cause the quality of your radiosity solution to suffer dramatically, as shown in Figure 12-6. In this example, a single IES Sun illuminates a teapot, and radiosity provides global illumination. Unfortunately, the illumination is extremely poor because of the wide variation in light energy distribution stored in the vertices of each face. To remedy this variation, 3ds Max needs to gather energy information from each face and redistribute as necessary to reduce variation. This process, which is also the next key setting that should be adjusted, is termed **Refine Iterations** (discussed in the next section of this chapter).

Figure 12-6. Radiosity imperfections in the illumination of an object

Enabling Radiosity

This exercise demonstrates how to quickly enable **radiosity** with the default parameters.

1. Open the file Ch12-Radiosity01.max, found in the 3dsMax8\Scenes\Friends_of_Ed folder.

2. Render the Camera view. Notice that light does not reach one corner of the room and half of the ball in the middle, because no light is bouncing around, as shown in the left image in the following illustration.

3. Press the keyboard shortcut F10 to open the **Render Scene** dialog box.

4. Click the **Advanced Lighting** tab.

5. In the **Select Advanced Lighting** rollout, click the drop-down list and select **Radiosity**.

6. In the **Radiosity Processing Parameters** rollout, click the **Start** button. This starts the radiosity calculation process.

7. In the **Interactive Tools** section of this rollout, click on the **Display Radiosity** in **View** option to disable this feature. Notice that the Camera view no longer shows light.

8. Render the Camera view. Now the areas of the room that were completely dark before are illuminated by the bounced light; however, some areas are illuminated poorly, and areas of reflected light, such as the shaded area of the ball, exhibit a large amount of noise. Notice also that the blue color of the walls is being reflected onto the white floor and ceiling, as shown in the right image in the following illustration. In the next exercise, we will remove these imperfections in the lighting.

9. Click on the **Display Radiosity** in **View** option again to reenable this feature.

10. Save this scene for use in the next exercise.

Refine Iterations

Refining the radiosity solution using the **Refine Iterations** feature will almost always be part of any scene utilizing radiosity. 3ds Max offers three ways to refine iterations. You can refine iterations globally, that is refine all objects; you can refine only objects selected at the time of rendering; or you can specify a refine iteration value for each individual object through its **Object Properties** dialog box (as shown at the bottom of the Figure 12-7). The first two methods, **Refine Iterations (All Objects)** and **Refine Iterations (Selected Objects)** are found in the **Radiosity Processing Parameters** rollout (Figure 12-5). In very large scenes, you may find it impractical to refine iterations globally, because doing so causes the radiosity solution to take too long to calculate. In addition, 3ds Max may leave certain objects out of the refining process if they don't visually benefit from refinement and don't degrade the visual quality of surrounding objects. A good **Refine Iterations (Selected Objects)** setting for test renders is 3, while a good setting for production renders is 10.

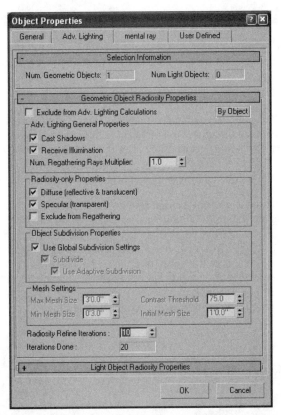

Figure 12-7. Advanced lighting settings for individual objects through the Object Properties dialog box

Figure 12-8 shows how using the **Refine Iterations** feature can improve the illumination of a scene. The image on the left shows the scene without the use of **Refine Iterations**. The image on the right shows how using **Refine Iterations** can remove the imperfections in light energy distribution.

Figure 12-8. Using Refine Iterations to correct the distribution of light energy in a scene

Light filtering

The last section of the **Radiosity Processing Parameters** rollout is the **Interactive Tools** section. Within this section, you can filter both direct and indirect light to further reduce the noise caused by uneven light energy distribution. This feature takes effect after the radiosity solution is calculated and, therefore, does not require recalculating the solution. Filtering the light with these features, especially **Indirect Light Filtering**, can supplement the process of refining iterations or sometimes even replace it.

Smoothing out the appearance of noise caused by uneven light energy distribution is almost always needed. Instead of using the **Refine Iterations** feature, which can add an enormous amount of time to your solution calculation, you might be able to get away with just increasing the **Indirect Light Filtering** setting to 10 or higher. The time needed to process indirect light filtering for the teapot shown in the right image of Figure 12-9 was less than a second. The time needed to use **Refine Iterations** was over a minute, yet this process did not produce significantly better results, as shown in the left image. Though this will not always be the case with your scenes and refine iterations will often be necessary, experimenting here might save you some valuable time.

Figure 12-9. Using Refine Iterations alone (left) and Indirect Light Filtering alone (right)

The same section of the **Radiosity Processing Parameters** rollout contains an option to disable or enable radiosity in your viewports, and a button that takes you to the **Environment and Effects** dialog box, where you can adjust the exposure control settings of your scene.

Radiosity Meshing Parameters rollout

The **Radiosity Meshing Parameters** rollout includes settings that let you set the size of the polygons for the invisible mesh objects used to calculate and store the radiosity solution. Breaking the invisible mesh scene into very small polygons using these settings is critical for storing accurate light energy data in the vertices of the polygons.

By selecting the **Enabled** option in this rollout, as shown in the top of Figure 12-10, 3ds Max divides the mesh objects into polygons with maximum and minimum sizes as specified in the **Mesh Settings** section of the rollout. Reducing the **Maximum Mesh Size** value improves radiosity but increases the time needed to calculate a solution. The **Use Adaptive Subdivision** option is great for letting 3ds Max determine the size each polygon should be relative to the others. This option, enabled by default and new to 3ds Max 8, reduces the size of the polygons that lie in areas of widely varying light energy values, areas that need more precise data stored in the vertices of the polygons. You only have to specify maximum and minimum mesh sizes, and 3ds Max determines what size, between these two values, each polygon should be. This option is similar to the **Optimize** modifier. If you do not enable the **Use Adaptive Subdivision** option, then you will be able to specify only the **Maximum Mesh Size** value, and every polygon in the invisible mesh that would otherwise be larger, will be reduced to the same maximum size.

When experimenting with radiosity, always enable global subdivisions and the **Use Adaptive Subdivision** option. Try a range of values for **Maximum Mesh Size** and **Minimum Mesh Size** to see how large your polygons can be before radiosity is degraded to an unacceptable level.

Figure 12-10. The Radiosity Meshing Parameters rollout

To make the process of subdividing your scene more flexible, 3ds Max gives you the ability to disable global settings and specify unique settings for individual objects that need different subdivision settings than the rest of the scene. To override the global subdivision settings in the **Render Scene** dialog box for individual objects, select the object(s), open the **Object Properties** dialog box, click the **Advanced Lighting** tab, and disable the **Use Global Subdivision Settings** option, as shown in Figure 12-11. Click **OK** to complete the command.

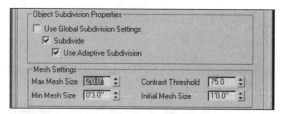

Figure 12-11. Using different subdivision settings for individual objects

If you understand the concepts discussed thus far in the chapter and want to experiment with more advanced **Radiosity** settings to fine-tune your results, try using the features in the **Light Painting** and **Rendering Parameters** rollouts.

Improving the radiosity solution

This exercise demonstrates how to improve the quality of the radiosity solution by using refine iterations, light filtering, and mesh subdivision.

1. Continue from the previous exercise or open the file Ch12-Radiosity02.max found in 3dsMax8\Scenes\Friends_of_Ed folder.

2. Press the keyboard shortcut F10 to open the **Render Scene** dialog box.

3. Click the **Advanced Lighting** tab.

4. In the **Radiosity Processing Parameters** rollout, type **10** in the **Refine Iterations (All Objects)** field.

5. Click the **Continue** button at the top of the rollout. This initiates the processing of refining the radiosity solution.

6. Render the Camera view. Now the imperfections in the reflected light are removed, such as the shaded area of the ball (shown in the following illustration).

7. Click the **Radiosity Meshing Parameters** rollout.

8. In the **Global Subdivision Settings** section, click the **Enabled** option. This tells 3ds Max to subdivide the invisible mesh to obtain and store more accurate light energy.

9. Disable the **Use Adaptive Subdivision** option.

10. Scroll back to the **Radiosity Processing Parameters** rollout and click the **Reset All** button. This removes the radiosity solution.

11. Click the **Start** button to recalculate a new radiosity solution. Notice that, when finished, the Camera view shows that the scene objects are subdivided so that no face is larger than the 3'3" specified in the **Maximum Mesh Size** field, as shown in the left image of the following illustration. 3ds Max evenly subdivides faces that require further division, so that each is the same size. Light energy is stored in the vertices of these faces, so as the faces are reduced in size, the radiosity becomes more accurate.

12. Render the Camera view. Notice that the rendering has improved significantly with mesh subdivision, as shown in the right image of the following illustration.

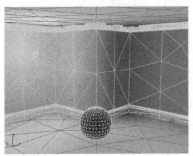 

13. In the **Radiosity Meshing Parameters** rollout, enable the **Use Adaptive Subdivision** option.

14. Scroll back to the **Radiosity Processing Parameters** rollout and click the **Reset All** button to remove the **Radiosity** solution again.

15. Click the **Start** button to calculate a new radiosity solution. Notice that the Camera view now shows that the scene objects are not subdivided evenly to a certain maximum size, as they were before. Instead, objects are subdivided into small faces in some areas and larger faces in others, as shown in the left image of the following illustration. Areas with smaller faces tend to be those where adjacent surfaces interact or where the edges of shadows lie.

16. Render the Camera view. Notice that the overall illumination of the scene has improved, particularly in the amount of red reflecting off the ball onto the white floor.

17. In the **Radiosity Processing Parameters** rollout, type **3** in the **Indirect Light Filtering** field.

18. Render the Camera view. The indirect light filtering has blurred the variations in light energy in the scene even further. Use of this feature is not apparent in all areas of your scenes; however, some area of your scene is sure to benefit. In this case, notice the area of reflected light underneath the ball. Increasing the **Indirect Light Filtering** value to 3 softened the variation between the red reflections on the floor coming from the ball and the blue reflections coming from the walls, as shown in the following illustration. The image on the left is rendered using no light filter and the image on the right is using the **Light Filtering** value of 3.

Considerations when using radiosity

When using radiosity, especially in conjunction with photometric lights, you must always ensure the geometry is to the correct scale. For example, you can not expect a single 100W light bulb to illuminate all the objects in a room the size of a stadium. Likewise, radiosity calculations won't be accurate if the objects that are broken up (through use of global subdivisions) are not to scale.

Another thing to consider with radiosity is the effect of geometry through which light can leak, or escape. If you calculate the radiosity solution within a small room, for example, and faces are missing from one of your walls, light might be allowed to escape through the opening. If allowed to do so, the escaping light can adversely affect objects outside the room or increase the time needed to calculate a solution (because the light is escaping into infinity and still being analyzed).

While preparing a radiosity calculation, you may realize that certain objects in your scene have little impact on the overall radiosity in your rendering or that including them in the calculation unreasonably increases your solution calculation time. If this is the case, consider excluding these objects from the radiosity calculation process. Doing so can save a tremendous amount of time in calculating a radiosity solution, especially when objects of a high face-count are excluded. Take trees for example, which often contain tens of thousands of faces. If you can verify that high-polygon trees in your scene do not need to benefit from radiosity, you can reduce the solution calculation time by excluding them from it. To exclude an object from advanced lighting calculations, right-click the object, click **Object Properties** in the quad menu, click the **Advanced Lighting** tab, and then click the **Exclude from Adv. Lighting Calculations** option, as shown in Figure 12-12. Click **OK** to complete the command. Try excluding objects with a high face-count that don't reflect a significant amount of light or that don't receive a significant amount of reflected light.

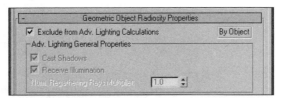

Figure 12-12. Excluding individual objects from advanced lighting calculations

Finally, because almost any adjustments to lights or objects in your scene will invalidate a radiosity solution, take care not to spend large amounts of time calculating a high-quality solution unless you are certain that your scene is finalized. When a solution is calculated, the solution is stored and saved with the file when the file is saved. Radiosity solutions can turn the smallest of scenes into a several-hundred-megabyte file, increasing load and save times for your files and complicating processes such as network rendering.

Summary

We have just discussed the most complex area of 3ds Max and the most important element of photo-realistic scenes—global illumination. Global illumination is all about realistic light reflections and is the pinnacle of architectural renderings. Although a difficult tool to master, radiosity provides a great means to achieving global illumination. The key to mastery is effectively balancing the mesh size and the refine iterations, not only to eliminate inaccurate light energy distribution, but also to achieve the feel you want in the render.

Most importantly, remember to keep your render times short during test renders and to render as often as possible when experimenting with global illumination. You will learn through trial and error how the numerous values affect the overall outcome. Realistic global illumination does not come easy, and often requires many experiments with seemingly endless variables. Whole books are written on the subject, and this chapter barely scratches the surface, intending to give you a starting point from which to expand your knowledge. The possibilities from here are boundless.

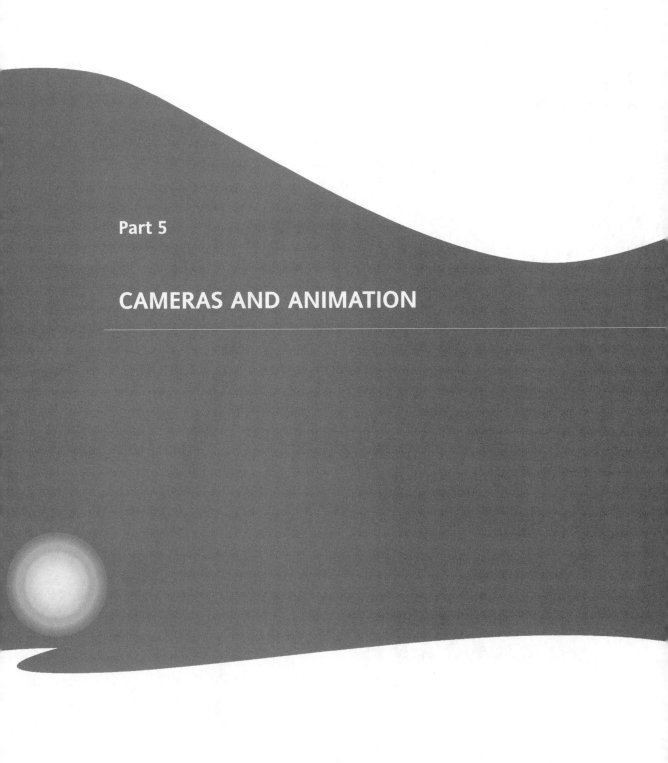

Part 5

CAMERAS AND ANIMATION

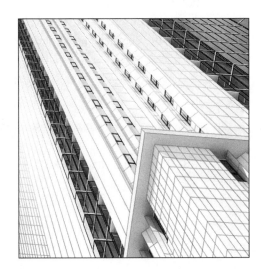

Quick Start 5

GETTING STARTED WITH CAMERAS AND ANIMATION

Approximate completion time: 20 minutes

Now it's time to create a camera for your scene and play the role of director. Everything a viewer sees in an animation is captured through the lens of your virtual camera, so setting up your camera and animating it properly is critical to producing a pleasing final product. In Quick Start 5, you'll pick up where you left off in the previous tutorial by creating a new camera and animating it in a way similar to how a movie director might move a camera during the production of a movie. Doing so will set you up for the final tutorial—on rendering—in which you'll make the final product come to life in the form of a rendered animation.

1. Open the file that you saved at the end of Quick Start 4, or open the file 3dsMax8\scenes\Friends_of_Ed\QuickStart05.max.

The initial scene file that was used at the start of Quick Start 1 contained a camera to facilitate viewport navigation and to prevent you from inadvertently changing the perspective of the view with which the scene will ultimately be rendered. In this tutorial, you'll start by seeing just how easy it is to create a new camera. First, let's delete the existing camera.

2. In the Command panel, click the **Display** icon.

3. In the **Hide** rollout, click **Unhide All**. This unhides the camera that was previously hidden from view.

4. Select the camera and press Delete. The camera is now deleted from the scene. Notice that the Camera view changes to the Perspective view since there is no longer a camera in the scene. The view does not change, as it takes on the same properties as the camera (which will be covered in this tutorial).

5. With the Perspective view active, press Ctrl+C to create a camera from the same vantage point that the Perspective view had. Notice also that the Perspective view is now the Camera view again.

6. In the Command panel, click the **Modify** icon.

7. In the **Parameters** rollout, click and hold the sliders next to the **FOV** field, and slowly drag up or down. Notice that the Camera view changes accordingly, as does the cone in the Top view that represents the field of view. Let's return the field of view to a reasonable setting.

8. In the **Stock Lenses** section of the **Parameters** rollout, click the **50mm** button. This is one of several preset buttons that change the view to a common camera lens setting. In this case, you set the virtual camera lens to 50mm, which provides a perspective similar to that of the human eye.

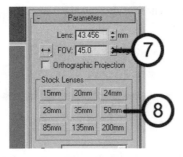

Now, you'll set the length of your animation.

9. In the bottom-right corner of the screen, click the **Time Configuration** icon. The **Time Configuration** dialog box opens.

10. In the **Animation** section, type **150** in the **End Time** field. Click **OK** to close the dialog box. This changes your animation from the default 101 frames to 151 frames (there's one extra frame because the first frame is 0). At the normal frame rate of 30 frames per second (fps), your animation length is now 5 seconds long. This is a very short animation, but for the purpose of this tutorial, it will suffice. Notice that the Time slider along the bottom of the screen now shows the animation ending at frame 150.

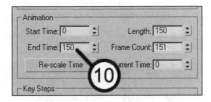

Next, you'll animate your camera.

11. Click the **Auto Key** button, located near the bottom-center of the screen. This tells 3ds Max to record any changes you make to the scene and create animation with those changes. When you click this button, it turns red.

325

12. Click the **Go to End** icon. This changes the current frame from frame 0 to frame 150. Now, any changes you make to your scene will be animated.

13. Make the Top view active and make sure the camera is selected.

14. Click the **Absolute Transform Type-In** icon to change the type-in fields to Offset mode.

15. In the **X:** field, type **40'**, and press Enter. This moves (offsets) the camera 40 feet to the right so that it's centered on the building. Next, center the camera target to the center of the building. This is important, otherwise, the camera will be looking in the wrong direction during the animation.

16. Click the **Auto Key** button to end the recording process.

17. Click the **Play** icon to see the camera in motion. The animation will keep looping until it is stopped.

18. While the animation is still playing, right-click inside the Camera view to see the animation from the camera's perspective. Notice that at the beginning of the animation, the camera accelerates from a stop to a constant speed. This is known as an "ease out," referring to how the camera slowly eases out of frame 0, rather than starting at a maximum speed right from the start. Likewise, when the animation ends, the camera slowly decelerates, or "eases in" to its final position, rather than going from full speed to an abrupt stop in one frame. If your software drivers and graphics card don't allow smooth playback, trying changing your Camera view to wireframe. This will allow you to see the effects of easing in and easing out. Remember to change the view back to **Smooth + Highlights**.

19. Click the **Go to Start** icon to stop the animation and return the Time slider to frame 0. You can also press Esc to stop the animation.

Next, you'll change the position of the camera at the start of the animation from its previous height of 15 feet to 6 feet. This will cause the camera to start at 6-feet high (eye level) and transition to 15-feet high by the end of the animation.

20. Select the camera in the Top view and click the **Auto Key** button. This will record the change to the camera height.

21. Click the **Offset Mode Transform Type-In** icon. This takes you back to Absolute Transform Type-In mode.

22. Type **6'** in the **Z:** field to change the height of the camera from 15 feet to 6 feet.

23. Click the **Auto Key** button to end the recording process.

24. Click the **Play** icon to start the animation again. Notice that the camera now starts at 6 feet above ground level, but transitions to 15 feet by the end of the sequence.

25. Click the **Pause** icon (same location as **Play**) to pause the animation.

26. Save your file as MyQuickStart05.max for use in the next Quick Start tutorial.

This concludes Quick Start 5. This tutorial has demonstrated how quickly and easily you can create cameras and put things into motion. Although you've prepared an animation for rendering, you've only brushed the surface on what's possible with cameras and motion control. In the following chapters, you'll delve deeper into the power of 3ds Max and see just what's possible. In the next and final Quick Start tutorial, you'll see the finished product come to life by rendering each frame of the animation sequence and compiling the individual images into a single animation file.

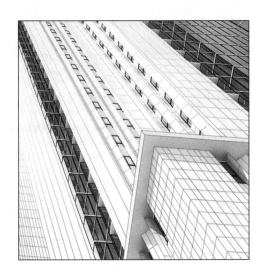

Chapter 13

CAMERA BASICS

Cameras in 3ds Max allow you to view a scene from a particular perspective, using all the controls you would expect to find in real-world cameras, as well as many other controls that are not available in the real world. Cameras can capture individual still images or animated sequences. Multiple cameras give you the ability to record the same scene from multiple perspectives and play the role of film director. Compared to other features in 3ds Max, the complexity of cameras is rather minor and the number of parameters involved is relatively small. Just like other features, however, the elements that you do control and the procedures you implement in the use of cameras require just as much skill and experience to master.

In the field of architectural visualization, the use of cameras is not always as simple and straightforward as an outside observer might think. Although the need for special effects, smoke and mirrors, and high-speed and erratic camera movement is not as great as it is in other industries, cameras used for architectural visualizations require just as much precision in their positioning and movement to achieve impressive and cost-effective presentations. Prior to beginning any work on a project, the modeler should have a good understanding of exactly what needs to be seen through the cameras when all elements have been added to the scene. Not having this understanding can result in the modeler spending far too much time creating models or adding too much detail that will not be seen or that will be out of the camera's point of view. Likewise, there will often be areas in your scenes that you must hide from the camera's view because of lack of detail. When you watch a TV show and hear someone say that it's "filmed before a live studio audience," you know that the cameras used on the set can only pan so far to either side before revealing technicians, set equipment, and the studio audience. Cameras in a studio have to be carefully positioned and oriented to capture all of the action, and constrained just as carefully to prevent showing too much. Equal care must be taken in the use of cameras in a visualization that maximizes cost efficiency and scene quality.

Finally, the user has the option to distort reality somewhat by making a scene appear bigger and better than it will actually be when the real structures are built. Using a wider-than-normal field of view on a camera, for example, can make a small room appear slightly bigger. Ultimately, it is through the lens of the camera that outside observers will view your presentation—thus, a good understanding of all the tools available for cameras and their use is critical in producing powerful presentations.

3ds Max provides many different ways to control the behavior of cameras. In Chapter 14, we'll cover the basics of camera animation, and in Chapter 15, you'll learn more advanced ways of controlling cameras through the use of the **Curve Editor** and controllers. For the remainder of this chapter, however, we'll focus on camera viewport navigation, camera placement, and the important camera parameters found in the rollouts of the **Modify** panel.

Camera types

There are two standard camera types in 3ds Max, both accessible through the **Camera** icon in the **Create** panel: **free cameras** and **target cameras**.

Both camera types are identical except for one major characteristic. Free cameras have only one component: the camera; whereas target cameras have two components: the camera and the target. Target cameras are always oriented to face the target, and because the target can move independently from the camera, the target can be animated. The left image in Figure 13-1 shows a target camera and the right image shows a free camera. Notice that both images are the same except for the small box (target) near the center of the left image. Target cameras always face their targets, so moving this target changes the direction that the camera faces. To change the direction of a stationary free camera, you can apply a rotate transform or use one of the viewport navigation control icons listed in Table 13-1. As a note, you can change the camera type from target to free and back again as needed.

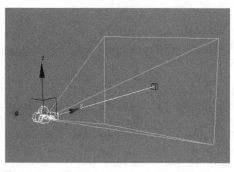
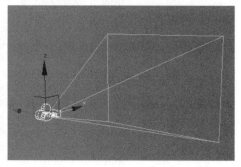

Figure 13-1. The target camera (left) and the free camera (right)

Creating cameras

To create a free camera using the Command panel, click **Create ➤ Cameras ➤ Free**, and click once in any viewport. The camera will face the direction of the view unless the viewport is displaying a User, Perspective, Camera, or Target Light view, in which case the camera will face in the negative z direction.

One way to create a target camera is to click **Target**, click and hold inside a viewport, and drag the mouse to position the target. Release the mouse button to place the target.

An even easier way to create a camera is by using the Create Camera from View command. This command creates a target camera (only) that matches the view of the active viewport and turns that viewport's display into a Camera view. To use this command, create the view you want in the active viewport and press Ctrl+C. If you already have a camera, and you want to move it to match the view in your active viewport, select the camera and then press Ctrl+C.

Once a camera is created, you can easily switch a viewport to the camera view by pressing C. If more than one camera exists, you will be asked which camera you want to switch views to.

Creating cameras

This exercise demonstrates how to create the two types of cameras.

1. Reset 3ds Max and create a few primitives in the Perspective viewport.
2. Within the **Create** panel, click the **Cameras** icon. The **Object Type** rollout appears with two types of camera available.
3. Click the **Free** button.
4. In the Front viewport, click, hold, and drag anywhere to create the camera and simultaneously move it into position. Release the mouse button to place the camera.
5. Right-click twice within the Perspective viewport; once to activate the viewport and one more time to end the camera-creation command.
6. Press C to change the Perspective view into the Camera view.
7. In any other viewport, apply a couple of transforms to the free camera to see their effect on the newly created Camera view.
8. Press Delete to delete the camera. Notice that the Camera view changes back to the Perspective view.
9. In the Command panel, click the **Target** button.
10. In the Top viewport, click, hold, and drag to create the camera and move the camera target into position. Release the mouse button to place the camera target.
11. Right-click the Perspective viewport, and then press C to change the Perspective view into the Camera view again.
12. In any other viewport, apply a couple of transforms to the target camera and the target to see their effect on the newly created camera view.
13. Delete the camera.
14. Activate the Perspective viewport and press Ctrl+C to create a camera from the view shown in the Perspective viewport.

Viewport navigation controls

When you create a Camera view, the viewport navigation controls in the bottom-right corner of the screen change to account for the source of the new view. Table 13-1 shows each of the new icons available when a camera view is active. The one icon you will probably want to steer clear of is **Roll Camera**, because it will cause your view to be tilted to one side or the other.

Table 13-1. Viewport navigation controls for the camera views

Icon	Name	Description
	Dolly Camera	Moves the camera along the axis in which the camera is pointing
	Dolly Target	Moves the target along the axis in which the camera is pointing
	Dolly Camera+Target	Moves camera and target along the axis in which the camera is pointing
	Perspective	Moves the camera closer to target, hence changing the FOV
	Roll Camera	Spins the camera along its local Z axis
	Orbit Camera	Rotates the camera around the target
	Pan Camera	Rotates the target around the camera

Some additional notes about the viewport navigation controls are as follows:

- By holding down the mouse scroll button, you can execute the Truck Camera command without having to click the icon.
- By holding down the Shift key, you can constrain camera movement to a single axis.
- By holding down the Ctrl key, you can magnify the effects of the viewport navigation controls.
- By holding down the Alt key, you can achieve finer control when using the viewport navigation tools.

Camera placement

In addition to offering transforms and viewport navigation controls, 3ds Max gives you the opportunity to place cameras precisely using two other helpful features: **Align Camera** and **Place Highlight**.

Align Camera

Not to be confused with the Align command (which can be used at any time to precisely place any object), the Align Camera feature aligns a camera to the normal of a specific face on a specific object. This allows you to precisely position and orient an existing camera so that it is directly in front of and facing a particular object.

To use this feature (shown in the top-left image of Figure 13-2), select a camera, click and hold the **Align** icon in the **Main** toolbar, and select the **Align Camera** icon from the flyout. Click and hold on top of any face inside the active viewport. A blue normal arrow will appear on the face that your mouse is over, as shown in the top-right image. Once you let go, the selected camera will move directly in front of and align itself with the normal of the face you choose, as shown in the bottom-left image. The image on the bottom-right shows the new view from the selected camera.

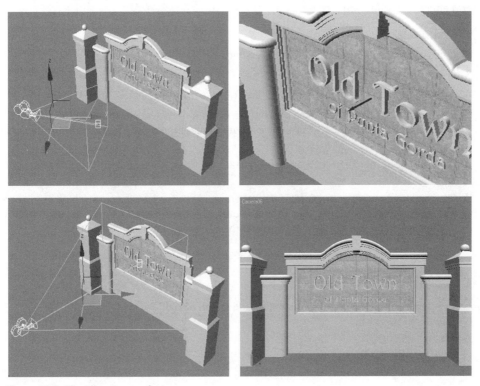

Figure 13-2. The Align Camera feature

Place Highlight

Another tool that you can use to align a camera to a specific face on a specific object is the Place Highlight command. This command works the same way as the Align Camera command, with one minor exception. Rather than showing you just a blue arrow to align the camera with, the Place Highlight command displays the camera in its new position as you move your cursor from one face to another.

The icon for the Place Highlight command is located directly above the **Align Camera** icon within the **Align** flyout icon. To use this command, click the **Place Highlight** icon and click and hold on top of any face inside the active viewport. A blue normal arrow will appear on the face that your mouse is over, and the camera will move into position. If you move the cursor over other faces, the camera will follow along and update its position. To finish the command, release the mouse button and the camera will remain in position, aligned with the normal of the last face your mouse was over.

Positioning cameras

This exercise demonstrates how to use the Align Camera and Place Highlight features to position cameras effectively within your scenes.

1. Reset 3ds Max.
2. Create a sphere of any size within the Perspective viewport.
3. Create a free camera anywhere in your scene.
4. Click and hold the **Align** icon to reveal the flyout icons and click the **Align Camera** icon.
5. Click and hold on top of any face of the sphere inside the active viewport. A blue normal arrow will appear on the face that your mouse is over. Release the mouse button and the camera will move into position.
6. Click and hold the **Align** icon again to reveal the flyout icons, and click the **Place Highlight** icon.
7. Click and hold on top of any face of the sphere inside the active viewport. A blue normal arrow will appear on the face that your mouse is over, and the selected camera will align itself with this normal. Release the mouse button and the camera will move into position.

Basic camera parameters

Cameras contain two unique rollouts: **Parameters** and **Depth of Field Parameters** (shown in Figure 13-3).

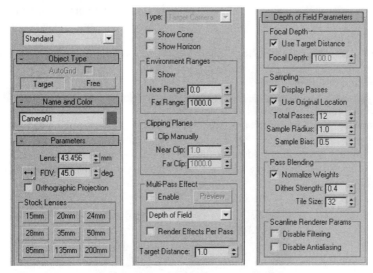

Figure 13-3. The standard camera rollouts

I'll discuss the most important of these features shortly.

Lens length and field of view

The first important parameter in the **Parameters** rollout, **Lens**, is linked directly to the next important parameter found directly below it, **FOV** (field of view). The **Lens** value is the focal length of the camera in millimeters, and controls the FOV seen through the camera. Changing either parameter causes the other parameter to change.

The **Lens** value in 3ds Max corresponds to the same FOV found on a camera in the real world. For example, using a standard 50mm lens will result in a FOV of 39.6 degrees in both 3ds Max and the real world. This and many other standard lens values can be found in the **Stock Lenses** section of this rollout. It is important to note that the typical camera that uses 35mm film does not use a 35mm lens. The typical everyday camera you buy in a store will use 35mm film, but will have a 50mm lens. A lens of 50mm provides the same type of image that your eyes perceive; anything else will distort the image to some degree.

By default, 3ds Max starts the first camera with a FOV of 45, which corresponds to a **Lens** value of 43.456mm. Although this is not a standard lens length, it is close to the standard 50mm and is perfectly suitable for most work. Personally, I use a 50mm or 35mm lens for almost every scene, depending on which one shows or hides the foreground the way I want. Occasionally, when rendering a scene such as a small room in which space is minimal, I use a wider-angle 28mm lens to make the room appear slightly bigger and more spacious. Any lens smaller than 28mm will produce unrealistic and distorted views and should only be used if a specific and necessary effect is desired.

The next options I find particularly useful are the **Show Cone** and **Show Horizon** options. When a camera is selected, light blue lines are displayed emanating from the camera. These lines represent the cone and show the boundaries of the camera's view. When the camera is not selected, the cone disappears unless the **Show Cone** option is enabled. Enabling the **Show Cone** option is particularly useful when using the Top view, moving objects around in a scene, and when you're trying to see when the objects come in and out of the camera's view.

The **Show Horizon** option displays a black line in Camera view to represent the horizon, as shown in Figure 13-4. Knowing where the horizon is when viewing your scene through a camera can be critical in the placement of distant objects. This option also helps you determine how far out you should place your terrain and where it should meet the sky. The closer your artificial horizon is to the true horizon, the more realistic your image will be. The horizon line can also show you if your camera is tilted to one side or another.

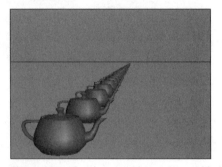

Figure 13-4. The Show Horizon option enabled

Using Lens length and FOV settings

This exercise demonstrates some of the important **Lens** length and **FOV** settings.

1. Reset 3ds Max and create a few primitives in the Perspective view.

2. In the Front view, create a free camera.

3. Activate the Left view, and then press C to change the view into a Camera view.

4. At the top of the **Parameters** rollout, click and drag on the slider arrows to the right of lens. Notice that the grid inside the Camera view and the cone inside the Perspective view change accordingly.

5. Click some of the various stock lenses to see their corresponding fields of view.

6. Click inside any viewport to deselect the camera. Notice that the camera cone is no longer visible.

7. Select the camera again and enable the **Show Cone** option (located below the **Stock Lenses** section).

8. Click inside any viewport to deselect the camera again. Notice that this time the camera cone is still visible.

9. Select the camera again and enable the **Show Horizon** option (located below the **Show Cone** option). This provides an artificial horizon as a display aid.

Environment ranges

In the next section of the **Parameters** rollout, **Environment Ranges**, you specify the distance from the camera for which environment effects, such as fog, are to be used. More detail regarding environment ranges will be covered in Chapter 18. For now, let's move on to the next set of parameters.

Clipping planes

The next important feature in the **Parameters** rollout is **Clipping Planes**. This feature lets you tell 3ds Max the distance at which you want the camera to begin viewing objects and the distance at which you want it to stop viewing objects. By default, cameras are not set to clip their views. To get a camera to clip its view, you must enable the **Clip Manually** option, as shown in Figure 13-5. With units set to US Standard, the default values for the Near Clip and Far Clip are 1.0" and 83'4" (1,000 units), respectively. This means that nothing within a distance of 1" from the camera will be seen, and likewise, nothing farther away than 83'4" will be seen.

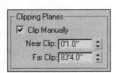

Figure 13-5. The Clipping Planes section, with the Clip Manually option enabled

The Clipping Planes feature comes in handy in a number of situations. One is when you want to show a cut-away section of a building, as the image in Figure 13-6. The top two images show a simple building elevation and floor plan with the camera used to view the elevation. The bottom two images show the same elevation and floor plan with Clipping Planes enabled. In the bottom-right image, the near clip plane cuts through the building and the far clip plane lies on the outside. The result is a building section view, as shown in the bottom-left image.

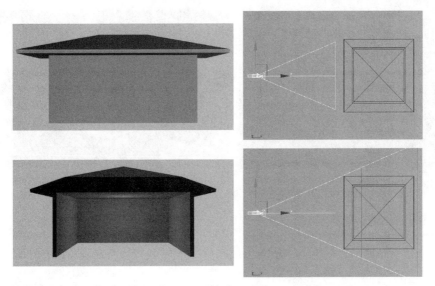

Figure 13-6. The Clipping Planes feature enabled to produce a building section

Another situation in which the Clipping Planes feature is useful is when you want to make an interior scene appear larger than it really is, as shown in Figure 13-7.

In the top-left image, you can see that the camera is placed just inside the walls of the room, and in fact, as close to the walls as possible in this corner of the room. The image on the top-right shows the resulting view from that location.

In the bottom-left image, you can see that the camera is placed outside the room, but with Clipping Planes enabled, you can hide the walls that block the view of the room. Notice that the near clip is placed just inside the walls. The bottom-right image shows the view from outside the room while using the Clipping Planes option. This result is an image that portrays a much more spacious room.

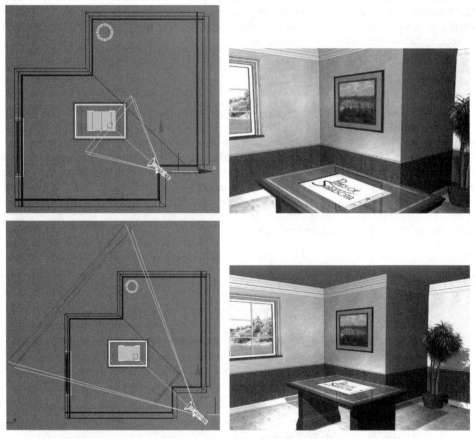

Figure 13-7. Clipping Planes enabled to make a room appear more spacious

Using clipping planes

This exercise demonstrates how to use clipping planes to hide the foreground of your scene. Though simplistic in nature, this same procedure can be used to hide objects that block the camera's view, as in the example in Figure 13-7.

1. Reset 3ds Max.
2. In the Perspective viewport, create a box of any size and click the **Zoom Extents All** icon. The view should look like the left image in the following illustration.
3. Press Ctrl+C to create a camera from the Perspective view.
4. Go to the **Modify** panel, and in the **Clipping Planes** section of the **Parameters** rollout, enable the **Clipping Manually** option.
5. To the right of the **Near Clip** value, click, hold, and drag the slider arrows upward until the front of the box is clipped, as shown in the right image of the following illustration.

 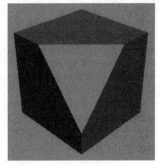

Summary

This chapter has covered the basics of viewport navigation, camera placement, and some of the important camera features found in the rollouts of the **Modify** panel. 3ds Max gives you an enormous amount of tools to control camera behavior—but as you saw in this chapter, a large portion of those tools are either just a different means to the same end, or they don't apply as well to visualizations as they do to other industries. Nevertheless, the features covered in this chapter are critical in everyday work, and along with the features covered in the next two chapters and Chapter 18, you'll have all the important tools needed to control camera behavior for your exact needs.

In Chapter 14, you'll learn the basics of camera animation, and in Chapter 15 you'll learn more advanced ways of controlling cameras through the use of the **Curve Editor** and controllers.

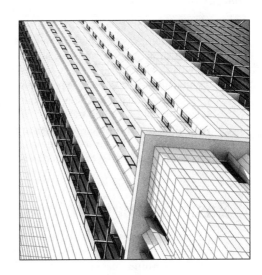

Chapter 14

ANIMATION BASICS

If someone were to ask me in what field I work, I would say, "3D computer animation." I could rightfully say, "3D computer renderings" or "3D computer stills," but it just wouldn't have the same pizzazz. Likewise, if you show people outside the 3D world your portfolio, they may be quite impressed with great stills, but if you show them quality animation, they will probably be left scratching their heads in amazement. We have reached the point where it is time to breathe life into what has been, until now, stillness.

Animations offer something unique that stills simply can't provide—a true sense of being immersed within a scene. They walk you through a project as if taking your hand and saying, "Look here, see that, watch this."

While an animation can give you much more, the final product comes at a hefty price. With a single still image, touching up blemishes or making enhancements to improve the overall appearance is easy. With an animation, you do not have the same kind of flexibility. Many post-production tools in 3ds Max and third-party programs allow you to improve the final look of an animation; however, the raw animation must have a certain level of quality to make the scene believable and free of glaring defects. In fact, faking 3D is not too difficult for individual objects or even an entire scene when the viewer is limited to a single perspective. However, when you take the viewer for a stroll into, out of, or through a project, it's quite clear just how three-dimensional a scene is. Of course, that clarity creates the problem of rendering up to 30 frames for each second of animation.

This chapter covers the basics of animation as they apply to architectural visualizations. In other industries, such as films and games, animation is an immense subject area that would require extensive coverage of nearly all the 3ds Max features. Fortunately for us, the animation requirements for an architectural visualization are relatively small. You will need to learn how to move cameras throughout your project and animate the elements in your scene that the viewer would expect to see in motion, such as people, cars, and water. But we won't need to cover the intricacies of complicated motion like you would if you were trying to perform character animation. In the next chapter, you will learn how to use the **Curve Editor** to provide greater control of your animated objects. With these two chapters, you will have all of the tools needed to animate an architectural visualization.

Basic animation interfaces

Before we create a simple animation sequence, we should discuss the basic animation interfaces. 3ds Max contains several powerful interfaces that give you more than enough control over your animations. The **Motion** panel and **Curve Editor**, covered in the next chapter, are two powerful interfaces that enable you to perform complex animation. For now, let's stick to those basic animation interfaces, so that we're prepared to dive into a discussion on key framing, which is arguably the most important concept of animation. After covering key framing, we will move on to the next chapter's discussion of the **Curve Editor**.

Time Configuration dialog box

The first and most basic interface that should be mentioned is the **Time Configuration** dialog box, shown in Figure 14-1. This dialog box controls the number of frames in your scene and the rate at which they are played back.

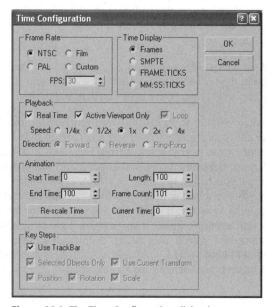

Figure 14-1. The Time Configuration dialog box

The **Frame Rate** section specifies the number of frames played per second for any animation you create. This rate can be designated as **NTSC** (National Television Standards Committee), **PAL** (Phase Alternating Line), or **Film** standard, or you can specify your own frames per second (fps) rate. The standard rate used in visualizations is the NTSC rate of 30 FPS, but if you are short on rendering time, because the project deadline is looming, you can get away with using the standard **Film** rate of 24 fps. This will shave 20% off your rendering time.

The **Time Display** section specifies how time is displayed in the time slider and throughout the other interfaces. I recommend leaving this setting on **Frames** as it provides the simplest and most straight-forward display.

The **Playback** section controls only the viewport playback rate. The **Real Time** setting allows you to play back animations at the rate specified in the **Frame Rate** section regardless of your graphics card's limitations. When a scene becomes so large that your graphics card can't refresh the display fast enough to keep up with the animation playback rate, this option allows 3ds Max to skip displaying as many frames as necessary to keep the animation playing smoothly in real time. If you need to see each frame displayed, regardless of how choppy the animation is, disable this option.

The last important section in this dialog box, **Animation**, defines a length of time known as the active time segment. The **active time segment** is the number of frames that are accessible through the time slider. By default, the time slider is set to a length of 100 frames, with the starting frame being 0; how-ever, the time slider may only dictate a small segment of the overall animation in a scene, hence, the term active time segment. You can have 1,000 frames in your animation, but by setting your **Start Time** to **0** and **End Time** to **200**, the active time segment will only be 200 frames. The rest of your animation will still exist but will not be accessible through the time slider.

Each scene may require a unique length, but you shouldn't need to change the start time. Although designating the first frame as 0 may seem strange, remember that frame 0 captures the scene before time starts. Therefore, by the time one second has passed, 31 frames have been played, not 30.

It is important to note that when you want to change the number of frames in your scene, you should always determine whether you need to rescale time. Clicking the **Re-scale Time** button opens the **Re-scale Time** dialog box with which you can change the number of frames and rescale time in the process. Rescaling time is sometimes necessary when your scene contains keyframes, which is a fea-ture in animation that we'll discuss in the next few pages of this chapter. As an introduction to the concepts of keyframes and rescaling time, imagine that you have a 100-frame scene in which to rotate an object 360 degrees. If you change the scene length to 200 frames without rescaling time, the object will still turn during the first 100 frames but stop at frame 100. If you rescale time as you change the number of frames, the object will turn 360 degrees during the entire 200 frames.

This exercise demonstrates how to configure a 3ds Max scene for a certain number of frames and how to change the frame rate, so animations play at a desired speed.

1. Reset 3ds Max.

2. Click the **Time Configuration** icon to the left of the viewport navigation controls.

3. In the **Frame Rate** section, select **Custom** and change the **FPS** (frames per second) to **15**, and press Enter. This changes the playback speed of animations from 30 to 15, which is a typical web video speed.

4. In the **Animation** section, change the **End Time** value to **900**, and click **OK**. This changes the animation length from the default 100 frames to 900 frames, which at 15 fps corresponds to an animation length of 60 seconds.

Now that we have covered the details of time configuration, let's look at the time slider and the animation playback controls.

Time slider

The time slider (Figure 14-2) is a feature positioned immediately below the viewports showing the active time segment, as defined within the **Time Configuration** dialog box.

Figure 14-2. The time slider and track bar

The time slider moves above the track bar from the first frame on the left to the last frame on the right, and displays its current frame location and the total frame count on the slider itself. As just mentioned, you can change the number of frames displayed in the track bar in the **Time Configuration** dialog box.

You can click the arrows to the left and right of the time slider to move forward or back one frame at a time. You can also move the slider to a specific frame by either clicking the empty area to the left or right of the slider arrows at the frame you want to move to or by clicking and dragging the slider to the desired frame.

Animation playback controls

To the immediate left of the viewport navigation controls are the animation playback controls, as shown in Figure 14-3.

The **Play** button, located in the middle of the controls, plays animations at the frame rate specified in the **Time Configuration** dialog box. Clicking again pauses the animation. This button is actually a flyout, and by holding down the **Play** flyout, you can access the **Play Selected** button, which is a handy feature that plays only those objects currently selected. When you use this feature, selected objects play, and all other objects are hidden from view. This is helpful when you want to focus on select objects or when your scene is so large that the graphics card can't keep up with the frame rate and display all your animated objects in real time.

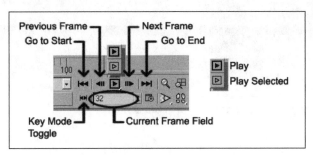

Figure 14-3. The animation playback controls

The arrows in the playback control area also move the time slider forward or back one frame at a time, or to the start or end frame, as shown in Figure 14-3. The greater-than sign (>) and less-than sign (<) keyboard shortcuts are a very handy way to move through time as well. One additional way to move the slider is to type a frame number in the current frame field.

At the bottom left of the time controls is the **Key Mode** toggle, which lets you change the **Next Frame** and **Previous Frame** buttons to the **Next Key** and **Previous Key** buttons. This toggle will be discussed further in the next section.

Keyframing

Before the advent of computers, animations were handdrawn one painstaking frame at a time. Since this was such a laborious process, a firm's junior animators would draw the majority of the individual frames while the senior animators concentrated on certain key frames, hence the term **keyframing**. The senior animator drew frames that showed key changes in action while the junior animator drew all the frames in between.

The process of keyframing is as important today as it has ever been. In computer animation, the animator dictates what a scene looks like at certain key frames, and the program fills in all of the frames in between with the necessary changes. Figure 14-4 shows our favorite teapot moving from left to right as it undergoes a massive squash transform during a simple seven-frame sequence. For display purposes, a feature known as ghosting, which will be discussed in the next chapter, is enabled to make the teapot's condition at each frame visible. A keyframe is created at frame 0 where the teapot is in its normal condition, and a second keyframe is created at frame 6 where the teapot is given its new position and the squash transform. Given the teapot's condition at frame 0 and frame 6, 3ds Max knows what condition the teapot must be in at each frame in between to provide a smooth and continuous transition.

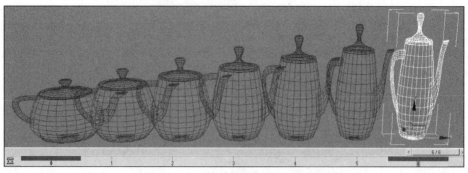

Figure 14-4. A simple seven-frame animation with two keyframes

Creating keyframes

Regardless of the type of action you need to animate in your scene, a keyframe is required at the start and end of the action to record the complete condition of the object at these frames and allow 3ds Max to figure out how to transition the object from one state to the other. There are numerous ways to assign keys in 3ds Max. Regardless of which method you use, keys are assigned to objects at particular frames; they are not assigned to frames, thereby affecting each object in the scene at those frames.

When a key is created at a particular frame, a key indicator will be displayed in the track bar at that frame, as shown in Figure 14-5. This indicator will display one, two, or three different colors for the three transform types depending on which transforms the object has received: red for position, green for rotation, and blue for scale. These color assignments are a great aid when working with keys in the **Curve Editor,** particularly manipulating the individual components of a key, which will be covered in the next chapter. For now, however, let's focus on how to create keys.

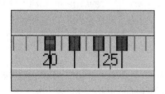

Figure 14-5. A key at frame 20 for all three transforms and keys for each individual transform at frames 22, 24, and 26

3ds Max provides several different methods of creating a keyframe. In each method, the object you want to assign a key to must first be selected.

One way to assign a key is to right-click the time slider, which brings up the **Create Key** dialog box shown in Figure 14-6. The default settings create a key for the position, rotation, and scale states at the current frame. Click **OK** to accept these settings and create a key.

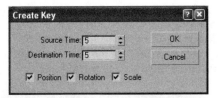

Figure 14-6. The Create Key dialog box

Another way to create a key is to click the **Auto Key** button (which turns red), move the slider to another frame, and transform the object. The **Auto Key** button, shown in Figure 14-7, automatically creates a key at the first frame in the scene and a key at the frame the transform was applied. If another key existed at an earlier frame in the scene before the **Auto Key** was used, a key will only be created where the transform was applied.

Figure 14-7. Auto and Set Key buttons

Similar to **Auto Key** is the **Set Key** feature which, when clicked, allows you to quickly create a key by clicking the larger button to the left displaying a key. The **Set Key** feature is used in conjunction with the **Set Key Filters**, a tool that determines which tracks will receive a key, while the **Auto Key** feature on the other hand creates a key for only those transforms that are applied. Note that the **Set Key** feature is not recommended unless you have a specific need that it addresses, as it seems to be bug-prone.

Keys can also be created in the **Motion** panel, the **Track View - Curve Editor**, and **Track View - Dope Sheet**, but for now, we will focus on the **Create Key** and **Auto Key** methods. Without understanding key creation using these methods, using the **Motion Panel** and **Track View** will be difficult.

Creating basic motion

Now that we've covered the basic animation interfaces and the concept of keyframing, let's move on to some basic examples of motion. The following example may seem simplistic, but it incorporates a great range of the procedures you will use in your own scenes.

The top image in Figure 14-8 shows a teapot with a trajectory path that includes two turns during a short 30-frame sequence. In the top image, the teapot starts at point A, makes a turn at points B and C, and comes to a stop at point D. How do you get an object to make such movements? As our previous discussion shows, keyframes need to be assigned to an object whenever you want the object to make an animated change in condition, whether that change is in trajectory, size, or shape.

The teapot has been assigned a key at frame 0 (point A), 10 (point B), 20 (point C), and at its final position at frame 30 (point D). If a key is created at frames 0 and 30 only, as shown in the bottom image, the teapot moves only in a straight line from point A to point D. Likewise, if you delete the keys at points B and C, the trajectory would change from the one shown in the top image to the one shown in the bottom. Now let's re-create this motion in a short tutorial.

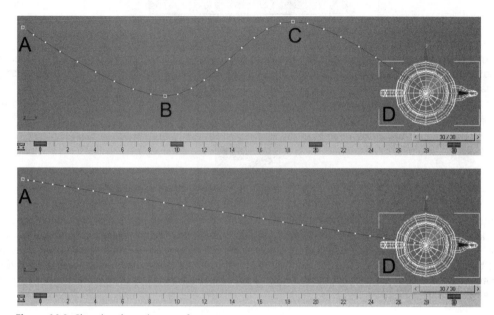

Figure 14-8. Changing the trajectory of a teapot

Creating basic motion

This exercise demonstrates how to create the motion shown in the top image of Figure 14-8, in which the teapot makes two distinct turns between its start and end points.

1. Reset 3ds Max.

2. Click the **Time Configuration** icon to the left of the viewport navigation controls. The **Time Configuration** dialog box opens.

3. In the **Animation** section, change the **End Time** to **30,** and click **OK** to close the dialog box. There is no need to rescale time, because there are no keys yet.

4. Make the Top viewport active, and click the **Maximize Viewport** toggle to maximize.

5. Create a teapot of any size, zoom away and pan the view to position the teapot at the left end of the screen, as shown by point A in Figure 14-8.

6. Right-click in the Top viewport and select **Properties** from the quad menus.

7. In the **Display Properties** section, enable the **Trajectory** option, and click **OK** to close the dialog box.

8. Click the **Auto Key** button. The button turns red.

9. Move the time slider to frame 10.

10. Move the teapot to the right, one-third across the screen and slightly down. If necessary, pan and zoom to make room on the screen. This creates a key at frame 0 and another key at frame 10.

11. Move the time slider to frame 20.

12. Move the teapot farther to the right the same distance as in the first move and move it slightly up. This creates a key at frame 20.

13. Move the time slider to frame 30.

14. Move the teapot once more to the right the same distance as in the first two moves and move it slightly down. This creates a key at frame 30. The trajectory should look similar to that shown in the top image of Figure 14-8.

15. Click the **Play** button. The teapot should move swiftly along the trajectory path.

16. Right-click the red key shown directly above frame 10.

17. Move the cursor over the **Delete Key** flyout and select **All** from the list. The key at frame 10 is deleted, and the trajectory of the teapot changes drastically.

18. Click the **Undo** icon to restore the key at frame 10.

19. Save this scene. It will be used in the next chapter.

Summary

This chapter covered three of the most basic animation interfaces in 3ds Max: the **Time Configuration** dialog box, the time slider, and the animation playback controls. The principles of keyframing were also discussed to show how to change the action of an object. Having completed this last tutorial, you should now have a good foundation in the basic concepts of animation.

In the next chapter, we will further analyze the animation of the teapot and use this example to illustrate the concepts of controllers and constraints. We will also cover the use of the **Motion** panel and the **Curve Editor**, the two main interfaces with which to work with constraints and controllers. After this next chapter, you will know everything needed to perform almost any type of animation in an architectural visualization.

Chapter 15

ANIMATION CONTROLLERS

3ds Max gives you the ability to create animations by making transforms and other changes to objects manually and using keyframes to record the changes. Not having to make changes to objects for every single frame of animation certainly makes life as an animator much easier than it used to be in the days when each frame was hand drawn. But 3ds Max contains far more power than we explored in the last chapter. One of the main concepts we covered, keyframing, is arguably the most important feature of computer animation; however, using features known as controllers and constraints in conjunction with your keyframes makes your potential as an animator almost limitless.

Controllers allow you to dictate long periods of complex and detailed action with just a few clicks of the mouse. For example, with controllers you can make a camera follow a long and complicated spline that represents the path of motion through a building, and specify with precise detail how the camera behaves at each step along the way. You can make a car follow the contour of a mountain road, slowing down the car during the turns and speeding it up during the straight sections of the road.

Numerous interfaces allow you to assign and edit controllers, but two interfaces stand out as the primary tools for working with controllers: the **Motion** panel and the **Curve Editor**. In this chapter, we will cover both of these and see just how easy it can be to work with controllers. After completing this chapter, you will have a great foundation for computer animation with 3ds Max.

Controllers

All animation in 3ds Max is dictated by special algorithms known as **controllers**. As the animator, obviously you dictate where an object goes and its condition at each keyframe. However, 3ds Max assigns default controllers to dictate how an object behaves between keyframes, at least until you make changes.

In the example used in the last tutorial of the previous chapter, a teapot moved from point A, to point B, to point C, and finally to point D, as shown in the top image of Figure 15-1. Notice that there are pronounced curves through points B and C, making the teapot's movements smooth as it moves from one point to another. These curves were created automatically as the default means of interpolating the teapot from one keyframe to another. The curves were created by a type of controller known as the **Bezier control**, perhaps the most versatile controller available in 3ds Max.

But what if you want the teapot to move in a straight line from one point to another, without the curves, as shown in the bottom image of Figure 15-1? All you have to do is change the type of controller assigned to the teapot from **Bezier** to **Linear**. The way to do this will be discussed later in this chapter during the introduction to the **Motion** panel.

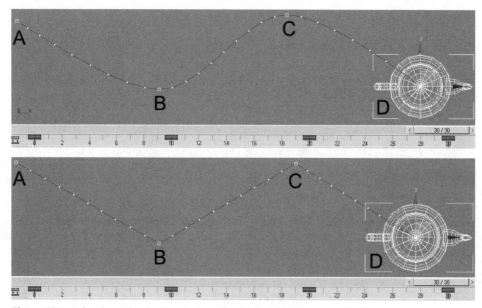

Figure 15-1. Animation using the Bezier controller (top) and Linear controller (bottom)

There are a few dozen different types of controllers that let you control your animations in just about any way imaginable. As an example, with the **Motion Capture Controller** you can use an external device such as a mouse to capture the motion you want a car to follow. Using the **Audio Controller**, you can use the amplitude from a music file to dictate how you want a radio to vibrate from the heavy bass coming from its speakers. You can assign random motion to the waves of water using the **Noise Controller**. The possibilities are as limitless as your imagination, and to completely cover every different type of controller and all of their possible uses would take volumes. But once again, in the world of architectural visualizations, it's not necessary to learn every possible feature. We are going to focus on a few key controllers that will give you the power to create great animations and the knowledge to experiment with the many other controllers.

Constraints

A **constraint** in 3ds Max is a type of controller tool that helps you automate action. Constraints are used to control one object's transformations through the use of another object. In the case of a car driving along a mountain road, the car is constrained by another object—the road. In the case of a camera walk-through, the camera is constrained to a specific path defined by a spline.

There are seven types of constraints in Max.

- The **Path Constraint** constrains the movement of an object to a path.

- The **Surface Constraint** constrains the movement of an object to the surface of another object.

- The **Position Constraint** constrains the movement of an object to the movement of another object.

- The **Attachment Constraint** constrains the movement of an object to the faces on another object.

- The **LookAt Constraint** constrains the orientation of an object, so that it always looks at another object.

- The **Orientation Constraint** constrains the rotation of an object so that it follows the rotation of another object.

- The **Link Constraint** constrains an object so that it's linked from one object to another.

Each of these seven constraints performs a unique function; together they give you the ability to constrain an object in just about any way you can imagine. Again, in the world of architectural visualizations, we need to focus on only a couple of these constraints. Although you may find an occasional use for each of the available seven, the two constraints that we are going to cover are the **Path** and **Surface Constraints**.

You can use two main methods to assign a constraint to an object. You can access constraints through the **Animation** menu, as shown in Figure 15-2, or through the **Motion** panel. In either case, constraints are only available when the object you want to constrain is selected. To assign a constraint through the **Animation** menu, select the object you want to constrain, select the type of constraint to use, and click on another object to which you want to constrain the first object.

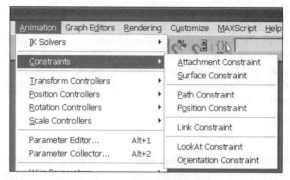

Figure 15-2. Assigning constraints through the Animation menu

Assigning a constraint through the Animation menu

This exercise demonstrates how to assign a path constraint using the **Animation** menu.

1. Reset 3ds Max.

2. In the Top viewport create a rectangle of any size, and inside the rectangle create a small teapot that is about one-quarter of the rectangle's size, as shown in the left image of the following illustration.

3. With the teapot selected, click the **Animation** menu, and select **Constraints ➤ Path Constraint**.

4. Click the rectangle in any viewport. Notice that the teapot is moved to one corner of the rectangle.

5. Click the **Play** button. The teapot moves around the rectangle during the course of the active time segment, as shown in the right image.

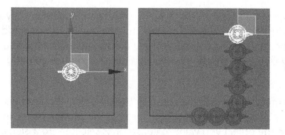

Motion panel

Now that controllers and constraints have been introduced, let's discuss one of the key interfaces used in conjunction with controllers and constraints—the **Motion** panel. The **Motion** panel, shown in Figure 15-4, is not only an interface through which you can assign controllers or constraints, it allows you to edit or manipulate those assignments, as well as create and edit keys.

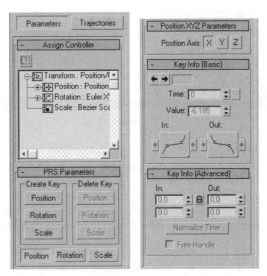

Figure 15-3. The Motion panel

The **Motion** panel is made up of two main areas: **Parameters** and **Trajectories**. The **Parameters** area lets you assign and edit controllers for the three transform types: position, rotation, and scale. Within this area you can also create, edit, and delete keys. In the **Trajectories** area, you can view and edit an object's trajectory. Both areas are invaluable in the controlling of animated objects.

Parameters

While the **Parameters** area of the **Motion** panel may look somewhat complicated and intimidating, it is really quite simple and not very large. The **Motion** panel interface itself is very straightforward, although some of the controllers and constraints that you can access through the **Motion** panel can be quite challenging to learn and use.

The first two rollouts, **Assign Controller** and **PRS Parameters**, are standard rollouts that appear for all controllers, while the additional rollouts change, depending on which controllers are assigned to an object.

Assign Controller rollout

As its name implies, the first rollout of the **Parameters** area, **Assign Controller**, allows you to assign or change controllers for an object. All objects are assigned default controllers upon their creation, but until an object is animated, the controllers are not activated and serve no purpose. The type of controller assigned depends on the type of transform or parameter that's being animated.

The **Motion** panel allows you to assign and edit controllers for transforms only. Later in the chapter, we'll discuss the **Curve Editor**, which gives the ability to assign or edit controllers for any object track type.

As Figure 15-4 shows, the default controllers assigned to position, rotation, and scale are **Position XYZ**, **Euler XYZ**, and **Bezier Scale**, respectively.

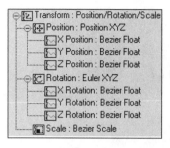

Figure 15-4. The Transform controllers

The **Position XYZ** and **Euler XYZ** controllers are both controllers that break down the X, Y, and Z components of an object's animation into three separate tracks: one each for X, Y, and Z. This compartmentalization allows each component to receive its own individual controller. By default, 3ds Max assigns the **Position XYZ** controller to each object's position transform track and the **Euler XYZ** controller for each object's rotation track. The **Bezier** Scale controller is assigned to the **Scale** transform.

So what does all of this mean? As I mentioned at the beginning of the discussion on controllers, the Bezier controller is perhaps the most versatile controller available in 3ds Max. It is also the default controller for many parameters, because 3ds Max assumes that whenever you want action, you want it to be smooth, rather than rough and abrupt. The Bezier controller provides a smooth interpolation between keyframes, so an object's animation is smooth. For example, if you animate a car leaving a four-way intersection from a complete stop, you shouldn't make the car instantly start moving at high speed in the first frame after it starts its movement. The car should gradually accelerate to its cruising speed. Likewise, when the car is coming to a four-way intersection, you should not take the car from its cruising speed to a complete stop in one frame. That would look unrealistic. If you want to animate a tree blowing in the wind, the tree's limbs should move smoothly back and forth, accelerating and decelerating with every movement. It would look unrealistic for a tree branch to be moving swiftly in one direction and in just one frame change direction and move swiftly in the opposite direction.

If, for some reason, you decide that you do want your car to go from 0 to 60 in one frame, you only need to assign a different controller—in this case the **Linear** controller, which provides linear (constant and straight) animation from one keyframe to another.

With that said, let's discuss how to assign or change a controller.

Assigning and changing controllers

To assign or change a controller, select an object, go to the **Motion** panel and open the **Assign Controller** rollout. In the **Assign Controller** window, highlight one of the three transforms types or one of the individual XYZ tracks within a transform. When you make a selection, the **Assign Controller** icon (shown to the right) becomes selectable. Click the **Assign Controller** icon, select a controller type from the menu that appears and click **OK** to complete the command. This will assign a new controller to the selected transform type or to the individual track you selected within the transform. You can highlight multiple XYZ tracks within a transform that has separate track assignments.

Changing controllers

This exercise demonstrates how to assign a new controller to an object.

1. Open the scene created in the last tutorial of Chapter 14, or open the file named Ch15-01.max from the 3dsMax8\Friends_of_Ed folder.

2. Select the teapot object.

3. Click the **Motion** panel tab.

4. Open the **Assign Controller** rollout.

5. In the **Assign Controller** window, highlight the Position transform, as shown in the left image of the illustration following step 7.

6. Click the **Assign Controller** icon.

7. Select **Linear Position** from the **Assign Controller** menu, as shown in the right image of the following illustration. Click **OK** to close.

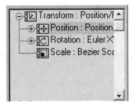
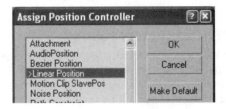

The teapot's X, Y, and Z movements are now controlled by the **Linear Position** controller, which causes the teapot to move in a straight line from one point to another, as shown in the following illustration. Notice also that the keyframe points indicated by the white dots along the trajectory are all evenly spaced. When the **Bezier Position** controller was assigned to the individual tracks of the **Position** controller, the keyframe points were not evenly spaced.

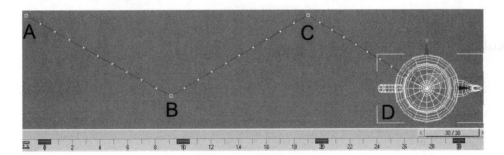

PRS Parameters rollout

The **PRS** (position, rotation, scale) **Parameters** rollout, shown in Figure 15-5, allows you to create or delete position, rotation, and scale keys without having to use the **Set Key** or **Auto Key** features. You can create or delete a key for only one of the three transforms at a time, depending on which transform button you click. The **Position**, **Rotation**, and **Scale** buttons across the bottom of the rollout determine which transform has its contents displayed in the **Key Info** rollout. To edit the rotation keys for an object, for example, click the **Rotation** button.

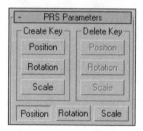

Figure 15-5. The PRS Parameters rollout

Position XYZ Parameters rollout

The **Position XYZ Parameters** rollout (Figure 15-6) appears by default when the **Position** button is highlighted in the **PRS Parameters** rollout, as shown in Figure 15-5, because the **Position XYZ** controller is the default controller assigned to an object's position transform when it is created. If the controller changes, this rollout will no longer be shown. Likewise, if you click the **Rotation** or **Scale** buttons in the **PRS Parameters** rollout, the **Position XYZ Parameters** rollout will disappear.

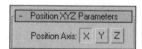

Figure 15-6. The Position XYZ Parameters rollout

Euler Parameters rollout

The **Euler Parameters** rollout, shown in Figure 15-7, appears by default when the **Rotation** button is highlighted in the **PRS Parameters** rollout, because the Euler controller is the default controller assigned to an object's rotation transform when it is first created. If you change controllers for the rotation transform, the **Euler Parameters** rollout will no longer be displayed.

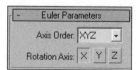

Figure 15-7. The Euler Parameters rollout

Key Info (Basic) rollout

Each key stores information for each of the three axes, X, Y, and Z. When the **Position XYZ** or Euler controllers are being used, the **Key Info (Basic)** rollout, shown in Figure 15-8, will display information for only one key at a time and one axis at a time, depending on which **axis** is highlighted in the **Position XYZ** or **Euler Parameters** rollouts.

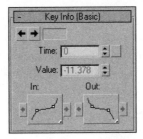

Figure 15-8. The Key Info (Basic) rollout for the Position XYZ and Euler controllers

As mentioned earlier, the **Bezier Float** controller is used by the individual tracks of the Position XYZ and Euler controllers. If the Bezier controller is assigned to an entire transform, rather than just the X, Y, or Z tracks of a transform, the **Key Info (Basic)** rollout changes to display X, Y, and Z parameters, as shown in Figure 15-9. Notice that the entire rollout is inaccessible until a key is created and the current frame is positioned on a keyframe.

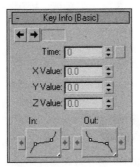

Figure 15-9. The Key Info (Basic) rollout for the Bezier controller

Once a key is created and the time slider is positioned on a key, the **Key Info (Basic)** rollout allows you to change several things related to the key.

The arrows at the top of the rollout allow you to quickly move from one keyframe to another, as long as more than one keyframe exists.

The **Time** field changes the time, or frame, at which the key is positioned. Since only one of the transforms is edited at a time, using this parameter moves only one transform key.

The **X**, **Y**, and **Z** values control the actual value of each of the X, Y, and Z components of an object's position, rotation, or scale, depending on which transform is being edited. For example, if a teapot is positioned at the world origin and the **Position** button is selected in the **PRS Parameters** rollout, the **X**, **Y**, and **Z** values will display a value of **0**. If the teapot is moved to the coordinates 10, 5, 20, then the **X**, **Y**, and **Z** values will display values of **10**, **5**, and **20**, respectively. Likewise, you can move the teapot along a particular axis by typing in the new position values directly into the fields or by using the slider arrows to the right of the fields.

The **In** and **Out** buttons, known as the **Key Tangent** flyouts, control the interpolation methods used by the selected key. Going back to the example discussed earlier in the chapter where a car accelerates or decelerates, the **In** and **Out** tangents control exactly how, or even if, that car accelerates or decelerates. If you click and hold either tangent flyout, a series of additional interpolation tangents is displayed, as shown in Figure 15-10. Selecting a different tangent changes the interpolation method and how the car moves from one keyframe to another. The next tutorial demonstrates the effect of some of the available interpolation methods.

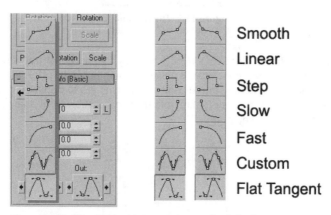

Figure 15-10. The standard interpolation methods for keys

Working with keys in the Motion panel

This exercise demonstrates how to create and edit keys in the **Motion** panel. To demonstrate these features, we will race three teapots to see how changing their assigned keys determines which teapot wins the race.

1. Reset 3ds Max.

2. In the far left side of the Top viewport, create a teapot of any size. Pan and zoom as necessary, so that the teapot takes up approximately one-fifth of the viewport's width.

3. Click the **Auto Key** button, move the time slider to frame **100**, and move the teapot to the far right side of the Top viewport.

4. Click the **Auto Key** button again to close the feature.

5. Move the time slider back to frame **0**.

6. Make two clones of the teapot using the **Copy** feature (not **Instance** or **Reference**), and position the three teapots side by side on the left-hand side of the Top viewport, as shown in the following illustration.

7. Click the **Play** button. Notice that each teapot finishes at the same time, because their motion is dictated by the same controllers and the same keys.

8. Click the **Stop** button.

9. Move the time slider back to frame **0**.

10. Click the middle teapot, and click the **Motion** panel tab.

11. Click and hold the **Out** tangent button and select the **Fast** tangent, as shown in the following illustration. The tangent buttons are only selectable on when the time slider is on a keyframe. Therefore make sure that you moved the time slider back to frame **0** (step 9).

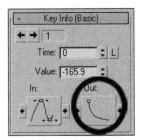

12. Click the **Play** button again. Now the middle teapot gets *out* to a *fast* start and takes a considerable early lead, as shown in the following illustration, but the other two teapots catch up with it at the finish. Notice the use of the words "out" and "fast" in the previous sentence. The teapot starts out quickly, because the **Out** tangent key at frame **0** was changed from **Flat** to **Fast**. Changing the **In** tangent at frame **0** would have no effect, because there is no frame before frame 0 and thus no way for the key to affect the speed that the teapot comes **in** to the keyframe. Also, notice the downward curve of the **Fast** icon. If you were to roll a ball down a hill shaped like this, the ball would start out rapidly but gradually slow down after coming out of the curve.

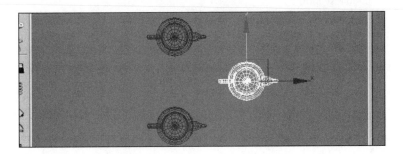

13. Click the **Stop** button and move the time slider to frame **100**.

14. Click the bottom teapot.

15. In the **Motion** panel, click and hold the **In** tangent button, and select the **Fast** tangent again as shown in the following illustration. The Fast tangent here is a mirrored version of the tangent you applied in step 11.

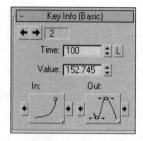

16. Click the **Play** button again. Notice now that the bottom teapot starts slowly, but comes *in* (to the finish) very rapidly and by frame **100** catches up with the other two teapots.

17. Click the **Stop** button and move the time slider to frame **0**.

18. Click the top teapot.

19. Click and hold the **Out** tangent button, and select the **Linear** tangent, as shown in the following illustration.

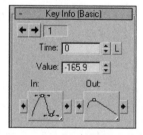

20. Click the **Play** button. Notice the constant speed of the top teapot throughout the entire **100** frames. You changed the **Out** tangent to linear so the teapot's speed was linear, or constant, during the first half of the animation. But how do you make one teapot finish before the others? Simple.

21. Click the **Stop** button.

22. Click the middle teapot.

23. Click and drag the key at frame **100** to frame **80**, as shown in the following illustration. When you click a key, it turns white.

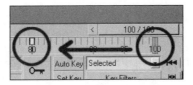

24. Click the **Play** button. Now the middle teapot gets to the finish line at frame **80** instead of frame **100**, clearly beating the competition.

Trajectories

The **Trajectories** area of the **Motion** panel, shown in the left image of Figure 15-11, displays an object's trajectory (path of travel) and allows you to edit the trajectory wherever keys exist. When you click the **Trajectories** button, the trajectory of the selected object appears as a red line with small squares at keyframe locations and small dots at every frame location, as shown in the image on the right.

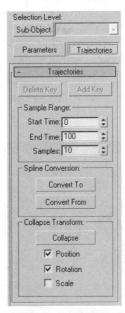

Figure 15-11. The Trajectories area of the Motion panel

To change the trajectory of an object that's already animated, select the object and click the **Trajectories** button. Then click the **Sub-Object** button above the **Trajectories** button, and, in any viewport, click one of the white squares and move it to a new location.

When the trajectory of an object is visible, you can add keys to any point on the trajectory by simply clicking the **Add Key** button at the top of the **Trajectories** rollout and clicking the trajectory at the point you want to add a key. Once a key is added, you can move it around as you like. You can just as easily delete a key by selecting it in a viewport and clicking the **Delete Key** button.

In the **Spline Conversion** section of the rollout you can create a spline from the trajectory of your object. Simply select your animated object, and click the **Convert To** button. When you do, a spline will appear that duplicates your object's trajectory. Conversely, you can quickly animate an object and assign a trajectory to it by selecting the object, clicking the **Convert From** button, and clicking the spline that you want the trajectory to simulate.

Curve Editor

The **Curve Editor**, shown in Figure 15-12, is a scene management tool that gives you great control over the creation and editing of keyframes. It uses curves on a graph to express animation, thereby allowing you to visualize the interpolation of your animations. With the **Curve Editor** you can assign controllers to your keys and manage animated parameters of an object, among numerous other things. This book introduces some of the best features the **Curve Editor** has to offer and shows you where further experimentation and exploration can take you.

The **Curve Editor** is one of two modes that make up a feature known as **Track View**. The other mode, the **Dope Sheet**, displays keyframes on a graph in a spreadsheet-like format, but is not covered in this book.

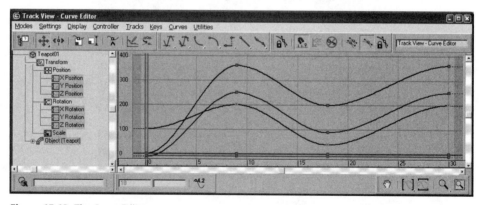

Figure 15-12. The Curve Editor

The **Curve Editor** is an extremely useful tool in editing animation. Although there are far too many features to cover in this chapter, one feature stands out for users in the architectural visualization industry—editing controllers. Although you can edit controllers in numerous other interfaces, such as the **Motion** panel or through the **Track Bar**, the **Curve Editor** gives you far more power and versatility to perform the editing and allows you to visualize the changes through the use of graphical displays. Earlier in the chapter we discussed the various interpolation methods used for keys, such as **Linear**, **Fast**, and **Smooth**, as shown in Figure 15-10. With the **Curve Editor**, these interpolation methods are graphically represented and can be easily edited to suit your needs.

The **Curve Editor** interface consists of a menu bar and toolbar across the top, a Controller window on the left that displays all scene objects and elements, and a Key window on the right that displays an object's animation graphically. Whenever you create an object, a material, a light, or any other type of scene element, it appears in the Controller window on the left, along with the parameters of the element. Whenever you select one or more objects in your scene, all keyframes for the selected objects are displayed in the Key window on the right.

To see these interfaces in action, let's complete two tutorials: one for editing controllers and one for editing animated parameters. After completing these tutorials, you should have a good understanding of the power of the **Curve Editor** and the skills for its basic use.

Editing controllers with the Curve Editor

This exercise demonstrates how to perform basic editing of controllers with the **Curve Editor**.

1. Reset 3ds Max.
2. Right-click inside the active viewport, select **Curve Editor** from the quad menu, and move the **Curve Editor** so that the Top viewport is completely visible.
3. Place the cursor over the open area of the controller window until the cursor changes into a hand symbol, as shown in the following illustration. Click and drag in the controller window, so that you can see word **Objects** in the bottom of the controller window. There are presently no objects in your scene, so no objects are displayed here.
4. In the far left side of the Top viewport, create a teapot of any size. Pan and zoom as necessary, so that the teapot takes up approximately one-fifth of the viewport's width. Notice that the teapot now appears under the **Objects** group in the controller window.
5. Pan up or down inside the controller window, so that you can see the X, Y, and Z position components of the teapot, as shown in the following illustration.

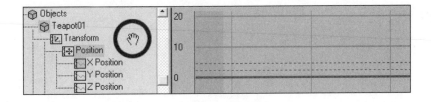

6. Click the **Auto Key** button and move the time slider to frame **100**.

7. On the main toolbar click **Select** and **Move**, then place the cursor over the X axis of the transform gizmo and drag the teapot to the far right side of the Top viewport along the X axis only. Notice that the X, Y, and Z components of the teapot's position transform are highlighted in the Controller window. Notice also that the teapot's position interpolation is now depicted graphically in the Key window, as shown in the following illustration.

8. Click the **Auto Key** button again to close the feature.

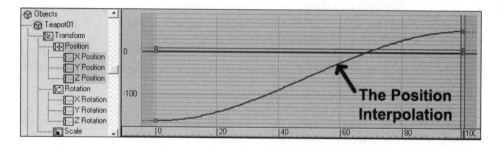

9. Click the **Play** button. Notice that the teapot starts off slowly, gradually accelerates to a cruising speed, and decelerates as it comes to frame **100**. Click the **Stop** button.

10. Right-click on top of the first key for the position interpolation, represented by a small gray square, as shown in the following illustration. This opens the Key Controller dialog box.

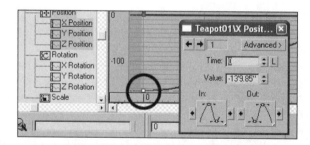

11. Click and hold the **In** tangent button and select the Linear tangent (second from top, showing the straight-line segment as in the following illustration). Notice that the interpolation curve did not change at all, because, as mentioned earlier, the **In** tangent only affects the frame coming into keyframe, and there are no frames before this first key.

12. Click and hold the **Out** tangent button and select the Linear tangent. Notice now that the left-hand side of the interpolation curve changes to a straight line, as shown in the following image.

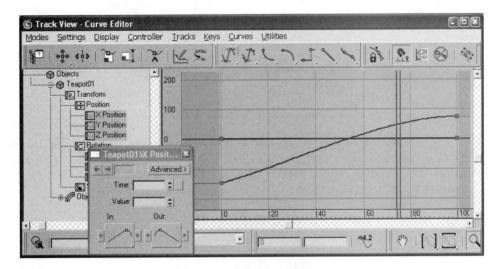

13. Right-click the last key, click and hold the **In** tangent button, and select the Linear tangent. Notice that the right-hand side of the interpolation curve changes to a straight line.

14. Click the **Play** button, and notice that the teapot moves at a constant, or linear, speed during the entire 100 frames. Click the **Stop** button.

15. Click the Add Keys button in the toolbar, as shown in the following image.

This changes Move Key mode to Add Key mode.

16. Click near the middle of the position interpolation to create a key, as shown in the following illustration. This creates a key with the default **Flat** tangent. Also notice just to the right of the arrows in the top left corner of the Key Controller dialog box that this key becomes key **2**. The key that used to be key **2** is now key **3**.

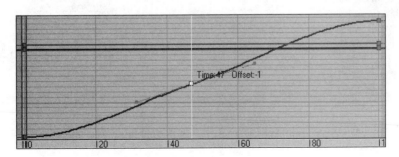

17. In the **Time** field of the Key Controller dialog box, type **50**, as shown in the following illustration. This moves the key to frame **50**.

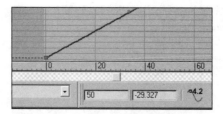

18. The Key window of the **Curve Editor** contains two vertical blue lines that represent the frame the time slider is on. Carefully place the cursor over these lines until left and right arrows appear. Click and drag the two lines so that they surround the key that you just created, as shown in the following illustration.

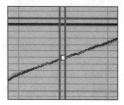

19. Right-click on top of the key you just moved to frame **50** (currently surrounded by the two vertical blue lines). This opens the Key Controller dialog box.

20. Move the Key Controller dialog box off to the side, so that you can see the key you created.

21. In the Key Controller dialog box, shown in the following image on the left, click and drag down the slider arrows to the right of the **Value** field until the interpolation is similar to the image on the right. This value represents the teapot's location along the X axis.

 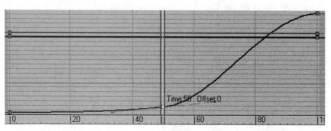

22. Click the **Play** button and let the animation play several times. Notice that the teapot starts off slowly but accelerates quickly near frame **50**. Click the Stop button.

23. Click and hold the **Move Keys** flyout in the **Curve Editor** toolbar and select the **Move Keys Vertical** icon, as shown in the following illustration.

24. Click and drag key **2** back to its original position, like the one shown in the following illustration. The **Move Keys Vertical** was used, so that the key only moves vertically and stays at frame **50**.

25. Click the **Display** menu at the top of the **Curve Editor** and select **All Tangents**. This turns on the tangent grips for all keys, rather than just the selected key.

26. Click either tangent grip (the light blue square) of key **2** and drag the grip, so that the interpolation looks like that shown in the following illustration.

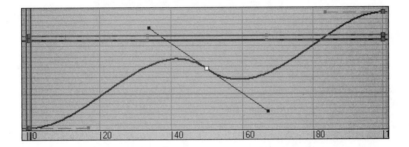

27. Click the **Play** button. Notice that the teapot moves from left to right, but near the middle of the sequence it reverses direction back to the left, and then reverses direction a second time back to the right. This is because we changed the teapot's **X Position** interpolation curve. The X value of the teapot's position goes up initially (which makes the teapot move to the right), and then goes down near frame **40** (which makes the teapot move back to the left).

28. With key **2** selected, click each of the standard interpolation tangent buttons in the **Curve Editor** toolbar shown in the following image. This illustrates the effect of each tangent on the graphical representation of the teapot's interpolation.

This exercise demonstrated how to animate controllers for an object's position, but the procedures are identical for animating other controllers, such as those for an object's parameters. To animate the radius of a primitive, for example, locate the word **Radius** in the Controller window of the **Curve Editor** and you will be able to edit the animation of the object's radius.

369

Summary

This chapter revealed some of the power and versatility of controllers in 3ds Max. Through the use of the **Motion** panel and the **Curve Editor**, you learned how to assign and edit controllers in order to dictate precisely how your animations should take place. With just a few clicks of the mouse, you can assign complex action to an object and edit that action at any point along the sequence.

Compared to other industries, the number and type of animated objects in an architectural scene is relatively small, but, for objects that do require animation in our line of work (such as cameras), getting the animation right is just as important as it is in other industries. Knowing how to work with controllers is critical to great animation.

Part 6

RENDERING

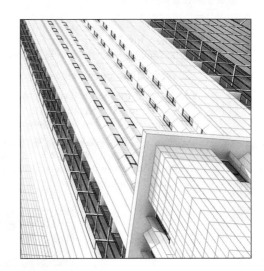

Quick Start 6

GETTING STARTED WITH RENDERING

Approximate completion time: 25 minutes

All phases of scene creation are now complete, and you're now ready to render. As with all areas of 3ds Max, rendering requires consideration of numerous settings and options. In this Quick Start tutorial, you'll begin by changing a setting that allows you to render to a different size, and another setting that allows you to render an entire scene of frames, rather than one single frame. Next, you'll tell 3ds Max to send you an email notification when the rendering is finished. Finally, you'll use the RAM Player to load your rendered images and save them as a movie file.

1. Open the file that you saved at the end of Quick Start 5, or open the file 3dsMax8\scenes\
   Friends_of_Ed\QuickStart06.max.

2. Press F10 to open the **Render Scene** dialog box.

3. Activate the Camera view and press the **Render** button at the bottom of the **Render Scene**
   dialog box. The **Render** button activates the Quick Render command. The Quick Render command renders whatever viewport is active. This is different from the Render Last command
   (F9), which renders the same viewport that was used in the last rendering. Notice here that the
   Camera viewport is rendered because it is the active viewport. When the rendering is complete,
   you should see a picture of the building surrounded by the site landscaping and parking area.
   Close the render window.

4. Right-click the Front view to make it active.

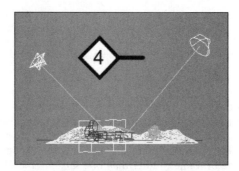

5. In the **Render Scene** dialog box, press the **Render** button again. This time, the Front view renders because it is the active view. Close the render window.

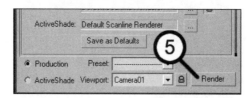

6. At the bottom of the **Render Scene** dialog box, click the **Viewport** drop-down list.

7. Select **Camera01** from the drop-down list. Notice that the Camera view becomes the active view.

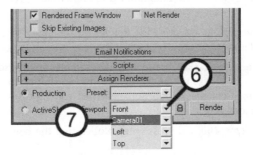

8. Click the **Lock View** icon (the icon that resembles a lock, located to the right of the **Viewport** drop-down list). It turns yellow when clicked to indicate that it's active.

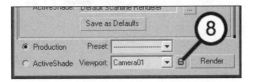

9. Right-click the Front view to make it active.

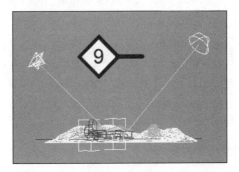

10. In the **Render Scene** dialog box, press the **Render** button again. This time, even though the Front view is active, the Camera view is rendered. This is because you used the Lock View feature to lock the render view to the view shown in the **Viewport** drop-down list. This is an immensely useful feature that can save you a great deal of time and aggravation by preventing you from accidentally rendering the wrong viewport. Close the render window.

Next, you'll change the render size to smaller dimensions so that the rendering process takes less time.

11. In the **Output Size** section of the **Common Parameters** rollout, click the preset button labeled **320x240**.

12. In the **Render Scene** dialog box, press the **Render** button again. Notice that the rendered window is much smaller than before—let's make it just a little bit larger.

13. In the **Output Size** section, click the icon that resembles a lock, located to the right of the **Image Aspect** field. This locks the image aspect ratio so that as you increase the width of the output size, the height changes proportionally. When you click this icon, it should turn yellow, indicating that the lock is now active.

14. In the **Width** field, type **400** and press Enter. Notice that the height changes automatically to **300**.

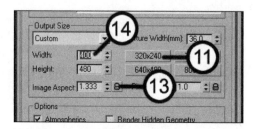

Now it's time to tell 3ds Max where to save the sequence of images that you're about to render.

15. In the **Render Output** section, click the **Files** button. This opens the **Render Output File** dialog box.

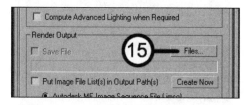

16. In the **File Name** field, type **MyRender**.

376

17. Click the **Save as type** drop-down list.

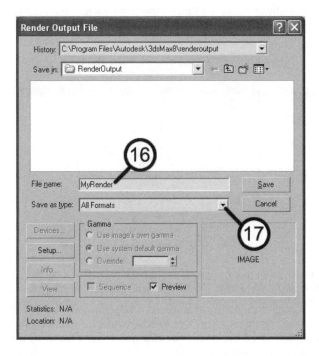

18. Select the **JPEG File** type. This is usually the best file type to save your individual rendered images.

19. Click the **Save** button. The **JPEG Image Control** dialog box opens.

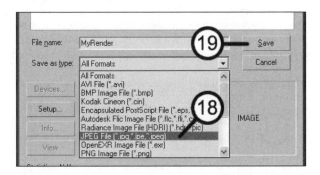

20. Click the slider directly under the **Quality** label.

21. Use the left and right arrow keys to move the slider so that the quality is set to **95**. This is a good setting for JPEG images.

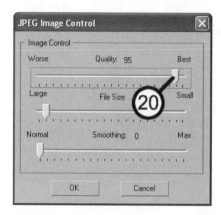

22. Click **OK** or press Enter to close the dialog box. Notice that now the **Save File** option in the **Render Output** section is automatically enabled. You can disable the saving of the output at any time by disabling this option.

23. In the **Render Scene** dialog box, click the **Render** button. The render window is a different size now, and you've just saved the image; however, you've rendered only one frame of the scene. Let's render the entire sequence of frames.

24. In the **Time Output** section at the top of the **Common Parameters** rollout, click the **Active Time Segment** option. If you press F9 now, the entire sequence will render, which will take some time. Let's assume for a moment that the scene will take several hours to render and you are at the office at the end of a long week and want to go home for the weekend. But you don't want to come back next week only to find that the computer at work crashed after rendering only a few frames. To prevent wasting the opportunity to render over the entire weekend, you can set up 3ds Max so that it sends an email notification to your computer at home not only when the scene is finished rendering, but also if 3ds Max or your computer crashes.

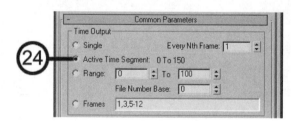

25. Scroll down (if necessary) to the bottom of the **Render Scene** dialog box and click the **Email Notifications** rollout.

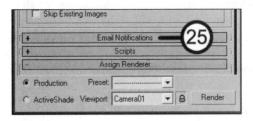

26. At the top of the rollout, click **Enable Notifications**.

27. Enable the **Notify Completion** option.

28. In the **Email Options** section, type your email address in the **To** field. This tells 3ds Max to send the email notifications to this email address. You can also type whatever email address you want in the **From** field to show where the notification is coming from.

29. In the **SMTP Server** field, type the name of your SMTP Server exactly as it appears in the configuration settings of your email account. You may have to obtain help from someone who knows how to change email account settings.

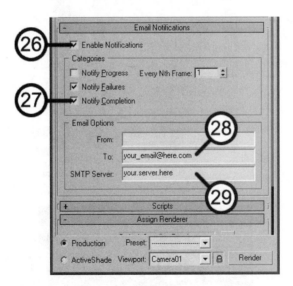

Now, let the rendering begin! This process will take around an hour, depending on the speed of your computer. If you wish to bypass this process, skip to step 31.

30. In the **Render Scene** dialog box, press the **Render** button. When the rendering process is complete, go to the next step.

31. Reset 3ds Max. By resetting 3ds Max, you close out of the scene and free up what is sometimes much needed RAM. The larger your scenes, the more RAM you will free up and the more you will be available to work with in the RAM Player.

32. Click the **Rendering** menu.

33. At the bottom of the **Rendering** menu, select **RAM Player**.

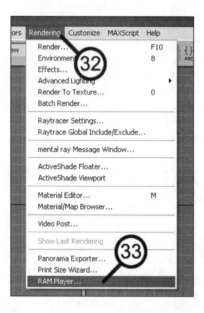

34. Click the **Open Channel A** icon (the leftmost icon in the RAM Player).

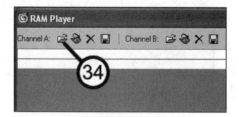

If you skipped the rendering process, you can download the rendered images (for use in the next step) from the download page at www.friendsofed.com. Save them to the 3dsMax8\RenderOutput folder.

35. Click once on any image in the sequence of images that you rendered except for the very first image (named **MyRender**). This image was created during the first time you saved to the hard drive, and because it was a single image, it was not given a numbered suffix at the end of the file name. All the other images are part of a numbered sequence, and loading one enables the entire sequence to load (by default).

36. Make sure the **Sequence** option at the bottom of the dialog box is enabled. This tells 3ds Max that you want to load the entire sequence of images rather than one single image.

37. Click the **Open** button. The **Image File List Control** dialog box opens.

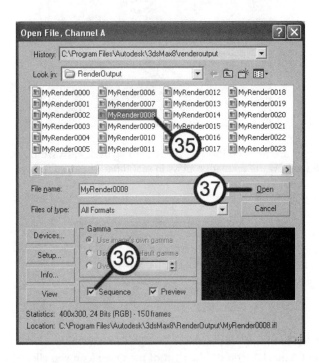

38. Click **OK**. This opens the **RAM Player Configuration** dialog box.

39. Click **OK** to accept the default settings. The **Load File** status window opens, showing you how many frames have been loaded, how much RAM has been used, and how much RAM is remaining. If you run out of RAM before the last image loads, the RAM player will not function properly because it will have to move data back and forth from the hard drive. This will cause the RAM Player to play too slowly.

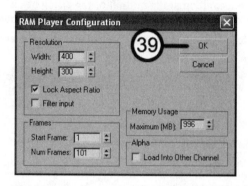

40. Once the images are finished loading, press the **Playback Forward** button in the RAM Player. You can now see how the animation plays in real time (i.e., at 30 fps).

Next, you'll save the sequence as a movie file.

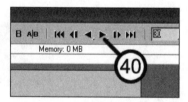

41. Click the **Playback Forward** button again to stop the animation.

42. Click the **Save Channel A** icon (to the right of the **Open** icon you clicked a moment ago).

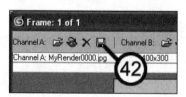

43. In the **File name** field, type **MyAnimation**.

44. Click the **Save as type** drop-down list.

45. Select the **AVI File** type.

46. Click the **Save** button. The **AVI File Compression Setup** dialog box opens.

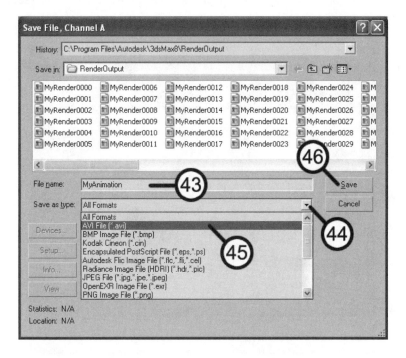

47. Click the **Compressor** drop-down list.

48. Select the **Cinepak Codec by Radius** compression type. This is a good compression algorithm that is playable on most computers.

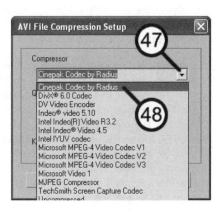

49. Using the slider, change the **Quality** to **95** and leave the **Keyframe Rate** at its default value of **15**.

50. Click **OK** to complete the movie-creation process. The movie may take several seconds to save.

51. Use Windows Explorer to locate the movie file you just created, and play the file.

This concludes Quick Start 6. You have just completed the final step in the creation of an architectural animation. Throughout these Quick Start tutorials, you've only scratched the surface of what's possible with 3ds Max. Although you may at this point be limited by your knowledge of 3ds Max, with enough practice you can eventually get to the point at which you're limited only by your imagination. The remaining chapters in this book cover rendering options in much greater depth, and give you the power to enhance your animations with effects and basic video-editing routines.

Regardless of how much time you spend creating your scene, there are always ways to improve the final product. Throughout these tutorials, you've created the very simple scene of a virtual 3ds Max welcome center. There are many ways to improve this scene, such as adding cars, people, more vegetation, signs, and perhaps even something unique like a small jet of water in the fountain. I invite and challenge you to explore ways to improve the scene you have just created by adding some additional content. On the web page for this book, located at www.friendsofed.com, there are numerous content files that you can download and use however you choose, courtesy of my friends at ArchVision (www.archvision.com) and CGarchitect.com (www.cgarchitect.com). They have graciously donated valuable RPCs and numerous image files (for use in the creation of materials) to complement the material discussed in this book. I urge you to give the RPC plug-in a try and see just how much it can bring your scenes to life. Likewise, the image files from CGarchitect.com can be invaluable in making an ordinary scene appear extraordinary.

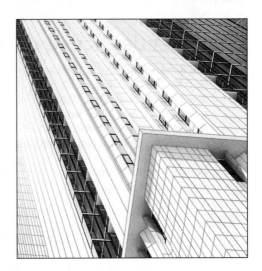

Chapter 16

RENDERING BASICS

The word "render" means, among other things, to cause to be or become. In 3ds Max, **rendering** is the process by which you create an image from the components of your scene. 3ds Max uses a program feature known as a **render engine** or **renderer** to perform the rendering process. 3ds Max ships with two unique render engines, although additional third-party renderers can be used. These are the default scanline renderer and the mental ray renderer.

The default scanline renderer provides a good mix of quality, speed, flexibility, and ease of use. The mental ray renderer, the other rendering option, offers the capability of producing higher-quality renderings with advanced lighting features. The mental ray renderer, however, is more difficult to use than the scanline renderer and can significantly increase render times. Although mental ray is used as the main rendering engine by a large percentage of veteran 3ds Max users, it is an advanced feature and therefore not covered in this book. This chapter focuses on the default scanline renderer and the critical settings that users in the visualization industry should be familiar with. The heart of the rendering process is the **Render Scene** dialog box—where most of the critical rendering settings lie.

In addition to the **Render Scene** dialog, this chapter also covers some great tools that can be a tremendous benefit to you during the rendering process. The RAM Player gives you the ability to load raw images into memory for playback at various rates, the **Print Size Wizard** helps you plan the rendering dimensions of a particular print size, and the Panorama Exporter lets you create and view 360-degree spherical panoramas.

The Render Scene dialog box

The **Render Scene** dialog box can be accessed by clicking the **Render Scene** icon on the **Main** toolbar, by using the **Rendering** menu, or by pressing F10. It contains five tabs when the default scanline renderer is used, as shown in Figure 16-1. The **Common** tab contains commands that are common to all renderers, while the **Renderer** tab contains commands that are specific to the selected renderer. The **Render Elements** tab contains features that allow you to render select elements of your scene, such as atmospheric effects, shadows, and alpha channels. The **Raytracer** tab controls advanced settings for raytracing, and the **Advanced Lighting** tab contains settings that control radiosity and other advanced lighting features, including Light Tracer. The **Render Elements**, **Raytracer**, and **Advanced Lighting** tabs are all advanced areas of 3ds Max, and with the exception of Advanced Lighting, are not covered in this book.

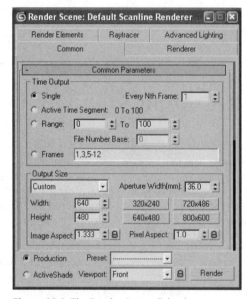

Figure 16-1. The Render Scene dialog box

Two buttons can initiate the rendering process. One is the **Render** button located at the bottom of the **Render Scene** dialog box, and the other is the **Quick Render** button located on the **Main** toolbar. The **Quick Render** button initiates the rendering process using the settings from the **Render Scene** dialog box, regardless of whether or not the dialog box is open.

The **Render** button in the **Render Scene** dialog box is visible at the bottom of the dialog box regardless of which tab is active. To the left of the **Render** button are some other handy features that are also always visible.

By default, all renders are set to **Production**, as shown in the bottom left corner of Figure 16-1. This means that your rendered images will be created in the best way possible, or as good as your work allows. The other option you can choose is **ActiveShade**, which gives you a preview of your rendering that shows you the effects of changing lighting or materials in your scene. If you change the lights or materials in your scene, the **ActiveShade** window automatically updates the rendering. This can be very useful and time-saving for large scenes that take a long time to render. You can also load a viewport with an **ActiveShade** display by right-clicking the viewport name and selecting **Views ➤ ActiveShade** from the drop-down list.

When you right-click an **ActiveShade** render window or viewport, a quad menu appears with various options, as shown in Figure 16-2. You can close the **ActiveShade** window or viewport by selecting **Close**. Several other options are available, and I invite you to explore them more if you find that the **ActiveShade** feature may benefit your work.

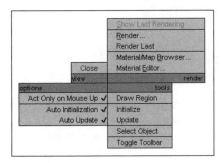

Figure 16-2. The ActiveShade quad menu

Another important feature at the bottom of the **Render Scene** dialog box is the **Lock View** feature. Few things in 3ds Max can be as frustrating as setting a time-consuming rendering in motion and leaving, only to come back and find that you've rendered the wrong viewport. You can render the wrong viewport by inadvertently activating a different viewport or by intentionally working in a different viewport and forgetting to reactivate the correct one when it's time to render. The active viewport displayed in the viewport drop-down list will always be the viewport that's rendered. To render the same viewport every time, regardless of which viewport is active, select the **Lock View** option.

Another feature at the bottom of the **Render Scene** dialog box is the **Preset** drop-down list. This feature lets you save several settings in numerous different categories, as shown in Figure 16-3. Saving these settings can be extremely handy and time-saving when you want to reuse settings that you've spent a great deal of time setting up. I find this feature particularly useful in saving and loading environment and render effects.

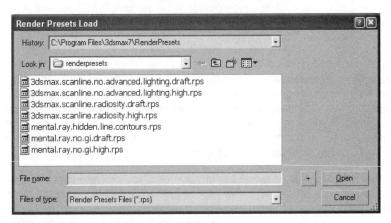

Figure 16-3. The Render Presets Load dialog box

389

The Common tab

The **Common** tab of the **Render Scene** dialog box, shown in Figure 16-4, contains three rollouts common to all render engines: **Common Parameters**, **Email Notifications**, and **Assign Renderer**. The **Assign Renderer** rollout is where you change the render engine type from the default scanline to any other type, such as mental ray or a third-party render engine.

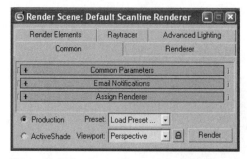

Figure 16-4. The three rollouts of the default scanline renderer

Time Output

The first section of the rollout, **Time Output** (Figure 16-5), deals with settings that control the specific frames to be rendered. The default **Single** option renders one frame—the current frame designated by the Time slider. The **Active Time Segment** option renders all of the frames shown in the Time slider. The **Range** option renders a range of frames designated in the two fields to the right of the option. The **Frames** option allows you to specifically designate the frames you want to render. You can specify individual frames or any range of frames using commas and hyphens. For example, if you want to render frames 1, 3, and 7 through 10, you would enter **1,3,5-12**.

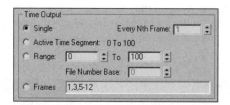

Figure 16-5. The Time Output section

When the **Active Time Segment** or **Range** option is used, you can render frames in selected increments using the **Every Nth Frame** option. If you have an animation with a large number of frames and want to perform a test render without spending the time to render each frame, you can render frames at regular intervals (that is, every *n*th frame) to get an overview of the entire sequence and find potential problems. Sometimes even rendering every fiftieth frame, if that's all you have time to render, can show you enough to know that your sequence is ready for a complete rendering.

When the **Active Time Segment** or **Range** options are used, you can also take advantage of the **File Number Base** setting. This setting allows you to designate the number given to the first rendered image file that is created during the rendering process. By default, whenever you render a sequence, the first file that is created is given the suffix of four zeros, or 0000. Each frame after that is followed by 0001, 0002, 0003, and so on, depending on the specific frames or range of frames you designate. With the **File Number Base** option, you can designate a different start suffix so that the first rendered file ends in some number other than 0000.

Output Size

You specify the dimensions, in pixels, of the final rendered output in the **Output Size** section, shown in Figure 16-6. The drop-down list provides standard categories of output such as high-definition, NTSC, PAL, and 35 mm. Selecting one of these categories causes 3ds Max to display the most common dimensions associated with the selected category in the four preset buttons to the right of the **Width** and **Height** fields. You can select from one of these preset buttons or type a specific width or height value yourself. The **Image Aspect** value shows the aspect ratio for the specified width and height values. The lock button to the right of the **Image Aspect** allows you to lock the aspect ratio, so that changing either the **Width** or **Height** value will cause the other value to change so that the aspect ratio is preserved. The **Pixel Aspect** ratio sets a value that can be changed to correct the way a rendering displays on a device other than your computer's display. If you change the pixel aspect ratio to something other than 1.0, the image might look squashed on your computer's display, but will look correct on a device with non-square-shaped pixels. You will probably never need to change this setting if your final product will be displayed on a computer or TV.

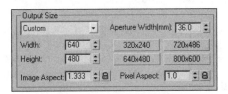

Figure 16-6. The Output Size section

Options

The **Options** section, shown in Figure 16-7, allows you to selectively include or exclude certain features in the rendering process. The options enabled by default are **Atmospherics**, **Effects**, and **Displacement**. This means that by default, any rendering you create will include all the active atmospheric and render effects that you created within your scene, as well as any applied displacement mapping. If you decide that you want to exclude atmospheric effects on a test render because of the added time it takes to complete the rendering, simply deselect the **Atmospherics** option.

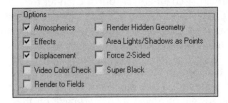

Figure 16-7. The Options section

Render Output

The **Render Output** section, shown in Figure 16-8, allows you to create an image or animation file during the rendering process. By default, the rendering output is set to **Rendered Frame Window** only. To save the output to a file, click the **Files** button, select a directory to save the file within, type a name, and select the file type from the **Save as type** drop-down list. When you save an output path with the **Files** button, the **Save File** option is automatically enabled.

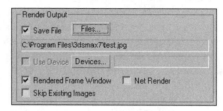

Figure 16-8. The Render Output section

In the visualization industry, I have found that the only file types that I need to render on a regular basis are the .jpg, .tga, and .tif. The following are descriptions of each file type and its typical uses:

- **JPEG** (Joint Photography Experts Group): The .jpg file is the best file type to use when rendering images for general purpose or for rendering a sequence of images to be animated later. When rendering a long sequence of images, I prefer using a .jpg, because there is no significant loss in quality, and a .jpg usually requires only a fraction of the storage space of a .tif or .tga. Long sequences of images with large file sizes can require an enormous amount of disk space and a great deal of RAM for video editing. A .jpg uses an algorithm that allows for extremely high compression with a minimal loss of quality. When you save to the .jpg format, I recommend using a quality level of 95.

- **TIFF** (Tagged Image File Format): The .tif file is the best file type to use if your final product is a high-resolution print and file size is not important. The several classes of .tif files each have different purposes. If you send a .tif file to a professional printing service, you may need to get specific guidance as to the type of .tif file they want to use. I also recommend saving without compression to allow for the highest possible quality.

- **TGA** (Targa): The .tga file is the best file type to use if the final product is an image with an embedded alpha channel. An **alpha channel** is a type of data embedded in an image file that assigns transparency information for each pixel. A typical image file will contain three channels of information for each pixel, corresponding to the three colors used to determine the appearance of each pixel. An alpha channel is a fourth channel that contains an additional piece of information for each pixel—a value from 0 to 255 that determines whether or not the pixel will be transparent or opaque. A value of 0 represents black (complete transparency). A value of 255 represents white (complete opacity).

All rendered images are created with an alpha channel. However, not all file types have the ability to save it; the .tga file type is commonly used to store this extra channel of information. The left image in Figure 16-9 shows a rendered teapot object, and the image on the right shows the alpha channel that is created with the rendering. When you want to save an alpha channel with a .tga file, make sure that you enable the 32-bit option on the setup menu that appears during the **Save As** operation. If you do not save a .tga with the 32-bit option, the alpha channel is lost.

Figure 16-9. Rendering of a teapot and the accompanying alpha channel

The **Net Render** option enables you to send your job to a network render manager so that you can use all of the computers at your disposal to help in the rendering process. Network rendering is discussed in detail later in this chapter.

The handy **Skip Existing Images** option skips the rendering process for files that have already been rendered. If you render a sequence of images and later find that a number of those images have problems that must be corrected, you can erase the problematic images and re-render the entire job without having to specify the exact frames to be rendered.

Using the Render Scene dialog box

This exercise demonstrates how to use some of the critical settings found within the **Render Scene** dialog box.

1. Reset 3ds Max.
2. In the Perspective view, create a teapot that rotates 360 degrees about the Z axis during 100 frames.
3. Click the **Render Scene** icon, or press F10.
4. In the **Time Output** section, select the **Active Time Segment** option.
5. Change the **Every Nth Frame** setting to 3. This will cause every third frame to render.
6. In the **Output Size** section, click the **320x240** preset. This sets the aspect ratio to a desirable value. You can now lock the aspect ratio and then increase the overall size of the output while still maintaining this desirable aspect ratio.
7. Lock the image aspect ratio by clicking the icon to the right of the **Image Aspect** field.
8. Change the **Width** of the output to **500**. The **Height** value changes to **375**.
9. In the **Render Output** section, click the **Files** button. The **Render Output File** dialog box opens.
10. Select a location on your computer to create a new directory to save this temporary rendering output.
11. Change the file type to .jpg, name the file **Test**, and click the **Save** button.
12. Change the quality of the .jpg output to **95,** and select **OK** to close.
13. Under the **Assign Renderer** rollout, click the **Preset** drop-down list, and select **Save Preset**. The **Render Presets Save** window appears.

14. Name the preset **test**, and click the **Save** button to close. Having done this, you can load these settings later, even after closing and reopening 3ds Max.

15. Click the **Render** button to save the 33 rendered images to the specified directory.

Email Notifications

Besides the **Common Parameters** rollout, **Email Notifications** is the only other rollout that needs to be discussed. The **Email Notifications** rollout, shown in Figure 16-10, gives you the ability to send email notifications to and from any email address you specify. These notifications include progress notifications of every *n*th frame, failure notifications, and completion notifications. All you need to do is specify a **From** address, a **To** address, and your **SMTP Server**.

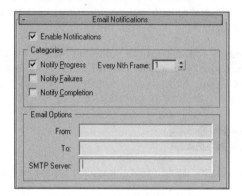

Figure 16-10. The Email Notifications rollout

If you work a typical work week—that is, from 8 a.m. to 5 p.m. Monday through Friday—weekends present the most useful times to render large jobs. In fact, you would have 63 hours from Friday at 5 p.m. until you return at 8 a.m. on Monday. By setting up 3ds Max to send progress or failure alerts from your office to your email account at home, you can save yourself a great deal of heartache by knowing about a failure when it happens instead of finding out about it Monday at 8 a.m. This gives you the opportunity to come back into the office to fix whatever problem caused the rendering failure before the entire weekend has come and gone with nothing to show for it. Of course, many veteran 3ds Max users might argue that they've never heard of an 8 a.m. to 5 p.m. 3ds Max job.

The Renderer tab

Up to this point, the discussion of the **Render Scene** dialog box has been limited to the **Common** tab. The next critical tab for users at the foundation level is the **Renderer** tab. When the assigned renderer is set to the default scanline, the **Renderer** tab contains only one rollout, the **Default Scanline Renderer** rollout (Figure 16-11). This rollout controls options and settings for the scanline renderer only.

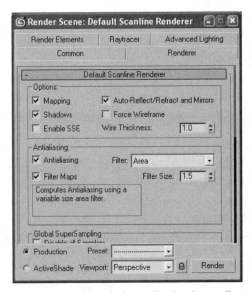

Figure 16-11. The Default Scanline Renderer rollout

Options

The **Options** section gives you the flexibility to turn on and off certain features that greatly impact rendering times. These features include such things as mapping, shadows, auto-reflections, and refractions. When doing test renders, I find it very handy to be able to turn off these options for the entire scene with just a couple clicks of the mouse. Likewise, I find it very handy to be able to render the entire scene in wireframe by simply turning on the **Force Wireframe** option, which you can use as another way of conducting a quick test render of a scene. The **Wire Thickness** setting can be used to change the wire thickness (measured in screen pixels) so that the objects display better.

Antialiasing

The **Antialiasing** section gives you the option to turn off anti-aliasing, a topic discussed in Chapter 6. Like the options just discussed, the **Antialiasing** option can be disabled to speed up test renderings, but under no circumstances should it be disabled for a final render.

The **Filter** drop-down menu, shown in Figure 16-12, contains a list of anti-aliasing filters that allow you to sharpen or soften your final output, depending on your needs. I have found a consistent use for only two of these filters: the default **Area** filter and the **Video** filter. The **Area** filter is the default filter type, and of all the available filters, usually provides the best and most practical rendering appearance for still images. Some of the other options provide too much sharpness or blurring. The **Video** filter causes slight blurring in a rendered image, so you may not particularly care for the appearance of a single image rendered with the **Video** filter. However, by not using the **Video** filter, you risk producing animations with noticeable flaws, such

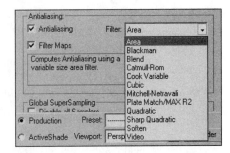

Figure 16-12. The available anti-aliasing filters

as flickering and texture crawl (also covered in Chapter 6). Although a single image from an animation may look excessively blurred, the animation itself will usually look fine, especially if you render at a higher-than-needed resolution and convert down to your desired output size. As an additional note, the **Filter Size** value should be left at **1.5**.

Global SuperSampling

This section allows you to enable **Global SuperSampling**, which is covered in chapter 6.

Object and Motion Blur

These sections control some of the parameters of Motion Blur, an effect covered in detail in chapter 18. These sections are likewise covered in chapter 18.

Auto Reflect/Refract Maps

The **Rendering Iterations** setting controls the number of interobject reflections with certain map types. Increasing this value may improve reflection quality, but can drastically increase rendering times. This value should remain at **1** until such time that you create scenes with advanced lighting methods.

Color Range Limiting

The options in this setting deal with advanced aspects of color management and are not covered in this book.

Memory management

3ds Max is a memory-hungry program, and as any veteran user will tell you, you should purchase as much memory as your budget allows. If you render a large scene that wants to consume more memory than is available, you risk crashing 3ds Max or your computer. If you simply don't have enough memory to render a particular scene, and you want to better your chances of avoiding such a crash, you can enable the **Conserve Memory** feature. This feature causes 3ds Max to render using 15 to 25% less memory, at the expense of render speed. Your scene may take a little longer to render, but you don't run as great a risk of crashing 3ds Max or your computer.

Choosing file dimensions

Whether your final product is a high-resolution print or a high-definition DVD, knowing what dimensions to use in your file output is critical. The standard computer screen displays approximately 72–130 pixels per inch (ppi), though your particular graphics card may allow you to alter this setting. While this range of resolution may look fine on a computer display, an image printed at the lower end of this range will look considerably pixilated and lack photographic quality. Learning the complexities of print and video resolution can be difficult and confusing, but the following discussion should give you a good understanding of the basics and the tools needed to produce high-quality presentations regardless of the format.

Before jumping into the details of video and print resolution, a discussion of what I refer to as the "final product" is warranted. In almost every visualization project I work on, the very first question I ask the client is "What is the final product?" The final product is the very thing that the client is paying you to create. It may be a single .jpg image that you send over the Internet, a high-definition DVD, a large-scale high-resolution print, or all of the above. Regardless of its form, the final product should drive your strategy towards completion of your project. If your final product includes a high-resolution image or high-definition DVD, you will need to incorporate a higher level of detail into your scenes than you will for an image to be viewed over the Internet or an animation to be viewed on a standard-definition TV. When it comes time to render your scene, the final product will dictate exactly what dimensions are needed for the file output. So let's see what the typical final products are and the dimensions that should be used for each.

Prints

Whether your image is going to be displayed in a magazine advertisement or on a street-side bill-board, images that get printed need to be at a considerably higher resolution than for any other media type. When you create an image for print, you should always attempt to use a resolution of at least 300 dpi, but under no circumstances should you allow the resolution to fall below 150 dpi. If time and resources permit, resolutions up to 600 dpi are warranted, but anything above 600 dpi is unnecessary, because the human eye is incapable of discerning better resolutions. 300 dpi is about the minimum resolution necessary to achieve photographic print quality; however, for a large-scale print such as a street-side billboard, 300 dpi may not be feasible. This may be especially true if your scene incorporates advanced lighting, effects, high polygon counts, or other characteristics that require too much RAM or too much time to render at such high resolution.

The billboard image in Figure 16-13 is a 36×18-inch print image rendered at 150 dpi and subsequently blown up to 8×4 feet. This resolution suffices, because the billboard should be viewed from at least a few feet away, and any pixilation will be unnoticeable.

Figure 16-13. A rendered image used in a billboard

How do you know exactly what dimensions to use as the file output? All you need to do is determine the actual size of the printed final product in inches, and multiply the length of each side by the dpi you want. For example, if your image is going to be a 36-inch-wide and 24-inch-high print, and you need 300 dpi, your file output size should be 36×300 by 24×300, or 10,800 pixels wide and 7,200 pixels high. If you do not have the great deal of RAM required to render such a high-resolution image, you can render the image in segments and splice the segments together in a photo-editing program. This procedure will be discussed later in this chapter. If you need to print a 3×3-inch image for a magazine advertisement or a brochure, try for a 600 dpi image, since RAM and time should not be as big a factor, and because the image will be viewed at a distance of only a few inches.

High-definition and standard DVDs

High-definition video has grown steadily in popularity since the late 1990s and will probably be the norm within a few years. I believe that by the release of 3ds Max 10, high-definition DVDs will be the standard for architectural visualizations incorporating DVD production.

720i and 1080i are currently two high-definition standards. **720i** is short for a resolution of 1080X720 interlaced pixels, and **1080i** is short for a resolution of 1920X1080 interlaced pixels. Creating an animation at a resolution of either type can be quite a challenge even with the best computer power available. However, this resolution will be more feasible as computers become faster. Recent developments in new chip technologies, such as the Cell multiprocessor (collaboratively created by Toshiba, Sony, and IBM), give a promising forecast of our future abilities to produce the highest-quality resolutions in high-definition digital video.

Standard DVDs use a video resolution of 640X480 dpi. If your final product is to be a standard DVD, you can use a video resolution of 640X480 to yield acceptable results.

Internet images

A good website will have a maximum pixel width of about 1,000 pixels because most computer users either do not have their monitors set beyond the standard 1024X768 resolution, or because most users don't typically view web pages in a maximized window. Because of this, images in websites are usually no larger than 1,000 pixels, and most of the time are much smaller than this. Therefore, renderings that you create for print or DVD will already be sufficient for displaying on the Internet. Although .jpg is the standard image type for Internet display, you always have the option of using the animated .gif file type to display animations.

Internet video

Chances are, if you need to create an animation for viewing on the Internet, you already need to create an animation for DVD. If that's the case, creating a video for the Internet is just a simple matter of using the raw images to create a video file. With each passing year, video compression gets better, and Internet connections get faster, giving you the ability to upload higher-quality videos with larger dimensions. Although 3ds Max comes with the ability to create decent video compressions, a professional video editor using top-of-the-line software can produce far better videos in much smaller files. If you don't have the resources to use a professional video editor, or if you would like to create a simple video to email your client for approval purposes, the following settings will allow you to create a high-quality video with decent video compression.

- **File Type**: MOV Quick Time File (*.mov)
- **Compression Type**: Sorenson Video 3
- **Frames per second**: 15
- **Key frame every**: 30 frames
- **Quality**: High

For more power and versatility in compressing your videos, you might want to try Autodesk's Cleaner software.

Additional rendering tools

3ds Max 8 contains several handy rendering tools that suit the architectural visualization industry very well. The **Print Size Wizard** gives you an easy way to determine the size at which your rendering must be created to accommodate the print resolution you need. The **RAM Player** gives you the ability to quickly load, play, and save image and video files with your computer's available RAM. Finally, the **Panorama Exporter** lets you create panoramic images that can give your clients the interactive capability of looking around a scene in any direction.

The Print Size Wizard

If you want an easy way to figure out what dimensions you need to render, 3ds Max can help you out with the **Print Size Wizard**. The **Print Size Wizard**, shown in Figure 16-14, is a user-friendly interface that does the math for you. To use this feature, simply select a dpi (dots per inch) value and enter a value for either the paper dimensions or image dimensions. As you change either one of these dimensions, the other dimension updates accordingly. The wizard even tells you the uncompressed file size of the image. As the image dimensions change in the wizard, the rendering dimensions in the **Render Scene** dialog box change as well.

In the **Print Size Wizard**, shown in Figure 16-14, notice that the image width and height are the default rendering dimensions. With the dpi set to **300** (the minimum needed for photographic quality), the image will only print 2.1 inches wide and 1.6 inches high, because there simply aren't enough pixels to make the print any larger without losing quality. Although this limitation may be readily apparent to you, assume that your clients know nothing about pixels, dpi, or print quality. If you don't make it abundantly clear that a 640×480 dpi rendering can't be printed at large scale, you may get a call from your client wondering why the image you sent looks so bad after he or she spent a great deal of money getting it blown up and laminated. Furthermore, don't assume that if you send the client an image for review or approval, the client won't sign off on the image and get it printed before you have a chance to send him a high-resolution image.

Figure 16-14. The Print Size Wizard

The RAM Player

The RAM Player, shown in Figure 16-15, is an invaluable rendering tool that lets you load a sequence of images into your computer's RAM and play them back at various speeds, without the effect of reduced quality that comes from video compression. You can also load two separate sequences into the two available channels and compare them. Finally, once the sequence is loaded, you can quickly save multiple versions of the sequence using varying dimensions and video compressors.

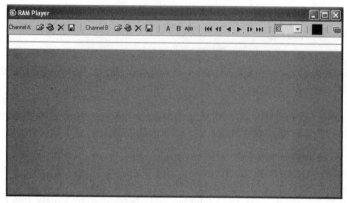

Figure 16-15. The RAM Player

To load a sequence of images, click the **Open Channel A** button (next to **Channel A**) and navigate through the explorer window, as shown in Figure 16-16, to locate the images. Select any numbered image, select the **Sequence** option at the bottom of the **Open File** dialog box, and click **Open**.

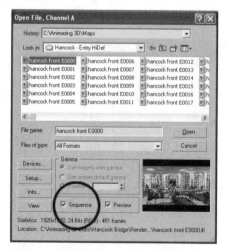

Figure 16-16. The Open File dialog box

The **Image File List Control** dialog box opens, as shown in the left image of Figure 16-17. Within this dialog box are options that let you load every nth frame, multiply the number of frames, or change the start and end frames. Click **OK** to load all of the frames. The final step is to confirm the settings in the **RAM Player Configuration** dialog box that opens (shown in the right image of Figure 16-17). In this dialog box, you can change the resolution dimensions or the total amount of memory used to load the images. To keep the default settings, click **OK**. The images will then load into the RAM Player.

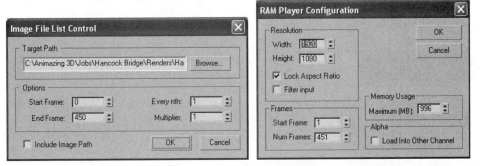

Figure 16-17. The Image File List Control dialog box (left) and the RAM Player Configuration dialog box (right)

As the images load into the RAM Player, you will see a status indicator appear, as shown in Figure 16-18. This indicator shows how many frames are loaded, the amount of memory used, and the amount of available memory remaining. In order for the images to play back smoothly, you must make sure that the memory doesn't run out before the images load. If the available memory runs out, the images will not load into RAM any longer and the sequence will probably not play back smoothly.

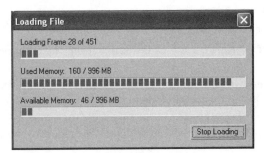

Figure 16-18. RAM status indicator

Once the images finish loading, you can play the sequence by clicking the **Playback Forward** button, or you can advance the images one frame at a time by clicking the **Next Frame** button.

A playback rate drop-down list, located to the right of the player controls, sets the number of frames that are played per second. Using a reduced frame rate is common for videos that play on websites. For example, reducing the playback rate of the typical animation from 30 fps to 15 fps means that you can halve the file size of animations that you load on your website. Videos at 15 fps still play well enough for most online purposes and load twice as fast as typical 30 fps animation. To see what your animations would look like at 15 fps, simply load every other frame in the RAM Player and change the playback rate to 15 fps using the drop-down list.

401

To the left of the play controls is the **Open Channel B** button. This is the same as the **Open Channel A** button except that any image loaded with this button is loaded into Channel B. By loading different images or sequences into the two channels, you can compare them during playback. Once you load both channels, you can use the **Channel A** and **Channel B** toggle buttons to hide or show the images in the two channels. By clicking and dragging in the channel display window, you can set the **A|B** divider between the two channels.

Finally, the **Open Last Rendered Image in Channel A** button does as its name implies. This tool is handy, because after using it, you can render the scene again with different settings, and click the **Open Last Rendered Image in Channel B** button to compare two different renderings of the same scene.

Using the RAM Player

This exercise demonstrates how to use the RAM Player to play a sequence of images and save the sequence as a movie file.

1. Reset 3ds Max.
2. In the **Rendering** menu, select **RAM Player**.
3. Click the **Open Channel A** icon, go to the directory 3dsMax8\Images\Friends_of_Ed\ EntryNorth, highlight any image in the sequence, enable the **Sequence** option, and click the **Open** button.
4. Click the **OK** button in the **Image File List Control** dialog box to accept the default settings.
5. Click the **OK** button in the **RAM Player Configuration** dialog box to accept the default settings. The sequence of images should begin to load in the RAM Player.
6. Click the **Save Channel A** icon.
7. In the **Save as type** drop-down list, select the **MOV** file type.
8. Name the movie **EntryNorth**, and click the **Save** button. The **Compression Settings** dialog box appears.
9. In the **Compression type** drop-down list, select **Sorenson Video 3**, and in the **Quality** section, use the slider bar to set the quality to **High**.
10. Click **OK** to save the movie. Depending on the number of frames and the image resolution, the saving process could take up to several minutes. This sequence, however, should take only a few seconds.

The Panorama Exporter

Here's another great tool that's as easy to use as any. The Panorama Exporter lets you create a 360-degree panorama from any camera and export the panorama as a QuickTime movie file. The Panorama Exporter works by rendering six separate views from a camera (Front, Back, Left, Right, Top, and Bottom) and splicing the images together to create one large image that is then wrapped around the camera spherically. The size of the wrapped image is determined by the dimensions you use to render the panorama. Since the typical camera only shows about a 45-degree section of that panoramic image (or one-eighth of a 360-degree view), the dimensions of the overall image must be about eight times larger than the dimensions of the final panorama. In other words, if you want your final panorama movie file to be displayed at 256×128 dpi and look every bit as clear and sharp as an image rendered at 256×128 dpi through the **Render Scene** dialog box, you must actually use dimensions of at least 2048×1024 dpi.

The Panorama Exporter feature is found under the **Rendering** menu, and once activated, can be found within the **Utilities** panel. When you select **Panorama Exporter**, the **Render Setup** dialog box opens, as shown in Figure 16-19, with a layout very similar to the **Render Scene** dialog box. The first rollout of the dialog box, **Interactive Panorama Exporter Common Parameters**, contains the only settings that are not featured in the **Render Scene** dialog box. At this point, you only have to tell 3ds Max the dimensions you want for the panorama movie file, but note that you must first have a camera in your scene to use the utility. Once the dimensions are set, click the **Render** button at the bottom of the dialog box.

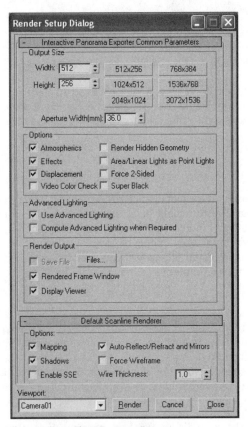

Figure 16-19. The Panorama Exporter

When the rendering process is finished, the Panorama Exporter Viewer opens, as shown in Figure 16-20. In the viewer, you can rotate your camera around the panorama by holding down the left or right button and moving the mouse, or you can rotate the panorama around your camera by holding down the right button and moving the mouse. You can also zoom in and out by holding down the middle (scroll) button and moving the mouse up and down.

Figure 16-20. The Panorama Exporter Viewer

The Panorama Exporter Viewer contains only one menu item, the **File** menu, which allows you to export the panorama to a movie file. To export a movie, select **File ➤ Export ➤ Export QuickTimeVR**, and save the movie file. You can then open the movie file independently of 3ds Max.

Video Post

Whether you manage or work for an animation company, act as a freelancer, or simply use 3ds Max as a student, you have a great deal to benefit from learning Video Post operations. Video Post, as the name implies, involves creating or modifying video files after the rendering process is completed. With Video Post, you can perform basic video editing or complex compositing. The information about the available Video Post techniques could fill many chapters; however, as with all areas of 3ds Max, this book concentrates on the foundation-level features that are most practical to the architectural production environment, and covers basic video editing, one of the most practical and useful facets of Video Post.

Whether or not you hire a professional video editor to create your final animation product, using Video Post to perform basic video editing is beneficial in numerous ways. Video Post cannot replace professional editing software; however, you can use Video Post to create test animations for your own continued work, or as a reference for your video editor. Being able to perform basic video editing gives you the freedom to test numerous ideas for your final products without having to pay top dollar for hours of professional editing.

The Video Post interface, shown in Figure 16-21, is made up of four areas: the toolbar, the status bar/view controls, the queue, and the event tracks area. Video Post operations revolve around events, which are input elements that either provide the content for the final output (i.e., images) or change the final appearance of the content. There are seven different event types accessible through the seven rightmost icons in the Video Post toolbar: Scene, Image Input, Image Filter, Image Layer, Image Output, External, and Loop. Some are only selectable when certain other event types are highlighted.

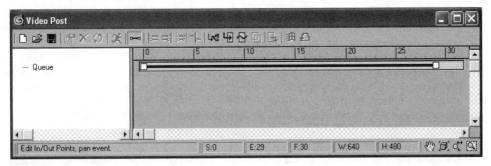

Figure 16-21. The Video Post interface

Image Layer events composite other images and scenes, while External events typically perform image processing with external programs. Both are advanced areas of Video Post and are not covered in this book.

The Scene event adds images to the queue by rendering a particular viewport. Essentially, the Scene event functions as a tool that lets you render multiple viewports or cameras in one operation, and send the output to a file. The Loop event causes other events to repeat over time.

The three events that this book focuses on are Image Input, Image Filter, and Image Output. The following list describes the functions of these three events;

- **Image Input event**: Adds already-rendered still or moving images to the queue
- **Image Filter event**: Performs image processing on another event
- **Image Output event**: Sends images processed by other Video Post events to a file

Video editing with Video Post

This exercise demonstrates how to perform basic video editing using Video Post.

1. Reset 3ds Max.
2. Select **Rendering ➤ Video Post**.
3. Click the **Add Image Input Event** icon on the Video Post toolbar (shown following).

4. Click the **Files** button, go to the directory 3dsMax8\Images\Friends_of_Ed\EntryNorth, highlight any image in the sequence, enable the **Sequence** option, and click the **Open** button.
5. In the **Image File List Control** dialog box, click **OK** to accept the default options. This tells 3ds Max that you want to load all 31 images. Remember that 31 images (not 30) yield one second of animation.

6. Click **OK** to close the **Add Image Input Event** dialog box. There is now an Image Input event loaded in the event tracks area, as shown in the following illustration. Notice that the loaded event is identified as an **Image Input Event** by the icon located to the left of the first image name in the queue. Also, notice that the track associated with the loaded event extends outward by as many frames as there are images loaded. If you load 500 images, the track will extend out to 500 frames; however, you won't see all 500 frames unless you use the view controls in the bottom-right corner of the Video Post interface. To see all of the tracks, click the **Zoom Extents** icon. To pan the view, click the **Pan** icon.

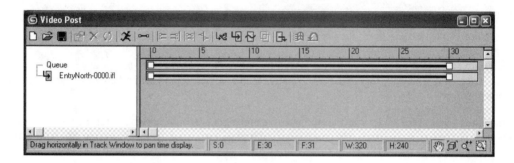

7. Click the **Add Image Input Event** icon again.

8. Click the **Files** button, go to the directory 3dsMax8\Images\Friends_of_Ed\EntrySouth, highlight any image in the sequence, enable the **Sequence** option, and click the **Open** button.

9. In the **Image File List Control** dialog box, click **OK** to load all 31 images.

10. In the **Video Post Parameters** section of the **Add Image Input Event** dialog box, change the **VP Start Time** to **31** and the **VP End Time** to **61**. This tells 3ds Max that the first of the 31 images is loaded into frame 31, and the last image is loaded into frame 61.

11. Click **OK** to close the dialog box. This puts the second sequence of 31 images immediately after the first, as shown in the following illustration.

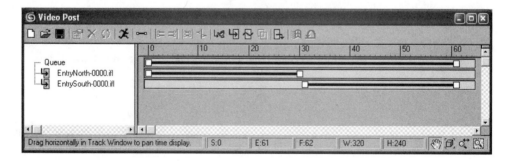

12. Click the **Zoom Extents** icon (shown following) to see all 61 frames of the sequences.

13. Click the **Image Filter Event** icon (shown following) on the Video Post toolbar. The **Add Image Filter Event** dialog box opens.

14. In the **Filter Plug-In** drop-down list, select **Fade** as the **Image Filter Event**, as shown in the following illustration.

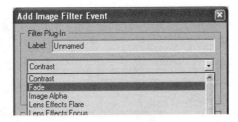

15. In the **Filter Plug-In** section, click the **Setup** button, select the **In** option, and click **OK** to close the **Fade Image Control** dialog box. This tells 3ds Max to perform a fade-in rather than a fade-out as the movie starts.

16. Click **OK** to close the **Add Image Filter Event** dialog box. Notice now that the **Fade Image Filter** event is loaded in the queue and its effects are spread from frame 0 to frame 60. This would produce a fade-in that lasts 60 frames, which would not look good. Let's change the effect so that it ends at frame 15.

17. Double-click the **Fade** event in the queue. The **Edit Filter Event** dialog box opens. Double-clicking any event in the queue or any event tracks area opens the corresponding dialog box.

18. Change the **VP End Time** to **15** so that the fade-in ends at frame 15, as shown in the following illustration. Select **OK** to close.

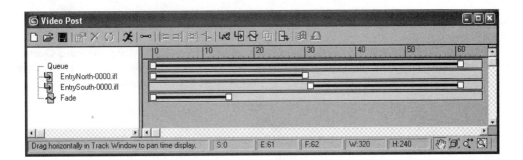

407

19. Click the **Add Image Output Event** icon (shown following) in the Video Post toolbar. The **Add Image Output Event** dialog box opens.

20. Click the **Image File** section, click the **Files** button, change the file type to **MOV**, name the movie file **test**, select a location on your computer to save the files, and click **Save**.

21. Set the compression type to **Sorenson Video 3** and the quality to **High**. Select **OK** to close.

22. In the **Add Image Output Event** dialog box, change the **VP End Time** to **61**.

23. Select **OK** to close the dialog box. The queue should now have four events loaded, as shown in the following illustration.

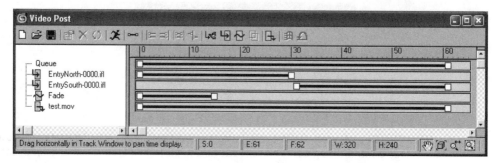

24. Click the **Execute Sequence** icon (shown following) in the Video Post toolbar.

25. In the **Time Output** section, select the **Range** option, and set the range from **0** to **61**. This ensures that all 61 frames of the sequences are included.

26. Click the **Render** button. Video Post now performs the video editing and produces a .mov file. You can play the file to see the results of combining the two video sequences and adding a fade-in.

You should also be aware of the following icons on the Video Post toolbar:

■ **Delete Current Event**: This icon deletes any selected event. By selecting the word **Queue** at the top of the event list within the queue, all events are highlighted. Clicking the **Delete Current Event** icon with all events highlighted will cause the entire queue to be deleted.

- **Edit Range Bar**: If you are using the view control icons at the bottom-right of the Video Post interface, you can either right-click the mouse or click this icon to re-enter range edit mode. In range edit mode, you can move an event track by clicking the middle of its range bar (which turns red when selected) and dragging it left or right. You can also change the start or end frame of the range by dragging either end of the bar.

- **Edit Current Event**: Selecting this icon opens the corresponding event dialog box. Double-clicking any event or track does the same thing.

Network rendering

Using one computer to produce a few renderings is not a problem, but when it comes time to create long animations of a complex scene, a single computer just won't do. Having multiple computers to produce these types of animations is critical, but just as critical is creating a system to divide the work among the computers. The network rendering capability of 3ds Max does just that.

Network rendering, simply enough, is the process of rendering with a network of computers. These rendering networks are sometimes called **render farms**. With network rendering, one computer must be set up to serve as the network manager, to farm out, or distribute, the work to other computers performing work as **rendering servers**. The entire process is monitored by a computer serving as the **queue monitor**. The queue monitor allows you to monitor the progress of the rendering job and each computer's contribution to finishing the job. It also allows you to edit job settings, start or stop a job, change the order of jobs, and much more. The same computer can serve simultaneously as the queue monitor, manager, and server.

To perform network rendering, enable the **Net Render** option at the bottom of the **Render Scene** dialog box, as shown in Figure 16-22.

Figure 16-22. The Net Render option in the Render Scene dialog box

Once you enable this option and click the **Render** button, the **Network Job Assignment** dialog box appears, as shown in Figure 16-23. At the top of the dialog box is the **Job Name** field, where you specify the name of the rendering job. You can name your jobs however you like, but each job name must be unique. Below this field is the **Description** field, where you can provide a description of your job.

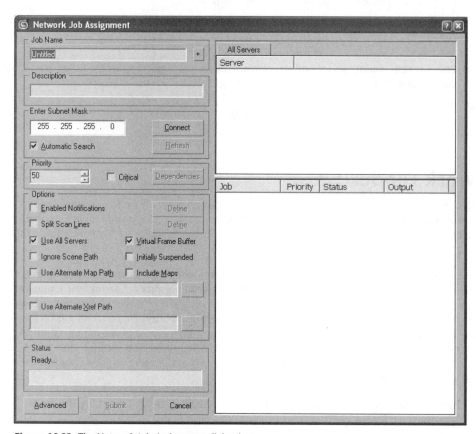

Figure 16-23. The Network Job Assignment dialog box

On the right-hand side of the dialog box is a listing of the servers that are available to receive network job assignments. However, before any servers can be available to receive job assignments, you must run the network Manager. The network Manager is one of the three components of a larger program named Backburner. The Manager, along with the Server and Monitor, is found in the Autodesk program directory, accessed through **Start ➤ Programs ➤ Autodesk ➤ Backburner**, as shown in Figure 16-24.

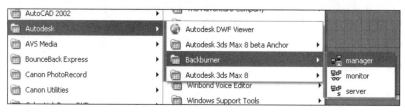

Figure 16-24. The Backburner components

Click the **manager** icon, return to the Backburner directory, and click the **server** icon. When you launch the Server, it immediately searches for the Manager, and when it connects to the Manager, it posts a statement saying **Registration to [IP address] accepted**. Likewise, the Manager will post a statement saying **Successful registration from [computer name]**. If either program is closed, a statement will be posted by the other program stating that closed program is "going down."

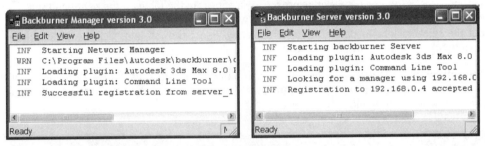

Figure 16-25. The Backburner Manager (left) and Server (right)

Now that both the Manager and Server are running, you can connect to the network through the **Network Job Assignment** window. Click the **Connect** button, and all of the computers running the Server program will appear in the **Server** listing, as shown in Figure 16-26.

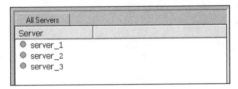

Figure 16-26. The connected servers

Now, all you have to do is click the **Submit** button at the bottom of the **Network Job Assignment** dialog box. When you do, the **Network Job Assignment** dialog box will disappear, and an independent **Render Frame** window and the **Render Progress** dialog box will appear. They will both remain visible for the duration of the rendering process, after which they will disappear. You can close the 3ds Max program after the network rendering process is underway without interrupting the rendering. You should not attempt to work in 3ds Max on a computer that is being used as a server, because the computer will have much less RAM and processor power available while trying to render as a server in the background. You can, however, run the Manager and Monitor programs on a computer that you are working on.

The Manager will always assign frames in a way that maximizes the efficiency of the rendering network. If a server becomes idle, the Manager automatically detects it and no longer considers it for a frame assignment. If a server is disconnected, the Manager takes that server's current frame and reassigns it to another server.

Once rendering begins, you can monitor its progress with the Queue Monitor program, shown in Figure 16-27. But before the Queue Monitor will show the progress of any job, you must first connect it to the network using the **Connect** icon (shown right), found on the far left of the only toolbar in the interface.

Once you connect, all of the jobs past and present will be displayed in the **Show All** table. When you select a job, the details of its progress will appear in the table on the right-hand side of the dialog box. The tabs at the top of the table will take you to other tables displaying more details about the selected job. To delete a job permanently, select the job and click the **Delete Job** icon (shown right).

At the bottom of the **Queue Monitor** dialog box is a table that displays all of the computers that the program has recognized at some point in the past. Those that are currently connected will appear in green, and their status should be listed as busy.

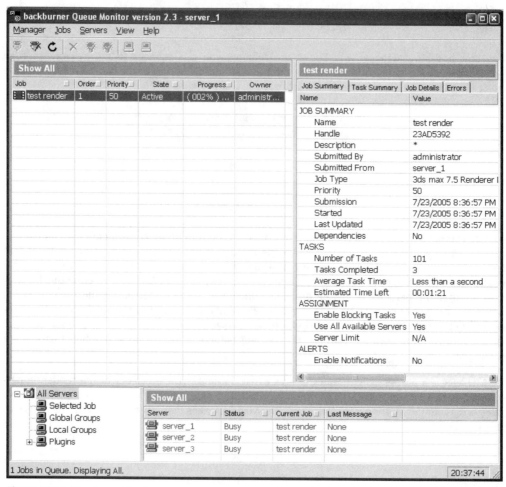

Figure 16-27. The Queue Monitor

Network rendering

This exercise demonstrates how to perform network rendering using a single computer.

1. Reset 3ds Max.
2. Start the Manager, Server, and Monitor programs from a single computer. For the sake of simplicity and training, this exercise demonstrates network rendering without having to place multiple computers on the network. The tutorial is the same regardless of the number of computers on the network.
3. In the Perspective view, create a teapot that rotates 360 degrees about the Z axis during 100 frames.
4. Click the **Render Scene** icon to open the **Render Scene** dialog box.
5. In the **Time Output** section, select the **Active Time Segment** option.
6. In the **Render Output** section, click the **Files** button.
7. Save the file as a .jpg, name the file, and click the **Save** button to close.
8. In the **JPEG Image Control** dialog box, select a quality of 95, and click **OK** to close.
9. In the **Render Output** section, enable the **Net Render** option.
10. Click the **Render** button to begin the rendering process.
11. In the **Network Job Assignment** dialog box, click the **Connect** button. The name of the computer you are using should appear in the window on the right in the dialog box under **Server**.
12. Click the **Submit** button at the bottom of the **Network Job Assignment** dialog box. The dialog box disappears.
13. Maximize the **Monitor** program that is running in the background.
14. Click the **Connect** icon on the far left-hand side of the **Monitor** toolbar.
15. The current job being rendered is displayed in the table on the left-hand side of the dialog box.

Summary

This chapter has focused on the critical settings within the **Render Scene** dialog box and some of the great tools that enhance the rendering process. Though the **Render Scene** dialog box contains a large number of settings for advanced lighting and the mental ray renderer, advanced lighting was sufficiently covered in Chapter 12, and mental ray is not presented in this book. Other nice features covered include rendering tools like the Panorama Exporter, the RAM Player, Video Post, and network rendering.

Rendering is the last step in the production process, unless you do your own video editing or DVD authoring. The next two chapters both present features to use before you begin to render a scene. However, they are placed after this chapter, because the information covered in both chapters is better understood with knowledge of the basics of rendering. After learning the features discussed in these next two chapters, you will have all the tools needed to create photorealistic architectural visualizations from start to finish. The only things left to cover at that point will be some practical, real-world production tips and tricks, which can be found in Appendix B.

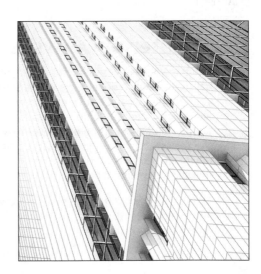

Chapter 17

SCENE ASSEMBLY

In the ideal 3D world, you could build all your scenes without regard to file size, available RAM, CPU speed, rendering times, or any number of things that complicate the design process. However, since most of us have to be aware of our computers' limitations, we have to manage the way we build objects and assemble our scenes. I've already discussed how creating objects with unnecessary detail results in longer rendering times and refresh rates. Likewise, assembling a scene improperly can result in unnecessarily long moments of waiting on your computer to update.

Creating a 3D scene is usually a long process—one that can take up to several months. Anything you can do to streamline your work should be considered. One practice that can save countless hours is building the major components of your scenes separately from each other. Your ability to work efficiently in 3ds Max can become significantly hindered when you allow too many highly detailed objects to reside unnecessarily in the background of your scene. Although it is usually necessary to have other objects visible in your scene as a reference, you should make an effort to prevent your scenes from becoming too large in file size or in polygon count.

This chapter covers the tools that allow you to assemble a scene from multiple files and work efficiently once the assembly process is complete. In addition, you will learn work practices that will reduce the time you wait on your computer to catch up with your commands. Knowing how to create the individual elements of a 3D scene is obviously important, but equally important is knowing how to assemble those elements without wasting countless hours waiting on your computer.

Computer power vs. scene complexity

Whether your project calls for a large golf course community with hundreds of homes or an individual single-family residence, great care should be taken in the methods you use to build and assemble your scenes. Whether your project requires the collective effort of dozens of individuals or you alone, your production process should be based on speed and efficiency. Someday, when computers are powerful enough, you may never have to worry about how complex your scenes become. But for the foreseeable future, you should employ practices and procedures that keep your wait time to a minimum. Before I cover some of the critical tools that allow you to assemble a scene from numerous individual elements, let's cover some of the realities of working in a 3D world.

There are several different situations in which the 3ds Max user is forced to wait on the computer. Three of these, in particular, are situations in which good procedures and practices can spare you from long and unnecessary waiting:

- Transferring files
- Refreshing viewports
- Rendering

Most other times, 3ds Max is waiting on the user for input, but for each of these you are forced to spend at least some time waiting on 3ds Max and your computer, depending largely on how you manage your scenes. So what are the attributes of a scene that affect each of these three situations, and what can you do to minimize your wait during each of these processes? In each case, I'll discuss how scene complexity affects the way 3ds Max transfers file data, and then I'll explain how it affects the time needed to refresh and render a viewport.

Transferring files

It goes without saying that larger files take more time to open, save, or merge. But what makes a file large, and what other characteristics of a scene cause the file commands to need more time to execute? If you were to open 3ds Max and save a file without having created any objects, you would notice that the file size is approximately 140K. As with any program, .max files saved with no user input still contain a certain amount of default data.

Except for the smallest scenes with virtually no objects, the vast majority of a scene's file size is dependent on the number of faces it has to keep track of. While most faces require a certain amount of data to be stored in order to define the normal and three vertices that make up a face, not all faces must be tracked. Parametric, instanced, and referenced objects are all examples of object types that contain faces whose data is not stored individually, but rather with the parent object. Let's look at a few examples of how all of this affects a scene's file size.

Figure 17-1 shows a single teapot with 25 segments and 40,000 faces. The file size for a scene that contains this object alone is 143K, only 3K more than a scene with no objects. Why is this? Because 3ds Max doesn't need to store the same amount of data for every face as it would if the scene were made up of 40,000 independent faces. The key information 3ds Max needs to store about this scene is that there is a single teapot with a particular radius value located at x, y, z, oriented x, y, z degrees, scaled a certain % along x, y, z, etc. There are, of course, numerous parameters and settings that go into defining the exact appearance and characteristics of this teapot, but this information only needs to be defined for the teapot, not all the individual faces that make it up.

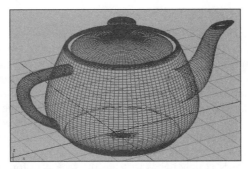

Figure 17-1. The 40,000 faces of a teapot

Now let's see what happens if you collapse this teapot into an editable mesh or poly. This same scene with the teapot collapsed to an editable mesh results in a file size of 1.85MB; when collapsed to an editable poly the resulting file size is 2.23MB. Both of these files are significantly larger, and when this result is compounded with hundreds of objects, the result can be a file size that is simply too large to open or save with today's computers.

Being able to minimize file size by keeping objects in their original parametric form is ideal; however, it's usually not practical for most scene elements. But there are equally effective ways of keeping file sizes under control with object types that typically make up a scene. Continuing on with the teapot example, let's use the Clone feature to create a scene with 25 of these teapots as collapsed editable meshes.

Figure 17-2 shows a scene with 25 meshes collapsed from the original teapot. If you create these meshes using the Copy command, each object becomes independent of the others, and 3ds Max has to track each and every face on each mesh. The result is a file size of 61.8MB and a scene that takes approximately 10 seconds to open and save. This same arrangement of meshes created with the Instance command, however, results in a file size of only 1.89MB and a scene that takes a fraction of a second to open or save. Clearly, whenever you need to duplicate highly detailed objects, it's better to use the Instance command than the Copy command. The trick is determining the point at which it becomes necessary to use the Instance command. After using the Copy command, you can attach all the copies to each other to make a single individual mesh. Instanced objects cannot be collapsed or attached without losing the quality that makes them instanced objects. There are some advantages to having few objects in your scene, even if it means slightly larger file sizes. Fewer objects result in easier object management for both you and 3ds Max. With fewer objects, the "Preparing Objects" step of rendering can be greatly reduced because 3ds Max doesn't have to run through the same process for as many objects.

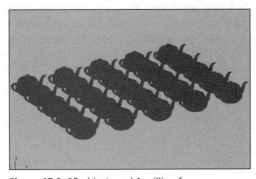

Figure 17-2. 25 objects and 1 million faces

Instance vs. copy

So when is it better to instance objects rather than copy and collapse them? Let's look at the example in Figure 17-3. This is a rendering of a medical office building that contains approximately 1 million faces. The blown-up image to the right of the rendering shows an area where the face count is substantially higher than other areas because of the curves needed to make the detailed balustrade. This is also an area that may be used for close-up shots, so the need for detail is even greater here. There are 20 small balusters and 2 large decorative column caps. To achieve the necessary level of detail, each baluster needed to contain approximately 10,000 faces and each column cap needed to contain approximately 20,000. These are both examples of objects that are suitable candidates for instancing. By creating instances of these objects, not only can you quickly change one and have the others update automatically, but 3ds Max only needs to store the face data for one object, thereby saving you from a much larger file size.

Figure 17-3. Using the Instance command to reduce file size

Once you instance objects like this, I highly recommend grouping them together to avoid seeing each individual instance displayed in the **Select Objects** dialog box, and so that you can quickly and easily change their display characteristics. Since objects like these increase your display refresh rates, it is often helpful to hide the objects or change their display to a box.

Let's look at one more example before moving on. Figure 17-4 shows a large condominium development with eight residential buildings and a clubhouse. In this development, there are six identical large residential buildings containing approximately 500,000 faces each, and two identical smaller buildings containing about 300,000 each. This is an example of when instancing objects would clearly be better than copying objects. The file size for a scene with just the larger building by itself is approximately 10MB, and a scene with the smaller building by itself is 8MB. If these buildings were copied rather than instanced, the file size for a scene with just the eight buildings alone would be almost 80MB.

Figure 17-4. A scene with instanced buildings to reduce file size

Using the Copy and Instance commands

This exercise demonstrates the differences between the Copy and Instance commands when used to populate a scene with multiple clones of a high face count.

1. Reset 3ds Max.
2. In the Perspective viewport, create a sphere of any radius, with 200 segments.
3. Save the file anywhere on your computer.
4. Using Windows Explorer, determine the size of the file you just saved. It should be approximately 180K. (Your file size may vary slightly from this value.)
5. Collapse the sphere to an editable mesh.
6. Resave the file and check the file size again. It should now be approximately 1.82MB, ten times the size of the previous save.
7. Hold down Shift and click the sphere. The **Clone Options** dialog box appears.
8. Select the **Copy** option and make 25 clones of the sphere.
9. Save the file and check the file size. It should be approximately 44MB.
10. Undo the Clone command.
11. Clone the sphere again using the **Instance** option and make 25 clones.
12. Save and check the file. It should now only be approximately 1.85MB (roughly 25 times smaller than the previously saved version). To summarize, instances reduce files size and use less RAM. Copies should be used when the individual objects need to retain unique appearances that aren't tied to the appearance of other objects.

Refreshing and rendering viewports

Everyone knows that the more faces that are displayed in a viewport, the longer it will take for the viewport to refresh. But what can be done to maximize the number of faces in your scene and minimize the amount of time it takes to refresh the viewports? Chapter 1 covered some of the great features that allow you to work in large, complex scenes without having to endure excessive refresh times. These included **Disable View**, **Rendering Levels**, and **Fast View**. Chapter 2 discussed the **Hide** feature, the **Display as Box** option, and the use of layers. All these features are critical to efficient work in 3ds Max. Now, let's cover some of the techniques of building and assembling scenes to minimize the time needed to refresh viewports.

Let's go back to the condominium example I just talked about. This project involved several sequences that went into the creation of a 4-minute animation. Numerous camera paths were set up throughout the site and not much was left out of the final animation. A scene with the entire project loaded contained approximately 1,000 objects and 4 million faces. Rendering a scene of 1,000 objects and 4 million faces can easily take 1 hour per frame, even without adding advanced lighting, rendering effects, or numerous other features that make an average rendering look photorealistic. If the final product were just a few individual images, the methods used to assemble the scenes would not be critical. However, since the animation needed to be 4 minutes long, or 7,200 frames, spending over an hour per frame was not an option. Even with a 10-computer render farm, the final animation could take over 720 hours of straight rendering time. These 7,200 frames don't even account for the numerous preview renderings and changes requested by the client. Needless to say, something needed to be done to make the project more manageable and allow for use of some of the advanced lighting and effects features.

The only solution was to break the project up into individual scenes of smaller size. On the set of a movie or TV show, scenes are created for filming from very specific camera angles so that the viewer doesn't see that just outside of the camera's view is the filming crew, the audience, and the studio walls. Just like the set of a movie, I assembled my scenes so that only those objects that would be seen by the camera were present. After developing a script, I created camera paths; and with the camera paths created, I knew exactly what I could leave out of each scene.

The sequence of images in Figures 17-5 through 17-8 show portions of a 30-second clip (900 frames) for the condominium project. In this particular scene, the camera moves around a virtual conference room and zooms into a set of architectural drawings resting on a table. As the camera moves closer, the first page is folded back, revealing a photo of the project. The camera continues to move closer, and the project is seen rising out of the photo. As the camera moves down to a street-level view, the conference room fades away and the viewer is led through the center of the project.

Frames 0 through 300 (Figure 17-5) only show the conference room objects, but in Figure 17-6 you can see the tops of the buildings rising out of the photograph. So for the first 300 frames, I was able to exclude the condominium objects, and the result was a very small file size of only 495K. Since the objects in the condominium project were not part of the scene for these first 300 frames, these frames rendered much faster. This was because the advanced lighting solutions did not have to take these objects into account; this is also because the RAM on the render farm computers was not completely expended loading this additional content. When you don't have enough RAM, your renderings may slow to a crawl because the processor will have to wait for information to move back and forth from the hard drive to the RAM before it can complete its work. If your RAM is completely expended and 3ds Max still wants more, your processor may work at as little as 10% efficiency, thereby increasing your rendering times as much as tenfold. Additionally, the cars in this project were RPCs. (**RPC** stands for Rich Photorealistic Content, a third-party plug-in from ArchVision—www.archvision.com—that I often use in my projects.) As the acronym implies, RPCs are a great source of content for architectural scenes. Available RPCs include vegetation, people, fountains, and in this case, vehicles. Since the cars were not visible in these frames, 3ds Max did not have to load the supporting plug-in files during the rendering process, which saved additional time. One final benefit to making the first scene this way was that these first 300 frames could be sent to Network Render while I continued to work on finalizing the condominium objects that were about to appear in the next sequence. By the time the second scene was ready for rendering, the first scene had already finished rendering.

 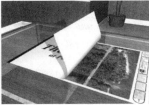 

Figure 17-5. Frames 0 through 300

I continued to break up the overall scene file into smaller files to take advantage of reduced file sizes, more available RAM, advanced lighting, and earlier final renders. In frames 301 through 400 (Figure 17-6), I was still able to exclude most of the site elements, such as streets, grass, and shrubs, but because the buildings and trees needed to be shown, the file size and face count jumped to over 40MB and 4 million, respectively.

Figure 17-6. Frames 301 through 400

Frames 401 through 600 (Figure 17-7) were the largest and most difficult to render, at over 5 million faces and 82MB. These frames showed the greatest number of objects and took much longer to render than any other frames in the clip.

Figure 17-7. Frames 401 through 600

421

In frames 601 through 900 (Figure 17-8), I was able to exclude two of the buildings and all their surrounding site elements. In addition, the conference room had faded away by this point, so these objects could also be excluded. The result was a significant reduction in file size, from 82MB to 58MB.

Figure 17-8. Frames 601 through 900

Figure 17-9 shows the final breakup of files for Scene 01. The files were named descriptively, with the scene name at the beginning (Conf.Rm) and the frame numbers at the end (0000-0300) so that I could easily keep track of them. Notice the varied file sizes involved. Even the largest file, at 82MB, contained only about half the objects used in all the scenes. Hundreds of objects that could not be seen from this scene's perspective were excluded from these files, such as the clubhouse pool objects, a small marina on the water, and much more. Had I not broken up the project into these smaller files, I would have had to work with a single file that contained all the project objects. This file would have been close to 200MB and required far more RAM than my computers had available.

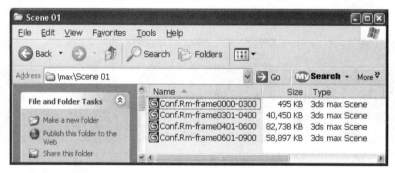

Figure 17-9. Files for Scene 01

Assembly tools

Now that we've covered some of the strategies for creating more manageable files, let's look at some of the tools in 3ds Max that make it possible to create these files. All the tools mentioned in this section are found in the File menu.

In addition to these tools, I'll cover some of the features that give you the ability to maintain an accurate picture of how complex your scenes become. These features will show you at any time exactly how many objects, faces, lights, plug-ins, and other elements your scene contains. They will also allow you to keep track of a scene's file size and the amount of RAM being used.

Save Selected

The Save Selected command is an important part of the scene-assembly process. It saves to a separate file any objects you have selected prior to executing the command. It's useful in a couple of different ways. If you open a file with numerous objects and want to save a particular object to a separate file as part of your library for future projects, select the objects and select the Save Selected command. This feature also works great when you simply want to break up a large file into smaller files for later assembly. While working in a scene, you may often find that you've just created some objects that contain a large number of faces, and these objects aren't needed until rendering time. Keeping these complex objects in your scene makes working in 3ds Max more difficult and places an unnecessary burden on your computer. Saving these select objects to a separate file makes it easier to continue working on the rest of the scene.

Figure 17-10 shows an example of a project in which several objects were saved to separate files because their face count became an issue. Keeping all these objects in the primary scene file made the file excessively large and consumed too much RAM. After saving these objects to separate files, they were later merged during scene assembly just prior to rendering. Notice the files in the Scene 04 folder are organized in a logical and easy-to-understand manner. The primary scene files are labeled Overhead-frame0000-0400 and Overhead-frame0401-0600, and the files to be assembled later are labeled with easy-to-recall names and the prefix x- so that Windows lists them together after the primary files.

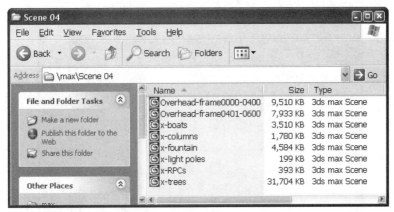

Figure 17-10. Using Save Selected to save smaller, high–face count files outside main scene file

Merge

The Merge feature lets you bring objects from another file into the file you are working on. When you merge objects, there is no link maintained between the two files involved, so changing the objects in either file has no effect on the other file. To perform a merge, select **File ➤ Merge** and select a file from the **Merge File** dialog box, as shown in Figure 17-11.

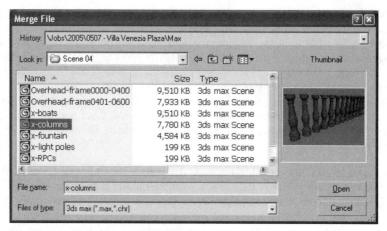

Figure 17-11. Merging files

After selecting the file, the **Merge** dialog box appears, as shown in Figure 17-12. This dialog box is nearly identical to the **Select Objects** dialog box, and works in the same way. Once you select the object or objects you want to merge, click **OK** to complete the merge.

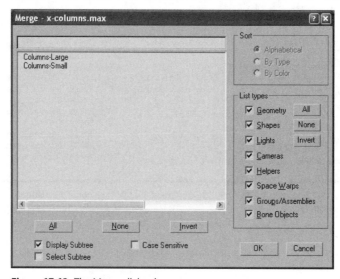

Figure 17-12. The Merge dialog box

Using the Save Selected and Merge commands

This exercise demonstrates how to use the Save Selected command to save select objects to separate files, and the Merge command to bring them back into the same file.

1. Reset 3ds Max.
2. In the Perspective view, create three spheres, three teapots, and three cylinders of any size.
3. Select the three teapots, and select **File ➤ Save Selected**. The **Save File As** dialog appears.
4. Name the file Teapots and save anywhere on your computer.
5. Select the spheres and use the Save Selected command to save them to a file with the name Spheres.
6. Select the cylinders and use the Save Selected command to save them to a file with the name Cylinders.
7. Reset 3ds Max.
8. Select **File ➤ Merge**. The **Merge File** dialog box appears.
9. Select the file named Teapots, highlight all three teapots, and click **OK** to complete the merge.
10. Run the Merge command again, select the file named Spheres, highlight any two spheres, and click **OK** to complete the merge.
11. Run the Merge command once more, select the file named Cylinders, highlight any one of the cylinders, and click **OK** to complete the merge.

Import

The Import command is similar to the Merge command, except that it works with file types other than the native .max file. Two file types you will become very familiar with in the visualization world are the .dwg and .3ds file types. The .dwg is the native AutoCAD file type that you will use for importing architectural drawings. The .3ds file is the old DOS 3D Studio mesh file format, which is still widely used as an exchange file format between various 3D software packages. Although you may never need it for exchange purposes, you may find it invaluable in its ability to create certain types of mesh objects, such as those from the polylines of a 2D CAD program. Figure 17-13 shows the **DWG Import** and **3DS Import** dialog boxes that appear when the command is executed. In most cases, you will want to click **OK** to merge the imported objects, rather than replace the entire scene.

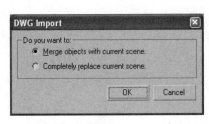
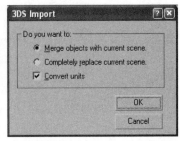

Figure 17-13. The DWG Import and 3DS Import dialog boxes

Export

The Export feature is used to export all the objects of your current file into another file type. Although you should rarely need to use this command, the most common file type you will probably need to export to is the native AutoCAD .dwg file type. One situation I have found this command very useful for is when I want to create linework in 3ds Max and export that linework into AutoCAD. I do this when I want to trace the exact position of 3D objects in a 3ds Max scene and use that linework as a reference to more work in AutoCAD.

Export Selected

The Export Selected feature works similarly to Export, except that it works only with those objects that are selected prior to executing the command.

XRef Objects

The XRef Objects feature, shown in Figure 17-14, is a great tool that allows you to load objects from other files and maintain a link to those files. You can maintain smaller working files by using the XRef command for select objects that contain a large number of faces. If changes are made to an object in the source file, the object is updated in the file that contains the XRef. These changes include any applied modifiers and changes to an object's parameters; however, they do not include transforms. If you change an object parameter in the source file, the XRef will update to show the change. However, if you move, rotate, or scale the object in the source file, the XRef will not show these transformations. All other changes to the source object will cause the XRef to update accordingly.

The XRef Objects feature is an alternative to the Merge feature. Which method you use is simply a matter of preference; however, breaking up large files into smaller, more manageable files is always a good choice.

To use the XRef Objects feature, select **File ➤ XRef Objects**. Click the **Create XRef Record from File** icon, locate the file you want to XRef into your scene, and click the **Open** button. Once you open the file, all the scene objects and materials will be displayed in the bottom half of the **XRef Objects** dialog box, and the new objects will appear in your scene. The objects are selected and can be transformed, but the parameters and modifiers that are available in the source file will not be available in your current file.

Within this dialog box are handy options that allow you to disable the XRef, merge the objects, and remove them from the XRef link. Within the **Modify** panel for any selected object, you can use a proxy object in place of the real object to reduce the number of visible faces.

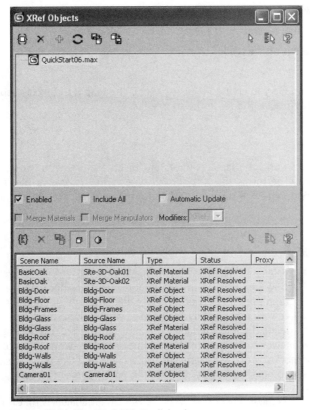

Figure 17-14. The XRef Objects dialog box

Using the XRef Objects command

This exercise demonstrates how to use the XRef Objects command to bring externally referenced objects into the current file, and how changing the objects in the source file causes the XRef to update automatically.

1. Reset 3ds Max.

2. In the Perspective view, create a teapot of any size.

3. Name the file teapot, and save anywhere on your computer.

4. Reset 3ds Max.

5. Select **File ➤ XRef Objects**.

6. Click the **Create XRef Record from File** icon and select the file you just saved.

7. Click the **Open** button to finish the command.

8. Save the file with the name teapot XRef.

9. Open the first file you created (teapot).

10. Increase the radius of the teapot twofold.

11. Save the file.

12. Open the second file you created (teapot XRef). The teapot in this file should now look twice the size it did before, as it does in the source file.

XRef Scenes

The XRef Scenes feature works the same as the XRef Objects feature, with two main exceptions. First, the XRef Scenes feature performs the XRef on all objects in the source file, rather than just the selected objects. Second, once the scene is XRef'd into the new file, the objects are not selectable or transformable.

File Link Manager

The File Link Manager creates XRef-like links to AutoCAD drawing files. Whenever I need to bring in linework from AutoCAD, however, I always use the Import feature rather than the File Link Manager. I do this because I prefer to import small, more manageable amounts of linework at a time, and then work on that imported linework immediately. In 3ds Max, when I finish modeling the objects I use the AutoCAD linework for, I delete the imported linework and start the process over again with a new area of the scene (and new linework). Because of this, I do not need linework to be continuously updated and reloaded. This method of work is a matter of preference, and like most areas of 3ds Max, there are numerous ways to accomplish the same thing. In this case, I prefer to import.

An additional problem you might encounter with the File Link Manager is that if you file link a scene and assign materials, and then make changes to the .dwg file, all the material assignments are lost.

File Properties

This feature gives you a great snapshot of some of the important characteristics of your scene, such as the total number of faces, objects, lights, and cameras. This particular information is found on the **Contents** tab of the **File Properties** dialog box, and is only updated when you resave the file. Figure 17-15 shows the contents of the scene with the 25 teapots and 1 million faces (discussed earlier).

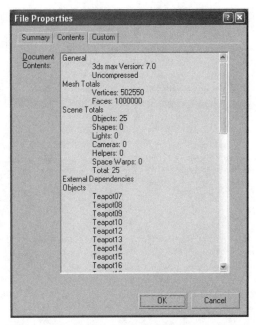

Figure 17-15. The File Properties dialog box

Summary Info

The Summary Info feature, shown in Figure 17-16, provides a more detailed view of the makeup of your scene than the File Properties feature. In addition to showing some of the information provided in the **File Properties** dialog box, the Summary Info feature also shows you important information such as how much RAM is being used. This information is updated as changes in the file occur, rather than only after the file is resaved.

In the **Summary Info** window (located at the lower half of the **Summary Info** dialog box) is detailed information that is shown only for the current frame that the Time slider is on. For example, if the number of faces in a teapot is changed from one frame to another, then the **Summary Info** dialog box will display the number of faces the teapot contains at the frame that the Time slider is on.

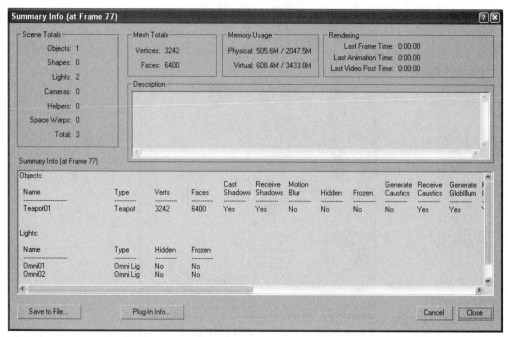

Figure 17-16. The Summary Info dialog box

Archive and Resource Collector

Although not completely related to scene assembly or other features covered in this chapter, the Archive feature and the Resource Collector are two additional features found within the File menu that are worth mentioning.

These tools are very handy in two particular situations. First, if you want to take a .max file and work with it on a different computer—maybe a laptop that you're taking on the road—the Archive and Resource Collector features are exactly what you need. Second, if you need to send your scene to someone else so that they can work on it, these features are invaluable.

The Archive feature creates a .zip file of every file 3ds Max needs to create your scene, including all image files used in materials and any plug-in resource files. To use the Archive feature, select **File ➤ Archive**, give the .zip file a name, and click **Save** to complete the command. You can only perform this command while in the 3ds Max file that you want to archive.

The Resource Collector feature does almost the same thing as the Archive feature; however, it does not automatically create a .zip file when it saves the files. To use the Resource Collector feature, go to the **Utilities** panel, open the **Utilities** rollout, and select **More ➤ Resource Collector**. The Command panel displays a **Parameters** rollout, as shown in Figure 17-17. Click the **Browse** button and select a location in which to save all the support files. Enable the **Include MAX File** option if you want a copy of the .max file to be saved along with the rest of the files.

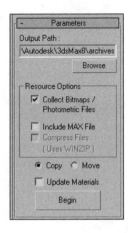

Figure 17-17. The Resource Collector

Summary

This chapter has shown why it's so important to know how to build and assemble a scene without excessive file sizes or face counts. Someday, we may no longer have to be concerned with such issues, but for the foreseeable future we should always try to use the tools available to allow for efficient work and prevent wasted time. I suspect that no matter how fast computers become, software developers will always fill your plates with more and more processor-hungry and memory-consuming programs and resources. If this is true, then the topics covered in this chapter will always apply.

At this point, there's not much left to cover at the foundation level. The next chapter will cover the last major area of 3ds Max I have yet to discuss—effects. After this chapter, you'll have looked at all the major areas in 3ds Max that apply to users in the visualization industry.

Chapter 18

EFFECT BASICS

In 3ds Max, the word "effect" can have many different meanings, depending on whom you talk to and what industry you work in. For 3ds Max, the features that employ the term "effects" fall into two categories: **atmospheric effects** and **render effects**. Atmospheric effects simulate real-world conditions or elements and are incorporated during the rendering process. Render effects simulate the effect of viewing the world through the lens of a camera, and are added after the initial rendering process is complete. Both types of effects can significantly improve an architectural visualization, but they can also have a dramatic impact on the time it takes to render a scene, so they should be used with some discretion.

This chapter covers each of the available atmospheric and critical render effects, all of which can enhance the quality and realism of an architectural visualization. When you first begin to explore these features, you may be surprised at just how easy they are to use. Some require very little explanation, but all of them usually require some amount of experimentation to achieve the desired effect. After reading this chapter, you will be able to add a great deal of quality to your visualizations with the following effects.

Atmospheric effects:

- Fire Effect
- Fog
- Volume Fog
- Volume Light

Render effects:

- Lens Effect
- Depth of Field
- Motion Blur

Atmospheric effects

3ds Max contains four types of atmospheric effects: Fire Effect, Fog, Volume Fog, and Volume Light. To access these effects, select **Environment** from the **Rendering** menu, or press 8. Doing so opens the **Environment and Effects** dialog box, as shown in the left image of Figure 18-1. In the **Atmosphere** roll-out, click the **Add** button to open the **Add Atmospheric Effect** dialog box (right image), select the effect you want to add, and click **OK** to close.

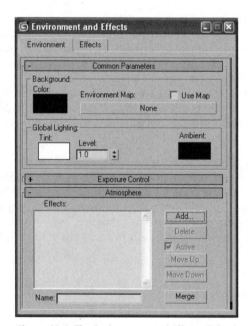
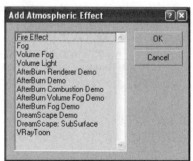

Figure 18-1. The Environment and Effects dialog box (left) and the Add Atmospheric Effect dialog box (right)

One of the first things to consider in adding an effect is where the effect is going to exist. Two of the effects, Fire and Volume Fog, require the use of an object called an atmospheric apparatus gizmo to define the space in which the effect is to exist. The Fog effect contains its own unique parameters to define its location, while the Volume Light effect uses a light's parameters to define its location.

The atmospheric effects will be discussed in alphabetical order, as they appear in the **Add Atmospheric Effect** dialog box—not in the order of their importance.

The Fire effect

Although not one of the more widely used effects in visualization, the Fire effect is very helpful in the simulation of one very important element of many visualizations. While you can use the Fire effect to create explosions, set things on fire, and numerous other things, the most useful application I have found for the Fire effect in visualizations is in the simulation of a simple fireplace. This one application alone makes learning the Fire effect worthwhile.

Before the Fire effect can be added to your scene, you must create an atmospheric apparatus gizmo. To access this type of gizmo, select the **Helpers** icon (shown right) from the **Create** panel.

The second helper type listed in the drop-down menu below the Create icons is **Atmospheric Apparatus**, as shown in the left image of Figure 18-2. Selecting this helper type opens a rollout with three gizmo types: **BoxGizmo**, **SphereGizmo**, and **CylGizmo** (right image). Although future releases of 3ds Max may contain more sophisticated types of volumes, currently you are limited to defining the area of the Fire and Volume Fog effects to the volume of a box, sphere, or cylinder. However, you can apply non-uniform scaling and position numerous gizmos throughout your scene to define more sophisticated volumes.

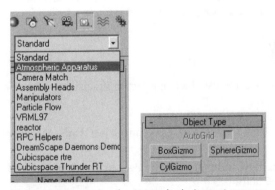

Figure 18-2. Accessing the Atmospheric Apparatus menu

To create a gizmo, select the gizmo type and click inside a viewport to define its volume, in the same way you would create the box, sphere, and cylinder primitives. Now when you add a Fire effect in the **Environment and Effects** dialog box, the **Fire Effect Parameters** rollout appears, as shown in Figure 18-3. In the **Gizmos** section, click the **Pick Gizmo** button; then, inside a viewport, click the gizmo you want to add the effect to.

435

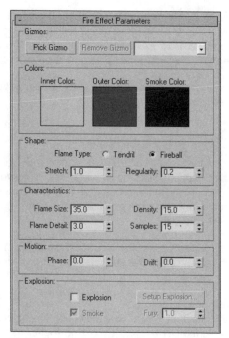

Figure 18-3. The Fire Effect Parameters rollout

The **Fire Effect Parameters** rollout contains numerous parameters to give you precise control over the appearance of the Fire effect. However, as I stated in the beginning of the chapter, most effects require some experimentation to achieve the desired look. The best way to learn the Fire effect is through the use of a practical exercise geared toward creating a typical fireplace.

Using the Fire effect

This exercise demonstrates how to use the Fire effect to simulate a typical fireplace.

1. Reset 3ds Max.
2. Click the **Helpers** icon in the **Create** panel and select **Atmospheric Apparatus** from the drop-down list.
3. Click the **SphereGizmo** button, and in the Perspective view, click and drag to define a gizmo with a radius of 50 units.
4. Enable the **Hemisphere** option, located directly below the **Radius** field. This changes the sphere into a hemisphere.
5. Perform a non-uniform scale by scaling the gizmo 300% along the Z axis. This will help stretch the flames of the fire.
6. Perform a Zoom Extents operation of the Perspective view.
7. Press 8 to open the **Environment and Effects** rollout.

8. In the **Background** section of the **Common Parameters** rollout, click the black color swatch to open the color selector.

9. Change the color to pure white, which will change the background to white.

10. In the **Atmosphere** rollout, click the **Add** button and select **Fire Effect**.

11. In the **Fire Effect Parameters** rollout, click the **Pick Gizmo** button, and click the **SphereGizmo** you created in the Perspective view. The effect is now added to the scene, and when rendered should look like the first fire on the left in the following illustration.

12. Within the **Shape** section, change the **Flame Type** to **Tendril**. This option creates pointed flames along the Z axis of the apparatus. Changing this option alone, however, will not produce the desired look—a few more adjustments must be made.

13. Change the **Stretch** value to **2**. The **Stretch** parameter scales flames along the Z axis of the apparatus. Values less than the default **1.0** cause the flames to appear shorter and thicker, while values greater than **1.0** cause the flames to appear longer and skinnier. The result should look like the second fire in the following illustration.

14. Next, change the **Flame Size** to **10**. Reducing the **Flame Size** makes more individual flames visible and keeps the effect from looking like a fireball. The result should look like the third fire in the following illustration.

15. Change the **Flame Density** to **30**. Increasing the **Flame Density** makes the fire less transparent and appear to burn hotter. The result should look like the fourth fire in the following illustration.

16. Finally, change the **Flame Detail** to **1** and render again to see the effect of changing this parameter. The result should look like the fifth fire in the following illustration, in which the fire appears blurred and less detailed. A **Flame Detail** value of 3 should work in most situations. Higher values increase render times, and may require an increase in the **Samples** values to produce a visible difference, which increases render times even further.

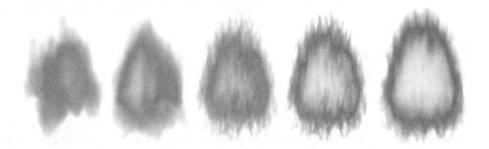

You can animate the fire by simply changing the phase over time. Over a 10-second period of time (i.e., 300 frames), try changing the **Phase** to **300**. This should produce a realistic animated fire.

The Fog effect

Fog is an extremely useful feature in 3ds Max that can give your work not only a greater sense of realism, but also inspire a greater sense of emotion. Adding fog to your scene can completely change the look of your visualization in numerous ways.

There are two types of fog effects in 3ds Max: **Fog** and **Volume Fog**. The Fog effect creates either a "standard" fog throughout the entire scene, which makes objects appear to fade with increasing distance from the camera, or a "layered" fog, in which the fog is confined to specific elevations. Image 1 in Figure 18-4 depicts a scene before fog is added. Image 2 shows the same scene with a standard fog that permeates everywhere. Image 3 shows the scene with layered fog, where the fog exists from the ground to approximately 5 feet above the ground. The Volume Fog effect creates fog in a volume defined by an atmospheric apparatus gizmo. Image 4 in Figure 18-4 depicts the scene with Volume Fog, where the gizmo occupies a volume confined to the first few feet above the lake. Because of this, the fog exists only above the lake in the foreground. I'll first cover the Fog effect and then move on to the Volume Fog effect.

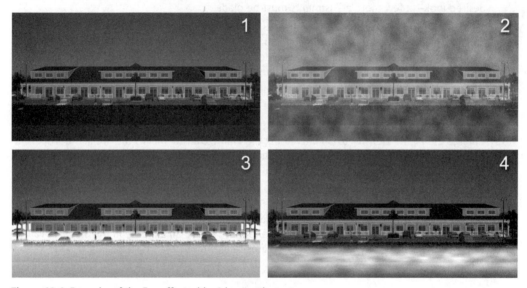

Figure 18-4. Examples of the Fog effect with various settings

The Fog effect contains only one rollout, **Fog Parameters** (shown in Figure 18-5). The color swatch sets the color of the fog, which can either be left as pure white or given a subtle amount of color to enhance the effect of penetrating light. You can also dramatically change the color of the fog to simulate something other than fog, such as the smoke from a fire.

The Environment Color Map lets you use a map to determine the color of the fog. Though I don't use this feature much, I use the Environment Opacity Map (located directly below the Environment Color Map) with almost all fog effects. The Environment Opacity Map lets you use a map to assign opacity to the fog. Once you load a map, you then drag the loaded map into the **Material Editor**, at which point you can control the parameters of the map as you would with any other map.

Below the map buttons is the **Fog Background** option, which should always be enabled if the background is visible (i.e., if there is no mapped object that represents the background).

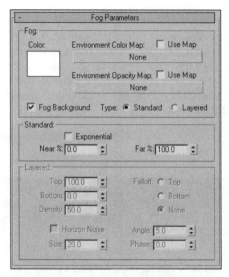

Figure 18-5. The Fog Parameters rollout

Standard fog

Enabling the standard fog option causes the entire scene to show fog. It acts like a filter causing all scene objects to fade from their normal appearance to whatever color the fog is. This fading increases with distance from the camera.

Within the **Standard** section of the rollout is the **Exponential** option. This option increases the density of the fog exponentially with distance, rather than linearly. I recommend always enabling this option because without it, transparent objects (such as vegetation created with opacity maps) will not render correctly.

The **Near** % and **Far** % values determine the strength of the fog at its beginning point and ending point. The beginning point is a distance from the camera defined by the **Near Range** value. This value is located in the **Environment Range** section of the **Parameters** rollout of a camera, as shown in Figure 18-6. The ending point is a distance from the camera defined by the **Far Range** value, which is located in the same place. Image 2 in Figure 18-4 used a **Near** % value of **0.0** and **Far** % value of **50.0**. I recommend leaving the **Near** % value at **0.0** and altering the **Far** % value to determine the overall strength of the fog for the entire scene. If the **Near** % value is set high, you might not see anything in your scene other than fog.

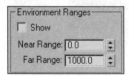

Figure 18-6. The Environment Ranges settings

Environment ranges

The **Environment Ranges** values allow you to specify the distance from the camera at which certain environment effects, such as Fog (standard), are to take place. By default, the **Near Range** is set to **0.0** and the **Far Range** is set to **1000.00** (or **83'4"**, with units set to **US Standard**). This means that the effect will begin at the camera with a strength specified in the **Near** % field located in the **Environment and Effects** dialog box, and extend out to 1,000 units from the camera, where it will end at a strength specified in the **Far** % field.

In the example in Figure 18-7, numbers are placed at their specified distance from the camera to demonstrate the use of environment ranges.

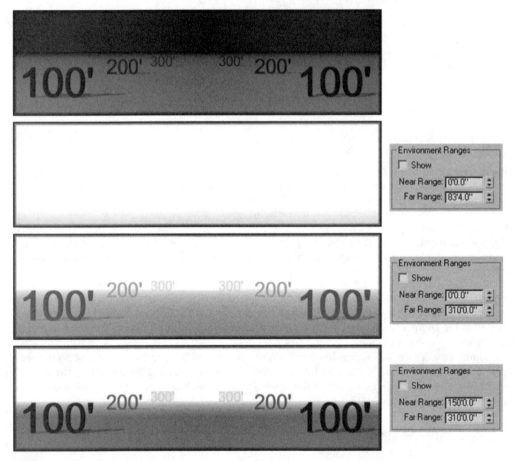

Figure 18-7. The effect of using environment ranges with Fog

In the top image, no environment effects are applied.

In the second image, a Fog effect is applied with the default settings. Since the Fog effect begins at the camera with 0% strength and reaches 100% strength at a distance of 83 feet, 4 inches from the camera, none of the numbers are visible.

In the third image, the fog still begins at the camera, but reaches 100% strength at a distance of 310 feet from the camera. For this reason, the numbers appear to fade as their distance from the camera increases. The objects 300 feet from the camera are barely visible.

In the bottom image, the fog still reaches 100% strength at a distance of 310 feet, but it doesn't begin until it is 150 feet away from the camera. For this reason, the objects 100 feet from the camera do not appear faded at all.

Using environment ranges to control an effect

This exercise demonstrates how to use environment ranges to control a Fog effect.

1. Reset 3ds Max.
2. Press 8 to open the **Environment and Effects** dialog box.
3. In the **Atmosphere** rollout, click the **Add** button. This opens the **Add Effect** dialog box.
4. Select **Fog** and click **OK** to close. The Fog effect is now added to your scene.
5. While in the Perspective view, press Ctrl+C to turn the view into a Camera view.
6. In the Camera view, create a teapot with a radius of 25 units.
7. Move the camera so that it captures a view of the teapot from the side.
8. Render the scene. The fog that you added to the scene should make the background white, as shown in the left image of the following illustration.
9. Select the camera, and go to the **Modify** tab. In the **Environment Ranges** section of the **Parameters** rollout in the Command panel, enable the **Show** option to display the environment range cone.
10. Reduce the **Far Range** value to **500** and render the scene. Fog should appear to whiten the teapot because the far range—which is the distance at which the fog is 100%—is closer to the teapot. The middle and right images in the following illustration show the scene with reduced **Far Range** values.

11. Continue to reduce the **Far Range** value until the environment range cone no longer encompasses the teapot, as shown in the following illustration. When this happens, render the scene, and the teapot should completely disappear. The fog is at 100% at a distance that is closer than the teapot.

Layered fog

Layered fog uses a top and bottom value to establish the elevation at which the fog exists, as shown in Figure 18-8. You set the lower extent of the fog in the **Bottom** field and the upper extent in the **Top** field. The **Density** value sets the strength, or thickness, of the fog.

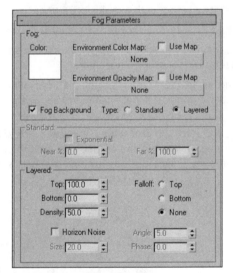

Figure 18-8. Layered fog settings

In the real world, fog does not instantly start and stop at certain elevations. Instead, it fades away. Likewise, 3ds Max does not automatically set the **Top** and **Bottom** values as the dramatic change between where fog exists and doesn't exist. You can, however, minimize the transition between fog and no fog using the **Falloff** option in the **Layered** section. Adding falloff at the bottom or top of the fog will cause the fog to fade away at an exponential rate rather than at a linear rate.

The **Horizon Noise** option can increase realism by adding noise to the fog in the area around the horizon. The **Size** value sets the size of the noise and the **Angle** value determines the angle from the horizon at which the noise begins to break up the fog. If the **Top** and **Bottom** values are so low that the fog crosses the horizon, the Horizon Noise feature will cause an undesirable effect in which the fog seems to be mirrored above and below the horizon. Although Horizon Noise is a great feature, you will probably have to experiment with the parameters in the **Layered** section to get just the look you want.

You can have multiple layers of fog by simply adding more Fog effects within the **Atmosphere** rollout.

The Volume Fog effect

The Volume Fog settings, shown in Figure 18-9, give you the flexibility of defining the limits of fog using an atmospheric apparatus gizmo, the same way as discussed for the Fire effect. The gizmos are created and used the same way for the Volume Fog effect as for the Fire effect. Furthermore, many of the settings discussed in the Fog effect work the same in the Volume Fog effect.

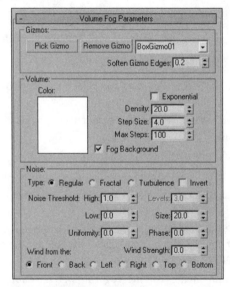

Figure 18-9. Volume Fog settings

The **Soften Gizmo Edges** value softens the fog around the edge of the gizmo. The default setting of 0.2 works fine in most cases, but even subtler edges can be achieved by increasing the value up to 1.0. A value of 0.0 will produce the undesirable effect of defining the gizmo with a harsh border.

The **Step Size** determines the coarseness of the fog. The smaller the value, the finer the fog becomes.

The **Max Steps** value sets the sampling of the fog. Increasing the value improves the sampling; however, it also increases the rendering time. The default value of 100 should work fine in most situations, and should not be set much higher without good reason, as high values could slow your computer to a crawl.

Within the **Noise** section of the **Volume Fog Parameters** rollout are settings to control the noise of the fog. The noise settings essentially control the design of the fog, and like so many of the effects discussed in this chapter, take a great deal of experimentation for the desired appearance to be achieved. The two settings I find particularly useful to control are **Size** and **Uniformity**. **Size**, as with the Fog effect, controls the puffiness of the fog. The **Uniformity** value, as the name implies, controls how similar the fog is throughout its volume. As you increase **Uniformity** to the maximum value of 1.0, the fog becomes less speckled.

By animating the **Phase**, you can make the fog appear to churn. By adding **Wind Strength**, you can make the fog appear to move in a direction defined by the **Wind from the** setting. Unless you animate the **Phase**, the **Wind Strength** setting will have no affect on the fog.

Creating Volume Fog

This exercise demonstrates how to create and modify the **Volume Fog** effect.

1. Reset 3ds Max.
2. Click the **Helpers** icon in the **Create** panel and select **Atmospheric Apparatus** from the drop-down list.
3. Click the **SphereGizmo** button, and in the Perspective view, click and drag to define a gizmo with a radius of 50 units.
4. Press 8 to open the **Environment and Effects** dialog box.
5. In the **Atmosphere** rollout, click the **Add** button. This opens the **Add Effect** dialog box.
6. Select **Volume Fog**, and click **OK** to close. The Volume Fog effect has now been added to your scene, but it hasn't yet been added to a gizmo.
7. In the **Volume Fog Parameters** rollout, click the **Pick Gizmo** button and then select the **SphereGizmo** you just created in the Perspective view. Render the scene, and the result should look like image 1 in the following illustration.
8. Within the **Noise** section of the **Volume Fog Parameters** rollout, reduce the size from the default value of **20** to **10**. Render the scene and the result should look like image 2.
9. Increase the **Uniformity** to **0.2**. Render the scene and the result should look like image 3.
10. Decrease the **Density** to 5. Render the scene and the result should look like image 4. This demonstrates how the settings can be altered to achieve just the right look.

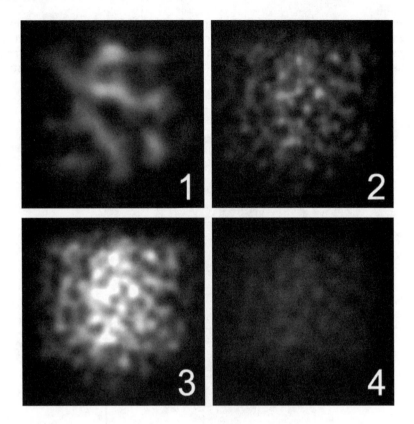

The Volume Light effect

Volume Light is probably the most widely used atmospheric effect, with numerous uses. It allows you to create the effect of light interacting with fog or other atmospheric particles. You can use it to simulate the glow around a light source, light coming through the windows of a building, or light shining from the headlights of a car, as shown in Figure 18-10.

Figure 18-10. Volume Light simulating the headlights of a car

To create a Volume Light effect, you must attach the effect to a light in your scene in the same way you attach Volume Fog to a gizmo. When you attach the effect to a light, a single rollout appears, as shown in Figure 18-11. Although the parameters in this rollout control most of the characteristics of the effect, they do not control the extent or intensity of the effect. These two characteristics are controlled through the light's settings within the Command panel.

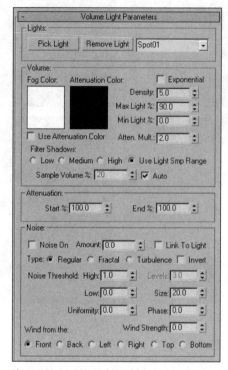

Figure 18-11. The Volume Light Parameters rollout

The Volume Light effect takes the shape of whatever light type is used, and is attenuated through the **Attenuation** parameters in the **Volume Light Parameters** rollout in the Command panel. In the example in Figure 18-10, a target spotlight is used with attenuation to create the light emitting from the headlights and attenuating after a certain distance. If the light type in this example were an omni light, the result would have been much different. The Volume Light would be cast in all directions, as shown in Figure 18-12.

Within the **Volume** section of the **Volume Light Parameters** rollout are several settings previously discussed in the sections on the Volume Fog and Fire effects. There are, however, several settings unique to Volume Light.

When enabled, the **Use Attenuation Color** option causes the Volume Light to attenuate from the **Fog Color** to the **Attenuation Color**. This option can be useful for creating unique effects. The **Atten. Mult.** option can be used to multiply the color change effect of the **Attenuation Color** feature.

Figure 18-12. Volume Light with an omni light source

The **Max Light** % is another way of controlling the intensity of the light. Although I recommend leaving this setting at the default value of 90, you can decrease this value to make the light appear less bright.

The **Min Light** % is a setting that should remain at 0 because any value other than 0 will cause the entire scene to be as bright as the **Fog Color**, unless the light is blocked by geometry. I highly recommend leaving both the **Max Light** % and **Min Light** % settings at their default values, and controlling the light through the other available settings.

The **Filter Shadows** settings control the blur applied to shadows cast within the volume of the Volume Light. These settings should work for almost any situation and should not have to be changed.

Just like the **Max Light** % and **Min Light** % values, the **Attenuation Start** % and **End** % values essentially perform the same function as other settings. In this case, you can change the start and end attenuation of the light as a percentage of the distance values specified in the settings found in the Command panel. I recommend leaving these settings alone to avoid confusion with the other settings that perform the same function.

The **Noise** section of the **Volume Light Parameters** rollout contains almost the same settings as the **Noise** section for the Volume Fog effect, with a couple exceptions. Noise is automatically enabled with Volume Fog; but with Volume Light, you must enable the **Noise On** option. Once it's on, you can control the amount of noise with the **Amount** value, which can be set from 0.0 (no noise) to 1.0 (full noise).

If you animate a light containing a Volume Light effect that also contains noise, you will almost always want the noise to remain linked to the world coordinates so that the noise doesn't move as the light moves. If you have a Volume Light attached to the headlights of a car, as in the example in Figure 18-14, you would want the noise to remain stationary as the car moves. Otherwise, it would appear as if the air and all the particles causing the noise were moving along with the car. Enabling the **Link To Light** option links the noise to the light, rather than the world coordinate system. For certain special effects, this may be desirable; but for most every situation, this option should remain off.

Other atmospheric effects are available as third-party plug-ins, but the four effects discussed in this chapter all perform their designed function in a very acceptable manner. Although other plug-ins may provide more power and flexibility, which could be very useful in other industries, these effects can be made to do the job in almost any visualization project.

Creating Volume Light

This exercise demonstrates how to create and modify the Volume Fog effect. This example can be applied to numerous situations, such as the headlights of a car, light coming through a window, and even the light from a film projector in a movie theater.

1. Reset 3ds Max.

2. In the center of the Perspective view, create a free spotlight.

3. Press 8 to open the **Environment and Effects** dialog box.

4. In the **Atmosphere** rollout, click the **Add** button. This opens the **Add Effect** dialog box.

5. Select **Volume Light**, and click **OK** to close. Volume Fog is now an effect added to your scene, but it hasn't yet been assigned to a light.

6. In the **Volume Light Parameters** rollout, click the **Pick Light** button and then select the light you just created in the Perspective view.

7. Render the scene. The volume light is very dense and should be reduced.

8. Within the **Volume** section of the **Volume Light Parameters** rollout, reduce the **Density** value from **5.0** to **1.0**. This reduces the density of the volume light to a fifth of its previous value.

9. Render the scene again and notice that the volume light is much less intense.

10. Experiment with the various volume light parameters and the parameters in the Command panel to see what type of look you can apply to your volume light.

Render effects

The render effects available in 3ds Max include all those shown in the **Add Effect** dialog box (Figure 18-13). To access these effects, click the **Add** button on the **Effects** tab of the **Environment and Effects** dialog box. Each acts as a type of filter that changes the rendering after the initial rendering process has been completed; once a rendering is completed and these effects have been added, they cannot be removed. While some of the available effects are best suited to be added during the rendering process, I strongly recommend not incorporating certain effects during the rendering process. These effects can be added in the post-production process through 3ds Max's Video Post feature, or with another program such as Photoshop. The four effects that shouldn't be added are as follows:

- Brightness and Contrast
- Color Balance
- Blur
- Film Grain

Each of these are very simple effects to add in post-production, and it is better to have the option of adding them or not adding them after your rendering process is completed.

Two additional effects listed in Figure 18-13 that will not be discussed are Hair and Fur and AfterBurn Glow. AfterBurn Glow is simply a demo plug-in effect. The Hair and Fur effect is geared toward other industries, but you might find it worthwhile to experiment with simulating grass in an architectural scene. In this way, the Hair and Fur effect has been a tremendous benefit to many visualization users because of its ability to simulate 3D grass at a minimal cost to RAM and file size.

The three effects that will be discussed in this chapter are **Lens Effect**, **Depth of Field**, and **Motion Blur**. Each of these effects contains very powerful features that cannot be added as effectively or with as much realism in post-production or in other programs. Therefore, they will be discussed in detail.

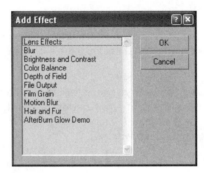

Figure 18-13. The Add Effect dialog box

The Lens effect

Lens effects simulate some of the real-world effects caused by sunlight hitting the camera at just the right angle. Lens effects are probably the most widely used of the render effects available in 3ds Max and, if not overdone, can add a great deal of realism to your scenes. There can be a tendency to put too much intensity into Lens effects, to the point that they don't look real and distract the viewer from the presentation's focus.

When you add the Lens effect to the effects list, two rollouts appear: **Lens Effects Parameters** and **Lens Effects Globals**, as shown in Figure 18-14. Within the **Lens Effects Parameters** rollout are effects for Glow, Ring, Ray, Auto Secondary, Manual Secondary, Star, and Streak. These effects each have their own unique rollouts, but also share the parameters within the **Lens Effects Globals** rollout. Changing a parameter for any loaded effect will change that parameter for all loaded effects. For example, if you double the **Size** value for Glow, the **Size** value is automatically doubled for Ring. If you want to double the size of the Glow without doubling the size of the Ring, you must use the **Size** parameter in the **Glow Element** rollout, rather than the **Size** parameter in the **Lens Effects Globals** rollout.

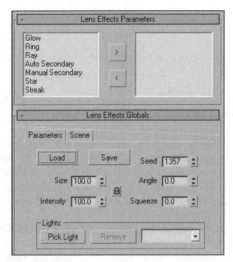

Figure 18-14. The Lens Effects Parameters and Lens Effects Globals rollouts

Because there are so many effects and so many unique parameters for each effect, I'll only cover the shared parameters found in the **Lens Effects Globals** rollout. You should explore each effect individually to get a feel for its function.

You can add and use as many effects as you want all at once by highlighting the effects in the left window of the **Lens Effects Parameters** rollout, and clicking the right arrow button to add them to the right window. You can unload them by moving them back to the left window using the left arrow button. You can also load effects by double-clicking them in the left window.

The **Lens Effects Globals** rollout contains two tabs: **Parameters** and **Scene**. The **Load** and **Save** buttons can be used to load existing parameter settings or save new ones for later use. This is very handy when you've spent a great deal of time to get an effect to look just right and want to use the same settings later without having to go through the same labor again.

Before an effect can be used, it must be attached to a light object. To attach an effect, click the **Pick Light** button and select the light in a view. You can attach the effect to multiple lights.

The **Size** is a percentage of the rendered frame. The **Intensity** controls the brightness and opacity of the effect, with higher values yielding brighter, more opaque effects. The **Angle** value can be used to rotate the effect around the viewer's perspective. The **Squeeze** value changes the aspect ratio of the effect to compensate for various frame aspect ratios. The effect is stretched horizontally with positive values up to 100, and stretched vertically with negative values down to –100.

Creating a Lens effect

This exercise demonstrates how to create and modify various Lens effects.

1. Reset 3ds Max.
2. Create an omni light in the center of the Perspective view.
3. Press 8 to open the **Environment and Effects** dialog box.
4. On the **Environment** tab, change the Background color to a medium-blue color, similar to a mid-day sky.
5. Select the **Effects** tab, click the **Add** button in the **Effects** rollout, and select **Lens Effects** from the **Add Effect** dialog box.
6. In the **Lens Effects Globals** rollout, click the **Pick Light** button and select the light object in any view.
7. In the **Lens Effects Parameters** rollout, double-click the first effect in the window on the left (Glow) and render the scene. It should look like image 1 in the following illustration.
8. Next, double-click **Ring** to load this effect. Render the scene. It should look like image 2.
9. Double-click **Ray** to load this effect. Render the scene. It should look like image 3.
10. Double-click **Auto Secondary** to load this effect. Render the scene. It should look like image 4.
11. The effect you just loaded, Auto Secondary, is very faint and difficult to see, so let's increase the intensity of the effect. With the Auto Secondary effect highlighted in the right window of the **Lens Effects Parameters** rollout, scroll down to the **Auto Secondary Element** rollout and increase the **Intensity** to **50**. Render the scene. It should look like image 5. Notice that this effect becomes brighter without affecting any of the other three loaded effects.
12. Finally, let's reduce the size of all the effects. With any effect highlighted, reduce the **Size** value in the **Lens Effects Globals** rollout to **75**. Render the scene. It should look like image 6. Notice that all of the effects are reduced in size by 25%.

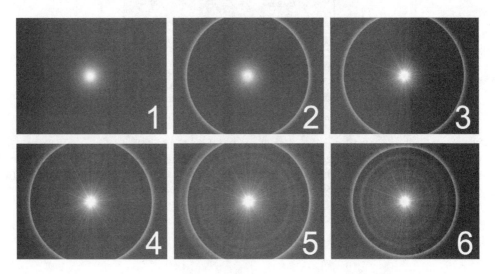

The Depth of Field effect

Depth of Field simulates the natural blurring effect of objects in the foreground and/or background when viewed through a camera. Adding Depth of Field in the right way can significantly increase the quality and realism of any scene. 3ds Max provides two ways to generate Depth of Field—as a render effect or a multi-pass effect. The multi-pass option will be discussed at the end of the chapter.

Depth of Field works by specifying a distance at which a camera is to focus. Anything closer to or farther away from the camera is blurred to some degree, depending on the distance from this specified distance, also known as the **target distance**. The farther an object is from the target distance, the greater the blurring effect.

When you load Depth of Field as a render effect, the **Depth of Field Parameters** rollout appears, as shown in Figure 18-15. Although you can apply the effect to a view without a camera, it is most practical to assign the effect to a specific camera. To do so, click the **Pick Cam.** button and select the camera. You must then tell the camera where to focus. There are two ways to do this. For one, you can click the **Pick Node** button and select an object in your scene that you want to have the camera focus on. The other option is to select the **Use Camera** option in the **Focal Point** section, select the camera in your scene with the applied effect, and set the **Target Distance** in the **Parameters** rollout of the Command panel.

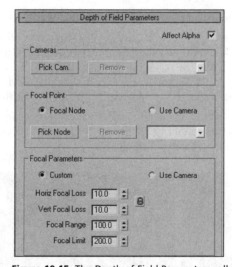

Figure 18-15. The Depth of Field Parameters rollout

The images in Figure 18-16 show an example of Depth of Field applied to a scene with two rows of teapots. Notice that in the image on the left, the target distance is set close to the teapots in the foreground. In the middle image, the target distance is set close to the teapots in the middle (third) row. Finally, the image on the right shows the target distance set near the teapots in the background.

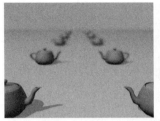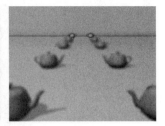

Figure 18-16. Depth of Field effects

Once you specify a target distance or a focal node, you must specify the range in which the camera will show objects in focus. This range is known as the focal range, and it is set in the **Focal Parameters** section of the **Depth of Field Parameters** rollout. Increasing the **Focal Range** value will make a greater area in your scene be in focus. You can also set the **Focal Limit** as the distance from the target distance at which blurring reaches a maximum value. If the blurring is too great too close to the target distance, simply increase the **Focal Limit** value until the blurring is acceptable. Finally, the **Horiz Focal Loss** and **Vert Focal Loss** values set the strength or intensity of the blurring. Reduce these values to reduce the overall blurring effect.

The Motion Blur effect

Motion blur adds a tremendous amount of realism to your scenes by simulating the effect of motion captured with a real camera. When an object moves in the short period of time that a camera shutter is open, the image of the object is blurred. This may be a result of the objects moving or the camera itself moving.

3ds Max generates motion blur in several different ways, but essentially there are two types of motion blur: Image Motion Blur and Object Motion Blur. **Image Motion Blur** creates the blur effect by smudging an object. **Object Motion Blur** renders multiple copies of an object and then superimposes them.

There are three primary means with which to add motion blur. One way is using **Scene Motion Blur**, a Video Post feature that blurs objects after the rendering process, and is generally less effective and realistic than the other two processes. Scene Motion Blur is not covered in this book. The two features that are covered are **Motion Blur**, found on the **Effects** tab of the **Environment and Effects** dialog box, and **Multi-Pass Effects**, found in the **Parameters** rollout of a camera object. Multi-Pass Motion Blur, along with Multi-Pass Depth of Field, will be discussed at the end of the chapter.

The Motion Blur effect is a render effect found on the **Effects** tab of the **Environment and Effects** dialog box. Before it can be used, it must first be activated for each individual object within the **Object Properties** dialog box. To activate it, select an object or group of objects to which you want to apply the Motion Blur effect, right-click inside the active viewport, select **Properties** from the quad menu, and select the **Image** option within the **Motion Blur** section, as shown in Figure 18-17. You can apply Motion Blur using either the **Object** or **Image** option; however, the **Image** option usually provides better results.

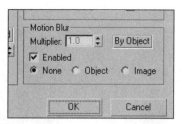

Figure 18-17. Motion Blur parameters within the Object Properties dialog box

You can deselect Motion Blur for any object or group of objects by deselecting the **Enabled** option. The **Multiplier** setting allows you to multiply the effect of the blur. However, I recommend just changing the basic settings that control the appearance of the blur to avoid confusion.

Those settings that control the appearance of the blur are found in the **Render Scene** dialog box, as shown in Figure 18-18. Here you can change the **Duration** of frames used to calculate the blur for either Object Motion Blur or Image Motion Blur. Within the **Image Motion Blur** section, there is an option to enable **Transparency**. If you don't enable this option, objects with transparent areas created with opacity maps will not show blurring behind the transparent areas. This option should always be enabled because visualizations usually have numerous uses of objects with transparent areas.

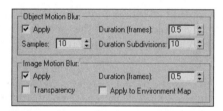

Figure 18-18. Motion Blur parameters within the Render Scene dialog box

As I mentioned before, you cannot use Motion Blur until you activate the option for each individual object; however, you can use Motion Blur without even loading it as an effect on the **Effects** tab of the **Environment and Effects** dialog box. In other words, as soon as you activate it in the **Object Properties** dialog box, Motion Blur will be used. If you do load Motion Blur into the effects list, the **Motion Blur Parameters** rollout appears, as shown in Figure 18-19. Only two settings are available, one to enable transparency and the other to control the duration of frames used to calculate the motion blur. When Motion Blur is added within the Environment and Effects dialog box, both of these settings override the same settings found in the **Render Scene** dialog box. Although not necessary, I recommend loading Motion Blur through the Environment and Effects dialog box and controlling the **Duration** setting here. This is the one central location you have to keep control and visibility over all your effects.

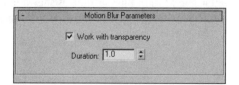

Figure 18-19. The Motion Blur Parameters rollout

Creating Motion Blur

This exercise demonstrates how to quickly and easily create a simple blur for any object.

1. Reset 3ds Max.

2. Create any object in the Perspective view.

3. Right-click the object in the active view and select **Properties** from the quad menu. The **Object Properties** dialog box opens.

4. In the **Motion Blur** section of the **Object Properties** dialog box, enable the **Image** option for the Motion Blur feature.

5. Animate the object so that it moves from one place to another during the course of the default 100-frame active time segment.

6. With the Time slider at frame 0, render the Perspective view. The image should look clear because at frame 0, the object hasn't begun moving yet.

7. Move the Time slider to frame 50 and render the Perspective view again. The object should look blurred now because it is moving at this point in time.

Multi-pass effects

Multi-pass effects are another more powerful option for the Depth of Field and Motion Blur effects. Multi-pass effects are found in the **Parameters** rollout of the Command panel when a camera object is selected. The available multi-pass effects include Depth of Field (mental ray), Depth of Field, and Motion Blur, as shown in Figure 18-20. Since Mental Ray is not covered in this book, the first option will likewise not be covered. In the following sections, I will cover Motion Blur and Depth of Field.

The Multi-Pass Motion Blur effect

The Multi-Pass Motion Blur effect is the most realistic means of adding motion blur to your scene—but it takes much longer to render than the Motion Blur effect because it renders the entire scene numerous times. 3ds Max achieves this effect by rendering several versions of the same frame with selective objects being offset from their normal locations. 3ds Max then combines these images with some processing to achieve the blurred effect. Although there is a process by which you can use layers to apply a multi-pass effect to only the objects to be blurred, this is an advanced process that is not always practical, and will not be covered in this book.

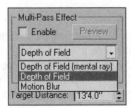

Figure 18-20. The available multi-pass effects

To enable Multi-Pass Motion Blur, select the **Enable** option (shown in Figure 18-20) and select **Motion Blur** from the drop-down list directly below it. When you select **Motion Blur**, the second rollout in the Command panel changes to the **Motion Blur Parameters** rollout, as shown in Figure 18-21. While each of the parameters in this rollout can have a dramatic effect on the overall appearance of the motion blur, there are only two parameters you should give specific attention to: **Total Passes** and **Duration (frames)**. If you take the time to investigate the other parameters in this rollout, you will probably find that either their manipulation does nothing to significantly improve the quality of your work, or that their manipulation degrades the quality of your work to an unacceptable level.

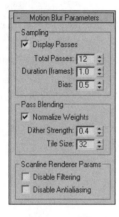

Figure 18-21. The Motion Blur Parameters rollout

The **Total Passes** value dictates how many times each individual frame will be rendered and, therefore, how many will be averaged to achieve the effect. Figure 18-22 shows the effect of changing the **Total Passes** value while leaving all other parameters at their default settings.

The top-left image shows a single frame of a car animation, but because Motion Blur is not enabled, the car appears to be motionless.

The top-right image shows the result of enabling Motion Blur and setting the **Total Passes** to its lowest possible value of 2. Close inspection of the blown-up image of the rear bumper shows two separate images combined into one. These are the two passes that 3ds Max uses to create one image in which only objects in motion are blurred.

The bottom-left image shows the result of increasing **Total Passes** to 3. The same blown-up image of the rear bumper shows three distinct passes; and because the passes are so distinct, the overall effect of motion blur is unrealistic. To achieve a believable effect, the number of passes should be high enough so that these distinctions can't be made.

The bottom-right image shows the result of increasing **Total Passes** to its default setting of 12. This image is much more realistic, but unfortunately 12 passes takes 12 times as long to render as a single frame with no motion blur. If your objects in motion are small enough or far enough away from the camera, you can achieve realism with much fewer than 12 passes. As with most effects, you should experiment adequately before settling on any particular setting. The **Preview** button directly above the **Multi-Pass Effect** drop-down list in the **Parameters** rollout allows you to preview the Motion Blur in Wireframe mode.

The other Motion Blur parameter that you should try experimenting with is **Duration (frames)**. This value tells 3ds Max how many total frames should be used to compute the blur for each individual frame. With a setting of 2, for example, 3ds Max uses one frame before and after an object's position to compute the blur. With a setting of 4, 3ds Max uses two frames before and two frames after, and so on. The more frames used, the more dramatic the blurred effect will be. Increasing this value may also require a greater number of total passes since the individual passes will be farther apart from each other and thus easier to see.

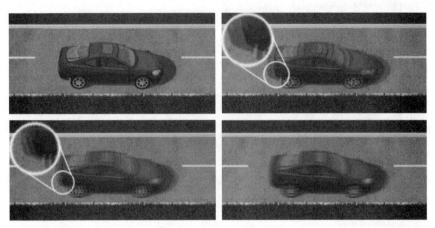

Figure 18-22. The effect of increasing the number of total passes using Multi-Pass Motion Blur

The Multi-Pass Depth of Field effect

Multi-Pass Depth of Field creates blurring based on distance from the camera. This effect simulates real-world cameras by allowing some objects to be in focus while objects at other depths are out of focus, as shown in Figure 18-23. Actually, in this case, it's people. That's me at the front-left and my long-time business partner Brian Zajac at the front-right.

Figure 18-23. An example of applying Multi-Pass Depth of Field to myself (front-left) and my cohort Brian (front-right)

To enable Multi-Pass Depth of Field, select the **Enable** option (shown in Figure 18-20) and select **Depth of Field** from the **Multi-Pass Effects** drop-down list directly below it. When you select **Depth of Field**, the second rollout in the Command panel changes to **Depth of Field Parameters**, as shown in Figure 18-24.

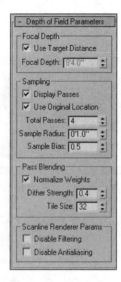

Figure 18-24. The Depth of Field Parameters rollout

To use Multi-Pass Depth of Field, you must determine where the camera should focus—everything closer to or farther from the camera will be blurred to some degree. That distance can be specified with one of two parameters: target distance and focal depth.

Target distance is the distance from the camera to the camera target. This parameter is the last in the **Parameters** rollout (partially shown at the top of Figure 18-24), and exists whether the selected camera is a target camera or a free camera. When a free camera is created, the target distance is set to the value of the last target camera created, even though a target doesn't exist.

Focal depth is the distance at which the camera is in focus. To use the **Focal Depth** parameter, you must disable the **Use Target Distance** option, which is enabled by default.

I prefer to use target distance to specify the point at which the camera should focus, because with this option, you can see at any time where in the scene the camera is focused. With the **Focal Depth** option, you don't have that visual clue, and unless you take a measurement or a test render, you don't know if the correct distance is specified. Figure 18-25 shows a perfect example of how the target distance option gives you the visual clue. The left image shows the Top view of a scene with several people at varying distances from the camera. Notice that the target of the camera is positioned exactly at the second set of people. The image on the right shows how this causes the second set of people to be in focus and the rest of them to be out of focus.

The only other two parameters I care about when using Multi-Pass Depth of Field are **Total Passes** and **Sample Radius**. **Total Passes** works the same here as with Motion Blur. Just as with Motion Blur, you will have to determine how many passes you can afford to spend your rendering time on, as well as the minimum number needed to produce a realistic effect.

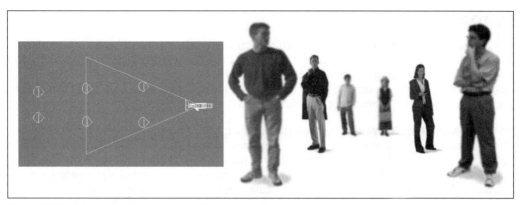

Figure 18-25. Using target distance to specify focus location on a camera

The **Sample Radius** parameter is the other critical parameter that you should pay attention to when applying Multi-Pass Depth of Field. This parameter specifies the potential distance that the scene can move around the focus point. Larger **Sample Radius** values produce greater blurring. The default setting of 0'1.0" produces an almost unnoticeable effect, so you might try 1'0" or 1'6".

Figure 18-26 shows several examples of a scene rendered using different **Sample Radius** values. In the top-left image, Depth of Field is applied with the default **Sample Radius** of 0'1". In the top-right image, the **Sample Radius** is increased to 0'3". In the bottom-left image, the **Sample Radius** is increased to 0'6". In the bottom-right image, the **Sample Radius** is increased further to 1'0".

It is important to note, however, that the **Sample Radius** values needed to produce these results require a scene with similar scale. The teapots in this scene are 3 feet wide. Therefore, if the entire scene were scaled up to twice the size, and the teapots were 6 feet wide, the **Sample Radius** values would have to be twice as large to produce the same results. The bottom line is that you will probably have to experiment several times to find the **Sample Radius** value that produces the result you're looking for. Again, the **Preview** button located in the **Parameters** rollout is a great way to experiment without having to render the scene each time.

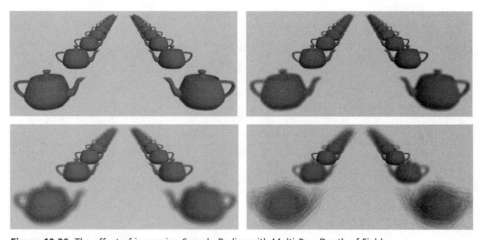

Figure 18-26. The effect of increasing Sample Radius with Multi-Pass Depth of Field

Summary

This chapter has covered many powerful effects that can drastically improve the quality and realism of your work with just a little effort. Each of these effects has a place in architectural visualization, and almost every award-winning image or animation has used at least one of the effects discussed in this chapter. When they are not used, it is much more difficult to pass off your work as a photorealistic presentation—and for the amount of time they take to implement, they're certainly worth the effort.

Deciding which effects to implement based on the time it takes to render with them is a critical part of the rendering process. If time is available, you may want to consider the multi-pass effects to achieve the highest possible quality. If, however, time is short, you may have to reduce the number or quality of your effects. Making the right decision can mean the difference between meeting a deadline with a high-quality product and missing a deadline and losing a customer forever.

APPENDIXES

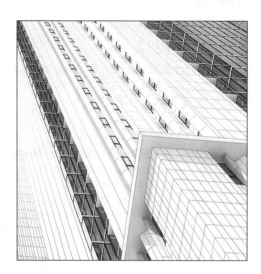

Appendix A

MARKETING YOUR SERVICES

In an ideal world, your business would grow so successfully that you would not need to focus time, energy, and resources on marketing your services. In the real world, however, such success usually only comes with time. How much time, obviously, depends on such things as the quality of your work and your general business savvy. But equally important is your ability to market yourself. Though good work sells itself, it only sells if someone knows you're selling. The next few pages discuss some of the key elements that you should consider when marketing your services and offer some suggestions that can help make you successful in this area of business management.

Your clients

It seems that with every year that goes by, more people become aware of and fascinated by 3D technology. Everyone knows the success Hollywood studios have had with animated films. Beyond these movies, however, the general public is not keenly aware of how this technology has been integrated into the world of architectural visualizations. One of the most common questions I'm asked when I tell someone what I do is, "Who do you sell to?" Before you market yourself in any business, you should know the answer to this question. Let's discuss some potential clients and some of the keys to successfully marketing to these clients.

Developers

A developer can be a single person, a large firm, or anything in-between. A developer's primary goal is to acquire land and build, or develop, on that land, and the 3D visualization services you offer can be an invaluable marketing tool in helping developers make those sales.

You will probably find developers to be the best source of large projects with the greatest profit margin, because their projects usually entail more than just a single residence or office building. If you're fortunate enough to land a large developer as a client, you many find yourself working on a large golf course community, a stadium for a metropolitan city, or a skyscraper—any of which may have a $500 million price tag. This type of client may be more inclined to offer payment for visualization services of this scale, knowing the marketing value of your services and understanding the small drop in the bucket that your service fees are when compared to the overall price tag. Take the $500 million golf course community, for example. A five-minute animation for such a project may require months of work for several people at the cost of $50,000 to the client. Even at $50,000, the total cost for your services would be no more than 1/10,000th or 0.01% of the project's cost. A developer probably understands, more than any other type of client, the ability of your services to produce sales. For these reasons, developers should comprise a good portion of your marketing effort.

As a freelancer or a small business owner, you might find completing a large project typically available through a developer difficult, and landing such a project even more difficult. Usually, the only way to do so is to create a good network of subcontractors, which is my first production tip discussed in Appendix B.

Architects

For many 3D visualizers, architects are the most typical type of client, especially for freelancers or small businesses that are not willing or able to work on the large projects possible through developers. Whether or not this is true for you, you should consider a number of things when marketing to architects. First of all, most projects you work on will require the services of an architect. Even though some states and countries don't require construction documents to be certified by a licensed architect (and you should know if yours does), an architect will usually be used for structures of any significant size and complexity. In addition, when hired by any client who is not an architect, you will almost certainly be required to deal with the architect who is designing the project for your client.

Depending on the complexity and scale of your project, you may be required to work closely with the architect for a long period of time. Helping you in any way possible to make your work a success is usually in the architect's best interests. An architect would be unwise to upset his client (who may also be your client), because he or she failed to communicate the design to you either verbally or in drawings. Because of this, the architect is usually willing to give you whatever is necessary for you to complete your work.

During the course of your dealings with the architect, you have the opportunity to win him or her over as a future client. By providing quality work and professional service, you will have made a great impression and given yourself unhindered access to one of the greatest potential clients in our industry.

Continuing education

Many states and countries require architects to undergo a certain amount of continuing education each year in order to maintain their licenses. In my home state of Florida, for example, architects are required to take 20 hours of instruction in state-certified courses. These courses range from Waterproofing Exterior Walls to Soundproofing a Residence to Changes in the Building Code. The lengths of these courses can range from one hour to 20 hours or longer. Some architects choose to attend formal classes to receive their training while others choose to receive the majority of their training at informal seminars or even in their own office.

If you have ever worked in an architectural office, you have probably witnessed some of these informal courses. Architects will receive a call from a firm asking if the architect would be willing to receive a catered lunch for his office in exchange for allowing the firm to give a presentation on their product. Although an architect might normally want employees to do something more viable than listening to a sales pitch from an unknown company, the architect might be willing to yield the time if the sales pitch is actually a state-certified continuing education course.

This continuing education requirement gives you a great opportunity to get your foot in the door of any architect's office. By becoming a certified architectural continuing education provider, you will be able to establish relationships with people who will be one of the greatest sources of future work.

One of the first things I did after starting my own business was to apply for such a certification. I was required to create a one-hour course of instruction with a detailed outline and slide-show presentation. I submitted the outline and a copy of the slide-show presentation along with an application to the Florida Department of Business and Professional Regulation, and two months later, I was given certification to teach a one-hour course entitled 3D CAD for Architectural Visualizations. Upon receiving this certification, I updated all of my marketing tools to make it known that I was a state-certified architectural continuing education provider. This became a great marketing help, not only because it offered something useful to architects, but also because it lent credibility to my business.

If you would like to receive the certification offered by your state, go to your state's official government website and search for "architecture continuing education." Feel free to use the outline and slideshow presentation on this book's web page at the www.friendsofed.com as a guide to creating your own course.

Individuals

Perhaps your most frequent calls for work will come from individuals that request your services for a one-time project. These calls can range from a couple who are building a dream home, to an entrepreneur who wants to build a small office complex, to a doctor who needs to move his practice into a larger building of his own design. This type of client should be given no less attention than any other, if for no other reason than that they may refer others to you down the road. If one of your long-term goals is to run a 3D visualization business without having to devote much effort to marketing, you will almost certainly have to rely on referrals to procure enough work, and the smallest of clients can refer the largest of clients. The doctor you are providing an animation for may have a brother that runs the largest development firm in your area. Such a situation presents another opportunity in which you are given unrestricted access to a great potential client.

Contractors

Another source of business for those of us in the architectural visualization industry comes from construction companies, or more simply, contractors. Contractors often design and draw plans for structures without the assistance of an architect. Some states and countries don't require an architect to approve the plans of a project. Even when the certification of an architect is required, the contractor may still perform all of the work (including designing and drawing the structure and coordinating with owner and subcontractors) and submit the plans to an architect for review and certification only. In these types of scenarios, contractors are just as likely to require your services as an architect.

Sometimes an architect or contractor will offer the option of your services to a client at an additional charge. The contractor may arrange a meeting with you and the owner, although this usually only happens when all three of you are in the same local area. When a meeting is not possible, you must usually rely on the architect or contractor to sell your services. Utilizing your services is often in the best interest of architects and contractors, because having your 3D visualization for their project can significantly increase their client's certainty in the design, facilitate the bidding process and reduce the overall bid prices, and provide them a sample project to use as a marketing tool for future projects. An architect or contractor who can offer 3D visualization services to a potential client may gain an edge on their competition; it may ultimately be the factor that separates them from the others.

Real estate agents

For many years after starting my own visualization firm, I did not believe real estate firms to be much of a source for potential business for those of us in the 3D visualization industry. But one day, when I started looking for a new office and contacted a few realtors, it occurred to me that I had stumbled upon possibly the greatest marketing strategy those of us in the visualization industry could employ. I had initially contacted three realtors about three different offices that I found while driving around town. While talking to them over the phone, each one asked what type of business I was in. After I told them, each one seemed enthusiastic about meeting with me to discuss the possibility of me doing work for them. I arranged a face-to-face meeting with each agent, and in each meeting we spent more time talking about my business and what I could do for them than talking about the office I was interested in purchasing. Two of the first three realtors I met with provided substantial 3D projects for my company and are still great clients of mine.

Although commercial realtors are not in the business of buying and developing property, they usually have long-term partnerships with developers, in which they act as selling agents for the developers' projects. In this situation, the real estate firm may be very willing to support the use of your services, whether you are paid directly by the real estate firm or the developer. In either case, the real estate firm is responsible for selling the developer's property, and anything that helps is worth investigating, especially something as interesting and eye-catching as 3D. Realtors have a vested interest in making their clients happy, and introducing a developer they work for to a great 3D visualization firm can make them very happy. For all of these reasons, real estate firms should never be overlooked as a source for potential business. I highly recommend contacting a few realtors and telling them you're interested in purchasing a new office. You might be amazed at what it leads to!

Your tools

Now that we've discussed some of your greatest sources of future visualization work, let's look at some of the marketing tools with which you can reach your potential clients. Even on a limited budget, you have numerous tools at your disposal. In the remaining pages of this appendix, we will look not only at some of the tools available, but some of the tricks to making the most out of them.

Websites

A website is easily your most important and ubiquitous form of marketing media. Unless you are a well-established firm with little need for marketing, an effective and eye-catching website is an absolutely critical tool to your business. With a website, you can show your work to anyone, anywhere in the world, at a minimal cost. But no matter how well-designed, a website will not be a marketing tool that brings in a large number of cold calls that lead to contracts. For this reason, I firmly believe spending a large amount of time and money on specific website marketing is not a good idea. What makes a website highly effective and important is that serves as an electronic brochure that anyone can access anywhere and anytime. This electronic brochure is the best way to follow up a conversation with a potential client. Whether the potential client is someone that you ran into on the street, someone that saw your advertisement in the phone book who calls to investigate your services, or someone that you just had a meeting with, your company's website serves as the ultimate marketing tool.

When a potential client calls you to get information about your company, they generally ask the same questions: What do you do? How do you do it? What do you need from me to start? How much does it cost? Rushing the conversation by simply saying, "Check the website; everything you need to know is there," can be a big turnoff for a client. Instead, you should attempt to feel out callers; answer some questions, and ask some of your own. But you can end conversations by informing the callers that they are welcome to visit your website to view your portfolio and find some additional information about your company and what you do.

What should your website contain, and how should it be designed? Without a doubt, it should contain the best work you have ever created. Your website should be easy to navigate and not contain an enormous number of large graphics or introductions that take excessive amounts of time to load. Your potential clients may be impatient and chose not to sit through fancy graphics or take the time to figure out how to navigate your site. More important, your company is being evaluated by the viewer at every moment, and an inability to create an efficient and effective website may give the viewer doubt in your ability to create an efficient and effective product for them.

I suggest creating a navigation menu with as few buttons as possible, just enough so that the viewer doesn't have to go through several pages to get to a particular point. My recommendation for the minimum page navigation buttons you should include are as follows:

- **Home**: This link takes the viewer back to the homepage and is an essential link that any website in any industry should have.

- **About Us**: This is a standard label for a link that takes the viewer to a description about your company. This link is important, because not revealing at least the basic information about your company cannot help but give the viewer doubts as to your company's candidness.

- **Gallery**: Display the best of your company's work here. For each category of content, I suggest creating a separate link. For example, on the gallery page of my website, I created three separate links: one for animations, one for renderings, and another for imagery.

- **Contact Us**: Another standard link, it should include at least one email address and phone number.

Brochures

Brochures are another type of media that I consider a must for those of us in the visualization industry. Brochures give you the ability to show your work to others during face-to-face meetings, tradeshows, or anyplace you run into potential clients. Your brochure can serve as your resume and is often the very first look others take at your work. Just like your website, your brochure should show off your best images and make a clear presentation of your company's services. If you offer animation services, state it clearly. If you offer unique services, state each one clearly—don't expect the viewer to know about them automatically. Like your website, your brochure is a demonstration of your presentation skills and a poorly designed brochure can kill your chances to receive work from the viewer.

I highly recommend using a professional printing service for your brochure, even for freelancers who only need a small number printed. But when and how should you distribute your brochures? If you believe only one thing in this discussion on marketing, let it be this—do not mass-mail your marketing materials. From my personal experience and that of many others I have spoken to, mass mailings waste time and money. A very small percentage of the brochures will ever make it to the person who actually has the influence to supply you with work. Those few that do make it to the right person, which could be as little as one percent, will likely be treated no better than the mounds of junk mail you receive at home. This marketing strategy sends the message that whatever you had to say was not important enough for you to say in person or with at least a phone call. You would be better off saving your money, printing fewer brochures, and handing them out as a follow-up to a phone call or a face-to-face meeting.

Phone books

If you can afford to splurge in any marketing area, an advertisement in the phone book would be a good choice. Many cities have more than one phone book, with one often being much more expensive than the others. In this situation, some caution should be taken and some research conducted, to determine which one to advertise in, or whether to advertise in more than one. In my hometown of Sarasota, Florida, we have two phone books, the *Verizon Yellow Pages* and the *Yellowbook*. The first year I was in business, I decided to splurge and advertise in both. I placed two ads in both phone books under the headings of "Architectural Illustrators" and "Graphic Design."

In the *Verizon Yellow Pages*, my ads cost three times as much as in the *Yellowbook*, even though their size was half that of the *Yellowbook* ads. I believed at the time that the circulation numbers justified spending more on the Verizon ads, but after more research, I learned that the greater circulation Verizon claimed was in residences. I realized in my second year that my primary focus should be on readers in businesses rather than in residences, and since the *Yellowbook* claimed to deliver to every business in the area, I didn't believe advertising in the more expensive book was justified. During that first year, I made it a point to ask people who called where they heard about my business. I received just as many referrals from the less expensive *Yellowbook* as I did from the more expensive *Verizon Yellow Pages*, which justified my decision to drop the Verizon ads.

Your decision to advertise in your local yellow pages should also depend heavily on your local area. If you live in an area like Sarasota, Florida, which is exploding in growth, advertising in the yellow pages should be a given. In areas with little growth, advertising in your local phone book might be a waste of money. If you decide to advertise in a phone book, I recommend placing an ad in the two separate locations I mentioned before, "Architectural Illustrators" and "Graphic Design." An ad placed under "'Architectural Illustrators" is likely to be seen by all of the architects listed, because their ads will appear right before yours. A listing under "Graphic Design" is a viable choice, because a large percentage of people think of the word "graphic" when looking for someone to provide visualization services. Other terms such as "architectural illustrator" or "visualizations" are not as well known outside the architectural world, but "graphic" is a generic word that describes our type of work better than any other word or term found in a typical phone book.

In addition, a listing under the category "Graphic Design" will draw the attention of those who are not necessarily looking for your type of business but who may decide to investigate hoping to find a better product than what they were looking for in the first place. For example, if a developer wants to create a brochure for a condominium being sold and needs a graphic image of each floor plan, he or she might call you to ask if you provide that type of service and find that you can provide much more than the ordinary floor plan graphic common in any brochure of that type. That developer may decide to spend a little more to have you create a 3D floor plan from a perspective view and, down the road, possibly an animation.

Finally, I have received many calls over the years from graphic designers who saw my listing next to theirs and called for help producing work for their clients. I received these calls, only because they were checking out their competition.

DVDs

If your company provides animation services, then DVDs are an essential component of your marketing strategy. DVDs provide your potential clients with the only true representation of what your animation services entail. Animation on your website can only provide a small glimpse of your company's capabilities, because even faster-than-normal connection speeds take too much time to download videos shown at DVD quality. Smaller resolutions allow you to put an entire demo DVD on your website, but even they are not as compelling or revealing as the full-size DVD resolution.

Going back to the discussion on mass mailing, DVDs should only be sent when preceded by a phone call, so that someone of authority expects to receive it. DVDs take a small amount of time to load or set up, but sometimes that's too much time for some people. A face-to-face meeting will allow you to combine both the best of what you have to say and the best visual imagery you have to show. A portable DVD player offers a great way to show your DVDs outside your own office.

Phone calls

Nobody likes receiving a telemarketing phone call, but when done with a certain style, placing a cold call can yield tremendous results. The main goal is to speak to someone with authority. For small companies, those with approximately ten staff members, you might try asking to speak to the owner or manager directly regarding visualization services. For larger companies, speaking to the owner will be much more difficult, but you might find a marketing division that is willing to meet with you to discuss your services.

Another approach I have found successful for larger companies is asking to speak to human resources. Employees in human resources tend to be more receptive to meeting with outsiders, because it's their job to do so. Even though human resources personnel are not the decision-makers that you need to speak with, they can arrange a meeting with the right ones.

Because of the unique nature of your services, and the fact that a quality visualization is fascinating and entertaining, the person you're meeting with can be hooked the moment they see your work. Above all, arranging a face-to-face meeting with someone in a firm is the critical first step.

E-mails

Under no circumstances should emails be sent when any other form of marketing is a viable option. E-mails should never be used locally, that is, within driving distance, when a phone call or face-to-face meeting is possible. Clearly, if you wish to market to prospective clients at great distances and you cannot afford the time and cost of phone calls or brochures, e-mail is a reasonable option. But e-mails must be exceptionally eye-catching and extremely brief to be considered by the viewer longer than the split-second it takes to find the delete button.

Spam is generally viewed with hostility, so you should be careful not to make a nuisance of yourself. Your e-mails should appear to be written directly to the company you're contacting rather than appearing as spam. Include an image or two of your best work, use a polite introduction and closing such as "Dear Sir" and "Sincerely," and include a link that takes the reader immediately to a page with eye-catching images that beg for more exploration. You should provide an easy mechanism to take addresses off your mailing list if people so desire and respect their wishes.

As a side note, my best two overseas subcontractors actually contacted me with advertising e-mails. I was impressed with their work and knew immediately that I wanted to work with them in the future.

Summary

Marketing a 3D business can be tricky. You can be the best animator in the business, but if the right people don't know your business exists or aren't introduced to your business in the right way, your business can't be successful. For most of us, building up the right clientele will simply take time, but the concepts discussed in this appendix should help speed up the process and also help you avoid some common marketing pitfalls. With every passing year, your business should only grow stronger.

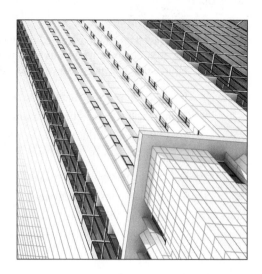

Appendix B

TOP 20 PRODUCTION TIPS

Few computer programs can claim to be as complex and difficult to learn as 3ds Max. Learning the program itself is challenging enough, but learning how to use the program in a production environment can be beyond the reach of many users. Many students learn 3ds Max thoroughly in a classroom environment and believe they have all the tools needed to be viable in the production environment. Like many technical fields, however, the visualization industry presents countless challenges that make simple program knowledge insufficient. Our industry is changing and advancing as rapidly as any other and knowing the program well is not enough.

Once you jump into a production environment, you soon learn tricks of the trade that you often can't find in any textbook or classroom discussion. The more 3D visualizers that you interact with, the more likely you are to pick up these tricks that would normally take many years to develop. If you manage your own business, the difficulties are even greater, and you must learn not only creative ways to work within 3ds Max as a user, but also ways to improve your production output from a business point of view.

The following is a list of my top 20 production tips. These tips represent the top 20 things I would teach a 3ds Max user coming out of training and preparing for a position in a production environment. Many of these tips cannot be found in any training document, and they highlight subject matter that new production users should concentrate on when preparing to work on an architectural visualization. They are listed in order of importance, and while some may seem too simple and obvious to even be placed on anyone's top 20 production tip list, they are all subjects that typically do not receive enough attention by the new 3ds Max user. By learning each of the following tips, you can implement procedures that normally take years for the typical user to develop in the workplace.

1. Build a network of subcontractors
2. Inspect the architectural drawings
3. Write a good script as soon as possible
4. Question poor designs
5. Master the keyboard shortcuts
6. Use additional input devices
7. Write a good contract
8. Break up a project into smaller projects
9. Use the Loft feature
10. Save incrementally and save often
11. Use advanced raytraced shadows and know when to use advanced lighting
12. Purchase the best available model and material libraries
13. Create assembly lines for doors and windows
14. Use material libraries
15. Use standard scene elements
16. Use the top third-party plug-ins
17. Use the Scatter command and Spacing tool to create vegetation
18. Use artificial shadows
19. Participate in website forums
20. Attend trade shows, seminars, and classes

1. Build a network of subcontractors

If you're a freelancer or the owner of a small firm, projects will always come along that are too large or have a deadline too soon for you or your firm to handle. Turning away any visualization project can be disheartening, especially when a large amount of money is involved. But because of staffing limitations, freelancers and smaller firms are often forced to turn away large projects with a high profit yields. Likewise, clients will be hesitant to give a large project to a small outfit without some clear and visible assurance that the project can be completed on time.

Hiring employees can be a risky move for small firms. Even more difficult might be the task of finding qualified employees that live locally. The solution is to build a network of subcontractors. By subcontracting your work out to others, you can accept larger jobs and complete any job in a shorter amount of time. Even as a freelancer, you can accept the largest of projects and complete them in a reasonable amount of time. In this way, you can compete with the larger visualization firms and win contracts at which you would otherwise have no chance.

Because of the unique nature of our industry, we can subcontract work out to anyone in the world while communicating completely through e-mail. Quality subcontractors can complete an entire visualization project with minimal guidance, turning the finished product over and leaving you with nothing more to do but bill the client. Depending on where your subcontractors are located, you may find that they charge much lower hourly rates than what you charge your clients, leaving you with a potentially large profit margin. 3ds Max is used worldwide and quality subcontractors can be found in any corner of the world.

To find a quality subcontractor, you can start by exploring the galleries of some of the top visualization websites such as www.cgarchitect.com, www.vismasters.com, or the official Autodesk 3ds Max discussion forum, located at http://support.discreet.com. At these and other websites, you can see who does great work and simply send an e-mail asking if they are interested in doing any subcontracting work. Another way is to post a message on a classified message board stating that you're looking for freelancers or firms interested in subcontracting work.

When dealing with subcontractors outside your home country, you always risk business dealings going bad and not having any legal recourse. However, by doing good research and communicating your needs clearly, the risk is minimal. Before engaging subcontractors in any large project, I highly recommend giving them a very small job to determine how well they can live up to your expectations. Some can produce fantastic work but have poor communication skills that make working by e-mail alone difficult. Others may display a great portfolio but be disgruntled employees of firms that produced the images and lack the skills needed to complete the work to the level of quality their images imply. You may also find that they cannot work with AutoCAD drawings.

One of the best ways to employ subcontractors initially is to give them the sole task of modeling a project. To model an architectural scene, a 3ds Max user should need nothing more than the architectural CAD files and some basic instructions. Hiring a subcontractor to complete the materials, lighting, or animation portion of a project can present many challenges that you may want to avoid until both of you are familiar with working and communicating with each other.

Until you make the leap of hiring full-time employees, subcontracting your work is the only way to compete with large firms and win the big visualization projects. Even if you only work on small projects that can be completed in just a few days, subcontracting your projects, even just the modeling portion, means that you can take in more work, turn around your work quicker, and keep your clients happier by not turning away work.

2. Inspect the architectural drawings

Most architectural visualizations begin with what I consider to be the foundation of 3D—the 2D line work. Sometimes, you may need to produce a visualization from nothing more than some simple hand-drawn elevations, in which case your best course of action is to trace the sketch in a 2D CAD program to produce some rough 2D line work. In most cases, however, you will begin a project with 2D CAD drawings already in hand, even when their creation is not finalized. These CAD drawings may be produced solely by the architect, by a freelance CAD drafter, or by numerous different firms working to complete their part of the final set of construction documents. Whatever the case may be, everyone has their own style for creating drawings and everyone leaves their own mark on their drawings. If you're lucky, you will receive a complete set of perfectly created drawings, but most of the time there are things in the drawings that, while not apparent on paper, may cause you hours of time to fix before the line work can be used in the creation of 3D models. These imperfections in the drawing process can eat away valuable production time and significantly impact your profits. The following sections describe some of the most common and troubling imperfections.

Lines that don't meet at their intended end points

Lines that don't meet at their intended points are nightmares for some 3D modelers. These imperfections occur when the drafter places the start point or end point of a line at some place other than the desired end point of another line. Take a simple set of four lines that together look like a rectangle, as shown in Figure B-1. While from a distance the rectangle appears to be intact, by zooming in on one of the corners you can see that the endpoints don't occupy the same point. The possible reasons for this are numerous, but the simple fact is that it's a common occurrence that can lead to numerous problems in the modeling phase of a project. Lines can cross over themselves, points may not weld properly, and vertical and horizontal lines can become askew, just to name a few issues.

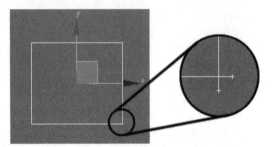

Figure B-1. An imported spline with unwelded endpoints

Line work on the wrong layer

Another common occurrence that adds work to a 3D visualization is when line work in a 2D CAD drawing is placed on the wrong layer. Sometimes it happens through poor drafting practices, and sometimes it's just a result of being rushed, but regardless of why, drafters often place line work on the wrong layer making it difficult to isolate the layers that the 3D modeler needs to concentrate on. You might find lines representing walls on a dimension layer or lines representing windows on a note layer. In these situations, you must take the time to move the line work to the correct layer or find some other way to accommodate the flaw.

Preparing architectural drawings for use in a 3D visualization can be a very time-consuming process, and until you explore the drawings you're given, you can never be sure how much time you're going to have to spend on preparation. Before quoting the cost of a visualization, you should either insist on seeing the drawings or let the client know you have to bid high to account for the possibility of poor drawings. Not doing so can be a costly and time-consuming mistake. Before becoming wise to these problems and covering myself during the bidding or contracting process, I often found myself spending endless hours fixing problems with the drawings. On a few occasions, the drawings I received were missing entire elevations and the clients expected me to deal with it at no additional cost to them, believing I should have accounted for that in the bid or contract.

The bottom line is that you must cover yourself by either refusing to start the visualization without good drawings or price your visualization higher to account for the worst-case scenario.

3. Write a good script as soon as possible

Clients will often not know what they want the final product to look like. When they see the final product before them, they will always know if they like it or not; however, it's not viable to keep making changes and reproducing the final product until they decide it's acceptable. By following tip 7, writing a good contract, you can minimize your risk of redoing work for free until the client accepts it, but a better approach would be to give the client a good final product the first time. When the final product is an animation, writing a good script is critical to ensuring you can do so.

A script is a play-by-play account of an animation sequence that tells the reader exactly what the viewer will be seeing and hearing every step of the way, as shown in Figure B-2. To be able to write a script, you or your client must know exactly what the final product should look like and sound like. By insisting on a script before proceeding to the animation phase of a project, you can force the client to give you all the information you need to produce exactly what he or she wants. I consider a script mandatory before the animation phase of a project and never proceed with setting up camera paths until I have it in hand. Failing to get a script ironed out will almost always lead to wasted time and reworking.

Action	Narration
Camera fades into overhead perspective view of clubhouse, begins moving back and away. Car pulls into view and parks under entryway. Camera turns to the right, moves upward, catches view of fountain, and comes to a stop 30 feet above ground. Camera fades out.	"At the Peace River Preserve in Port Charlotte, enjoy a relaxing afternoon at our luxurious clubhouse, featuring a wide variety of amenities, including an olympic size pool, hot tub, weight room, office center, and indoor movie theater." *Music fades in at beginning and volume reduced as narration begins.*
Camera fades into the entry of clubhouse. Double-doors open and camera moves through. Camera moves back into corner to obtain a view of entire interior, coming to a stop 8 feet above floor, panning to front desk and fading out.	"Host your next dinner party or banquet at our 2000 sq ft banquet room, featuring a full size kitchen, 15-foot bar, piano, and indoor fountain, while taking in the breathtaking view of the Gulf of Mexico." *Music volume increases at end of narration.*
Camera fades into view of marina while boat moves from left to right	"You'll marvel at the beautiful marina directly behind the clubhouse, where

Figure B-2. A simple animation script

Instead of waiting until the animation phase of a project, you would be wise to try to obtain a script early on in the project. Having a script before doing any work at all is the ideal situation, because by knowing exactly what the viewer should see at every step in the animation, you can also know exactly what objects should receive more detail and the objects where the detail can be left out.

With a script, you can even determine if objects need to be created or inserted in the scene at all. Take for example a sequence in which a camera captures the view from only the front of a house. If the camera never views the back of the house, there's no reason to model those features and place objects in the scene that won't be viewable. Doing so will only waste time and increase your file sizes.

The earlier you obtain a script, the less time you will spend performing the same work over and over again and the less time you will waste working on parts of your scene that will never be viewed.

4. Question poor designs

One of the most practical uses for a 3D visualization for a client is being able to see their project before it's built and change a poor design before construction begins. Your work may begin while a project is still in its design development stage, in which case its design is not set in stone and construction documents have not been produced. In this situation, you may find yourself modeling a portion of the project that appears poorly designed. Sometimes an architect or drafter will create drawings based on their interpretation of what their client wants or what their client's sketches show. These drawings do not always represent what their clients have in mind. Sometimes their clients don't even know what it is they want.

You may be asked to model a poor design when your client, whether it's an architect, a developer, or the owner himself, jumps the gun and has you begin your work before the design has been thoroughly analyzed by all of the necessary personnel. In any case, whenever you come across a drawing that appears to be a poor design or a design that simply doesn't make sense, you should question it and stop working until a resolution is found.

You should also question drawings in which different parts of them are in conflict with one another before continuing work. This problem is a very common especially with drawings that haven't been completely finalized. An example would be a floor plan that shows a window not shown on the elevations, or vice versa. Another example is when the front elevation shows one roof height, and a side elevation shows a much different roof height. These types of problems should be questioned before continuing work, and if you manage to find numerous problems like these before you accept a job or quote a certain price, you should cover yourself by not accepting the drawings from your client or by explaining that you will have to charge more to account for these problems. You will probably regret not doing so later.

5. Master the keyboard shortcuts

I consider the keyboard shortcut to be the single most important interface element for efficient work in a 3D program. Veteran 3ds Max users, many of whom started 3D in the pre-Max days of DOS, will usually agree that keyboard shortcuts are an important part of their work. In the days of 3D Studio for DOS, users relied more heavily on inputting commands from the keyboard, and keeping one hand on the mouse and the other hand on the keyboard was common practice. As I have stated in numerous places throughout this book, I highly recommend such a practice. Proper use of the keyboard can shave many hours off your larger projects and a significant amount of time off even your smallest.

See Appendix D for a list of what I consider to be the most practical default shortcuts as well as a list of additional shortcuts that I believe are important enough to assign.

6. Use additional input devices

In recent years, several great input devices have been developed that can significantly increase your speed and improve your efficiency in 3ds Max. Two of my favorites are the keypad and 3D motion controller. Both of these have streamlined my inputs to the program, and I highly recommend investigating their potential with your work.

The keypad, shown in the left image of Figure B-3, is a device similar to the keyboard with keys that can be programmed to execute a command or display text with a single key press. As an outspoken supporter of keyboard shortcuts, I believe that programming and learning a keypad can significantly improve anyone's speed and efficiency. Efficiency in 3ds Max requires rapid input and few devices compare to the input capability a programmable keypad has. Hot keys offer the shortest path to action, and the keypad provides a clearly labeled, physical location for these complex or redundant functions, so you don't have to think about them. Keypads come in many different shapes and sizes, but should you decide to purchase one, make sure you choose one that contains enough keys for all the commands you wish to use with it. Two added benefits of the keypad over the keyboard are the ability to write the names of the commands on the keys and the ability to input text with a key.

The second input device that I have found to be a tremendous asset is the 3D motion controller, shown in the right image of Figure B-3. With six degrees of freedom, you can navigate comfortably with one hand while editing with your mouse in your other hand. This device gives you unparalleled view navigation control, allowing you to zoom in and out and rotate your view with an easy-to-use controller cap. View navigation commands are, for many 3ds Max users, the most commonly used commands. Anything that can aid in their execution can save a tremendous amount of production time and should be considered for use.

I purchased the keypad shown below-left at www.xkeys.com and the 3D motion controller at www.3dconnection.com.

Figure B-3. The keypad (left) and 3D motion controller (right)

7. Write a good contract

This tip ties into tip 4, in which I suggested that you cover yourself with higher prices to account for the possibility of working with poor drawings. Writing a good contract is a crucial step in most visualization projects. You might feel the urge to do away with a contract for certain clients, but caution should be taken in these situations. Obviously, if you've known your client for a long time and trust in their way of doing business, doing without a contract is a reasonable option for most projects. However, even for these clients, large projects with large price tags should usually include a contract.

When working with new clients, contracts should be used for even small projects, because sometimes only when the details of the scope of services are laid out in writing will the client truly understand what you are going to produce for them. Good contracts prevent you from incurring the cost of additional services not explicitly set forth in writing. They also explain in detail what is expected from each party and the limitations of your services. You do not need to have a lawyer write or review your contracts to have them be upheld in court, but they should be well written to avoid any chance of misinterpretation.

See this book's webpage on the friends of ED website for a sample contract that I have developed and used as a template for most of my projects. This contract covers all the bases and should help give you an idea of some of the ways a contract can protect you. Feel free to use this as a template for your own work.

8. Break up projects into smaller jobs

Large 3D projects can be difficult to manage and complete on schedule. The further you get into a project, the more harrowing the adventure gets, and with deadlines looming, you can easily begin to wonder how it's all going to be finished in time. Breaking your projects into smaller jobs can help you manage them and keep production on schedule. Regardless of the project size, and whether you work on it by yourself or with the help of others, a project should be broken up into several smaller and more manageable jobs. Doing so helps you to keep track of what's finished and what remains to be finished. Breaking up a project can also help you better estimate the time and staff that will be needed to complete it and aid in the development of a contract.

You can start the process by breaking up a project into the major areas of 3D work such as drawing preparation, modeling, materials, lighting, animation, and postproduction. Some firms assign specialists to perform work solely in these specific areas, and in this way, projects can be easier to manage. Modeling should be broken up further because of the large amount of time this area requires. When I begin the modeling phase of a project, I usually break the work into major scene elements, save the files separately, and merge them together later when all of the modeling is complete. In Figure B-4, for example, I modeled the building in one file and in a completely separate file modeled the site elements, which included terrain, streets, sidewalks, curbs, and so forth. Following the site elements, I created the entry signage in a file by itself, and after that the vegetation. Lastly, I added miscellaneous objects, such as cars and people, and assembled all of these elements together to finish the modeling phase of the project. At any point along the way, I could have determined I was falling behind and needed help to get back on schedule. In this situation, I could have subcontracted part of the modeling, such as the site, to another person or firm. Had I tried working on all of the elements at the same time, subcontracting out work would not be a practical option.

Figure B-4. A finished scene built as separate smaller elements

By breaking up your projects, you can better gauge how much time is required for each component and for the project as a whole, and at any point along the way, you can determine how well production is staying on schedule. Finally, by breaking up your project, you can send work out to others the same way a network manager sends out work to servers during a network rendering.

9. Use the Loft feature

Like the previous tip, I've included use of the **Loft** feature to highlight what I consider to be one of the very best features in 3ds Max. In the area of modeling, I have found **Loft** to be the most productive and useful feature.

In visualizations, lofts can be used to model numerous object types, such as curbs, columns, trim, and furniture, just to name a few, but perhaps the most valuable use of a loft is in the creation of a wall. With a loft you can quickly and easily create complex and highly detailed walls from two shapes or splines, and you can modify the loft by making changes to either. You can also apply multi/subobject materials to a loft using material IDs.

Chapter 4 explains the use of lofts in great detail. I highly recommend taking advantage of this tremendous feature and exploring some of the ways it can save you valuable production time.

10. Save incrementally and save often

If you're like me, you hate to lose work when your computer or 3ds Max crashes or when your files become corrupted in some way. Restarting the computer and interrupting your workflow is bad enough, but having to backtrack and redo work is painful. Equally as bad is going back to a certain point in your work to retrieve a scene (or objects) in a previous state, only to find that you didn't save a copy of the scene at the right time. The solution here is to save incrementally and save often.

When you click the **Save As** command in the **File** menu, the **Save As** dialog box opens and displays a + symbol to the left of the **Save** button. Clicking this button saves a copy of the file and places a number at the end. The first time you save a file with this button, the number "01" will be placed at the end of the file name (unless a number is already used at the end of the name). Each additional click of the + button will cause an additional file to be saved with the next number: 02, 03, and so on. In the course of any project, I make dozens of incremental saves, which allows me to go back to just about any point in the creation process and retrieve objects in a previous state, such as before being collapsed or before Boolean operations were performed. Before performing a critical procedure that can't be undone, I always save my work. Figure B-5 shows an example of the incremental saves made during a past project. Notice the numerous versions of different scene elements. Notice also the names of the files: **clubhouse**, **entry_signage**, **room**, **site**, and **vegetation**. As I suggest in tip 8, each of these elements was created separately and merged together at the end.

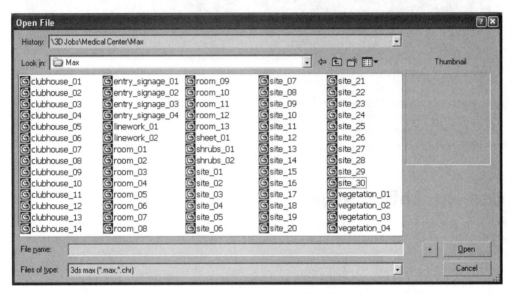

Figure B-5. Incremental saves made throughout the course of a 3D project

Good file management is critical to efficient production and nonexistent in a large percentage of the 3D firms with which I have worked. Saving incrementally and saving often are two good practices that can go long way toward improving your production output.

11. Use advanced raytraced shadows and know when to use advanced lighting

I've included this tip in my top 20 list to highlight the usefulness of advanced raytraced shadows and some of the benefits and drawbacks of advanced lighting. As I mention in Chapter 10, advanced raytraced shadows are a personal favorite of mine for scenes with an extremely large polygon count or for long animations with a short production deadline. They combine the best characteristics of all the available shadow types. They are very accurate and physically realistic. They also support transparency and opacity maps, use a small amount of RAM, render much faster than raytraced shadows, and can be used to produce soft edges. Advanced raytraced shadows have become an important part of my production process, and if you haven't used them to their full capacity, you are missing out on one of the best features of 3ds Max. Figure B-6 shows the advanced raytraced option.

Figure B-6. The advanced raytraced option

Advanced lighting features in 3ds Max can make a dramatic difference in the quality and realism of any scene. While the benefits of **Radiosity**, **Light Tracer**, and **raytracing** are clear, each of these features has one significant drawback—increased rendering times. For projects where only a few still renderings are needed, advanced lighting is usually the best option. However, when projects call for lengthy animations, and the rendered scenes contain several million polygons, advanced lighting can cause excessive rendering times that make it difficult to meet a production deadline.

Before beginning work on any project, every detail of how the finished product will be created should be planned. The decision whether or not to incorporate advanced lighting does not have to be made from the start, but in most cases, it should be made before the first scene is rendered. You shouldn't create half your scenes with advanced lighting only to realize that you don't have enough time to produce the remaining scenes the same way. Scenes with different lighting qualities will often look out of place and utilizing the same lighting style throughout each sequence of an animation is usually best.

Creating photorealistic and believable scenes does not always require advanced lighting. When in doubt about the feasibility or viability of utilizing advanced lighting features, you may be better off to err on the side of caution, choosing to avoid the burden these features place on your network rendering process. Knowing when to use advanced lighting and when to make the most of 3ds Max's basic lighting features can make a dramatic difference in your ability to stay profitable and meet deadlines.

12. Purchase the best available model and material libraries

The importance of a good model and material library cannot be overstated. Like so many other components of a 3D scene, good models and materials are critical to the final product. The quality of your libraries is not only dependent on the quality of the individual models or materials, but also the quantity of each. If you have a very small number of either, you might be able to produce exterior renderings without much difficulty; however, you will almost certainly find it impossible to produce interior renderings without giving your clients the ability to choose exactly the type of furniture or appliances they want along with the exact type of look they want for their floors, walls, furniture, etc. Exterior scenes usually allow only a small portion of the objects to be stock models from your library. With the exception of objects such as street lamps, cars, and signs, most of the objects in an exterior scene are specifically called for in the architectural drawings. Interior scenes, on the other hand, require far more use of library models and materials. Most clients are not willing to pay for custom furniture or appliances and the only alternative is to use stock content from your library. Without an extensive selection to provide your client, you will almost never be able to provide the exact look your client desires.

It is not enough to have good materials and models. You must have an easy and efficient way for you or your clients to find what's needed. If you spend an extensive amount of time looking for a specific piece of content, then you are usually wasting time. Adding content to any scene can be a simple thing

483

if your libraries are arranged and labeled in a logical and easy-to-understand manner. On the other hand, if your content is not categorized logically and labeled correctly, you can easily spend days adding models and materials to your scenes.

I have found that the best way to select content for any scene is to maintain an up-to-date digital and printed catalog of all models and materials, categorized by specific content type. This is even more important when my clients need to select the content for themselves. Clients can be quickly over-whelmed when making furniture or material selections, and providing them the means to make their selections with minimal difficulty is critical. Nothing makes working on interior projects with a client easier than handing them a nice catalog (digital or printed) and telling them to get back with you when they've made their selection. If they are making furniture selections, I recommend giving them a floor plan, having them draw simple shapes to represent each piece of furniture they've selected, and then labeling those selections with the furniture names provided in the catalog. For material selections, I recommend giving the client elevations and having them label each area of the elevation with the materials they've selected, again, using the names in the catalog. This process streamlines what could otherwise be an ordeal for any visualizer.

To develop great model and material libraries, you will probably have to make a sizeable investment in the purchase of each. Before deciding to do so, I struggled for a long time with free content I down-loaded from numerous websites. I found such a method to be a waste of time, because the quality and quantity available was usually not sufficient. The following two companies sell some of the best con-tent available on the market, and I have purchased nearly all of my model and material content from these two companies alone:

- **Materials**: Marlin Studios (www.marlinstudios.com)
- **Models**: Evermotion (www.evermotion.org)

13. Create assembly lines for doors and windows

Windows and doors comprise a significant portion of the modeling required for most buildings and homes. Many 3ds Max users choose to create these two building elements separately in CAD programs such as Architectural Desktop or using the **Doors** or **Windows** feature within 3ds Max; however, both methods have big downsides.

The problem with the **Doors** and **Windows** features in 3ds Max is that the available door and window types are very limited and rarely provide the flexibility to create all of the types needed for even the simplest building or home. In addition, these features only work with the **Wall** feature in the **Create ➤ Geometry ➤ AEC Extended** group, which also has very limited capability.

A problem with modeling these elements in other programs such as Architectural Desktop is the amount of time needed to initially set up all the different window and door types needed for your projects. If you used the same standard types for each project and didn't need to create any custom types, then modeling in other programs might be an option. Someday, programs may be developed with effective parametric door and window generators, but for now, I prefer to model doors and win-dows (along with the walls they rest in) in 3ds Max, using the imported 2D line work.

After years of trying countless ways of creating these critical building elements, I have found one way that stands out above all the other methods I have tried: the assembly line. It worked for Henry Ford in the production of automobiles, and it can work just as well in the creation of windows and doors in 3ds Max.

By using an assembly line, you can reduce the creation time per door and window type to a fraction of what it would take to create each using other methods. If you decide to try this method, the first thing you need to do is to line up a single copy of each door and window type in a row, as shown in Figure B-7. If your line work originates in AutoCAD or another 2D CAD program, simply make the copies somewhere off to the side and import the line work. If you don't have 2D CAD line work, and instead have to create the windows and doors from scratch in 3ds Max, create the line work off to the side in your 3ds Max file. Figure B-7 shows a project that contained 14 different styles, which would have been extremely time-consuming to create one by one.

Figure B-7. Preparing windows and doors for assembly line creation

An important thing to remember about doors and windows in an architectural visualization is that they will usually not require a great deal of detail because your cameras will usually not be very close to them. The detail shown in architectural plans will usually suffice, and in most cases, you can simulate these elements very well with just a few key object types: Booleans, frames, trim, and glass (as described in the following list). *All of these object types are created from splines or shapes, and whether they are created in 3ds Max or a 2D CAD program, they must always be closed and nonoverlapping.* If the line segments aren't welded together properly, you will get strange results.

- **Boolean**: The Boolean object will be the object whose volume will be subtracted from the wall object using the Boolean feature. The Boolean object is created from the line(s) that lie on the outside of the window frame. Simply extrude those closed lines with enough thickness to penetrate your walls on both sides with room to spare, as shown in the left image of Figure B-8. I use 24 inches as a rule, but anything greater than the wall thickness will suffice. After placing the entire window assembly and all of its necessary copies in the correct 3D location, attach all of the Boolean objects together (to include the Boolean objects for doors) and subtract from wall object(s).

- **Frame**: To create a frame, use the Attach command in the **Edit Spline** feature to attach all of the closed lines into one editable spline. Extrude the editable spline to the desired thickness (three inches usually works for me), and you have your window frame, like the one shown in the middle image of Figure B-8. Of course, if your line work isn't created properly, your frames will not look right.

■ **Glass**: The glass of a window is the easiest part of the window to model. Simply collapse the closed spline or shape to an editable mesh or poly object, as shown in the right image of Figure B-8.

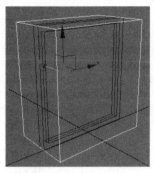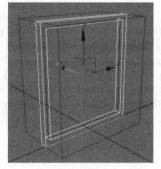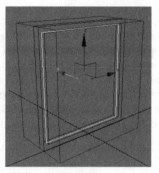

Figure B-8. A simple window with a Boolean, frame, and glass object highlighted, respectively

The best part about this method of creation is that you can create all of the window and door types at once. After positioning the line work for each window and door type side by side, and importing into 3ds Max if necessary, you can isolate the line work needed to create each component (Boolean, frame, glass, and so on) and create each component at the same time. You can even attach all of the lines together for each type, use the **Extrude**, **Edit Mesh**, or **Edit Poly** command to create the mesh or poly objects, attach each finished object type together, and then detach the entire window or door as an individual object (comprised of the individual elements).

14. Use material libraries

Working with materials in 3ds Max can be a long and arduous process, made more difficult if you don't use material libraries. Material libraries allow you to store and retrieve your favorite and most frequently used materials in easy-to-access files. As discussed in Chapter 6, creating the same materials over and over again for each project would be a waste of time. Hopefully, your image library, which you use for materials, contains tens of thousands of images. However, if this is the case, the simple act of locating an image to apply to a map channel can end up being not so quick and simple. For scenes with dozens of materials, this can translate to large amounts of wasted time.

The solution is to create and maintain good libraries. If you create a material that you think you will want to use again in the future, take a moment to give the material a relevant name and add it to a library. If you've never spent much time creating libraries, try opening some of your best scenes, reviewing the materials you applied, and putting the best ones in your library.

Like other areas in 3ds Max, a little bit of time spent in program maintenance can save you a tremendous amount of production time and help you meet your deadlines.

15. Use standard scene elements

Like the application of materials to your scene, placing common and everyday scene elements can be a laborious and time-consuming process if not done wisely. Most scenes contain ordinary elements such as lampposts, street signs, houseplants, TVs, and so on. Creating these objects again for each project is clearly not a viable option for you or your client, and therefore using objects from earlier projects is usually the only reasonable alternative. You can always purchase additional 3D objects or download free content from numerous websites. Since the focus of a visualization is usually other elements such as buildings, interior or site design, clients will often not care one way or another how you populate your scenes with ordinary objects, so long as they do not distract the viewer from the focus of the scene. For these reasons, I highly recommend using objects from past projects to populate your scene with ordinary scene elements.

Using objects from past projects, however, can be time-consuming if you must open numerous large or hard-to-find files to locate the objects you're looking for. Just like with material libraries, you should create and maintain object libraries containing these common and ordinary objects. Your libraries should not, however, be limited to just the ordinary objects that you tend to use for all your projects; rather, they should include virtually all well-created objects that you would be proud to display in future projects. These can be furniture, vegetation, picture frames, or kitchen accessories, as shown in Figure B-9. How you organize the files that contain your objects is not important as long as you can keep track of them and locate them in the future. Maintaining and using a good object library will save time on any visualization.

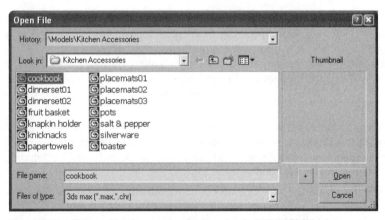

Figure B-9. A library of kitchen accessories saved as individual files for later use

16. Use the top third-party plug-ins

Another great characteristic of 3ds Max is its ability to allow the use of plug-ins, which are third-party programs that run within 3ds Max. Plug-ins offer expanded or specialized capability of specific functions, such as rendering or the creation of trees. While 3ds Max provides tremendous power and capability through a seemingly endless list of features, some plug-ins provide unequalled power and capability in select areas of 3D.

Over the years that 3ds Max has been around, some plug-ins have become so ubiquitous and so successful, that they have been acquired by Autodesk and fully integrated into the program. Freelancers or small firms should take caution and conduct research to ensure that a particular plug-in is truly needed. Purchasing plug-ins can quickly become expensive, and if you don't perform adequate research beforehand, you may regret making a purchase. However, if a plug-in can shave enough time off the production process or significantly improve the quality of your work, then the price should not stop you.

There are far too many plug-ins available to provide an adequate analysis here, but certain functions that some plug-ins perform bear mentioning. If you haven't already explored the following types of plug-ins, you should take some time to see how they could benefit your production:

- **Render engines**: One of the most common types of plug-ins is a render engine to replace the default scanline renderer. Some of these provide much greater realism than the default scanline, and some users prefer them over the mental ray render engine that ships with 3ds Max. The popular VRay rendering engine is one example. Most of the gallery images in this book were created using VRay.

- **Vegetation**: Many programs aid in the creation of trees to fill an area of 3ds Max that, in the view of almost any architectural visualizer, hasn't received enough native support. Plug-ins can provide vast libraries of vegetation with parameters for controlling height, age, seasonal appearance, as well as the ability to move with the application of wind. ArchVision's RPC plug-in is a great tool for the creation and placement of trees as well as other category types, such as people and cars.

- **People**: Modeling people with adequate detail in any 3D program would require millions of polygons. While many years from now this may be a possibility, in the foreseeable future the best way to use people in your scene is through the use of photographs. Several plug-ins are available that use photographs and alpha channels along with parametric controls to allow for the easy creation and integration of people into your scenes. The best plug-ins allow for either animated people or a 3D view of a person, that is, a different image displayed for each perspective.

- **Cars**: Many architectural visualizations require the use of numerous cars to fill large parking lots. When using upward of 100 cars or more, each car must be represented in a way that doesn't burden your computer with too many faces. Some plug-ins offer amazing realism with the use of less than a few hundred faces per car.

- **Water**: You can simulate moving water in numerous ways in 3ds Max. You can use animated materials, animate modifiers applied to a mesh or poly object, or use one of a number of great plug-ins. Like other object types, water can be created and animated with relative ease with the power of the top plug-ins.

Some other great plug-ins include the following:

- **Npower Software's Power Booleans**: Performs fast, reliable, and clean polygonal Boolean operations. See www.npowersoftware.com.

- **Reyes Infografica's DirtyReyes**: Adds natural and realistic wear and tear to objects in your scenes. See www.reyes-infografica.com.

- **Digimation's Seascape**: Allows for the easy creation of realistic water surfaces, waves, and wake effects. See www.digimation.com.

17. Use the Scatter command and Spacing tool to create vegetation

In a 3D scene, one of the most difficult elements to simulate realistically is vegetation. This is especially true when your scenes are animated, and your cameras move in and around the vegetation. Whether a scene contains 2D vegetation, 3D vegetation, or a combination of both depends on numerous factors, such as rendering time available, your vegetation libraries, distance of the vegetation from the camera, camera paths, and available RAM. Too many 3D plants or trees can lead to extremely large files sizes and rendering times, which is why I recommend using a combination of 2D and 3D vegetation in most scenes. When you do decide to use 3D vegetation, one of the ways you might want to create your plants is with the Scatter command.

As Chapter 4 discussed, the Scatter command is used to create copies of one object over the surface or within the volume of another object. In this way, it gives you a quick and easy method to create realistic 3D plants for an entire project, regardless of size. Creating plants this way can produce effective and realistic results with minimal burden on your computer.

It's often unimportant to the client exactly what type of plants they see in their visualization and since landscape drawings are usually one of the last things created during a project's planning, landscaping will often not even be decided by the time your work begins. When this is the case, the client may want you to play landscaper and tell you to simply create something that looks good. This can be a double-edged sword. Although it is nice to not be constrained by placing the exact required vegetation type throughout your scenes, the client may not like what you use. Good communication about landscaping requirements and exactly how you will meet them cannot be overstated. In fact, if anything should be highlighted in your contract, it should be details regarding the landscaping. Whenever possible, I highly recommend gaining flexibility from the client in this area.

When you aren't constrained by creating plants of particular type, I recommend using the Scatter command to create at least a portion of your plants. Doing so can save an enormous amount of time, especially for larger projects. Some projects call for the use of thousands of plants and placing each of these plants one at a time can take hours. With the Scatter command, you can create the appearance of a beautifully landscaped scene in a fraction of the time. Figure B-10 shows a few examples of images that can be used to create 3D shrubs and plants. These same types of images can also be scattered around the volume of an object to create the canopy of a tree.

Figure B-10. Examples of leaves that can be scattered to create plants and shrubs

Regardless of the landscaping constraints detailed in your contract, another great tool that facilitates the placement of landscaping throughout your scenes is the Spacing tool. You can use a spline (path) or two points separated by a certain distance to specify exactly where your vegetation is placed.

18. Use artificial shadows

Another one of the things that makes vegetation difficult to work with is the creation of realistic shadows. Vegetation can be simulated in 2D through the use of photographs and alpha channels, or it can be modeled with a wide variety of detail. Regardless of which method you use, each has pros and cons and tricks that can make working with it easier.

In the previous tip, I discuss how to create shrubs and plants using the Scatter command. By creating shrubs and plants this way, you can create fairly accurate shadows, depending on the size of the leaf object being scattered. When using 2D shrubs and plants, the shadows are not quite as accurate but will suffice in most situations if the camera is not too close, because the shadows are usually small and closely surrounded by other shadows.

The real difficulty in shadow creation comes with the use of trees. Because trees are larger and more sparsely placed, their shadows stand out more and their detail, or lack thereof, is more noticeable.

A 2D tree is represented by an image placed on a simple polygon object, as shown in the left image of Figure B-11. The advantage of this type of tree is that it requires only a few faces, or polygons, per tree object, and therefore it renders quickly. This type of 2D object, however, casts poor shadows. In default mode, only raytraced shadows use an image's alpha channel to cast shadows. Unless the alpha channel is used, the entire object will cast shadows and result in unrealistic rectangular shadows. Another disadvantage is that the images must always be oriented to face the camera, unless you use two crisscrossing duplicates (shown in the center image of Figure B-11), which rarely looks good. The images also become distorted when viewed at high perspectives, such as those greater than 45 degrees above the horizon, as shown in the right image.

Figure B-11. Examples of how 2D vegetation is used

3D trees use models containing sometimes hundreds of thousands of polygons per tree, depending on the type of tree and the level of detail. The obvious advantage of 3D trees is that they have depth and look completely 3D. They also look different at every angle and cast great shadows. The clear disadvantage with this type of tree is that it significantly increases your refresh rate and render time. 3D trees slow down render times, not only because the tree must be displayed, but also because the shadows must be displayed. Figure B-12 shows a 3D generic oak created with 3ds Max's **Foliage** feature. The tree has depth and casts realistic shadows, but at a price of 24,000 faces.

Figure B-12. A 3D tree with 24,000 faces

All of this being said, you can simulate shadows realistically for 2D in a couple of ways, and you have one option to increase render speed when using shadows with 3D trees as well.

Again, by default, only raytraced shadows use the alpha channel of an image to produce realistic shadows. However, you can create realistic shadows in the same way using advanced raytraced shadows by enabling the **Transparent Shadows** option, as shown in Figure B-13. This option uses the alpha channel to cast shadows.

Figure B-13. A 2D tree casting shadows with the help of an alpha channel

Regardless of which shadow type you are using in your scene, another way to simulate realistic shadows is by using a projector map with a light positioned directly above each tree, as shown in Figure B-14. By applying a negative value to the light (approximately –0.5), you can create a shadow where there would normally be light cast. This method creates a shadow for each tree, regardless of whether the tree is 2D or 3D. For 2D trees, the shadows make the tree look 3D with minimal burden on the computer and minimal increase in render time. For 3D trees, you can disable the shadow option for each tree and use the projector map to simulate shadows in the same way. By disabling the shadow option of a tree with a large polygon count, you can save a tremendous amount of rendering time.

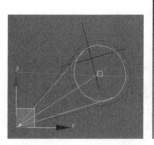

Figure B-14. A 2D tree casting shadows with the help of a projector map

One additional method of creating shadows you might want to try is disabling the shadows option of a 2D tree, and using a 3D tree with the render option disabled. This causes the 3D tree to be hidden from render, yet still cast shadows for the 2D tree. Chapter 10 explains how to create shadows using projector maps.

Although your computer has to calculate shadows for the 3D tree, by replacing the burden of rendering a 3D tree with that of a 2D tree, you can significantly reduce your render times.

Vegetation is a vital component of most 3D scenes. Poor vegetation can ruin an otherwise great scene, and when not used wisely, vegetation can be a tremendous burden on your computer. By using methods discussed in this tip, you can save a significant amount of production time.

19. Participate in website forums

Many of us in the 3ds Max community, new and experienced, fix some of our most difficult 3D problems with the help of others in the 3D community. To find this help, we often post our questions in 3ds Max online forums and review the replies at a later time. Because of the expertise of the readers in these forums, few problems go unsolved. As long as the question is relevant and posted in a professional manner, it will almost always be answered by one or more readers.

Online forums and chat rooms offer all of us a limitless pool of knowledge from which to draw information, and they are often the only places users can turn for answers to difficult problems. This is especially true for freelancers or sole proprietors who work on projects alone and don't have other experts working by their side.

Two of the best forums in the 3ds Max community are the official 3ds Max forum administered by Autodesk at www.autodesk.com, shown in Figure B-15, and the forum hosted by CGarchitect at www.cgarchitect.com. Both sites are monitored by industry experts.

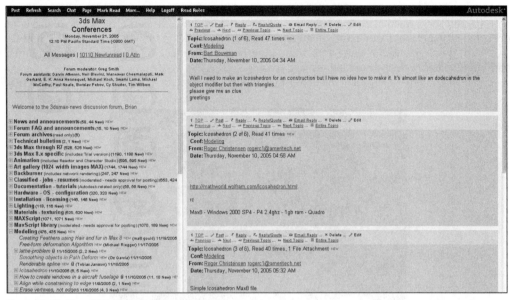

Figure B-15. The official 3ds Max discussion forum

This tip simply highlights the fact that website forums should play an important role in the work of the 3ds Max user, especially the less-experienced user. When a deadline is fast approaching, and you have a problem affecting your production, turn to the experts of a 3ds Max online forum or chat room.

20. Attend trade shows, seminars, and classes

On several occasions each year, the 3D community gathers together to participate in trade shows to display and learn about the latest technological advancements in 3D. Vendors of all types of 3D software, hardware, and media exhibit their most advanced products, while others explore and seek out the products that can aid their production. To maximize your production capabilities, you usually need to use the latest and greatest, and by attending trade shows, you can stay informed and know what that is. Otherwise, you may take quite some time to stumble upon the newest products that can help your production.

Seminars and classes offer all of us the opportunity to improve our work practices and increase our productivity. Generally, the more experienced a 3ds Max user is, the less willing and able they are to change their habitual ways of doing things. But the fact remains that everyone will always have room for improvement, and with the way 3D technology advances, you have to be willing to learn new things or eventually you will fall behind your peers. Even certified instructors and specialists learn new tips and tricks when attending seminars and classes taught by other experts. When you have the opportunity, you should give some of these a try. The largest 3D gathering in the United States is SIGGRAPH (see Figure B-16), a weeklong trade show held each summer in one of a number of different metropolitan cities. Also held at and during SIGGRAPH is the annual VisMaster's Design Visualization Conference, arguably the densest gathering of architectural visualization talent each year.

Figure B-16. SIGGRAPH 2005

Summary

Our business demands innovation and creativity. Every year that goes by, the software we use makes creating stunning visualizations easier and easier. But at the same time, our clients expect a better product. That combined with increasing competition, refusing to learn innovative ways to improve our own business will eventually lead to lower profits or even business failure.

The tips and tricks presented here took me many years to learn, often as a great expense and grief. Hopefully these ideas will help you avoid some unnecessary expense and grief of your own.

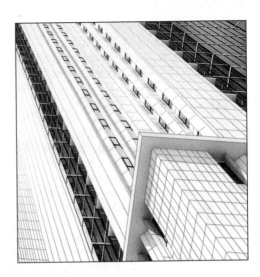

Appendix C

CUSTOMIZING 3DS MAX

3ds Max contains powerful customization features that enable you to streamline your work beyond those methods discussed throughout the chapters in this book. Customizing a program as complex as 3ds Max, however, is not effective unless you have a thorough understanding of the commands and features with which you arrange your interface. For this reason, I have placed an explanation of customization in this appendix. The first chapter in this book briefly highlighted some critical customization features that were necessary to mention during a discussion of the 3ds Max interface. This appendix picks up where Chapter 1 left off.

Although 3ds Max is used by numerous industries, its default interface layout is configured to provide the greatest efficiency for users in the entertainment industry. If you have finished reading this book, you now have a good foundation level understanding of 3ds Max and should take a look at some customization features that will make the interface more efficient and effective for your work in architectural visualizations.

The Customize menu

The bottom half of the **Customize** menu shown in Figure C-1 contains access to critical customization features in 3ds Max. These areas include **Configure User Paths**, **Units Setup**, **Grid and Snap Settings**, **Viewport Configuration**, and **Preferences**. The critical features of these areas were discussed in Chapter 1, and although they represent only a small fraction of all the customization features available, coverage of these areas is sufficient for the foundation level user. Playing around with these features and making numerous changes is easy and sometimes tempting, but exercise caution. Unless you read about a specific feature or explicitly understand what effect a particular change has on the program, you will probably be better off not to make the change. The next few pages discuss areas of customization in 3ds Max where change is much more justifiable.

UI schemes

When 3ds Max starts, it uses a file in the 3dsMax8\UI directory called MaxStartUI.ui to decide how to arrange the user interface. The very first time you run 3ds Max, that file is identical to the DefaultUI.ui file, but every time you close the program, the MaxStartUI.ui file is resaved with any changes made to any part of the user interface. If you move a toolbar or undock the Command panel, those changes will be saved in this file. To reload the original default user interface and revert back to the way 3ds Max appeared when you first installed it, click the **Customize** menu, select **Load Custom UI Scheme** (as shown in Figure C-1), and open the DefaultUI.ui file. If you make changes to the interface and want to revert back to the way 3ds Max was configured when you started your current session, simply select **Revert to Startup Layout** from the **Customize** menu, also shown in Figure C-1. To prevent the need of reverting to your startup layout because of inadvertent clicks of the mouse, you can lock the user interface by selecting **Lock UI Layout**, or use the keyboard shortcut Alt+0.

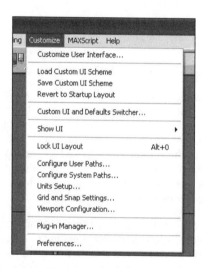

Figure C-1. The Customize menu

Custom UI and Defaults Switcher

Before going any further in the customization of 3ds Max, let's discuss the default user interface a little more. As I stated in the previous paragraph, 3ds Max is streamlined for the entertainment industry, not ours. Autodesk, however, kept the visualization industry in mind by preparing a way for us to make one simple customization change in our favor that has widespread effect over the entire program.

If you select **Custom UI and Defaults Switcher** from the **Customize** menu (see Figure C-1), a window appears which displays four different global configurations for 3ds Max. The default 3ds Max configuration shown at the top of the list provides a version of 3ds Max, as I mentioned, geared towards the entertainment industry. As the program clearly states in the center window, "The Max initial settings are configured to provide as much interactive performance as possible with small scenes, containing only a few shadow casting lights. Your application will be directed towards modeling, animating and rendering characters or models related to the entertainment industry."

Third in the list, the **DesignVIZ** configuration configures 3ds Max in a way that saves users in the visualization industry enormous amounts of time over the course of a project. Here the program states, "The DesignVIZ initial settings are configured to provide as much rendering performance as possible with large scenes, containing many lights. Your application will be directed towards photo realistic rendering of typical architectural models."

As an example, when you create a light with the default Max configuration, no shadows are cast unless you manually enable them. This lack of shadows suits the entertainment industry, however it does little to serve the visualization industry where lights almost always need to cast shadows. While changing this setting manually takes very little time, over the course of a project, you could easily make tens of thousands of similar changes that could otherwise be avoided by simply enabling the **DesignVIZ** configuration. I avoided a discussion of this feature in Chapter 1, because anyone missing this one area of discussion could be easily confused with what I would later call default settings. Because you are exploring more methods of useful customization, now would be a good time to begin using this feature. By reading the discussion of the **DesignVIZ** configuration in the center window, you can gain an understanding of just how broad the changes to the program are.

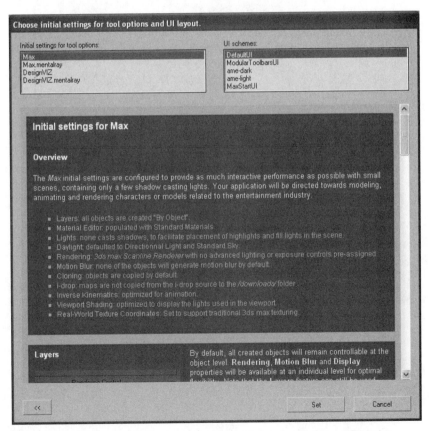

Figure C-2. A feature to globally change the UI to a design visualization configuration

Customize User Interface

The **Customize User Interface** feature, found at the very top of the **Customize** menu, provides access to another very large area of customization in 3ds Max. Selecting this first item in the menu opens the **Customize User Interface** dialog box. You can also access this dialog box by right-clicking certain icons in the **Main** toolbar, such as **Layer Manager,** or by right-clicking any empty space to the right of the toolbar.

When you open the **Customize User Interface** dialog box, shown in Figure C-3, five tabs appear at the top. With four of these tabs you can customize specific interfaces within the overall 3ds Max interface; the keyboard, toolbars, quads, and menu. The fifth tab provides a way to make color changes to just about any area of the program. Though users commonly change the viewport background from the default gray to black, you should take caution in doing so. Often changing one color causes a ripple effect which requires you to change another so that you can see the tools you need to use. You might find that making color changes is simply more trouble than it's worth, but it's all a matter of preference. If you want a dark background, you might be better off loading the amedark.ui interface.

Figure C-3. The Customize User Interface dialog box

In each of the first four tabs, 3ds Max displays a list of commands by group type. These group types include many areas, such as **Material Editor** and **Video Post**. With some groups, the available commands (or features) can be further separated by categories. What is important here is that just about every command in 3ds Max can be found in these groups and linked to each of these four interface types. In the **Customize User Interface** dialog box, you can assign keyboard shortcuts, referred to here as **Hotkeys**. Within the **Toolbars** tab you can create, delete, or rename toolbars. Within the **Quads** tab, you can create, delete, and even edit quad menus. Finally, within the **Menus** tab you can create, delete, and edit not only the menus at the top of the program, but virtually every menu found in the program.

Use of each tab is fairly straightforward and takes little time to master. As an example, you can quickly assign hot keys by highlighting a command in the left scroll window, pressing a key on the keyboard and then clicking the **Save** button at the bottom of the dialog box. By holding down the Ctrl, Alt, or Shift keys while pressing any other key, you can create a shortcut from a combination of keys pressed simultaneously. Using the existing hot keys and setting up your own hot keys are good practices for speeding up your production time. It is always faster to use a hot key than to click on a menu item in the interface.

Summary

Once you have a strong foundation in 3ds Max, the **Customize User Interface** dialog box is truly an area worth exploring. The most beneficial way you can take advantage of this dialog box is to study how you work, figure out what commands you use most often and then customize the various interfaces around those commands. When you do, you'll find yourself working at top speed and efficiency.

Appendix D

KEYBOARD SHORTCUTS

Among the greatest time-saving features in 3ds Max are the keyboard shortcuts. Keyboard shortcuts allow you to execute a command by pressing a single key or a combination of keys on the keyboard. Using keyboard shortcuts saves enormous amounts of time over using interface elements such as menus, icons, or the Command panel. Instead of clicking in numerous places to execute a single command, you can use the keyboard to do it in a fraction of a second. Veteran 3ds Max users will usually keep one hand on the keyboard to quickly execute a command in less time than it would take to visually locate an icon.

While some commands are only accessible through certain menus or through the Command panel, the vast majority of all commands in 3ds Max can be executed with a keyboard shortcut. This appendix provides a default list of keyboard shortcuts that I have found to be the most useful as well as additional keyboard shortcuts that I have set up for myself because of their frequency of use.

Default keyboard shortcuts

Table D-1 lists handy default keyboard shortcuts. It is important to not try to learn every available default shortcut or to try to create a shortcut for every command that you find yourself using throughout the course of a project. Doing so will only confuse you. Instead, try to learn the default shortcuts for the commands you use most often and set up the additional shortcuts for the commands that you find yourself using most frequently. In this way, you will be able to recall the shortcuts quickly instead of pondering over a long list in your mind or on paper.

If a shortcut does not exist for a particular command, refer to Appendix C to learn how to create your own.

Table D-1. Default keyboard shortcuts in 3ds Max

Command	Shortcut
Adaptive Degradation	O (zero)
Advanced Lighting Panel	9
Align	Alt+A
Auto Key Mode Toggle	N
Bottom View	B
Camera View	C
Clone	Ctrl+V
Create Camera From View	Ctrl+C
Cycle Active Snap Type	Alt+S
Default Lighting Toggle	Ctrl+L
Disable Viewport	D
Display as See Through Toggle	Alt+X
Environment Toggle	8
Fetch	Alt+Ctrl+F
Front View	F
Go to Start Frame	Home
Go to End Frame	End
Hide Cameras Toggle	Shift+C
Hide Geometry	Shift+G
Hide Grids	G
Hide Lights	Shift+L
Hide Shapes	Shift+S
Hold	Alt+Ctrl+H
Isolate Selection	Alt+Q

Command	Shortcut
Isometric User View	U
Left View	L
Lock User Interface Toggle	Alt+0
Material Editor	M
Maximize Viewport Toggle	Alt+W
New Scene	Ctrl+N
Open File	Ctrl+O
Percent Snap Toggle	Shift+Ctrl+P
Perspective User View	P
Place Highlight	Ctrl+H
Play Animation	/
Polygon Counter	7
Quick Align	Shift+A
Quick Render	Shift+Q
Redo Scene Operation	Ctrl+Y
Redo Viewport Operation	Shift+Y
Render Last	F9
Render Scene Dialog Toggle	F10
Restrict to Plane Cycle	F8
Restrict to x	F5
Restrict to y	F6
Restrict to z	F7
Save File	Ctrl+S
Select All	Ctrl+A
Select and Move	W

Continued

Table D-1. Default keyboard shortcuts in 3ds Max *(continued)*

Command	Shortcut
Select and Rotate	E
Select and Scale	R
Select By Name	H
Select Invert	Ctrl+I
Select None	Ctrl+D
Selection Lock Toggle	Space
Set Key Mode	'
Set Keys	K
Showing Floating Dialogs	Ctrl+`
Show Safeframes Toggle	Shift+F
Snaps Toggle	S
Spot/Directional Light View	Shift+4
Top View	T
Transform Gizmo Size Down	-
Transform Gizmo Size Up	=
Transform Gizmo Toggle	X
Transform Type-In Dialog Toggle	F12
Undo Scene Operation	Ctrl+Z
Undo Viewport Operation	Shift+Z
View Edged Faces Toggle	F4
Wireframe/Smooth+Highlights Toggle	F3
Shade Selected Faces	F2
Zoom Extents All Selected	Z

Additional keyboard shortcuts

The shortcuts in Table D-2 are additional ones that I have set up for commands that are used often or require numerous mouse clicks to access. Some of these shortcuts override default shortcuts, and whenever possible, I have used single keys for the shortcuts to make executing the commands as easy as possible. As with many of the default shortcuts, creating a shortcut with the first letter of the command the shortcut represents is not always possible.

When making your own shortcuts, you might want to consider matching your 3ds Max shortcuts to the shortcuts for commands found in Photoshop. Doing so might help you learn them more easily and prevent you from having to remember two different shortcuts for the same command.

In addition to the shortcuts discussed in this appendix, several companies manufacture keypad devices that allow you to program hundreds of keys as shortcuts to commands or to replace frequently typed words and phrases. This type of device, similar to a computer tablet, can save a tremendous amount of time, and I highly recommend its use, as I mentioned in Appendix B.

Table D-2. Additional 3ds Max keyboard shortcuts

Command	Shortcut
Affect Pivot Only Mode Toggle	0
Array	Alt+Shift+A
Asset Browser	J
Backface Cull	Alt+B
Boolean	Ctrl+B
Convert to Editable Mesh	[
Convert to Editable Polygon	]
Convert to Editable Spline	\
Curve Editor (Open)	Y
Display Floater	I
Edit Mesh Modifier	Page Up
Edit Spline Modifier	Page Down
Group	1
Group Attach	2
Group Close	3

Continued

Table D-2. Additional 3ds Max keyboard shortcuts *(continued)*

Command	Shortcut
Group Detach	4
Group Explode	5
Group Open	6
Hide Selection	Up Arrow
Hide Unselected	Down Arrow
List Lister	Alt+L
Mirror	Ctrl+M
RAM Player	Alt+R
Tape Measure	Q
Unfreeze All	, (comma)
Unfreeze by Hit	. (period)
Unfreeze by Name	/
Unhide All	Left Arrow
Unhide by Name	Right Arrow
UVW Map Modifier	Ctrl+U

INDEX

Numbers and symbols

2-Pass Antialias value
  Adv. Ray Traced Params rollout, 286
2-Sided option
  Shader Basic Parameters rollout, 179
2 Sided Shadows option
  Area Shadows rollout, 285
  Shadow Map Params rollout, 284
2D maps
  types of maps in 3ds Max, 229
2D modeling
  working with shapes and splines, 81–88
3D maps
  types of maps in 3ds Max, 229
3D modeling
  working with meshes and polys, 88–104
3D motion controller
  tips for production environment, 479
3DS Import dialog box
  scene element assembly, 425
3ds Max
  customizing 3ds Max, 81, 497–501
  discussion forum, 475
  screen interfaces, 16–19

A

About Us
  marketing your services on websites, 467
Absolute Map Bias option
  Shadow Map Params rollout, 284
Absolute Transform Type-In icon
  Quick Start with animation, 326
Absolute:World column
  Transform Type-In dialog box, 54
Acquire button, Parameters rollout
  Quick Start with materials, 148, 150
Acquire option
  UVW mapping, 233
    Quick Start with materials, 148

Acquire UVW Mapping dialog box, 233
  Quick Start with materials, 148, 150
Active Time Segment option
  Common Parameters rollout
    Quick Start with rendering, 378
  Render Scene dialog box, 390, 393
ActiveShade quad menu, 389
ActiveShade setting
  Render Scene dialog box, 388
Adaptive Degradation command, 504
Adaptive option
  Interpolation rollout, 87
Adaptive Path Steps option
  Skin Parameters rollout, Lofts, 114
Add Atmospheric Effect dialog box, 434
Add Effect dialog box, 449
Add Image Input Event dialog box, 406
Add Image Input Event icon, 405
Add Image Output Event dialog box, 408
Adv. Ray Traced Params rollout, 286
  advanced raytraced shadows, 275
Advanced Effects rollout, 279–280
  Affect Surfaces section, 279
  Cast Shadows option, 280
  Projector Map section, 279
Advanced Lighting Panel command, 504
Advanced Lighting tab
  Render Scene dialog box, 388
    Quick Start with lights, 259
advanced raytraced shadows, 275
  Quick Start with lights, 249
  tips for production environment, 482
  using, 276
Advanced Transparency section
  Extended Parameters rollout, 184
AEC Extended option, Command panel
  Quick Start with modeling, 70
Affect Backfacing option
  Soft Selection rollout, 96

Affect Indirect Only option
    Logarithmic Exposure Control Parameters rollout, 292
Affect Pivot Only Mode Toggle command, 507
Affect Surfaces section
    Advanced Effects rollout, 279
AfterBurn Glow effect, 449
algorithms
    shaders, 308
aliasing
    anti-aliasing, 186
    description, 184
Align Camera feature, 333
    illustrated, 269
    light placement, 269
    positioning cameras, 334
    positioning lights, 270
Align command, 504
Align section
    Lathe modifier, 140
Alignment section, Parameters rollout
    UVW Map modifier, 232
alpha channel
    file types for rendering, 392
Ambient color swatch
    Blinn Basic Parameters rollout, 181
Amount value
    Extrude modifier, 129
Amplitude value
    Waves map, 222
Angle parameters
    Coordinates rollout, 210
Angle value
    Lens Effects Globals rollout, 450
Animate Noise option
    Noise modifier, 132
animation
    animation script, 477
    Assign Controller rollout, 355
    controllers, 352
    creating basic motion, 347–349
    creating keyframes, 346–347
    Curve Editor, 364–369
    Euler Parameters rollout, 358
    exposure control, 292
    file types for rendering, 392
    introduction, 341
    Key Info (Basic) rollout, 359
    keyframing, 345

    Motion panel, 354–364
    network rendering, 409, 413
    playback controls, 344
    Position XYZ Parameters rollout, 358
    PRS Parameters rollout, 358
    Quick Start tutorial, 323–327
    Time Configuration dialog box, 342
    time slider, 344
animation controllers
    assigning and changing controllers, 356
    Audio Controller, 352
    changing controllers, 357
    constraints, 353
        assigning through Animation menu, 354
    Motion Capture Controller, 352
    Noise Controller, 353
Animation Offset value
    Scatter Objects rollout, 124
Animation section
    Time Configuration dialog box, 343
        Quick Start with cameras, 325
anti-aliasing, 186
    Raytracer Parameters rollout, 200
Antialiasing Options section
    Adv. Ray Traced Params rollout, 286
    Area Shadows rollout, 285
Antialiasing section
    Default Scanline Renderer rollout, 395
Apply Mapping option
    Surface Parameters rollout, Lofts, 111
Apply Material to Selection icon
    Quick Start with materials, 151
Arc Rotate icon, 28, 29
Arc Rotate Selected icon, 28, 29
Arc Rotate SubObject icon, 28, 29
architects
    marketing your services, 464
architectural drawing inspections
    tips for production environment, 475
architectural units
    setting up 3ds Max with, 76
architectural work
    setting up 3ds Max for, 73, 74
Archive feature
    assembling scene elements, 430
ArchVision
    RPCs (Rich Photorealistic Content), 421
area light, 293

Area Light Dimensions section
  Area Shadows rollout, 285
Area Light Parameters rollout, 294
area shadows, 274
Area Shadows rollout, 274, 285
  using, 276
Array command, 507
artificial shadows
  tips for production environment, 490
assembling scene elements
  see scene element assembly
assembly tools
  assembling scene elements, 422–429
Asset Browser command, 507
Asset Browser tool
  Utilities panel, 24, 25
Assign Controller rollout, 355
Assign Material to Selection icon, 168, 169
  Material Editor, 173
  Quick Start with materials, 145, 147, 149, 155, 156, 160
Assign Renderer rollout
  Render Scene dialog box, 390, 393
Atmosphere rollout
  creating and modifying Volume Fog, 444
  using Fire effect, 437
atmospheric apparatus gizmo, 435
  Helpers icon, 435
Atmospheric Apparatus menu, 435
atmospheric effects, 434–448
  accessing, 434
  description, 433
  Fire effect, 435–437
  Fog effect, 437–443
  Volume Fog effect, 443–444
  Volume Light effect, 445–448
Atmospheric Shadows section
  Shadow Parameters rollout, 282
Atmospherics option
  Render Scene dialog box, 391
Attach button
  Edit Geometry rollout, Modify panel, 99
Attach List dialog box, 100
Attachment Constraint
  animation controllers, 353
Atten. Mult. option
  Volume Light Parameters rollout, 446
attenuation
  Far Attenuation Start/End values, 277, 278
  Intensity/Color/Attenuation rollout, 277

near and far attenuation illustrated, 278
  Near Attenuation Start/End values, 277, 278
  photometric lights, 264
  standard lights, 264
  working with attenuation settings, 278
Attenuation End % values
  Volume Light Parameters rollout, 447
Attenuation Start % values
  Volume Light Parameters rollout, 447
Audio Controller
  animation controllers, 352
Auto Backup section, Files tab
  Preference Settings dialog box, 79, 80
Auto Key button
  creating and editing keys in Motion panel, 360
  creating keys, 347
  editing controllers with Curve Editor, 366
  Quick Start with animation, 325
Auto Key Mode Toggle command, 504
Auto Reflect/Refract Maps setting
  Default Scanline Renderer rollout, 396
Auto Secondary Element rollout
  creating Lens effect, 451
Auto Smooth option
  Smooth modifier, 131
AutoCAD
  example of floor plan drawing in, 82
AutoGrid option
  Object Type rollout, 84
  placing shape on surface of object, 84
Automatic exposure control, 292
Automatic Exposure Control value
  Exposure Control rollout, 256
AVI File Compression Setup dialog box
  Quick Start with rendering, 383
axonometric view, 26

B

Backburner components
  network rendering, 410
Backburner Manager dialog box, 411
Backburner Server dialog box, 411
Backface Cull command, 507
Backface Cull option
  Display floater/panel, 49
Background icon
  Material Editor, 164, 174

Background section
    Common Parameters rollout, 437
Backlight icon
    Material Editor, 173
Backup Interval
    Preference Settings dialog box, 79
Banking option, Skin Parameters rollout
    Lofts, 115
    Quick Start with modeling, 64
Base Scale value
    Scatter Objects rollout, 124
Basic Options section
    Area Shadows rollout, 285
Before/After value
    Optimize modifier, 133
Bezier control
    animation controllers, 352
Bezier Float controller, 359
Bezier Position controller
    changing controllers, 357
Bezier Scale controller
    Motion panel, animation, 356
Bias setting
    Shadow Map Params rollout, 283
billboards
    choosing file output dimensions for rendering, 397
Bitmap map, 207–214
    Coordinates rollout, 208
    Noise rollout, 213
    Output rollout, 214
    Time rollout, 214
Bitmap Parameters rollout, 207
    Diffuse Color and Opacity channels, 192
    illustrated, 208
Bldg-Glass object
    Quick Start with materials, 156
Bldg-Roof object
    Quick Start with materials, 161
    Quick Start with modeling, 68
Bldg-Walls object
    Quick Start with materials, 151, 152
    Quick Start with modeling, 67
Bldg-Walls-path object
    Quick Start with modeling, 64
Blinn Basic Parameters rollout
    Material Editor, 180
        color swatches, 181
        Opacity field, 166

Self-Illumination section, 182
        Specular Highlights section, 181
    Quick Start with materials, 155, 158
Blinn shader, 309
Blur value
    Displace modifier, 136
Blur/Blur offset parameters
    Coordinates rollout, 211
blurring
    Depth of Field effect, 452
    Motion Blur effect, 453, 455
    Motion Blur Parameters rollout, 454
    Multi-Pass Depth of Field effect, 457
    Multi-Pass Motion Blur effect, 455, 457
Boolean button, Command panel
    Quick Start with modeling, 67
Boolean command, 507
Boolean compound objects, 116–119
    caution: closed surfaces, 119
    caution: inconsistent face normals, 119
    caution: linked objects, 119
    caution: object faces long/skinny, 119
    caution: objects have modifiers in modifier stack, 119
    creating, 119
    Cut operation, 118
    Intersection operation, 118
    performing Boolean operations, 119
    Pick Boolean rollout, 116
    rollouts illustrated, 116
    Subtraction operation, 117
    tips for production environment, 485
    Union operation, 117
Boolean operations
    tips for production environment, 488
Bottom View command, 504
Bounding Box rendering level, viewports, 31
Box option, mapping coordinates
    UVW Map modifier, 231
        Quick Start with materials, 154
brochures
    marketing your services, 468
Bubble parameter
    Soft Selection rollout, Modify panel, 97
Bump channel
    Maps rollout, 195–197
business development
    marketing your services, 463–470
By Hit option
    Display floater, 48

By Name option
   Display floater, 48
By Vertex option
   Selection rollout, Modify panel, 93, 95

C

Camera view
   configuring, 12
   enabling radiosity, 312
   Quick Start with lights, 247
Camera View command, 504
camera viewport navigation, 332
cameras, 329–339
   Align Camera feature, 269, 333
   camera parameters, 334–339
   camera placement, 333–334
   camera rollouts illustrated, 335
   camera types, 330
   clipping planes, 337–339
   creating, 331
   Dolly Camera icon, 332
   Dolly Camera+Target icon, 332
   Dolly Target icon, 332
   environment ranges, 337
   free cameras, 330
   lens length and field of view, 335–336
   Orbit Camera icon, 332
   Pan Camera icon, 332
   Parameters rollout, 335
   Perspective icon, 332
   Place Highlight command, 334
   positioning cameras, 334
   Quick Start tutorial, 323–327
   Roll Camera icon, 332
   target cameras, 330
Candela value
   photometric lighting, 296
Cap End option
   Skin Parameters rollout, Lofts, 114
Cap Holes modifier, 141
Cap Start option
   Skin Parameters rollout, Lofts, 114
Capping options
   Extrude modifier, 129
cars, modeling
   tips for production environment, 488

Cast Shadows option
   Advanced Effects rollout, 280
   Quick Start with lights, 248
Choose New External Files Path window, 6
Cinepak Codec by Radius compression type
   Quick Start with rendering, 383
circles
   steps defining, 86
Circular Selection Region
   available shapes for selecting objects, 42
clients
   marketing your services, 463–466
Clip Manually option
   Clipping Planes section, cameras, 337
clipping planes
   hiding foreground, 339
Clipping Planes section
   Parameters rollout, 337
Clone command, 504
Clone Options dialog box
   Quick Start with lights, 251
Clone Part of Mesh dialog box
   editing mesh objects, 91, 92
Clone To Element option
   Clone Part of Mesh dialog box, 91
Clone To Object option
   Clone Part of Mesh dialog box, 91
color
   exposure control, 292
   Intensity/Color/Attenuation rollout, 277
   photometric lights, 264
   working with color settings, 278
color bleeding
   radiosity, 309
Color by Elevation rollout
   terrain compound objects, 121
Color option
   Blinn Basic Parameters rollout, 182
Color Range Limiting setting
   Default Scanline Renderer rollout, 396
Color section
   Intensity/Color/Distribution rollout, 295
Color Selector dialog box, 171
Color Selector: Diffuse Color
   Quick Start with materials, 155
Combine Objects by Layer option
   Quick Start with modeling, 61

Command panel
 docking/undocking, 18
 illustrated, 18
 interface elements described, 18
 tabs for panels within, 19
 using, 19–25
commands
 additional keyboard shortcuts, 507–508
 default keyboard shortcuts, 503–506
 keyboard shortcuts, 503–508
Common Parameters rollout
 Background section, 437
 Options section, 391
 Output Size section, 391
 Render Output section, 392–394
 Render Scene dialog box, 390
 Time Output section, 390
Common tab
 Render Scene dialog box, 388, 390–394
compound objects, 107–127
 Booleans, 116–119
 lofts, 108–116
 scatter objects, 123–126
 terrain, 120–122
Compound Objects group
 Geometry tab, Create panel, 107
 Quick Start with modeling, 62
Compression Settings dialog box
 RAM Player, 402
computer power
 assembling scene elements, 416–422
cones
 Show Cone option, 336
configuration
 configuring user paths, 5
 DesignVIZ configuration option, 499
 Quick Start tutorial, 4–13
 Viewport Configuration dialog, 9
Configure Modifier Sets icon/dialog box
 configuring 3ds Max, 10
Configure System Paths dialog box, 77, 78
Configure User Paths dialog box, 5, 77, 78, 79
Connect icon
 network rendering, 412
Conserve Memory feature
 Default Scanline Renderer rollout, 396
constraints
 animation controllers, 353
 assigning through Animation menu, 354

Contact Us link
 marketing your services on websites, 467
continuing education
 marketing your services, 465
contractors
 marketing your services, 466
contracts
 tips for production environment, 480
Control Parameters rollout, 301, 302
 North Direction setting, 301
 Orbital Scale value, 301
controllers, animation, 352
 assigning and changing controllers, 356
 Audio controller, 352
 Bezier control, 352
 Bezier Float controller, 359
 Bezier Scale controller, 356
 changing controllers, 357
 constraints, 353, 354
 Curve Editor, 365
 editing controllers, 365
 Euler XYZ controller, 356
 Linear controller, 356
 Motion Capture controller, 352
 Noise controller, 353
 Position XYZ controller, 356
Convert to Editable Mesh command/option
 additional keyboard shortcuts, 507
 Quick Start with materials, 152
 Quick Start with modeling, 60, 61
Convert to Editable Polygon command, 507
Convert to Editable Spline command, 507
cool materials, 168
coordinates
 generating mapping coordinates, 229
Coordinates rollout
 Bitmap map, 208
  Angle parameters, 210
  Blur/Blur offset parameters, 211
  Offset parameter, 209
  Tiling parameter, 209
 Noise map, 220
 UVW Map modifier, 237
Copy command
 managing file size, 417
 using, 419
Copy feature
 creating and editing keys in Motion panel, 361

Copy method
    Creation Method rollout, 109
copying objects
    instance objects compared, 418–419
Create Camera From View command, 504
Create Key dialog box, 346
Create New Set icon, 43
Create panel, 20
    creating an object, 20
    creating Booleans, 116–119
    creating lofts, 108–116
      with Get Path and Get Shape, 108
    creating scatter objects, 123–126
    creating terrain, 120–122
    Creation Method rollout, 85
    icons explained, 20
    illustrated, 20
    Interpolation rollout, 86
    Keyboard Entry rollout, 85
    Name and Color rollout, 20, 85
    Object Type rollout, 20
    Parameters rollout, 85
    Rendering rollout, 85
Creation Method rollout
    Create panel, 85
Creation Method rollout, Loft feature, 108
    Copy method, 109
    Instance option, 109
    Move method, 109
    Quick Start with modeling, 64
Cropping/Placement section
    Bitmap Parameters rollout, 195
Crossing icon
    see Window/Crossing icon
crossing selection, 41
Curve Editor (Open) command, 507
Curve Editor, animation, 364–369
Custom Sample Object
    Material Editor, 165
Custom UI and Defaults Switcher option
    Customize menu, 498
customization
    3ds Max interface, 81
    caution, 497
    DesignVIZ configuration option, 499
    locking user interface, 498
    reverting to original defaults, 498

Customize menu
    Custom UI and Defaults Switcher option, 498
    customizing 3ds Max, 497–501
    illustrated, 498
    Load Custom UI Scheme, 498
    Lock UI Layout option, 498
    Revert to Startup Layout option, 498
Customize User Interface dialog box, 500
    keyboard shortcuts, 501
Cut operation
    Boolean compound objects, 118
    Quick Start with modeling, 68
Cycle Active Snap Type command, 504
Cylindrical option, mapping coordinates
    UVW Map modifier, 231

D

dark/nighttime scenes
    exposure control, 292
Daylight feature, 301–303
    Control Parameters rollout, 301, 302
Daylight Parameters rollout, 303
decay
    Intensity/Color/Attenuation rollout, 277
Default Lighting Toggle command, 504
Default Scanline Renderer rollout
    Antialiasing section, 395
    Global SuperSampling section, 396
    Options section, 395
    Render Scene dialog box, 394
defaults
    Custom UI and Defaults Switcher option, 498
DefaultUI.ui file
    reverting to original defaults, 498
Deformations rollout, Loft objects, 116
Delete button
    Edit Geometry rollout, Modify panel, 104
Delete Current Event icon
    Video Post interface, 408
Delete Job icon
    network rendering, 412
Dens./Density setting
    Shadow Parameters rollout, 281, 298
Depth of Field effect, 452–453
    Multi-Pass Depth of Field effect, 457–459
    target distance, 452

Depth of Field Parameters rollout, 452, 458
  focal depth, 458
  Focal Limit value, 453
  Focal Parameters section, 453
  Horiz Focal Loss value, 453
  Pick Cam. button, 452
  Pick Node button, 452
  Sample Radius parameter, 459
  target distance, 458
  Total Passes parameter, 458
  Use Target Distance option, 458
  Vert Focal Loss value, 453
deselecting objects individually, 42
design
  questioning poor designs, 478
DesignVIZ configuration option
  customizing 3ds Max, 499
Detach as Clone feature, 103
Detach button
  Edit Geometry rollout, Modify panel, 101, 103
Detach to Element feature, 103
developers
  marketing your services, 464
dialog boxes
  3DS Import, 425
  Acquire UVW Mapping, 148, 150, 233
  Add Atmospheric Effect, 434
  Add Effect, 449
  Add Image Input Event, 406
  Add Image Output Event, 408
  Attach List, 100
  AVI File Compression Setup, 383
  Backburner Manager, 411
  Backburner Server, 411
  Clone Options dial, 251, 252
  Clone Part of Mesh, 91, 92
  Color Selector, 171
  Compression Settings, 402
  Configure Modifier Sets, 10
  Configure System Paths, 77, 78
  Configure User Paths, 77, 78, 79
  Create Key, 346
  Customize User Interface, 500, 501
  DWG Import, 425
  Edit Filter Event, 407
  Environment and Effects, 256, 292, 434
  Exclude/Include, 272
  Fade Image Control, 407
  File Properties, 428

  Flag Properties, 217
  Graphics Driver Setup, 76
  illustrated, 19
  Image File List Control, 381, 401, 402, 405, 406
  interface elements described, 19
  JPEG Image Control, 377, 413
  Layer Manager, 50
  Material Editor Options, 164
  Merge, 424
  Merge File, 424
  Move Transform Type-In, 61
  Named Selection Sets, 43, 44
  Network Job Assignment, 410, 411, 413
  Object Properties, 453, 454
  Open File, 400
  Preference Settings, 77, 79, 80
  Queue Monitor, 412
  RAM Player Configuration, 401
  Render Output File, 376, 393
  Render Presets Load, 389
  Render Scene, 387, 388–396, 454
  Render Setup, 403
  Select File to Import, 61
  Select Objects, 38, 39
  Summary Info, 429
  System Unit Setup, 75
  Time Configuration, 342–344
  Transform Type-In, 52, 54
  Units Setup, 7, 74
  Viewport Configuration, 9, 244
Diffuse Color channel
  Bitmap Parameters rollout, 192
  Maps rollout, 190–192
Diffuse color swatch
  Blinn Basic Parameters rollout, 155, 181
diffuse distribution, 295
Digimation's Seascape
  tips for production environment, 488
dimensions
  specifying for final rendered output, 391
Diplay Properties section
  Display floater/panel, 48
direct illumination, 308
direct lights, 265, 266
Directional Parameters rollout, 287
directory structure, 78
Disable Viewport command, 504
disabling viewports, 30
discussion forum, 475

Displace modifier, 136, 137
Displacement Approx. modifier, 201
Displacement channel
  Maps rollout, 200–202
Displacement section
  Displace modifier, 136
Display Alpha Channel icon, 195
Display as Box option
  Display floater/panel, 48
Display as See Through Toggle command, 504
display drivers, 76
Display floater, 48
  By Hit option, 48
  By Name option, 48
  displaying objects, 47
  Hide By Category option, 48
  Hide/Freeze tab, 48
  Object Level tab, 48
  Tools menu, 23
  using, 49
Display Floater command, 507
Display floater/panel, 48
Display icon, Command panel
  Quick Start with cameras, 324
  Quick Start with modeling, 66
Display panel, 23, 24
  Display Properties rollout, 48
  displaying objects, 47
  Freeze rollout, 48
  Hide By Category rollout, 48
  Hide rollout, 48
Display Properties rollout
  Display panel, 48
Display rollout
  scatter compound objects, 123
Display/Update rollout
  Boolean compound objects, 116
displaying objects, 47–51
  Layer Manager dialog box, 50
Distance option
  Path Parameters rollout, Lofts, 113
Distribute Using variable
  scatter compound objects, 124
Distribution drop-down list
  Intensity/Color/Distribution rollout, 294
distribution objects, scatter compound objects
  Hide Distribution Object option, 123
  Perpendicular parameter, 124
  Pick Distribution Object button, 123

distributions, light
  diffuse distribution, 295
  isotropic distribution, 294
  web distribution, 295
Dolly Camera icon, 332
Dolly Camera+Target icon, 332
Dolly Light icon, 268
Dolly Light+Target icon, 268
Dolly Target icon, 268, 332
Doors feature
  tips for production environment, 484
Dope Sheet mode, animation
  Track View feature, 364
downloads, 4
Duplicates value
  Scatter Objects rollout, 123
Duration (frames) setting
  Multi-Pass Motion Blur effect, 456, 457
DVDs
  choosing file output dimensions for rendering, 398
  marketing your services, 469
DWG Import dialog box
  scene element assembly, 425
Dynamic Properties rollout
  Material Editor, 187

E

easing
  Quick Start with animation, 326
Edge Distance option
  Soft Selection rollout, 98
Edges Only option
  Display floater/panel, 49
Edit Current Event icon
  Video Post interface, 409
Edit Filter Event dialog box
  video editing with Video Post, 407
Edit Geometry rollout, Command panel
  Quick Start with modeling, 68
Edit Geometry rollout, Modify panel, 98, 99
  Attach button, 99
  Delete button, 104
  Detach button, 101, 103
  Explode button, 101
  Grid Align feature, 102
  Remove Isolated Vertices, 102
  View Align feature, 102, 103
  Weld feature, 104

Edit Mesh modifier, 90
  editing mesh objects, 90
  Quick Start with materials, 154
  working with map channels, 238
Edit Mesh Modifier command, 507
Edit Named Selection Sets icon, 43
Edit Range Bar icon
  Video Post interface, 409
Edit Spline modifier, 110, 122
Edit Spline Modifier command, 507
editing mesh objects, 90
educational courses
  marketing your services, 465
effects, 433–460
  AfterBurn Glow effect, 449
  atmospheric effects, 433, 434–448
    Fire effect, 435–437
    Fog effect, 437–443
    Volume Fog effect, 443–444
    Volume Light effect, 445–448
  Depth of Field Parameters rollout, 458
  Fire Effect Parameters rollout, 435
  Hair and Fur effect, 449
  Lens Effects Globals rollout, 449
  Lens Effects Parameters rollout, 449
  multi-pass effects, 455
  post-production effects, 448
  render effects, 433, 448–459
    Depth of Field effect, 452–453
    Lens effect, 449–451
    Motion Blur effect, 453–455
    Multi-Pass Depth of Field effect, 457–459
    Multi-Pass Motion Blur effect, 455–457
  using environment ranges to control, 441–442
Email Notifications rollout
  Quick Start with rendering, 379
  Render Scene dialog box, 394
Email Options section
  Email Notifications rollout, 379
emails
  marketing your services, 470
Enable In Renderer option
  Rendering rollout, Create panel, 85
Enable In Viewport option
  Rendering rollout, Create panel, 85
Enable option
  Multi-Pass Depth of Field effect, 458
  Multi-Pass Motion Blur effect, 456

Enabled option
  Radiosity Meshing Parameters rollout, 315, 316
end points
  imported spline with unwelded endpoints, 476
  lines not meeting at intended end points, 476
environment
  setting up work environment, 74–81
Environment and Effects dialog box, 292, 434
  Quick Start with lights, 256
Environment Color Map
  Fog effect, 438
Environment Opacity Map
  Fog effect, 438
Environment Ranges section
  Parameters rollout, 337
Environment Ranges values
  Fog effect, 440–442
Environment Toggle command
  default keyboard shortcuts, 504
error messages
  Missing Map Coordinates error message, 154, 237
Euler Parameters rollout, 358
Euler XYZ controller
  Motion panel, animation, 356
Every Nth Frame option
  Render Scene dialog box, 390, 393
Exclude button
  General Parameters rollout, 271
Exclude from Adv. Lighting Calculations option
  Geometric Object Radiosity Properties rollout, 318
Exclude/Include dialog box
  excluding object from shadow casting illustrated, 272
Execute Sequence icon
  video editing with Video Post, 408
Exit Isolation Mode button
  Quick Start with modeling, 65, 67
Explode button
  Edit Geometry rollout, Modify panel, 101
explosions
  Fire effect, 435
Exponential option
  Fog Parameters rollout, 439
Export command
  scene element assembly, 426
Export Selected command
  scene element assembly, 426
exposure control, 291–293
  animations, 292
  exposure control parameters, 292

Logarithmic Exposure Control Parameters rollout, 292
types of exposure control, 292
Exposure Control Parameters rollout, 292
Render Preview button, 293
Exposure Control rollout, 292
Quick Start with lights, 256
Extended Parameters rollout
index of refraction, 202
Material Editor, 183
Advanced Transparency section, 184
Reflection Dimming section, 183
Wire section, 184
Exterior daylight option
Logarithmic Exposure Control Parameters rollout, 293
Extrude modifier, 129, 130
Quick Start with modeling, 60, 67, 68

F

face icon, Selection rollout
Quick Start with modeling, 68
Face Map option
Shader Basic Parameters rollout, 180
Face Thresh parameter
Optimize modifier, 133
Faceted option
Shader Basic Parameters rollout, 180
Fade Image Control dialog box, 407
Fade Image Filter event, 407
Falloff map, 223
Falloff Parameters rollout, 224
Falloff option
Layered fog, 443
Falloff parameter
Soft Selection rollout, Modify panel, 96, 97
Falloff Parameters rollout
Falloff map, 224
Falloff/Field diameter value
Light Falloff icon, 268
Falloff/Field parameter
Spotlight/Directional Parameters rollouts, 288
Far Attenuation Start/End values, 277, 278
Far Range value
Fog Parameters rollout, 439
using environment ranges to control Fog, 441
Fast tangent
creating and editing keys in Motion panel, 361
Fast View option
enabling, viewports, 32, 33

Fence Selection Region
available shapes for selecting objects, 42
Fetch command, 504
Field of View icon, 28, 29
File Link Manager
scene element assembly, 428
File Number Base setting
Render Scene dialog box, 390
File Properties dialog box
scene element assembly, 428
files
choosing output dimensions for rendering, 396–399
configuring paths, 77
file types for rendering, 392
importance of good directory structure, 78
managing file size, 416
transferring, 416–419
Filter Color swatch, Color section
Intensity/Color/Distribution rollout, 296
Filter Plug-In drop-down list
video editing with Video Post, 407
Filter Shadows settings
Volume Light Parameters rollout, 447
filters
Selection Filter, 43
final product
choosing file output dimensions for rendering, 396
Fire effect, 435–437
Fire Effect Parameters rollout, 435
Flame Density parameter, 437
Flame Detail parameter, 437
Flame Size parameter, 437
Gizmos section, 435
Shape section, 437
Stretch parameter, 437
Flag Properties dialog box, 217
Flame Density parameter
Fire Effect Parameters rollout, 437
Flame Detail parameter
Fire Effect Parameters rollout, 437
Flame Size parameter
Fire Effect Parameters rollout, 437
Flame Type option
Fire Effect Parameters rollout, 437
Flat Mirror map
Reflection channel, 198, 199
flickering, 185
Flip Normals option
Skin Parameters rollout, Lofts, 115

floaters
    Display floater, 48
    illustrated, 19
    interface elements described, 19
focal depth
    Depth of Field Parameters rollout, 458
Focal Limit value
    Depth of Field Parameters rollout, 453
Focal Parameters section
    Depth of Field Parameters rollout, 453
Fog Background option
    Fog Parameters rollout, 438
Fog effect, 437–443
    description, 438
    Environment Ranges values, 440–442
    using environment ranges to control, 441–442
    Volume Fog effect, 443–444
    Volume Fog Parameters rollout, 444
Fog Parameters rollout, 438
    Exponential option, 439
    Falloff option, 443
    Far Range value, 439
    Horizon Noise option, 443
    Layered section, 442
    Near Range value, 439
    Standard section, 439
Foliage button, Object Type rollout
    Quick Start with modeling, 70
foreground
    hiding using clipping planes, 339
Form section
    terrain compound objects, 121
forums
    3ds Max discussion forum, 475
    website forums, 492
FOV (field of view)
    camera parameters, 335
    using FOV settings, 336
Fractal option
    Noise modifier, 132
Frame Rate section
    Time Configuration dialog box, 343
frames
    controlling specific frames to be rendered, 390
    tips for production environment, 485
Frames option
    Render Scene dialog box, 390
frames, video clips
    Time rollout, 214

free cameras, 330
    creating cameras, 331
free lights
    creating lights, 266, 268
free spotlights, 267
freelancing
    see tips for production environment
Freeze option/rollout
    Display floater/panel, 48
Frequency value, Animate Noise option
    Noise modifier, 132
Front View command
    default keyboard shortcuts, 504

G

gallery link
    marketing your services on websites, 467
General Parameters rollout, 271–276
    Exclude button, 271
    illustrated, 271
    Light Type section, 271
    Shadow map type, 272
    shadow type drop-down list, 272
    Shadows section, 271
    turning lights off, 271
Generate Material IDs option
    Surface Parameters rollout, Lofts, 111
Geometric Object Radiosity Properties rollout, 319
    Exclude from Adv. Lighting Calculations option, 318
Geometry Options section
    Quick Start with modeling, 61
Geometry tab, Create panel
    Compound Objects group, 107
    groups within, 107
    Loft command, 108
    Particle Systems group, 107
    Standard Primitives group, 107
Get Material icon, 169, 174
    Material Editor, 173, 174
Get Path option
    creating lofts, 108
Get Shape button, Creation Method rollout
    Quick Start with modeling, 64
Get Shape option
    creating lofts, 108
gizmos
    atmospheric apparatus gizmo, 435
    creating, 435

modifier gizmo, 231
Soften Gizmo Edges value, 443
SphereGizmo button, 436, 444
transform gizmo, 38, 52, 53, 92, 98, 122
Transform Gizmo commands, 506
types, 435
UVW Map gizmo, 231, 232, 233
Gizmos section
Fire Effect Parameters rollout, 435
glass
tips for production environment, 486
global illumination, 307–319
description, 263, 307
principles of, 308–309
radiosity, 309–319
shaders, 308–309
Global Ray Antialiaser option
Raytracer Global Parameters rollout, 200
Global SuperSampling section
Default Scanline Renderer rollout, 396
SuperSampling rollout, 184
Glossiness value
Blinn Basic Parameters rollout, 181
Go Forward to Sibling icon
Material Editor, 173
Go to End Frame command, 504
Go to End icon
Quick Start with animation, 326
Go to Parent icon, 191
Material Editor, 173
Quick Start with materials, 157
Go to Start Frame command, 504
Go to Start icon
Quick Start with animation, 327
Graded Solid option, Form section
terrain compound objects, 121
Graded Surface option, Form section
terrain compound objects, 121
Gradient map, 215
Gradient Parameters rollout, 215
Gradient Ramp map, 216
Gradient Ramp Parameters rollout, 216
Graphics Driver Setup dialog box, 76
Grid Align feature
Edit Geometry rollout, Modify panel, 102
grids
viewports, 30
Group commands, 507

H

Hair and Fur effect, 449
Helpers icon
atmospheric apparatus gizmo, 435
using Fire effect, 436
Hemisphere option
using Fire effect, 436
Hide button
Selection rollout, Modify panel, 94
Hide By Category option
Display floater, 48
keyboard shortcuts, 49
Hide By Category rollout
Display panel, 48
Hide Cameras Toggle command, 504
Hide Geometry command, 504
Hide Grids command, 504
Hide Lights command, 504
Hide option/rollout
Display floater/panel, 48
Quick Start with cameras, 324
Quick Start with modeling, 66
Hide Selection command, 508
Hide Shapes command, 504
Hide Unselected command, 508
Hide/Freeze tab
Display floater, 48
Hierarchy panel, 21
changing object's pivot point, 22
IK (Inverse Kinematics) button, 21
Link Info button, 22
Pivot button, 21
high-definition video
choosing file output dimensions for rendering, 398
high-resolution print
file types for rendering, 392
Highlight Selected Objects icon, 43
highlights
Place Highlight command, 270
specular highlights, 308
Hold command, 504
Horiz Focal Loss value
Depth of Field Parameters rollout, 453
Horizon Noise option
Layered fog, 443
horizons
Show Horizon option, 336

Horizontal section, Simplification rollout
    terrain compound objects, 121
hot materials, 168
hotkeys
    see keyboard shortcuts
Hotspot/Beam parameter
    high/low values illustrated, 288
    Light Hotspot icon, 268
    Spotlight/Directional Parameters rollouts, 288

I

icons
    Material Editor, 172
IES (Illuminating Engineering Society), 293
IES Sky
    creating sunlight and skylight photometric lights,
        299–301
    Quick Start with lights, 257
    standard lights compared, 303
IES Sky Parameters rollout, 299
IES Sun
    creating sunlight and skylight photometric lights,
        299–301
    Quick Start with lights, 254
    Shadow Parameters rollout, 298
    standard lights compared, 303
    Sun Parameters rollout, 298
Ignore Backfacing option
    Selection rollout, Modify panel, 93, 95
Ignore Extents option
    Display floater/panel, 49
Ignore Visible Edges option
    Selection rollout, Modify panel, 94
IK (Inverse Kinematics) button
    Hierarchy panel, 21
illumination
    see also lighting
    direct illumination, 308
    global illumination, 307–319
Image Aspect value
    Render Scene dialog box, 391, 393
Image File List Control dialog box
    Quick Start with rendering, 381
    RAM Player, 401, 402
    video editing with Video Post, 405, 406
Image Filter event
    Video Post interface, 405
Image Filter Event icon, 407

Image Input event
    Video Post interface, 405, 406
Image Motion Blur
    Motion Blur effect, 453
Image Output event
    Video Post interface, 405
Image section
    Displace modifier, 136
image with embedded alpha channel
    file types for rendering, 392
images
    choosing file output dimensions for rendering, 398
    configuring user paths, 5
    file types for rendering, 392
    rendering, 387–413
    rendering tools, 399–404
Import command
    scene element assembly, 425
Import Options section
    Preference Settings dialog box, 80
importing files
    Quick Start with modeling, 61
In button
    editing controllers with Curve Editor, 366
    Key Info (Basic) rollout, 360
index of refraction
    Extended Parameters rollout, 202
Indirect Light Filtering feature
    Radiosity Processing Parameters rollout, 314
Indirect Light Filtering value
    Radiosity Meshing Parameters rollout, 318
industry
    see tips for production environment
Initial Quality values
    Radiosity Processing Parameters rollout, 310
input devices
    tips for production environment, 479
inspecting architectural drawings
    tips for production environment, 475
Instance cloning method
    Clone Options dialog box, 252
Instance command
    managing file size, 417, 418
    using, 419
instance objects
    copying objects compared, 418–419
Instance option
    Creation Method rollout, Loft feature, 109

instanced lofts
  power of instanced lofts, 109
intensity
  Intensity/Color/Attenuation rollout, 276
  Multiplier settings illustrated, 276
  working with intensity settings, 278
Intensity section
  Intensity/Color/Distribution rollout, 296
Intensity setting
  Lens Effects Globals rollout, 450
Intensity/Color/Attenuation rollout, 276–279, 297
  attenuation, 277
  color, 277
  decay, 277
  illustrated, 276
  intensity, 276
  Quick Start with lights, 253
Intensity/Color/Distribution rollout, 294
  preset photometric lights, 297
Interactive Panorama Exporter Common Parameters
    rollout
  Render Setup dialog box, 403
Interactive Tools section
  Radiosity Processing Parameters rollout, 314
interface, 3ds Max
  customizing 3ds Max, 81, 497–501
  discussion forum, 475
  screen interfaces, 16–19
interface elements, 16–19
  main screen interfaces of 3ds Max illustrated, 16
interfaces
  keyboard shortcuts, 16
  mouse, 17
internet images/videos
  choosing file output dimensions for rendering, 398
Interpolate Points *4 option, Simplification rollout
  terrain compound objects, 121
interpolation methods
  Curve Editor, animation, 365
Interpolation rollout, 86
  Create panel, 86, 87
Intersection operation
  Boolean compound objects, 118
Inverse Decay option
  options for setting decay, 277
Inverse Square option
  options for setting decay, 277

Isolate Selection command
  default keyboard shortcuts, 504
  illustrated, 47
  keyboard shortcut, 46
  selecting objects, 46
  using, 47
isolating objects
  Quick Start with materials, 149
isolation mode
  Exit Isolation Mode button, 67
Isometric User View command, 505
isotropic distribution, 294
Iteration value
  TurboSmooth modifier, 135
Iterations setting, Fractal option
  Noise modifier, 132

J

JPEG Image Control dialog box
  network rendering, 413
  Quick Start with rendering, 377
.jpg file
  file types for rendering, 392

K

Kelvin option, Color section
  Intensity/Color/Distribution rollout, 295
Key Info (Basic) rollout, 359
  determining transform contents displayed, 358
  In and Out buttons, 360
  Key Tangent flyouts, 360
  standard interpolation methods for keys, 360
  Time field, 359
  x, y, and z values, 360
Key Mode toggle
  animation playback controls, 345
Key Tangent flyouts
  Key Info (Basic) rollout, 360
Keyboard Entry rollout
  Create panel, 85
keyboard shortcuts, 503–508
  additional keyboard shortcuts, 507–508
  benefit of learning, 16
  creating, 507
  Customize User Interface dialog box, 501
  default keyboard shortcuts, 503–506
  editing mesh objects, 90

Hide By Category option, Display floater, 49
Isolate Selection, 46
menus, 17
Select and Move icon, 51
Select and Rotate icon, 53
Select icons, 38
Selection Region icons, 42
tips for production environment, 478
toolbars compared, 17
Transform Type-In dialog box, 54
viewports, 27
    using/not using, 29
keyframing
animation, 345
creating keyframes, 346–347
keypads
tips for production environment, 479
keys
creating and editing in Motion panel, 360
standard interpolation methods for, 360

L

large projects
tips for production environment, 474
Lasso Selection Region
available shapes for selecting objects, 42
Lathe button, Modify panel
Quick Start with modeling, 69
Lathe modifier, 138, 139
Layer Manager dialog box, 50
Layered section
Fog Parameters rollout, 442
Layered Solid option, Form section
terrain compound objects, 121
layers, 50
line work on wrong layer, 476
using, 51
Layout tab
Viewport Configuration dialog, 9
layouts
viewports, 9, 34
Left View command, 505
Length Repeat parameter
Surface Parameters rollout, Lofts, 111
Lens effect, 449–451
Lens Effects Globals rollout, 449
Angle value, 450
creating Lens effect, 451

Intensity setting, 450
Parameters tab, 450
Size setting, 450
Squeeze value, 450
Lens Effects Parameters rollout, 449
creating Lens effect, 451
lens length
using Lens length settings, 336
Lens value
Parameters rollout, cameras, 335
libraries
material libraries, 175–177
tips for production environment, 486
Light Affects Shadow Color feature
Shadow Parameters rollout, 282
Light Falloff icon, 268
Light Hotspot icon, 268
Light Tracer feature, 303
using in production environment, 303
Light Type section
General Parameters rollout, 271
lighting
animations, 292
area light, 293
creating lights, 266–268
Daylight feature, 301–303
exposure control, 291–293
free lights, 266, 268
global illumination, 263, 307–319
IES Sky, 299–301
    standard lights compared, 303
IES Sun, 298
    standard lights compared, 303
importance of good lighting, 263
Lens effect, 449
light parameters, 270–282
light placement, 269–270
    Align Camera feature, 269
    Place Highlight command, 270
linear light, 293
photometric lighting, 291–304
    light types, 293–298
    photometric lights, 263, 264
photometric spotlight, 294
point light, 293
positioning lights, 270
preset photometric lights, 297–298
Quick Start tutorial, 243–261

rollouts
  Adv. Ray Traced Params, 286
  Advanced Effects, 279–280
  Area Light Parameters, 294
  Area Shadows, 274, 285
  Control Parameters, 301, 302
  Daylight Parameters, 303
  Directional Parameters, 287
  Exposure Control, 292
  Exposure Control Parameters, 292
  General Parameters, 271–276
  Geometric Object Radiosity Properties, 319
  IES Sky Parameters, 299
  Intensity/Color/Attenuation, 276–279, 297
  Intensity/Color/Distribution, 294
  Linear Light Parameters, 294
  Logarithmic Exposure Control Parameters, 292
  Optimizations, 286
  Radiosity Meshing Parameters, 315–318
  Radiosity Processing Parameters, 310–314
  Ray Traced Shadow Params, 286
  Select Advanced Lighting, 310
  Shadow Map Params, 282–285
  Shadow Parameters, 280–282, 298
  Spotlight Parameters, 287, 294
  Sun Parameters, 298
  Volume Light Parameters, 446
  Web Parameters, 295
  standard lights, 264
    common standard light rollouts, 271
    description, 263
    IES Sun and IES Sky compared, 303
  Sunlight feature, 304
  target lights, 266, 268
  Volume Light effect, 445–448
Lights icon
  Quick Start with lights, 245
Linear controller
  Motion panel, animation, 356
Linear exposure control, 292
linear light, 293
Linear Light Parameters rollout, 294
Linear Position controller
  changing controllers, 357
lines
  line work on wrong layer, 476
  not meeting at intended end points, 476
Link Constraint
  animation controllers, 353

Link Info button
  Hierarchy panel, 22
Link To Light option
  Volume Light Parameters rollout, 448
linked objects
  Boolean compound objects, 119
List Lister command, 508
List Types section
  Select Objects dialog box, 39
Load Custom UI Scheme option
  Customize menu, 498
Local Exclude option
  Raytracer Parameters rollout, 200
Lock UI Layout option
  Customize menu, 498
Lock User Interface Toggle command, 505
Lock View feature
  Render Scene dialog box, 389
Lock View icon
  Quick Start with rendering, 375
locking
  Selection Lock toggle icon, 46
Loft command
  Geometry tab, Create panel, 108
Loft feature
  tips for production environment, 481
Loft objects
  Creation Method rollout, 108
  Deformations rollout, 116
  illustrated, 108
  Path Parameters rollout, 112
  Skin Parameters rollout, 114
  Surface Parameters rollout, 110
lofts
  compound objects, 108–116
  creating, 109
  creating with Get Path and Get Shape, 108
  definition, 108
  modifying shape steps and path steps of, 115
  power of instanced lofts, 109
  Quick Start with modeling, 64
  requirements, 108
  rollouts for, 108
Logarithmic exposure control, 292
Logarithmic Exposure Control Parameters rollout, 292
LookAt Constraint
  animation controllers, 353
Lower Interface bar
  interface elements described, 18

lumen value
    photometric lighting, 296
lux value
    photometric lighting, 296

M

Main section
    TurboSmooth modifier, 135
Main toolbar, 17
Make Material Copy icon, 167, 169
    Material Editor, 173
Make Unique icon
    Material Editor, 173
Make, Play, Save Preview icon
    Material Editor, 174
map channels
    changing value in Material Editor, 237
    changing value in UVW Map modifier, 237
    multi/sub-object material, 235
    working with, 237
Map section
    Displace modifier, 136
mapping
    2D/3D map requirements for, 229
    coordinates differentiating from modeling, 229
    generating mapping coordinates, 229
    UVW mapping, 229
mapping coordinate options
    UVW Map modifier, 231
maps
    Bitmap map, 207–214
    capital M and lowercase m, 191
    Falloff map, 223
    Gradient map, 215
    Gradient Ramp map, 216
    loading and removing, 170
    Mix map, 218
    Noise map, 220
    removing, 169
    showing maps in viewport, 172
    Smoke map, 221
    types of maps in 3ds Max, 229
    UVW mapping information, 232
    Waves map, 222
Maps rollout
    Material Editor, 190–204
        Bump channel, 195–197
        Diffuse Color channel, 190–192

        Displacement channel, 200–202
        enable/disable switch for maps, 190
        Opacity channel, 195
        percentage of map displayed, 190
        Quick Start with materials, 157
        Reflection channel, 197–200
        Refraction channel, 202–203
marketing your services, 463–470
    architects, 464
    brochures, 468
    clients, 463–466
    contractors, 466
    developers, 464
    DVDs, 469
    educational courses, 465
    emails, 470
    individuals, 465
    marketing tools, 466–470
    phone books, 468
    real estate agents, 466
    telemarketing, 469
    websites, 467
Material drop-down list, 172
Material Editor, 163–187
    see also materials
    icons, 172
        Assign Material to Selection icon, 173
        Background icon, 164, 174
        Backlight icon, 173
        Get Material icon, 173, 174
        Go Forward to Sibling icon, 173
        Go to Parent icon, 173
        Make Material Copy icon, 173
        Make Unique icon, 173
        Make, Play, Save Preview icon, 174
        Material Effects Channel icon, 173
        Material Map Navigator icon, 174, 177
        Options icon, 164, 174
        Pick Material from Object icon, 173
        Put Material to Scene icon, 173
        Put to Library icon, 173
        Reset Map/Mtl to Default Settings icon, 173
        Sample Type icon, 165, 173
        Sample UV Tiling icon, 174
        Select by Material icon, 174
        Show End Result icon, 173
        Show Map in Viewport icon, 173
        Video Color Check icon, 174
    Quick Start with materials, 145, 147

rollouts, 177–187
    Blinn Basic Parameters rollout, 180
    Dynamic Properties rollout, 187
    Extended Parameters rollout, 183
    illustrated, 177
    Maps rollout, 190–204
    Mental Ray Connection rollout, 187
    Shader Basic Parameters rollout, 178
    SuperSampling rollout, 184
  sample slots, 164
    available layouts, 164, 166
    changing object type, 165
    magnifying, 165
Material Editor command, 505
Material Editor Options dialog box, 164
Material Effects Channel icon, 173
material libraries, 175–177
  creating and editing, 176
  tips for production environment, 483, 486
Material Map Navigator, 174, 177
Material Type button/icon, 172, 174
Material/Map Browser, 174–175, 191
materials, 163–187
  see also Material Editor
  assigning to objects, 167
  cool and hot materials, 168
  creating new, 167
  creating/naming/assigning new materials, 168
  loading and removing, 170
  loading in sample slots, 169
  naming, 167
  Quick Start tutorial, 145–161
  removing, 169
  selecting objects by, 171
Materials section
  Surface Parameters rollout, Lofts, 111
Max Light % setting
  Volume Light Parameters rollout, 447
Max Quadtree Depth setting
  Ray Traced Shadow Params rollout, 286
    Quick Start with lights, 250, 256
Max Steps value
  Volume Fog Parameters rollout, 444
Maximize Viewport Toggle command, 505
Maximize Viewport Toggle icon, 28
  Quick Start with lights, 244
MaxStartUI.ui file
  customizing 3ds Max, 498

measurements
  Units Setup dialog box, 7
memory management
  Default Scanline Renderer rollout, 396
Mental Ray Connection rollout
  Material Editor, 187
mental ray renderer, 265
  description, 387
menus
  Customize menu, 497–501
  default 3ds Max menus illustrated, 17
  interface elements described, 17
  keyboard shortcuts, 17
Menus tab
  Customize User Interface dialog box, 501
Merge command
  scene element assembly, 424, 425
Merge dialog box, 424
Merge File dialog box, 424
Mesh option
  Surface Parameters rollout, Lofts, 111
Mesh Settings section
  Radiosity Meshing Parameters rollout, 315
meshes
  creating mesh objects, 89
    methods of converting objects, 89
  editing mesh objects, 90–98
    adding/subtracting selections, 91
    entering sub-object mode, 90
  managing file size, 417
  modeling, 88–104
  subdividing a mesh, 310
Min Light % setting
  Volume Light Parameters rollout, 447
minus signs
  rollouts, 19
Mirror command, 508
Missing Map Coordinates error message, 237
  Quick Start with materials, 154
Mix Amount parameter
  Mix Parameters rollout, 218
Mix map, 218
Mix Parameters rollout, 218, 219
modeling, 73–105
  coordinates differentiating from mapping, 229
  meshes, 88–104
  modifiers, 129–142
  people, 488
  polys, 89

Quick Start tutorial, 59–71

setting up work environment, 74–81

shapes, 82, 83–88

splines, 82, 88

tips for production environment, 483

modifier gizmo, 231

Modifier Stack

Boolean compound objects, 119

converting object to mesh, 89

editing mesh objects, 90

modifiers, 129–142

Cap Holes modifier, 141

Configure Modifier Sets dialog box, 10

configuring 3ds Max, 10, 11

description, 20

Displace modifier, 136

Edit Mesh modifier, 90

Edit Spline modifier, 110, 122

Extrude modifier, 129, 130

history of modifiers applied to object, 21

Lathe modifier, 138

Noise modifier, 132

Optimize modifier, 133

Smooth modifier, 131

STL Check modifier, 140

TurboSmooth modifier, 135

UVW Map modifier, 230

Modify panel, 20

converting object to mesh, 89

Edit Geometry rollout, 98, 99

editing mesh objects, 91

illustrated, 21

Modifier drop-down list, 20

Modifier Stack, 21

modifying an object, 21

Selection rollout, 92

Soft Selection rollout, 95

Monitor program

network rendering, 413

Mono Channel Output section

Bitmap Parameters rollout, 193, 194

Morph option

Skin Parameters rollout, Lofts, 114

motion

creating basic motion, 347–349

Motion Blur effect, 453–455

activating, 453

creating, 455

Default Scanline Renderer rollout, 396

Image Motion Blur, 453

Multi-Pass Motion Blur effect, 455–457

Object Motion Blur, 453

Render Scene dialog box, 454

Scene Motion Blur, 453

Motion Blur Parameters rollout, 454

Motion Capture Controller

animation controllers, 352

motion controller, 3D

tips for production environment, 479

Motion panel, animation, 23, 354–364

Assign Controller rollout, 355

assigning and changing controllers, 356

Bezier Scale controller, 356

changing controllers, 357

creating and editing keys in, 347, 360

Euler Parameters rollout, 358

Euler XYZ controller, 356

Key Info (Basic) rollout, 359

Linear controller, 356

Parameters area, 355–363

Parameters button, 23

Position XYZ controller, 356

Position XYZ Parameters rollout, 358

PRS Parameters rollout, 358

Trajectories area, 363–364

Trajectories button, 23

mouse

scroll button, 17

using in viewports, 29

Mouse Control section, Viewports tab

Preference Settings dialog box, 80

Move method

Creation Method rollout, 109

move transform, 51

performing, 53

Move Transform Type-In dialog box

Quick Start with modeling, 61

mR Area Omni light source, 265

mR Area Spot light source, 265

multi-pass effects, 455

Multi-Pass Depth of Field effect, 457–459

Enable option, 458

Multi-Pass Motion Blur effect, 455–457

Duration (frames) setting, 456, 457

Enable option, 456

Total Passes setting, 456

Multi/Sub-Object Basic Parameters rollout, 235

working with map channels, 238

multi/sub-object material, 235
Multiplier setting, Intensity section
    Intensity/Color/Attenuation rollout, 276
        Quick Start with lights, 253
    Intensity/Color/Distribution rollout, 296

N

Name and Color rollout
    Create panel, 20, 85
Named Selection Sets
    using, 45
Named Selection Sets dialog box, 43, 44
Named Selection Sets drop-down list, 44
Named Selections
    Selection rollout, Modify panel, 94
naming
    materials, 167
    Named Selection Sets, 44, 45
    objects, 39
navigation controls
    camera viewport navigation, 332
    viewport navigation controls, 27, 28, 268–269
Near Attenuation Start/End values, 277, 278
Near Range value
    Fog Parameters rollout, 439
Net Render option
    Render Scene dialog box, 393
        network rendering, 409
Network Job Assignment dialog box
    network rendering, 410, 411, 413
network of subcontractors
    tips for production environment, 474
network rendering, 409–413
    Backburner components, 410
    Backburner Manager dialog box, 411
    Backburner Server dialog box, 411
    Network Job Assignment dialog box, 410, 411
New Scene command, 505
Next Frame button
    animation playback controls, 345
Next Key button
    animation playback controls, 345
Noise Controller
    animation controllers, 353
Noise map, 220
    Coordinates rollout, 220
    Noise Parameters rollout, 220

    reducing pixilation, 213
    reducing tiled effect of bitmaps, 214
Noise modifier, 132, 133
Noise Parameters rollout, 220
Noise rollout, 213
Noise section
    Volume Fog Parameters rollout, 444
    Volume Light Parameters rollout, 447
North Direction setting
    Control Parameters rollout, 301
Notify Completion option
    Email Notifications rollout, 379
Npower Software's Power Booleans
    tips for production environment, 488
Num Wave Sets value
    Waves map, 222
NURBS, 73

O

Object Level tab
    Display floater, 48
Object Motion Blur
    Motion Blur effect, 453
Object Properties dialog box
    activating Motion Blur effect, 453, 454
Object Properties menu
    turning lights off, 271
Object Shadows section
    Shadow Parameters rollout, 281
Object Type rollout
    AutoGrid option, 84
    available shapes in 3ds Max, 83
    common shape rollouts, 84
    Create panel, 20
    photometric lighting, 293
    Quick Start with modeling, 70
    Start New Shape option, 85
objects
    applying multi/sub-object material, 235
    assigning materials to objects, 167
    attaching objects, 99, 101
    changing display of object, 24
    changing pivot point, 22
    compound objects, 107–127
    creating an object, 20
    creating mesh objects, 89
    detaching, 103, 104
    displaying, 47–51

editing mesh objects, 90
limiting number of objects, 101
modifying an object, 20, 21
naming, 39
selecting, 37–47
    Select icons, 38
selecting by material, 171
selecting by region, 40, 42
selecting object by name, 40
transforming, 51–55
transforming inadvertently, 38
working with objects, 37–55
Offset Mode Transform Type-In icon
    Quick Start with animation, 327
Offset parameter, Coordinates rollout
    Bitmap map, 209
Offset:World column
    Transform Type-In dialog box, 54
omni lights
    creating lights, 266
    creating parallel/non-parallel shadows, 265
    illustrated, 265
    light parameters, 270–282
    standard light source types, 265
    Volume Light effect, 447
On/Off option
    turning lights off, 271
opacity
    changing material opacity, 166
Opacity channel
    Bitmap Parameters rollout, 192
    Maps rollout, 195
Opacity field, Blinn Basic Parameters rollout
    Material Editor, 166
    Quick Start with materials, 158
Opacity option
    Blinn Basic Parameters rollout, 183
Open Channel A icon
    RAM Player, 400, 402
Open Channel B icon
    RAM Player, 402
Open File command, 505
Open File dialog box
    RAM Player, 400
Optimizations rollout, 286, 287
Optimize modifier, 133, 134
    Quick Start with modeling, 70

Optimize option
    Interpolation rollout, Create panel, 86
        enabled/disabled illustrated, 87
Optimize Path option
    Skin Parameters rollout, Lofts, 114
Optimize Shapes option
    Skin Parameters rollout, Lofts, 114
Options icon
    Material Editor, 164, 166, 174
Options section
    Common Parameters rollout, 391
    Default Scanline Renderer rollout, 395
    Skin Parameters rollout, Lofts, 114
Orbit Camera icon, 332
Orbit Light icon, 268
Orbital Scale value
    Control Parameters rollout, 301
Orientation Constraint
    animation controllers, 353
Out button
    editing controllers with Curve Editor, 367
    Key Info (Basic) rollout, 360
Output rollout
    Bitmap map, 214
Output section
    Surface Parameters rollout, Lofts, 111
Output Size section
    Common Parameters rollout, 391
        Quick Start with rendering, 376
    Render Scene dialog box, 393
Overshoot option
    Spotlight/Directional Parameters rollouts, 288

P

Paint Selection Region
    available shapes for selecting objects, 42
Pan Camera icon, 332
Pan icon, 28, 29
    video editing with Video Post, 406
Pan Light icon, 268
panning
    viewports, 28
    viewports using mouse, 29
Panorama Exporter feature
    Render Setup dialog box, 403
    Rendering menu, 403
    rendering tools, 387, 399, 402–404

Panorama Exporter Viewer, 404

Parameters area

Motion panel, animation, 355–363

Parameters button

Motion panel, 23

Parameters rollout, 335

Boolean compound objects, 116

camera parameters, 335

Clipping Planes section, 337

Environment Ranges section, 337

Lens value, 335

Show Cone option, 336

Show Horizon option, 336

Stock Lenses section, 335

Create panel, 85

Displace modifier, 136

Quick Start with cameras, 324

Quick Start with materials, 146, 148

Quick Start with modeling, 60

terrain compound objects, 121

UVW Map modifier, 231

UVW Mapping modifier, 150

Parameters tab

Lens Effects Globals rollout, 450

Particle Systems group

Geometry tab, Create panel, 107

patches, 73

Path Constraint

animation controllers, 353

Path Parameters rollout, Loft objects, 112

Path Steps field, Skin Parameters rollout

Quick Start with modeling, 64

Path Steps option

Path Parameters rollout, Lofts, 112

Path Steps parameter

Skin Parameters rollout, Lofts, 114

paths

Choose New External Files Path window, 6

configuring paths, 77, 79

configuring user paths, 5

Pause icon

Quick Start with animation, 327

people, modeling

tips for production environment, 488

Percent Snap Toggle command, 505

Percentage option

Path Parameters rollout, Lofts, 112

performance

limiting number of objects, 101

Perpendicular parameter

scatter compound objects, 124

Perspective icon, 332

Perspective User View command, 505

perspective view, 26

Perspective view

Quick Start with cameras, 324

Phase value

Waves map, 222

Phase value, Animate Noise option

Noise modifier, 132

phone books

marketing your services, 468

photometric lighting, 291–304

creating photometric lights, 296–297

creating sunlight and skylight photometric lights, 299–301

description, 263

global illumination, 307

light types, 293–298

Object Type rollout, 293

photometric spotlight, 294

preset photometric lights, 297–298

Quick Start with lights, 254, 256

standard lights compared, 264

Pick Boolean rollout

Boolean compound objects, 116

Pick Operand button, 116

Pick Cam. button

Depth of Field Parameters rollout, 452

Pick Distribution Object button

scatter compound objects, 123

Pick Material from Object icon, 169, 171

Material Editor, 173

Quick Start with materials, 159

Pick Node button

Depth of Field Parameters rollout, 452

Pick Operand button

Pick Boolean rollout, 116

Pinch parameter

Soft Selection rollout, Modify panel, 97

Pivot button

Hierarchy panel, 21

pivot point

changing for object, 22

Pixel Aspect ratio

Render Scene dialog box, 391

pixilation

choosing file output dimensions for rendering, 396

Place Highlight command, 334
  default keyboard shortcuts, 505
  light placement, 270
  positioning cameras, 334
  positioning lights, 270
Planar option, mapping coordinates
  UVW Map modifier, 231
Play Animation command, 505
Play button
  animation playback controls, 344
  creating and editing keys in Motion panel, 361, 362
Play icon
  Quick Start with animation, 326, 327
Play Selected button
  animation playback controls, 344
playback controls, animation, 344
Playback section
  Time Configuration dialog box, 343
plug-ins
  Filter Plug-In drop-down list, 407
  RPCs (Rich Photorealistic Content), 421
  third-party plug-ins, 487
  tips for production environment, 487
  Utilities panel, 24
plus/minus signs
  rollouts, 19
point light, 293
Polygon Counter command, 505
polys
  modeling with, 89
Position Constraint
  animation controllers, 353
Position controller
  changing controllers, 357
Position section
  Daylight Parameters rollout, 303
Position XYZ controller
  Motion panel, animation, 356
Position XYZ Parameters rollout, 358
Preference Settings dialog box
  Auto Backup section, Files tab, 79
  changing settings, 79
    original settings, 80
  illustrated, 77
  Mouse Control section, Viewports tab, 80
  Zoom Extents on Import section, Files tab, 80
Preset drop-down list
  Render Scene dialog box, 389
preset photometric lights, 297–298

Previous Frame button
  animation playback controls, 345
Previous Key button
  animation playback controls, 345
Print Size Wizard
  file output dimensions for rendering, 387, 399
prints
  file output dimensions for rendering, 397
production environment
  see also tips for production environment
  file types for rendering, 392
Production setting
  Render Scene dialog box, 388
projection
  projector light simulating, 280
  projector map simulating shadow, 280
Projector Map section
  Advanced Effects rollout, 279
projects
  dividing project into smaller parts, 480
PRS (position, rotation, scale) Parameters rollout
  changing controllers, 358
Pseudo exposure control, 292
  exposure control parameters, 292
Put Material to Scene icon, 168
  Material Editor, 173
Put to Library icon
  Material Editor, 173

Q

Quad menus
  illustrated, 19
  interface elements described, 18
Quads tab
  Customize User Interface dialog box, 501
queue monitor
  network rendering, 409
Queue Monitor dialog box
  network rendering, 412
Quick Align command, 505
Quick Render button
  Render Scene dialog box, 388
Quick Render command, 505
Quick Start support files, 4
Quick Start tutorials
  getting started, 4–13
  getting started with cameras and animation, 323–327
  getting started with lights, 243–261

getting started with materials, 145–161
getting started with modeling, 59–71
getting started with rendering, 373–384
overview, 3

R

radiosity, 309–319
  color bleeding, 309
  considerations when using, 318–319
  enabling, 312
  excluding objects from calculation, 318
  Geometric Object Radiosity Properties rollout, 319
  imperfections in illumination of objects, 311
  improving radiosity solution, 316–318
  missing faces affecting, 318
  scale, 318
  Select Advanced Lighting rollout, 310
  subdividing a mesh, 310
Radiosity Meshing Parameters rollout, 315–318
  Enabled option, 315, 316
  improving radiosity solution, 316–318
  Indirect Light Filtering value, 318
  Mesh Settings section, 315
  Use Adaptive Subdivision option, 315
  Use Global Subdivision Settings option, 315
Radiosity Processing Parameters rollout, 310–314
  Indirect Light Filtering feature, 314
  Initial Quality values, 310
  Interactive Tools section, 314
  Quick Start with lights, 259
  Refine Iterations feature, 312–314
RAM Player
  Image File List Control dialog box, 401
  Open File dialog box, 400
  RAM status indicator, 401
  rendering tools, 399, 400–402
  using, 402
RAM Player command, 508
RAM Player Configuration dialog box, 401, 402
  Quick Start with rendering, 380, 381
Range option
  Render Scene dialog box, 390
Ray Traced Shadow Params rollout, 286
  Quick Start with lights, 250, 255
Raytrace map
  Reflection channel, 198
    Quick Start with materials, 157

raytraced shadows, 274
  advanced raytraced shadows, 275
  IES Sun, 298
  illustrated, 275
  Quick Start with lights, 250
  tips for production environment, 482
  using, 276
Raytracer Global Parameters rollout, 199, 200
Raytracer Parameters rollout, 199, 200
Raytracer tab
  Render Scene dialog box, 388
Re-scale Time button
  Time Configuration dialog box, 343
real estate agents
  marketing your services, 466
Real Time setting
  Time Configuration dialog box, 343
Rectangular Selection Region
  available shapes for selecting objects, 42
Redo Scene Operation command, 505
Redo Viewport Operation command, 505
Refine Iterations feature
  Radiosity Processing Parameters rollout, 312–314
Refine option, Cut operation
  Boolean compound objects, 118
Reflection Amount field
  Quick Start with materials, 157
Reflection channel, Maps rollout
  Material Editor, 197–200
  Quick Start with materials, 157
  simulating artificial reflection, 197
Reflection Dimming section
  Extended Parameters rollout, 183
Refraction channel
  Maps rollout, 202–203
refreshing viewports, 30, 420–422
Region Zoom icon, 28, 29
regions
  selecting objects by region, 40, 42
Remove Isolated Vertices
  Edit Geometry rollout, Modify panel, 102
Render button
  Render Scene dialog box, 388
    Quick Start with rendering, 374
  video editing with Video Post, 408
render effects, 448–459
  Depth of Field effect, 452–453
  description, 433
  Lens effect, 449–451

Motion Blur effect, 453–455
Multi-Pass Depth of Field effect, 457–459
Multi-Pass Motion Blur effect, 455–457
post-production effects, 448
Render Elements tab
    Render Scene dialog box, 388
render engines
    default, 387
    description, 387
    mental ray renderer, 387
    tips for production environment, 488
render farms
    network rendering, 409
Render Iters feature
    TurboSmooth modifier, 135
Render Last command, 505
Render Output File dialog box, 393
    Quick Start with rendering, 376
Render Output section
    Common Parameters rollout, 392–394
        Quick Start with rendering, 376
    Render Scene dialog box, 393
        network rendering, 413
Render Presets Load dialog box, 389
Render Presets Save window
    using Render Scene dialog box, 393
Render Preview button
    Exposure Control Parameters rollout, 293
Render Scene dialog box, 199, 387, 388–396
    ActiveShade setting, 388
    Advanced Lighting tab, 388
    Assign Renderer rollout, 390
    Common Parameters rollout, 390
    Common tab, 388, 390–394
    Default Scanline Renderer rollout, 394
    Email Notifications rollout, 394
    Lock View feature, 389
    Motion Blur effect, 454
    network rendering, 413
    opening, 310
    Preset drop-down list, 389
    Print Size Wizard affecting, 399
    Production setting, 388
    Quick Render button, 388
    Quick Start with lights, 259
    Quick Start with rendering, 374
    Raytracer tab, 388
    Render button, 388

Render Elements tab, 388
Renderer tab, 388, 394–396
Transparency option, 454
using, 393–394
Render Scene Dialog Toggle command, 505
Render section
    IES Sky Parameters rollout, 299
Render Setup dialog box
    Interactive Panorama Exporter Common Parameters
        rollout, 403
    Panorama Exporter feature, 403
Rendered Frame Window option
    Render Scene dialog box, 392
Renderer tab
    Render Scene dialog box, 388, 394–396
rendering, 387–413
    choosing file output dimensions, 396–399
    controlling specific frames to be rendered, 390
    description, 387
    file types, 392
    network rendering, 409–413
    Print Size Wizard, 399
    Quick Start tutorial, 373–384
    refreshing and rendering viewports, 420–422
    rendering tools, 399–404
    Panorama Exporter, 399, 402–404
        RAM Player, 399
        RAM Player, 400–402
    scene elements, 415–431
    selectively including/excluding features in rendering
        process, 391
    specifying dimensions of final rendered output, 391
    Video Post interface, 404–409
Rendering Iterations setting
    Default Scanline Renderer rollout, 396
rendering levels, viewports, 31
    changing, 32
Rendering menu
    accessing atmospheric effects, 434
    Panorama Exporter feature, 403
    Quick Start with rendering, 380
    RAM Player, 402
Rendering rollout, Create panel, 85
    Enable In Renderer option, 85
    Enable In Viewport option, 85
Reset Map/Mtl to Default Settings icon
    Material Editor, 173
Reset Material/Maps to Default Settings icon, 169, 171

resolution
  choosing file output dimensions for rendering, 396–399
  map types losing, 213
Resource Collector feature
  assembling scene elements, 430
Restore Active Viewport option, 35
Restrict to Plane Cycle command, 505
Restrict to x/y/z commands, 505
Revert to Startup Layout option
  Customize menu, 498
Reyes Infografica's DirtyReyes
  tips for production environment, 488
Roll Camera icon, 332
Roll Light icon, 268
rollouts
  accessing controls within, 19
  Adv. Ray Traced Params, 286
  Advanced Effects, 280
  Area Light Parameters, 294
  Area Shadows, 274, 285
  Assign Controller, 355
  Assign Renderer, 390
  Atmosphere, 437
  Auto Secondary Element, 451
  Bitmap Parameters, 207
  Blinn Basic Parameters, 180
  Boolean compound objects, 116
  camera rollouts, 335
  clicking and dragging, 19
  Color by Elevation, 121
  Common Parameters, 390
  Control Parameters, 301, 302
  Coordinates, 208, 220, 237
  Creation Method, 108
  Daylight Parameters, 303
  Default Scanline Renderer, 394
  Deformations, 116
  Depth of Field Parameters, 452, 458
  described, 19
  Directional Parameters, 287
  Display, 123
  Dynamic Properties, 187
  Email Notifications, 379, 394
  Euler Parameters, 358
  Exposure Control, 292
  Exposure Control Parameters, 292
  Extended Parameters, 183
  Falloff Parameters, 224
  Fire Effect Parameters, 435, 437

Fog Parameters, 438
General Parameters, 271–276
Geometric Object Radiosity Properties, 319
Gradient Parameters, 215
Gradient Ramp Parameters, 216
IES Sky Parameters, 299
Intensity/Color/Attenuation, 276–279, 297
Intensity/Color/Distribution, 294
Interactive Panorama Exporter Common Parameters, 403
Interpolation, 86
Key Info (Basic), 359
Lens Effects Globals, 449
Lens Effects Parameters, 449
Linear Light Parameters, 294
Loft compound objects, 108–116
Logarithmic Exposure Control Parameters, 292
Maps, 190, 204
Material Editor, 177, 187
Mental Ray Connection, 187
Mix Parameters, 218
Motion Blur Parameters, 454
Multi/Sub-Object Basic Parameters, 235
Noise, 213
Noise Parameters, 220
opening/closing, 19
Optimizations, 286
Output, 214
Parameters, 121, 335
Path Parameters, 112
plus/minus signs, 19
Position XYZ Parameters, 358
PRS Parameters, 358
Radiosity Meshing Parameters, 315–318
Radiosity Processing Parameters, 310–314
Ray Traced Shadow Params, 286
Raytracer Global Parameters, 199
Raytracer Parameters, 199
Rendering, 85
Scatter Objects, 123
Select Advanced Lighting, 310
Shader Basic Parameters, 178
Shadow Map Params, 282–285
Shadow Parameters, 298, 280–282
Simplification, 121
Skin Parameters, 114
Smoke Parameters, 221
specific shadow types, 282–289
Spotlight Parameters, 287, 294

Sun Parameters, 298
SuperSampling, 184
Surface Parameters, 110
Surface Properties, 235
terrain compound objects, 120
Time, 214
too large for screen, 19
Transform, 125
typical shape rollouts, 84
Volume Fog Parameters, 444
Volume Light Parameters, 446
Web Parameters, 295
rotate transform, 53
rotating view using mouse, 17
rotating viewports, 28
using mouse, 29
Rotation values, Transform rollout
scatter compound objects, 125, 126
Roughness setting, Fractal option
Noise modifier, 132
RPCs (Rich Photorealistic Content), 421

S

Sample Radius parameter
Depth of Field Parameters rollout, 459
Sample Range setting
Shadow Map Params rollout, 283
sample slots
loading materials in sample slots, 169
magnifying, 165
Material Editor, 164
Sample Type icon
Material Editor, 173
flyout icon, 165
Sample UV Tiling icon
Material Editor, 174
Save Active Viewport option, 35
Save File command, 505
Save Selected command
scene element assembly, 423, 425
saving work
tips for production environment, 481
Scale flyout menu, 52
scale transform, 52
non-uniform scale illustrated, 53
performing, 53
squash scale illustrated, 53
uniform scale illustrated, 53

Scaling values, Transform rollout
scatter compound objects, 125
scanline renderer
default render engine, 387
Default Scanline Renderer rollout, 394
rollouts of default scanline renderer, 390
tips for production environment, 488
scatter command
tips for production environment, 489
scatter compound objects, 123–126
creating, 125
Display rollout, 123
Transform rollout, 125
Scatter Objects rollout, 123
Source Object Parameters section, 123
Quick Start with modeling, 70
scene element assembly, 415–431
Archive feature, 430
assembly tools, 422–429
computer power and scene complexity, 416–422
Export command, 426
Export Selected command, 426
File Link Manager, 428
File Properties dialog box, 428
Import command, 425
Merge command, 424
Resource Collector feature, 430
Save Selected command, 423
Summary Info dialog box, 429
transferring files, 416–419
XRef Objects command, 426
XRef Scenes command, 428
scene elements
rendering, 387–413
tips for production environment, 487
Scene Motion Blur
Motion Blur effect, 453
screen interfaces, 16–19
scripts
animation script, 477
need to write good scripts early, 477
scroll button, mouse, 17
See-Through option
Display floater/panel, 49
Seed value
Noise modifier, 132
Segments field, Parameters rollout
Quick Start with modeling, 69

Segments value
Extrude modifier, 129
Select Advanced Lighting rollout, 310
Quick Start with lights, 259, 260
Select All command, 505
Select and Move command, 505
Select and Move icon
keyboard shortcuts, 38, 51
Quick Start with modeling, 61
Select and Rotate command, 506
Select and Rotate icon, 38, 53
Select and Scale command, 506
Select by Material icon, 171
Material Editor, 174
Select By Name command, 506
Select File to Import dialog
Quick Start with modeling, 61
Select icons, 37, 38
Select Invert command, 506
Select None command, 506
Select Object icon
avoiding inadvertent transforms, 38
Select Objects dialog box, 38
List Types section, 39
Quick Start with materials, 145, 156
Quick Start with modeling, 59
selecting object by name, 40
Selection Sets drop-down list, 40
Sort feature, 39
wildcard characters, 39
Select Objects in Set icon, 43
selecting objects, 37–47
by material, 171
by region, 40
available shapes for selection, 42
completely/partially enclosed objects, 40, 41
Window/Crossing icon, 40, 41
clicking multiple objects, 42
deselecting objects individually, 42
Isolate Selection, 46
named selection sets, 43
other ways of, 46
restricting selection to object type, 43
Select icons, 37
Select Objects dialog box, 38
Selection Filter, 43
Selection Lock toggle icon, 46
Selection Filter, 43

Selection lock, 46
illustrated, 43
Selection Lock Toggle command, 506
Selection Lock toggle icon, 46
Selection Region flyout menu, 42
Selection Region icons, 42
Selection rollout, Command panel
Quick Start with modeling, 68
Selection rollout, Modify panel, 92
By Vertex option, 93, 95
editing mesh objects, 92
Hide button, 94
Ignore Backfacing option, 93, 95
Ignore Visible Edges option, 94
illustrated, 93
Named Selections, 94
Show Normals option, 94, 95
using Selection rollout options, 95
Selection sets
creating, 43, 44
Selection Sets drop-down list
Select Objects dialog box, 40
Self-Illumination section
Blinn Basic Parameters rollout, 182
services
marketing your services, 463–470
Set ID field, Surface Properties rollout
Quick Start with materials, 153
Set Key button
creating keys, 347
Set Key Mode command, 506
Set Keys command, 506
sets
Named selection sets, 43
Shade Selected Faces command, 506
Shader Basic Parameters rollout, Material Editor, 178
2-Sided option, 179
Wire option, 178
shaders
Blinn shader, 309
global illumination, 308–309
specular highlights, 308
Shadow Integrity/Quality settings
Area Shadows rollout, 285
Shadow Map Params rollout, 282–285
2 Sided Shadows option, 284
Absolute Map Bias option, 284
Bias setting, 283
illustrated, 282

Quick Start with lights, 248
resolution of applied map, 272
Sample Range setting, 283
Size value, 283
shadow maps
    changing quality of, 285
    General Parameters rollout, 272
    light sources close/distant illustrated, 272
    transparent illustrated, 273
    using, 273, 274
Shadow Parameters rollout, 280–282, 298
    Atmospheric Shadows section, 282
    changing color/strength of shadows, 282
    Dens. field, 281
    illustrated, 281
    Light Affects Shadow Color feature, 282
    Object Shadows section, 281
shadows
    2 Sided Shadows enabled/disabled illustrated, 284
    Adv. Ray Traced Params rollout, 286
    advanced raytraced shadows, 275
    area shadows, 274
    Area Shadows rollout, 285
    Cast Shadows option, 280
    changing color/strength of, 282
    color swatch changing shadow strength illustrated, 281
    Directional Parameters rollout, 287
    effect of increasing shadow map size illustrated, 283
    IES Sun, 298
    loading map into shadow illustrated, 281
    Optimizations rollout, 286
    Ray Traced Shadow Params rollout, 286
    raytraced shadows, 274
    rollouts for specific shadow types, 282–289
    sample ranges illustrated, 284
    shadow map, 272
    Spotlight Parameters rollout, 287
    tips for production environment, 490
    Transparent Shadow On option, 287
Shadows section, General Parameters rollout, 271, 272
    Quick Start with lights, 249, 253
Shape section
    Fire Effect Parameters rollout, 437
Shape Steps parameter, Skin Parameters rollout, 114
    Quick Start with modeling, 64
shapes
    AutoGrid placing shape on surface of object, 84
    available shapes in 3ds Max, 83
    creating renderable shapes and splines, 85
    definition, 82
    examples of shapes in 3ds Max, 83
    modeling, 83–88
    splines compared, 83
    typical shape rollouts, 84
    using interpolation with, 88
shortcuts
    see keyboard shortcuts
Show Cone feature
    Spotlight/Directional Parameters rollouts, 288
Show Cone option
    Parameters rollout, 336
Show End Result icon, 173
Show Frozen in Gray option
    Display floater/panel, 49
Show Horizon option
    Parameters rollout, 336
Show Map in Viewport icon, 172, 173
    Quick Start with materials, 146, 147, 149
Show Map in Viewport option, 175
Show Normals option
    Selection rollout, 94, 95
Show Safeframes Toggle command, 506
Showing Floating Dialogs command, 506
Simplification rollout
    terrain compound objects, 121
Single option
    Render Scene dialog box, 390
Site-Fountain object
    Quick Start with modeling, 69
Site-Grass object
    Quick Start with materials, 145, 148
    Quick Start with modeling, 59
Site-Mulch object
    Quick Start with materials, 149
Site-ParkingLines object
    Quick Start with materials, 154
    Quick Start with modeling, 61
Site-Shrubs object
    Quick Start with modeling, 70
Site-Streets object
    Quick Start with materials, 147
    Quick Start with modeling, 60
Site-Terrain object
    Quick Start with materials, 160
    Quick Start with modeling, 62
Size setting
    Lens Effects Globals rollout, 450

Size value
Shadow Map Params rollout, 283
Volume Fog Parameters rollout, 444
Skin Parameters rollout, Loft objects, 114
Quick Start with modeling, 64
Skip Existing Images option
Render Scene dialog box, 393
sky
IES Sky light, 299–301
skylight
standard light source types, 265
Skylight feature, 303
slots
changing sample slot background, 164
changing sample slot object type, 165
loading materials in sample slots, 169
magnifying sample slots, 165
Material Editor, 164
working with sample slots, 166
Slots section, Material Editor, 166
Smoke map, 221
Smoke Parameters rollout, 221, 222
Smooth + Highlights rendering level, viewports, 31
Quick Start with lights, 245
Smooth modifier, 131
Quick Start with modeling, 63, 65
Smooth option
Extrude modifier, 130
Smoothing Length option
Surface Parameters rollout, Lofts, 110
Smoothing Width option
Surface Parameters rollout, Lofts, 110
SMTP Server field
Email Notifications rollout, 379
Snaps Toggle command, 506
Soft Selection Curve graph, 96
Soft Selection rollout, Modify panel, 95
Affect Backfacing option, 96
Bubble parameter, 97
Edge Distance option, 98
enabled/not enabled, 96
Falloff parameter, 96, 97
Pinch parameter, 97
Use Soft Selection option, 96
using soft selections, 98
Soften Gizmo Edges value
Volume Fog Parameters rollout, 443
Soften value
Blinn Basic Parameters rollout, 181

Sort feature
Select Objects dialog box, 39
Source Object Parameters section
Scatter Objects rollout, 123
Quick Start with modeling, 70
spacing tool
tips for production environment, 489
Specular color swatch
Blinn Basic Parameters rollout, 181
specular highlights
shaders and, 308
Specular Highlights section
Blinn Basic Parameters rollout, 181
Specular Level value
Blinn Basic Parameters rollout, 181
SphereGizmo button
creating and modifying Volume Fog, 444
using Fire effect, 436
Spherical option, mapping coordinates
UVW Map modifier, 231
spinners
Update During Spinner Drag option, 30
Spline Conversion section
Trajectories area, Motion panel, 364
splines
creating renderable shapes and splines, 85
definition, 82
modeling, 88
shapes compared, 83
using interpolation with, 88
Split option, Cut operation
Boolean compound objects, 118
Quick Start with modeling, 68
Spot/Directional Light View command
default keyboard shortcuts, 506
Spotlight Parameters rollout, 287, 294
spotlights
free spotlight illustrated, 267
high/low Hotspot/Beam values illustrated, 288
illustrated, 265, 266
photometric spotlight, 294
standard light source types, 265
target spotlight illustrated, 267
Squeeze value
Lens Effects Globals rollout, 450
standard lights
description, 263
exposure control, 292
IES Sun and IES Sky compared, 303

photometric lights compared, 264
standard light source types, 264–266
    direct lights, 266
    omni lights, 265
    skylight, 265
    spotlights, 265
Standard Primitives group
    Geometry tab, Create panel, 107
standard scene elements
    tips for production environment, 487
Standard section
    Fog Parameters rollout, 439
Start New Shape option
    Object Type rollout, 85
state-certified courses
    marketing your services, 465
Status bar type-in fields, 55
Status section
    STL Check modifier, 140
Step Size value
    Volume Fog Parameters rollout, 444
steps
    Interpolation rollout, Create panel, 86
still images
    exposure control, 292
STL Check modifier, 140
Stock Lenses section, Parameters rollout, 335
    Quick Start with cameras, 324
Strength values
    Displace modifier, 136
    Noise modifier, 132
Stretch parameter
    Fire Effect Parameters rollout, 437
sub-object material
    multi/sub-object material, 235
sub-object mode
    editing mesh objects, 90
subcontractor network
    tips for production environment, 474
Subtraction operation
    Boolean compound objects, 117
Summary Info dialog box
    scene element assembly, 429
Sun Parameters rollout, 298
    Quick Start with lights, 255
sunlight
    Lens effect, 449
Sunlight feature, 304

SuperSampling rollout
    Material Editor, 184
support images
    configuring user paths, 5
Surface Constraint
    animation controllers, 353
Surface Parameters rollout, Loft objects, 110
Surface Properties rollout
    illustrated, 236
    multi/sub-object material, 235
    Quick Start with materials, 153
    working with map channels, 238
System Unit Setup dialog box, 75
System Units setting
    setting up 3ds Max for architectural work, 74
    setting up 3ds Max for architectural work, 75

T

Tape Measure command, 508
target cameras, 330
    creating cameras, 331
target distance
    Depth of Field effect, 452
    Depth of Field Parameters rollout, 458
target lights, 266, 268
target spotlights, 267
telemarketing
    marketing your services, 469
terrain compound objects, 120–122
    adding additional splines, 120
    Color by Elevation rollout, 121
    rollouts, 120
terrain features
    Quick Start with modeling, 62
    Soft Selection rollout, Modify panel, 95, 96
Tessellate modifier
    Boolean compound objects, 119
texture crawling, 186
.tga file
    file types for rendering, 392
third-party plug-ins
    tips for production environment, 487
three dimensional (3D) maps, 229
three dimensional (3D) modeling
    working with meshes and polys, 88–104
thumbnails
    displaying different sizes of, 25

.tif file
  file types for rendering, 392
Tiling parameter, Coordinates rollout
  Bitmap map, 209
Time Configuration dialog box, 342–344
  Animation section, 343
  creating basic motion, 348
  Frame Rate section, 343
  Playback section, 343
  Quick Start with cameras, 325
  Re-scale Time button, 343
  Real Time setting, 343
  Time Display section, 343
Time Configuration icon
  Quick Start with cameras, 325
Time Display section
  Time Configuration dialog box, 343
Time field
  Key Info (Basic) rollout, 359
Time Output section
  Common Parameters rollout, 390
    Quick Start with rendering, 378
  Render Scene dialog box, 393
    network rendering, 413
  video editing with Video Post, 408
Time rollout
  Bitmap map, 214
time slider
  animation, 344
tips for production environment, 473–494
  additional input devices, 479
  advanced raytraced shadows, 482
  artificial shadows, 490
  assembly lines for doors and windows, 484
  building subcontractor network, 474
  contracts, 480
  creating cars, 488
  creating people, 488
  creating vegetation, 488, 489
  dividing project into smaller parts, 480
  inspecting architectural drawings, 475
  keyboard shortcuts, 478
  Loft feature, 481
  material libraries, 486
  model and material libraries, 483
  questioning poor designs, 478
  saving work incrementally, 481
  simulating moving water, 488
  standard scene elements, 487

  third-party plug-ins, 487
  trade shows/seminars/classes, 493
  website forums, 492
  writing good scripts early, 477
toolbars
  interface elements described, 17
  keyboard shortcuts compared, 17
  Main toolbar, 17
Toolbars tab
  Customize User Interface dialog box, 501
tools
  assembling scene elements, 422–429
  rendering tools, 399–404
Tools menu
  Display floater, 23
Top View command, 506
Total Passes parameter
  Depth of Field Parameters rollout, 458
Total Passes setting
  Multi-Pass Motion Blur effect, 456
Track View feature
  Curve Editor mode, 364
  Dope Sheet mode, 364
trade shows
  tips for production environment, 493
training architects
  marketing your services, 465
Trajectories area
  Motion panel, 363–364
Trajectories button
  Motion panel, 23
Trajectory option
  Display floater/panel, 49
transferring files
  computer power and scene complexity, 416–419
Transform Degrade option
  Skin Parameters rollout, Lofts, 115
transform gizmo, 38
  creating terrain object, 122
  editing mesh objects, 92
  illustrated, 52
  moving objects, 52
  spinning object around, 53
  using soft selections, 98
Transform Gizmo Size Down command, 506
Transform Gizmo Size Up command, 506
Transform Gizmo Toggle command, 506
Transform rollout
  scatter compound objects, 125

Transform Type-In dialog box, 52, 54
Transform Type-In Dialog Toggle command, 506
transforming objects, 51–55
    move transform, 51
    rotate transform, 53
    scale transform, 52
    Status bar type-in fields, 55
transforming objects inadvertently, 38
transforms
    creating keyframes, 346
    move, scale, and rotate transforms, 53
transitions
    keyframing, 345
Transparency option
    Render Scene dialog box, 454
Transparent Shadows section
    On option enabled/disabled illustrated, 287
    Optimizations rollout, 286
    tips for production environment, 491
Truck Camera command
    executing, 332
TurboSmooth modifier, 135, 136
    Quick Start with modeling, 62
two dimensional (2D) maps, 229
two dimensional (2D) modeling
    working with shapes and splines, 81–88
Two-Sided option
    Shader Basic Parameters rollout, 179

U

Undo Scene Operation command, 506
Undo View Change option, viewports, 35
Undo Viewport Operation command, 506
Unfreeze commands, 508
Unhide All button, Hide rollout
    Quick Start with cameras, 324
    Quick Start with modeling, 66
Unhide commands, 508
Uniformity value
    Volume Fog Parameters rollout, 444
Union operation
    Boolean compound objects, 117
units
    centering on the world origin, 75
    engineering scales, 76
    System Units setting, 74

Units Setup dialog box, 7, 74
Update During Spinner Drag option
    viewports, 30
Use 1/2 of Lines option, Simplification rollout
    terrain compound objects, 121
Use 1/2 of Points option, Simplification rollout
    terrain compound objects, 121
Use Adaptive Subdivision option
    Radiosity Meshing Parameters rollout, 315
Use Attenuation Color option
    Volume Light Parameters rollout, 446
Use Global Subdivision Settings option
    Radiosity Meshing Parameters rollout, 315
Use Selected Faces Only option
    scatter compound objects, 124
Use Shape IDs option
    Surface Parameters rollout, Lofts, 111
Use Soft Selection option
    Soft Selection rollout, 96
Use Target Distance option
    Depth of Field Parameters rollout, 458
user interface
    Customize User Interface feature, 500
    customizing 3ds Max, 498
Utilities panel, 24, 25
    Asset Browser tool, 24, 25
    converting object to mesh, 89
    plug-ins, 24
UVW coordinates, 208
UVW Map gizmo, 231
    alignment, 232
    size and tiling options, 232
    sizing and tiling, 232
    working with, 233
UVW Map modifier, 230
    changing map channel value, 237
    changing U and V Tile values, 237
    Parameters rollout, 231
        Alignment section, 232
    Quick Start with materials, 146, 147, 154, 161
    working with map channels, 237
UVW Map Modifier command, 508
UVW mapping, 229
    Acquire option, 233
    Acquire UVW Mapping dialog box, 233
UVW Mapping modifier
    Parameters rollout, 150

V

vegetation, creating
  tips for production environment, 488, 490
Vert Focal Loss value
  Depth of Field Parameters rollout, 453
Vertex Chaos value
  Scatter Objects rollout, 124
Vertex Ticks option
  Display floater/panel, 49
Vertical section, Simplification rollout
  terrain compound objects, 121
vertices
  Remove Isolated Vertices feature, 102
  steps, 86
  welding vertices, 105
video clips
  choosing file output dimensions for rendering, 398
  rendering tools, 399–404
  Time rollout, 214
Video Color Check icon
  Material Editor, 174
video editing
  Video Post interface, 405–409
Video Post interface
  Delete Current Event icon, 408
  Edit Current Event icon, 409
  Edit Range Bar icon, 409
  Image Filter event, 405
  Image Input event, 405
  Image Output event, 405
  rendering, 404–409
  Scene Motion Blur, 453
  video editing with, 405–409
Video Post Parameters section
  Add Image Input Event dialog box, 406
View Align feature
  Edit Geometry rollout, 102, 103
View Edged Faces Toggle command, 506
Viewport Configuration dialog box
  Quick Start with lights, 244
Viewport drop-down list
  Quick Start with rendering, 374
viewport navigation controls, 268–269
  camera viewport navigation, 332
  light view icons illustrated, 268
viewports, 25–35
  active viewports, 30
  changing viewport type, 26

changing views within, 27, 30
configuring 3ds Max, 8
  Camera view, 12
converting object to mesh, 89
current viewport, 30
default 3ds Max viewports, 18
default viewport layout, 26
description, 25
disabling, 30
enabling Fast View option, 32, 33
grids, 30
increasing update speed, 30
indicating currently active viewport, 26
indicating viewport type, 26
interface elements described, 18
keyboard shortcuts, 27
  using/not using, 29
layouts, 9, 34
navigation controls, 27, 28
navigation icons, 29
panning in, 28
Quad menus, 18
refreshing, 30
refreshing and rendering, 420–422
rendering levels, 31
  changing, 32
Restore Active Viewport option, 35
rotating in, 28
Save Active Viewport option, 35
saving view changes, 35
showing maps in viewport, 172
types of views, 26
Undo View Change option, 35
undocking Command panel, 18
undoing view changes, 35
Update During Spinner Drag option, 30
view types, 27
Viewport Configuration dialog, 9
Viewport Configuration option, 34
viewport layouts, 34
zooming in, 28
views
  axonometric view, 26
  perspective view, 26
  rotating using mouse, 17
  zooming in/out using mouse, 17
visualization industry
  see tips for production environment

Volume Fog effect, 443–444
  creating and modifying, 444
  description, 438
Volume Fog Parameters rollout, 443, 444
Volume Light effect, 445–448
  omni light source, 447
Volume Light Parameters rollout, 446
  Atten. Mult. option, 446
  Attenuation End % values, 447
  Attenuation Start % values, 447
  Filter Shadows settings, 447
  Link To Light option, 448
  Max Light % setting, 447
  Min Light % setting, 447
  Noise section, 447
  Use Attenuation Color option, 446
  Volume section, 446
Volume section
  Volume Light Parameters rollout, 446

W

Walk Through icon, 28
water simulation
  tips for production environment, 488
Wave Len Max value, Waves map, 222
Wave Len Min value, Waves map, 222
Wave Radius value, Waves map, 222
Waves map, 222, 223
wear and tear
  tips for production environment, 488
web distribution, 295
Web Parameters rollout, 295
website forums
  tips for production environment, 492
websites
  marketing your services, 467
Weld feature
  Edit Geometry rollout, 104
    welding vertices, 105
Width Repeat parameter
  Surface Parameters rollout, Lofts, 111
wildcard characters
  Select Objects dialog box, 39
Wind Strength setting
  Volume Fog Parameters rollout, 444
window selection, 41
  Quick Start with materials, 159
Window/Crossing icon, 40

Quick Start with materials, 152
Windows feature
  tips for production environment, 484
Wire option
  Shader Basic Parameters rollout, 178
Wire section
  Extended Parameters rollout, 184
Wireframe mode
  Quick Start with modeling, 65
Wireframe rendering level, viewports, 31
Wireframe/Smooth+Highlights Toggle command, 506
work environment
  setting up, 74–81
working in industry
  see tips for production environment
World Coordinate System, 75
  centering on the world origin, 75

X

XRef Objects command
  scene element assembly, 426
XRef Scenes command
  scene element assembly, 428
XYZ coordinates, 208

Y

Yellowbook
  marketing your services, 468

Z

Zoom All icon, 28, 29
Zoom Extents All icon, 28, 29
  configuring 3ds Max, 13
  Quick Start with lights, 245
Zoom Extents All Selected icon/command, 28, 29
  keyboard shortcut, 506
Zoom Extents icon, 28, 29
  video editing with Video Post, 406, 407
Zoom Extents on Import option, Files tab
  Preference Settings dialog box, 80
Zoom Extents Selected icon, 28, 29
Zoom icon, 28, 29
zooming
  viewports, 28
  viewports using mouse, 29
zooming in/out using mouse, 17

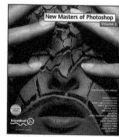

friendsofed.com/forums

Join the friends of ED forums to find out more about our books, discover useful technology tips and tricks, or get a helping hand on a challenging project. *Designer to Designer*™ is what it's all about—our community sharing ideas and inspiring each other. In the friends of ED forums, you'll find a wide range of topics to discuss, so look around, find a forum, and dive right in!

■ **Books and Information**

Chat about friends of ED books, gossip about the community, or even tell us some bad jokes!

■ **Flash**

Discuss design issues, ActionScript, dynamic content, and video and sound.

■ **Web Design**

From front-end frustrations to back-end blight, share your problems and your knowledge here.

■ **Site Check**

Show off your work or get new ideas.

■ **Digital Imagery**

Create eye candy with Photoshop, Fireworks, Illustrator, and FreeHand.

■ **ArchivED**

Browse through an archive of old questions and answers.

HOW TO PARTICIPATE

Go to the friends of ED forums at **www.friendsofed.com/forums**.

Visit **www.friendsofed.com** to get the latest on our books, find out what's going on in the community, and discover some of the slickest sites online today!

CGarchitect
.com

The leading online magazine and
user community for Architectural
Visualization Professionals

Image courtesy Yiran (BHAA)

GALLERY CREDITS

Brian L. Smith

Visualizer: Brian L. Smith (author); email: brian.smith@3das.com; firm: 3DAS; country: USA; website: www.3das.com
Top image: rendering time: 2 hours; equipment: (1) Pentium 3 GHz, 2GB RAM, scanline; face count: 2.3 million
Bottom image: rendering time: 30 minutes; equipment: (1) Pentium 3 GHz, 2GB RAM, scanline; face count: 0.7 million

Visarty

Visualizers: Nadiya Tarasyuk (top), Oleg Melnyk (middle), Volodymyr Kvasnytsya (bottom); email: info@visarty.com; firm: Visarty; country: Ukraine; website: www.visarty.com
Top image: rendering time: 8 hours; equipment: (2) Athlon 64 4200+, 2GB RAM, VRay; face count: 0.8 million; designer: Nadiya Tarasyuk
Middle image (book cover): rendering time: 3 hours; equipment: (1) Pentium 3 GHz, 2GB RAM, VRay; face count: 2.3 million; designer: Oleg Melnyk
Bottom image: rendering time: 12 hours; equipment: Dual Xeon 3 GHz, 3GB RAM, VRay; face count: 1.3 million; designer: Nadiya Tarasyuk

Thomas Livings

Visualizer: Thomas Livings; email: thomaslivings@gmail.com; firm: none (freelancer); country: England; website: www.thomaslivings.com
Top image: rendering time: 6 hours, 30 minutes; equipment: (1) Pentium 3.2 GHz, 2GB RAM, VRay; face count: 0.8 million
Bottom image: rendering time: 40 minutes; equipment: (1) Pentium 3.2 GHz, 2GB RAM, VRay; face count: 134,000; architect: Brewster-Bye Architects

Reza Bahari

Visualizer: Reza Bahari; email: visual3d@streamyx.com; firm: Visual 3D; country: Malaysia; website: www.visual3d.50megs.com
Top image: rendering time: 6 hours; equipment: (1) Dual Xeon 3.6 GHz, 3GB RAM, VRay; face count: 2.1 million; architect: Indra Ramanathan (Woods Bagot)
Bottom image: rendering time: 2 hours, 30 minutes; equipment: (1) Dual Xeon 3.6 GHz, 3GB RAM, VRay; face count: 1.3 million; architect: Martin Axe (SL+A)

Beno Saradzic and Massimo Ruggeri

Visualizers: Beno Saradzic, Massimo Ruggeri; email: beno@eim.ae, maxrug@eim.ae; firm: E*Clips Visual Communications; country: United Arab Emirates
Top image: rendering time: 14 hours; equipment: (5) Dual Athlon MP 2800, 4GB RAM, finalRender; face count: 4.6 million; architect: Waleed Shaalan, BrainStorm
Bottom image: equipment: (16) AMD Athlon 3400, 3GB RAM, finalRender; face count: 3.8 million; architect: DIAR CONSULT

Serge Vasiliew

Visualizer: Serge Vasiliew; email: caesar@cat-a-pult.com; firm: Catapult; country: Ukraine; website: www.cat-a-pult.com
Top image: rendering time: 10 minutes; equipment: (8) Pentium 3 GHz, 2GB RAM, VRay; face count: 0.4 million
Bottom image: rendering time: 6 hours; equipment: (1) Dual Xeon 3 GHz, 2GB RAM, VRay; face count: 1.2 million

Alexandr Sharovsky

Visualizer: Alexandr Sharovsky; email: artspline@mail.ru; firm: ARTspline; country: Russia; website: www.artspline.ru
Top image: rendering time: 3 hours; equipment: (2) Athlon 64 Dual-Core 4800, 2GB RAM, VRay; face count: 120,000
Bottom image: rendering time: 8 hours; equipment: (1) Pentium 3 GHz, 1GB RAM, VRay; face count: 5 million

Zhu Tianyi

Visualizer: Zhu Tianyi (yiran); email: yiran-tianyi@hotmail.com; firm: BHAA; country: China; website: www.bhaa.com.cn
Image: rendering time: 2 hours; equipment: (1) Pentium 2.2 GHz, 512MB RAM, VRay; face count: 1.5 million